子連れ狼

LONE
WOLF
AND
子連れ狼 CUB

story
KAZUO KOIKE

art
GOSEKI KOJIMA

DARK HORSE COMICS

translation
DANA LEWIS

lettering & retouch
DIGITAL CHAMELEON

cover artwork
FRANK MILLER with **LYNN VARLEY**

publisher
MIKE RICHARDSON

editor
MIKE HANSEN

assistant editor
TIM ERVIN-GORE

consulting editor
TOREN SMITH for **STUDIO PROTEUS**

book design
DARIN FABRICK

art director
MARK COX

Published by Dark Horse Comics, Inc., in association
with MegaHouse and Koike Shoin Publishing Company., Ltd.

Dark Horse Comics, Inc.
10956 SE Main Street, Milwaukie, OR 97222
www.darkhorse.com

First edition: July 2001
ISBN: 1-56971-512-2

1 3 5 7 9 10 8 6 4 2

Printed in Canada

Lone Wolf and Cub Vol. 11: Talisman of Hades

To find a comics shop in your area, call the
Comic Shop Locator Service toll-free at 1-888-266-4226

TALISMAN OF HADES

By KAZUO KOIKE
& GOSEKI KOJIMA

子連れ狼

VOLUME

11

A NOTE TO READERS

Lone Wolf and Cub is famous for its carefully researched re-creation of Edo-Period Japan. To preserve the flavor of the work, we have chosen to retain many Edo-Period terms that have no direct equivalents in English. Japanese is written in a mix of Chinese ideograms and a syllabic writing system, resulting in numerous synonyms. In the glossary, you may encounter words with multiple meanings. These are words written with Chinese ideograms that are pronounced the same but carry different meanings. A Japanese reader seeing the different ideograms would know instantly which meaning it is, but these synonyms can cause confusion when Japanese is spelled out in our alphabet. *O-yurushi o* (please forgive us)!

LONE WOLF AND CUB

TABLE OF CONTENTS

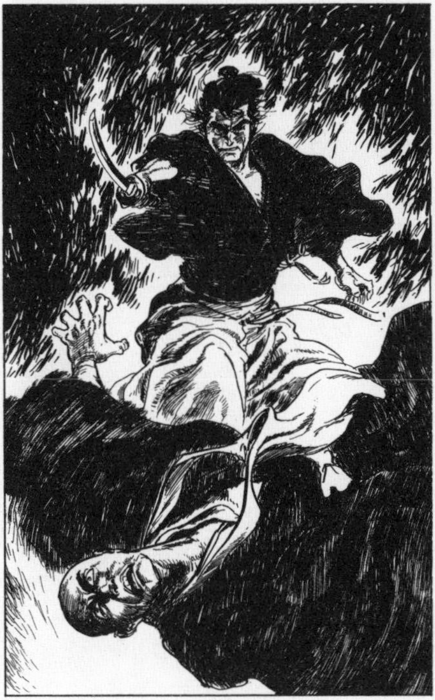

the fifty-fifth

Talisman of Hades

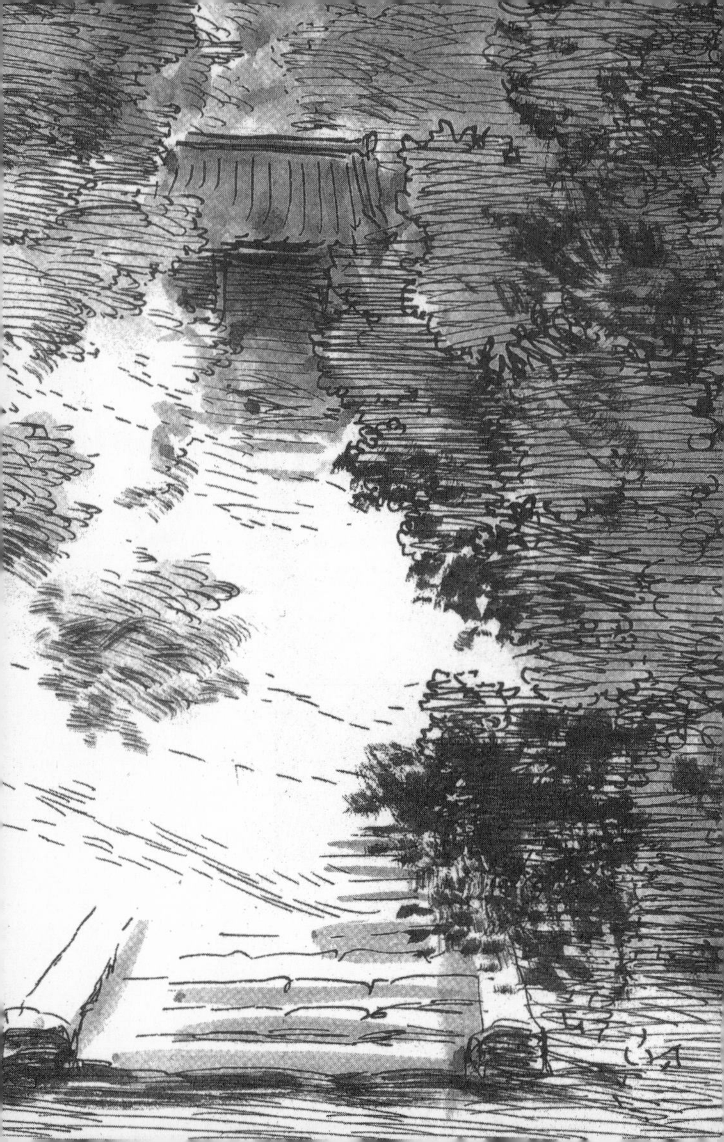

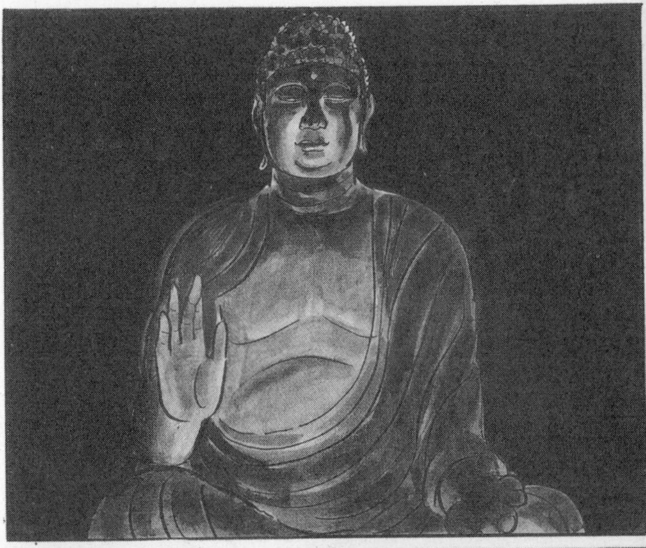
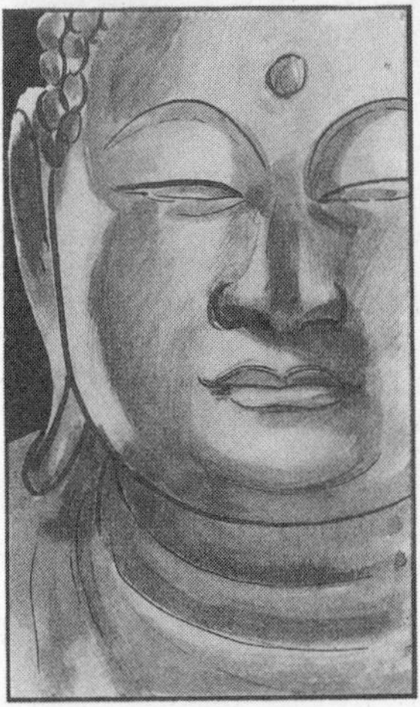
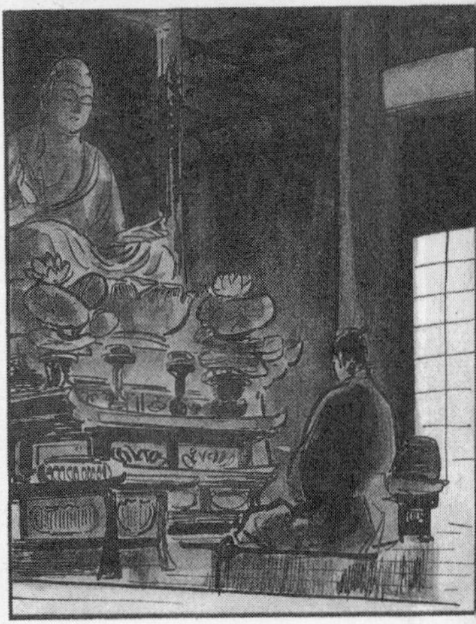

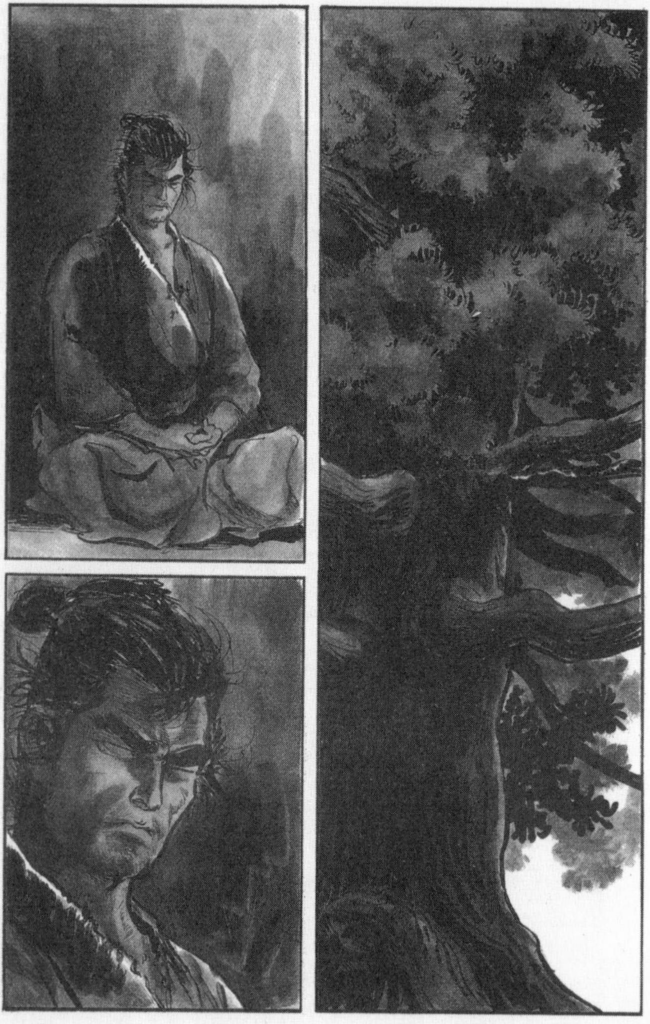

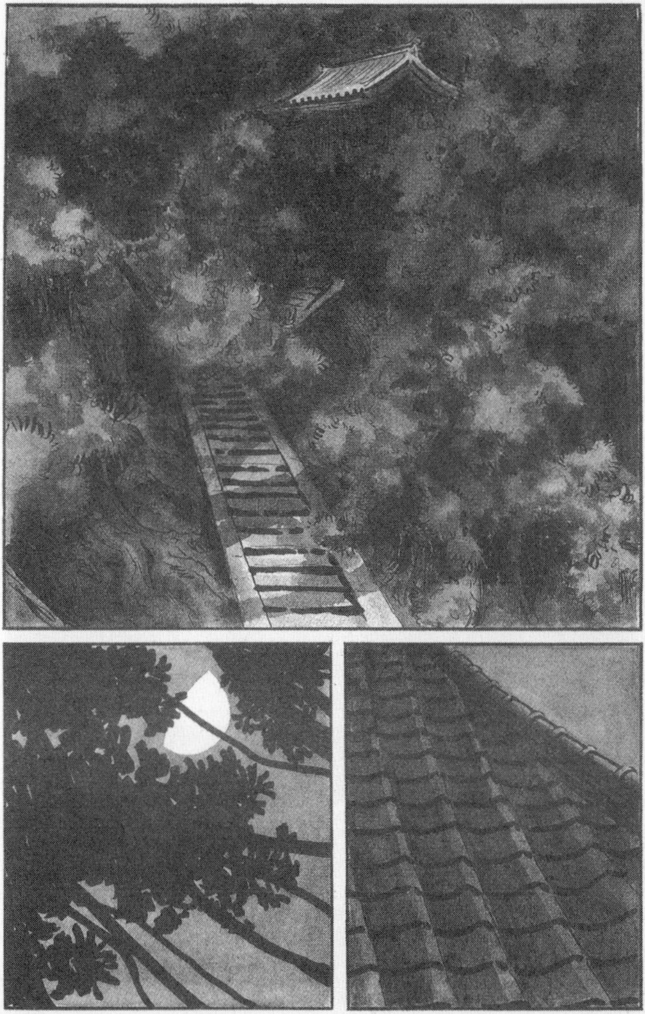

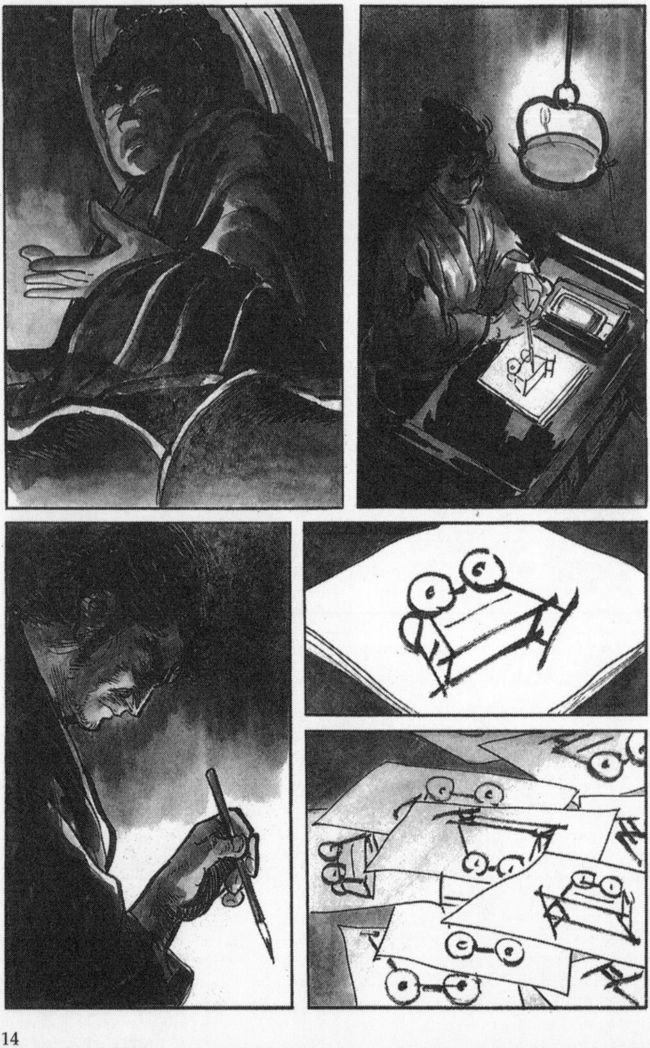

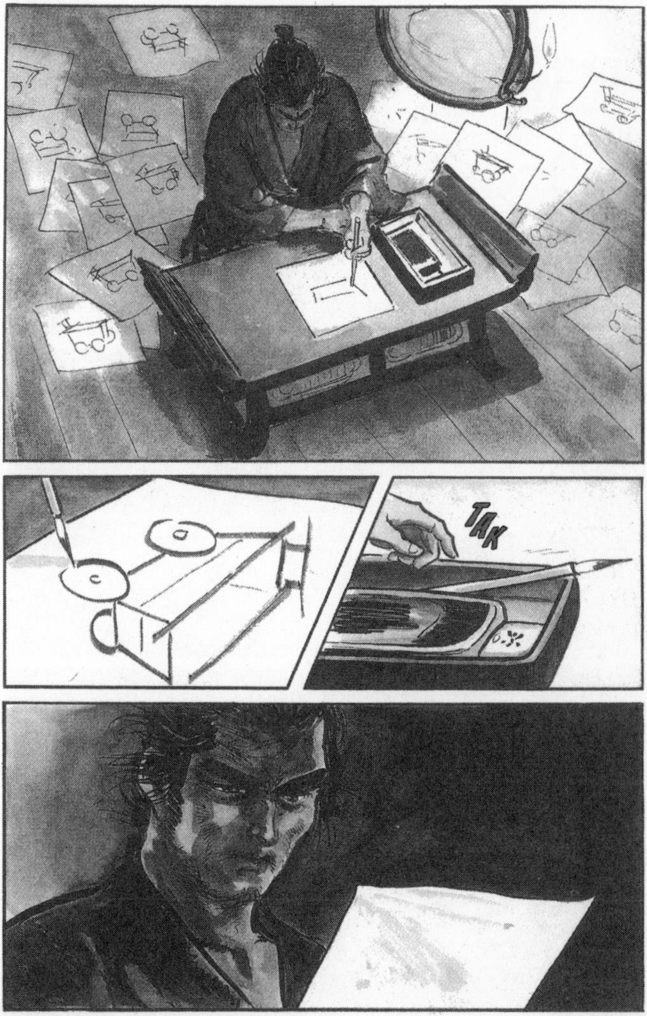
TAK

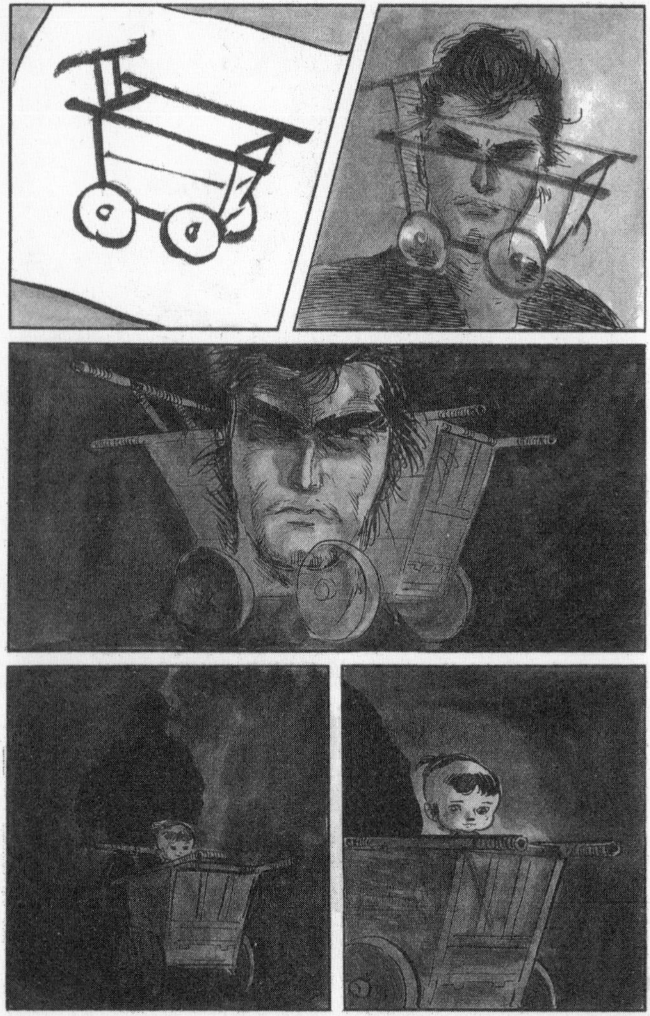

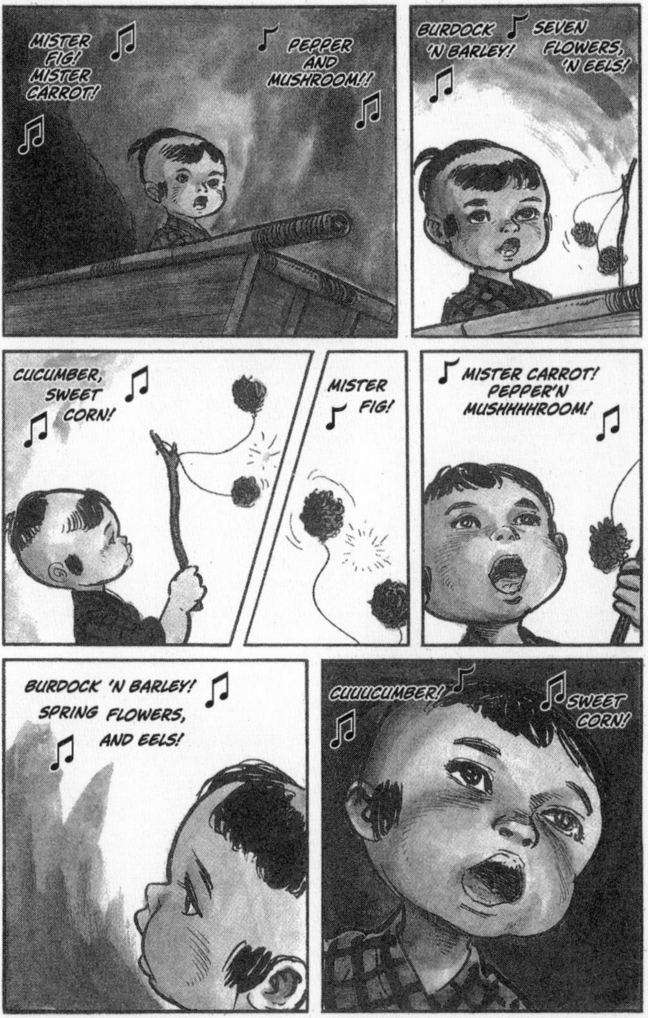
MISTER FIG! MISTER CARROT!
PEPPER AND MUSHROOM!!
BURDOCK 'N BARLEY!
SEVEN FLOWERS, 'N EELS!
CUCUMBER, SWEET CORN!
MISTER FIG!
MISTER CARROT! PEPPER'N MUSHHHHROOM!
BURDOCK 'N BARLEY! SPRING FLOWERS, AND EELS!
CUUUCUMBER!
SWEET CORN!

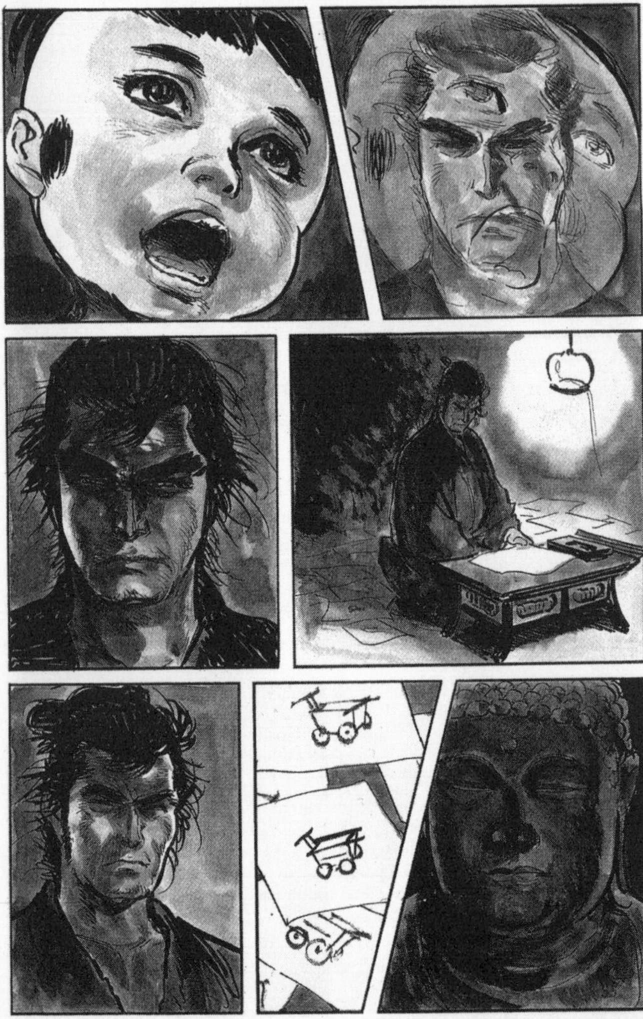

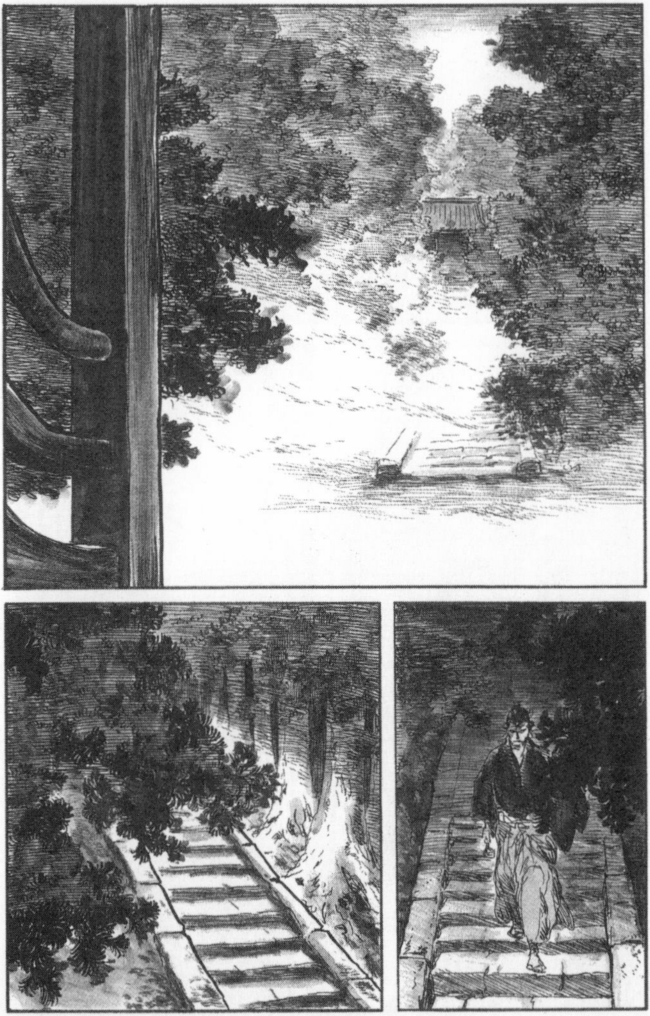

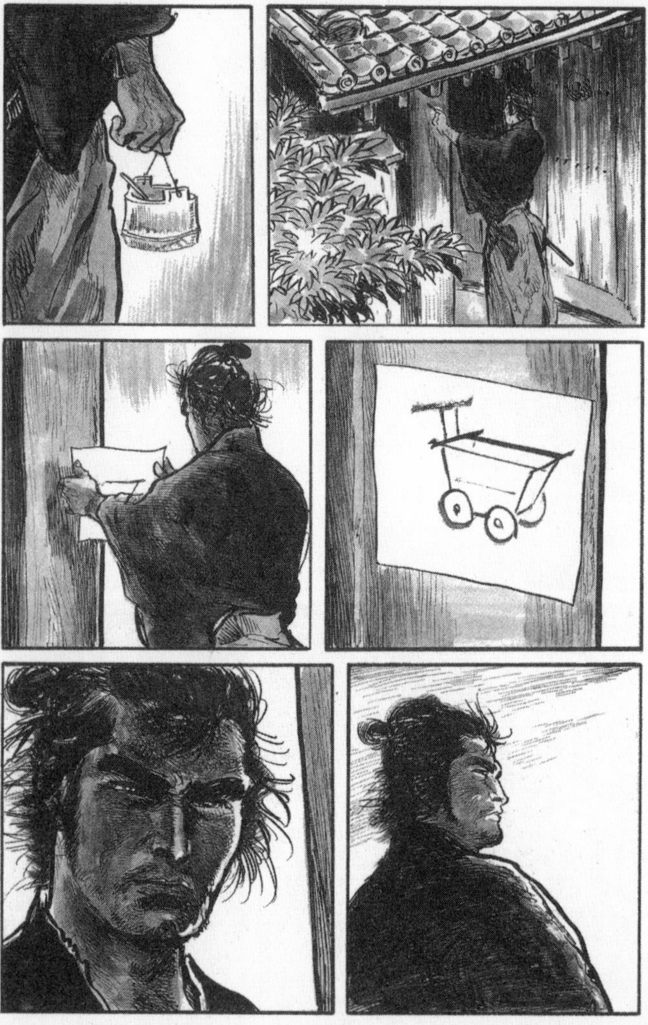

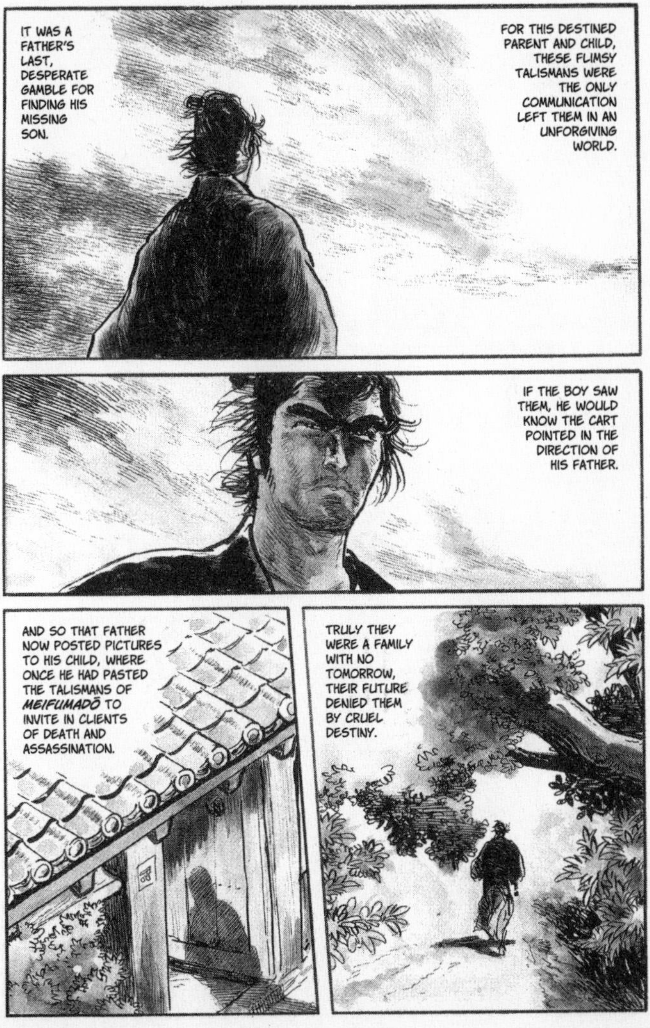
IT WAS A FATHER'S LAST, DESPERATE GAMBLE FOR FINDING HIS MISSING SON.
FOR THIS DESTINED PARENT AND CHILD, THESE FLIMSY TALISMANS WERE THE ONLY COMMUNICATION LEFT THEM IN AN UNFORGIVING WORLD.
IF THE BOY SAW THEM, HE WOULD KNOW THE CART POINTED IN THE DIRECTION OF HIS FATHER.
AND SO THAT FATHER NOW POSTED PICTURES TO HIS CHILD, WHERE ONCE HE HAD PASTED THE TALISMANS OF *MEIFUMADŌ* TO INVITE IN CLIENTS OF DEATH AND ASSASSINATION.
TRULY THEY WERE A FAMILY WITH NO TOMORROW, THEIR FUTURE DENIED THEM BY CRUEL DESTINY.

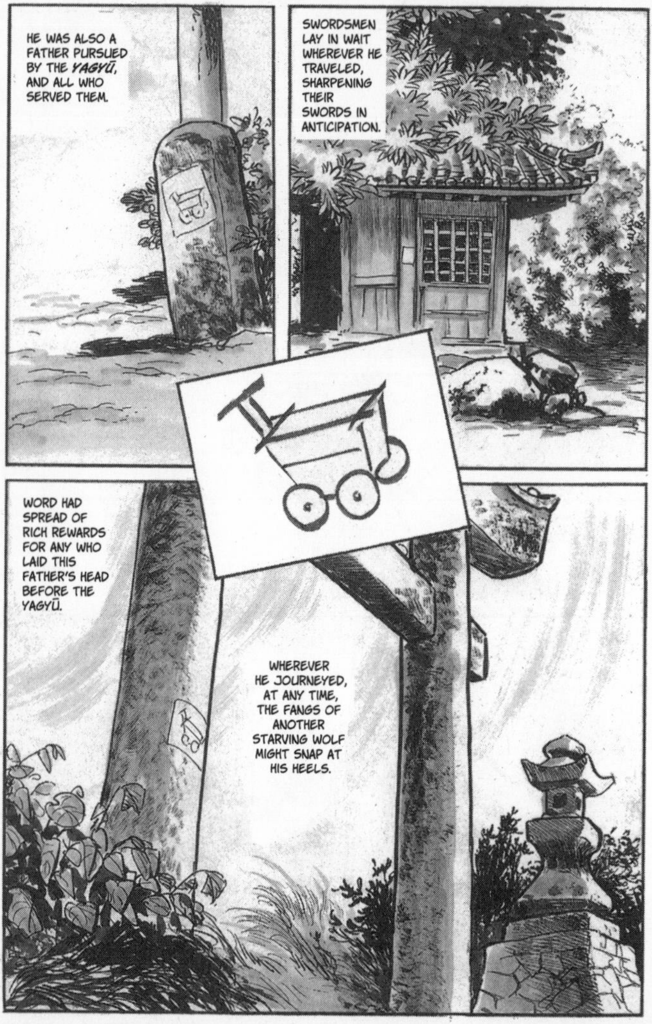
HE WAS ALSO A FATHER PURSUED BY THE *YAGYŪ*, AND ALL WHO SERVED THEM.
SWORDSMEN LAY IN WAIT WHEREVER HE TRAVELED, SHARPENING THEIR SWORDS IN ANTICIPATION.
WORD HAD SPREAD OF RICH REWARDS FOR ANY WHO LAID THIS FATHER'S HEAD BEFORE THE YAGYŪ.
WHEREVER HE JOURNEYED, AT ANY TIME, THE FANGS OF ANOTHER STARVING WOLF MIGHT SNAP AT HIS HEELS.

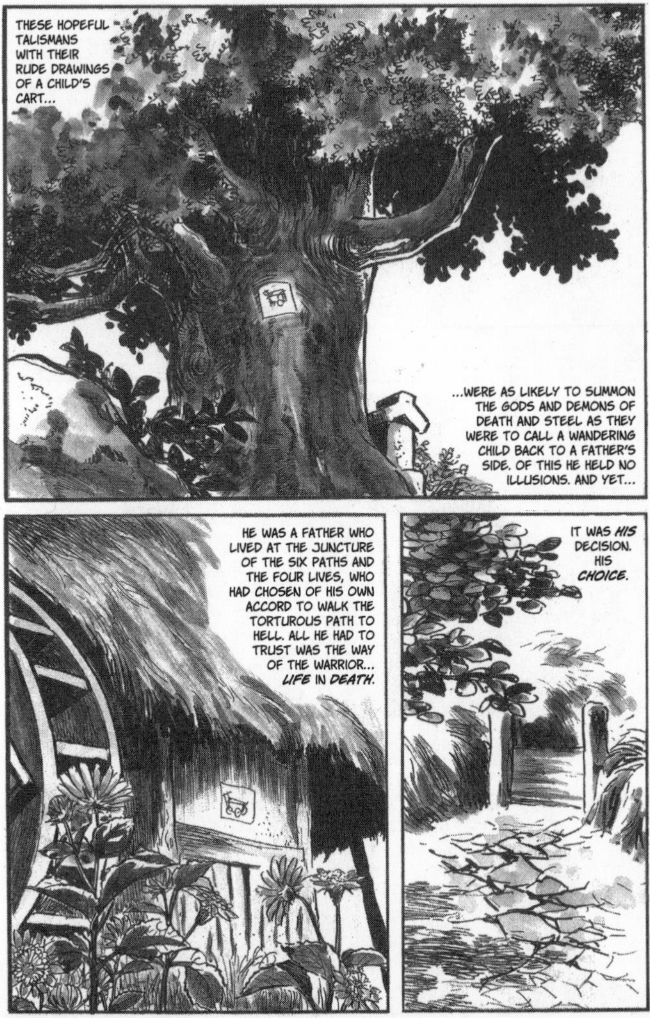
THESE HOPEFUL TALISMANS WITH THEIR RUDE DRAWINGS OF A CHILD'S CART...
...WERE AS LIKELY TO SUMMON THE GODS AND DEMONS OF DEATH AND STEEL AS THEY WERE TO CALL A WANDERING CHILD BACK TO A FATHER'S SIDE. OF THIS HE HELD NO ILLUSIONS. AND YET...
HE WAS A FATHER WHO LIVED AT THE JUNCTURE OF THE SIX PATHS AND THE FOUR LIVES, WHO HAD CHOSEN OF HIS OWN ACCORD TO WALK THE TORTUROUS PATH TO HELL. ALL HE HAD TO TRUST WAS THE WAY OF THE WARRIOR... *LIFE* IN *DEATH*.
IT WAS *HIS* DECISION. HIS *CHOICE*.

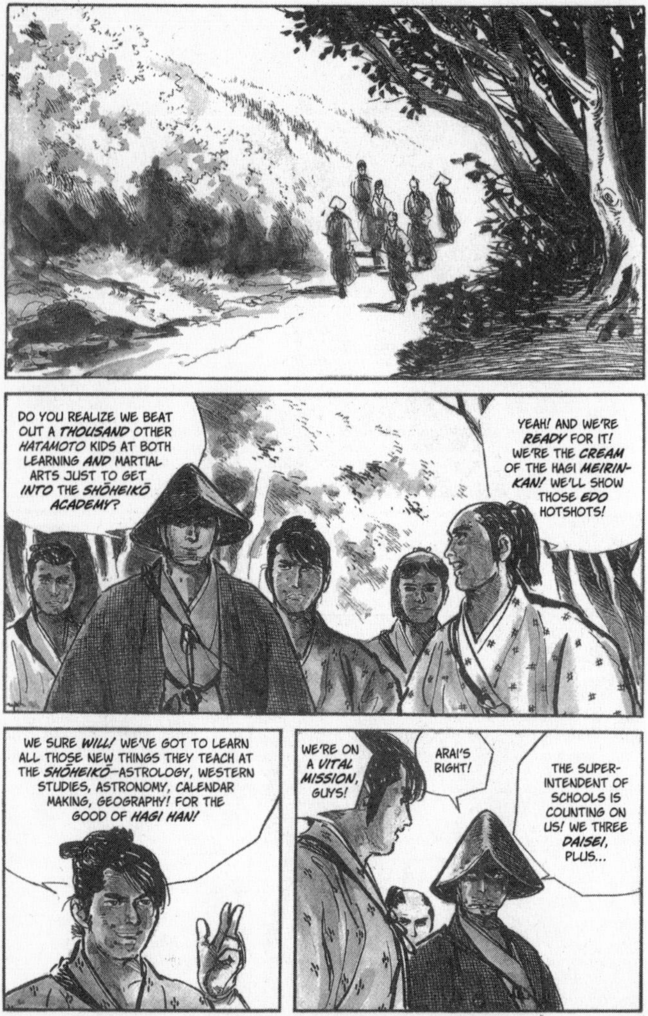
DO YOU REALIZE WE BEAT OUT A THOUSAND OTHER HATAMOTO KIDS AT BOTH LEARNING AND MARTIAL ARTS JUST TO GET INTO THE SHŌHEIKŌ ACADEMY?
YEAH! AND WE'RE READY FOR IT! WE'RE THE CREAM OF THE HAGI MEIRIN-KAN! WE'LL SHOW THOSE EDO HOTSHOTS!
WE SURE WILL! WE'VE GOT TO LEARN ALL THOSE NEW THINGS THEY TEACH AT THE SHŌHEIKŌ—ASTROLOGY, WESTERN STUDIES, ASTRONOMY, CALENDAR MAKING, GEOGRAPHY! FOR THE GOOD OF HAGI HAN!
WE'RE ON A VITAL MISSION, GUYS!
ARAI'S RIGHT!
THE SUPER-INTENDENT OF SCHOOLS IS COUNTING ON US! WE THREE DAISEI, PLUS...

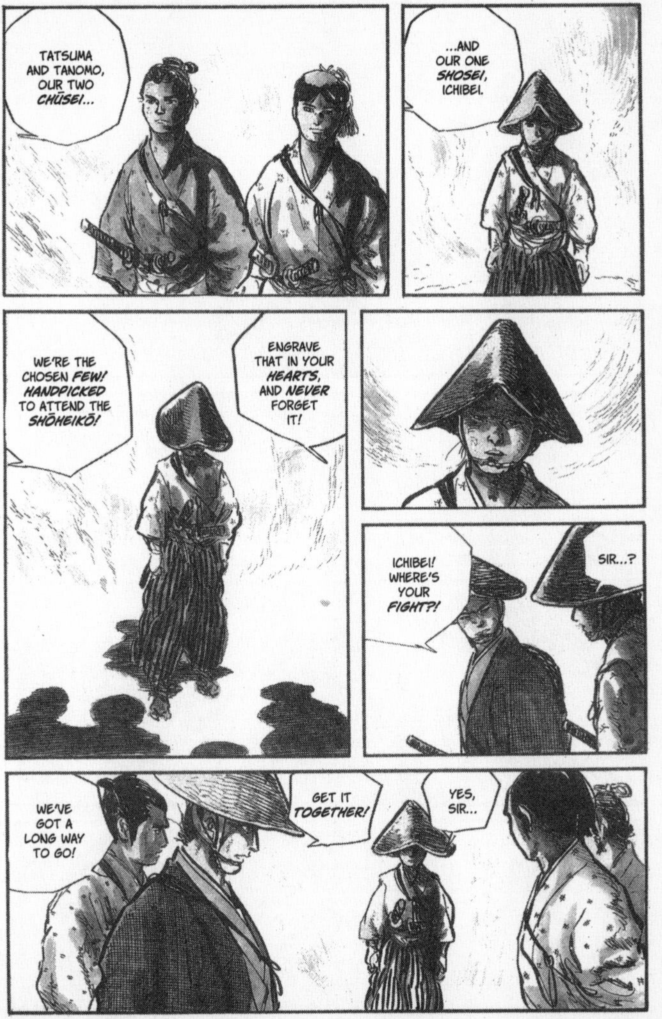
TATSUMA AND TANOMO, OUR TWO *CHŪSEI*...
...AND OUR ONE *SHOSEI*, ICHIBEI.
WE'RE THE CHOSEN *FEW! HANDPICKED* TO ATTEND THE *SHŌHEIKŌ!*
ENGRAVE THAT IN YOUR *HEARTS*, AND *NEVER* FORGET IT!
ICHIBEI! WHERE'S YOUR *FIGHT?!*
SIR...?
WE'VE GOT A LONG WAY TO GO!
GET IT *TOGETHER!*
YES, SIR...

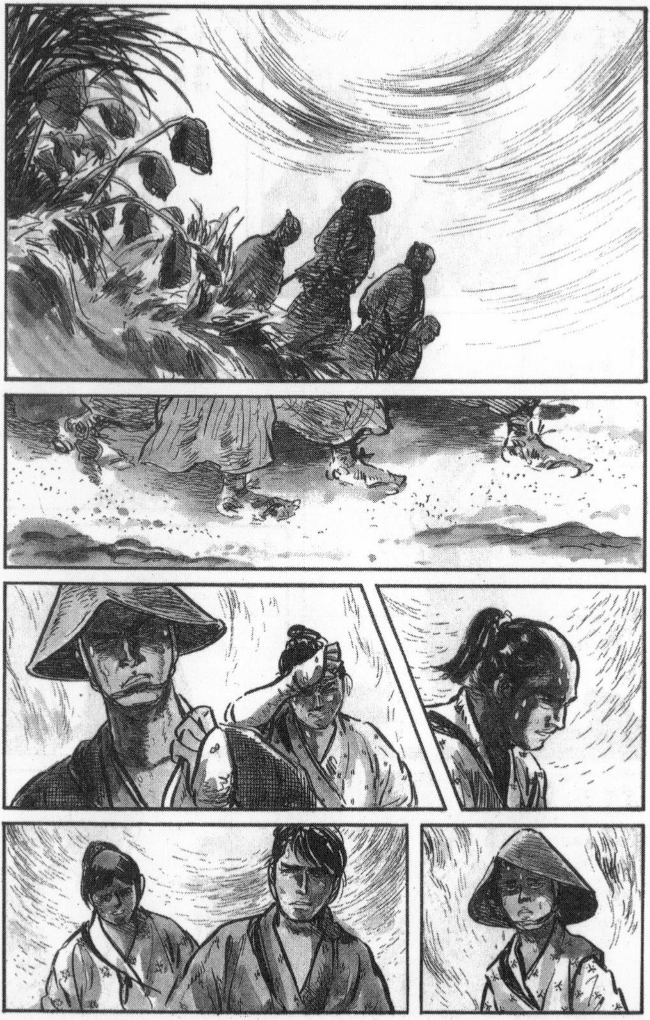

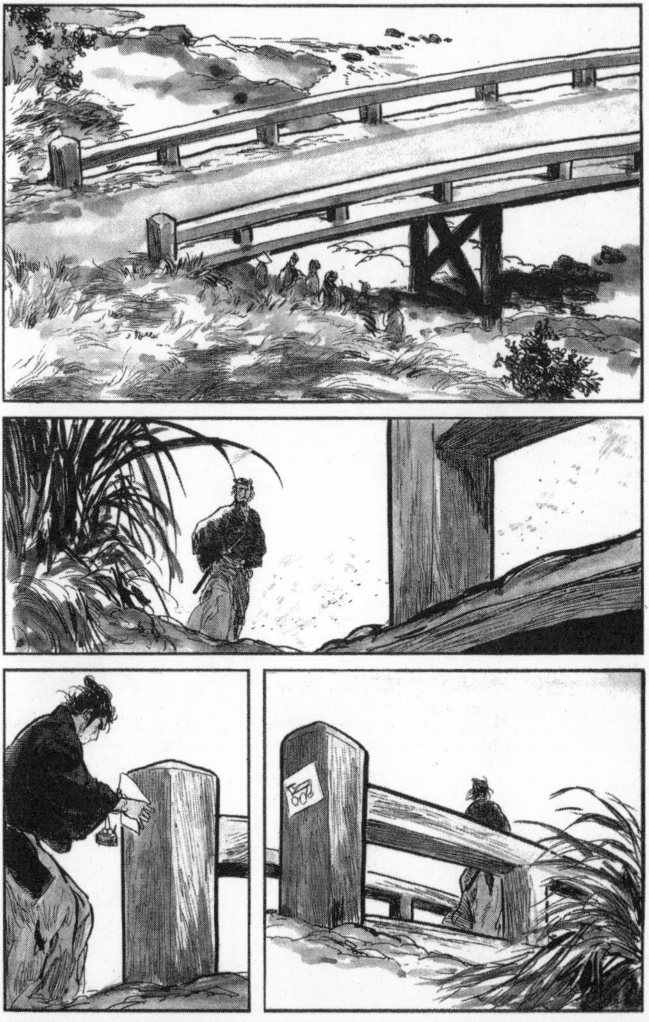

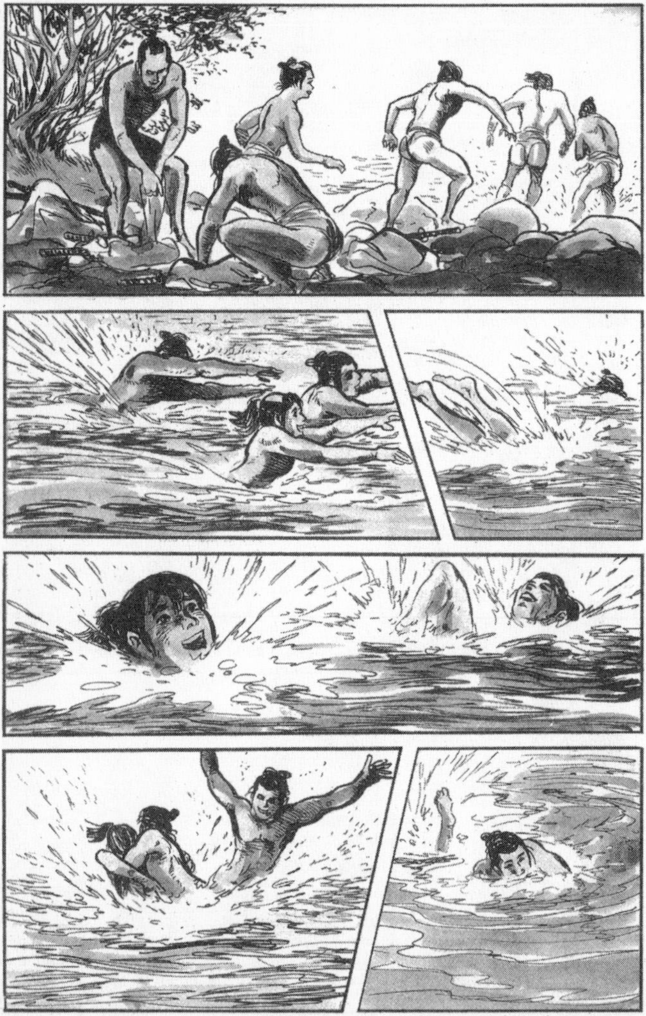

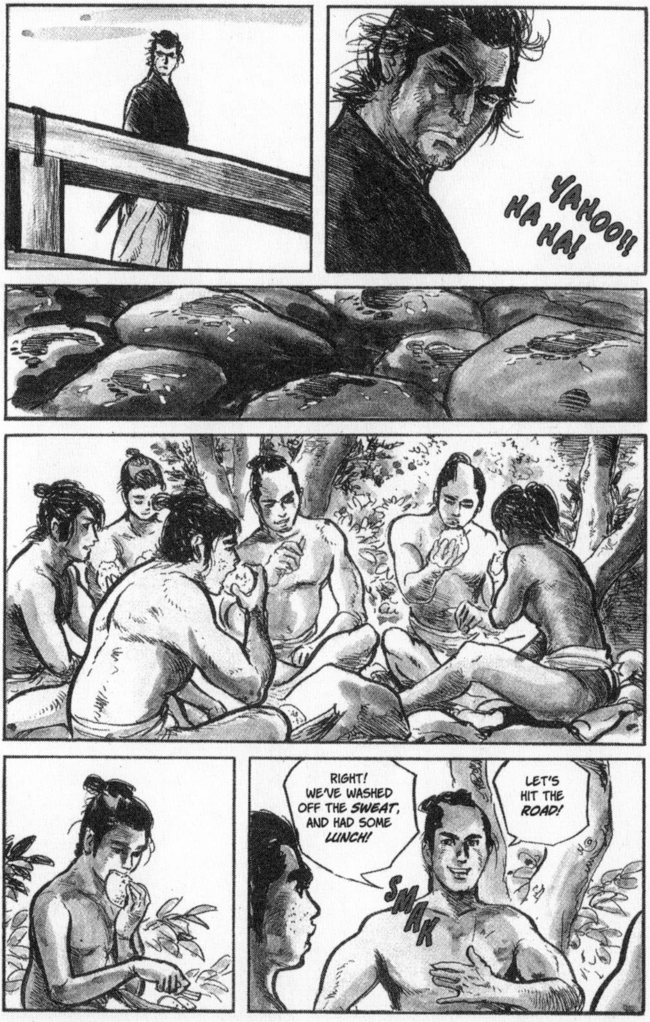
YAHOO!! HA HA!
RIGHT! WE'VE WASHED OFF THE SWEAT, AND HAD SOME LUNCH!
SMAK
LET'S HIT THE ROAD!

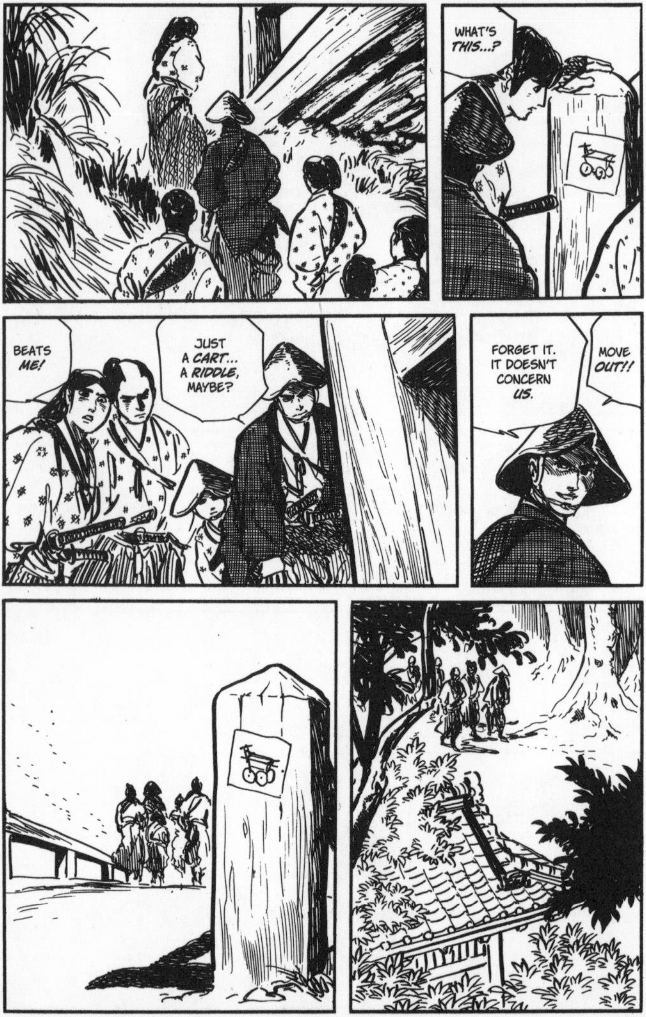

WHAT'S *THIS...?*
BEATS *ME!*
JUST A *CART*... A *RIDDLE,* MAYBE?
FORGET IT. IT DOESN'T CONCERN *US.*
MOVE *OUT!!*

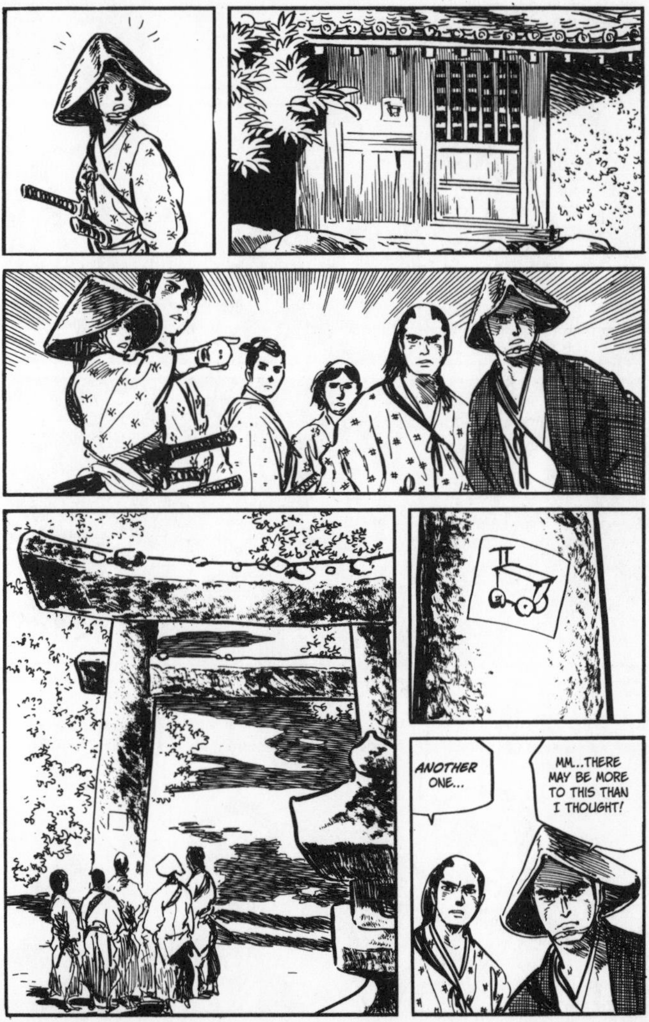
ANOTHER ONE...
MM...THERE MAY BE MORE TO THIS THAN I THOUGHT!

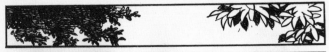

ELDER BROTHER...? MAYBE IT'S A *CODE*... FOR A *RENDEZVOUS* OR SOMETHING?

HMM. IF SOMEONE'S BEEN POSTING THEM ALL ALONG THE *HIGHWAY*, IT'S GOTTA BE *BIG*. BIGGER THAN A SINGLE VILLAGE.

IN WHICH CASE...*BANDITS?* A MESSAGE FOR A GANG OF *GRIFTERS?* HRMM...

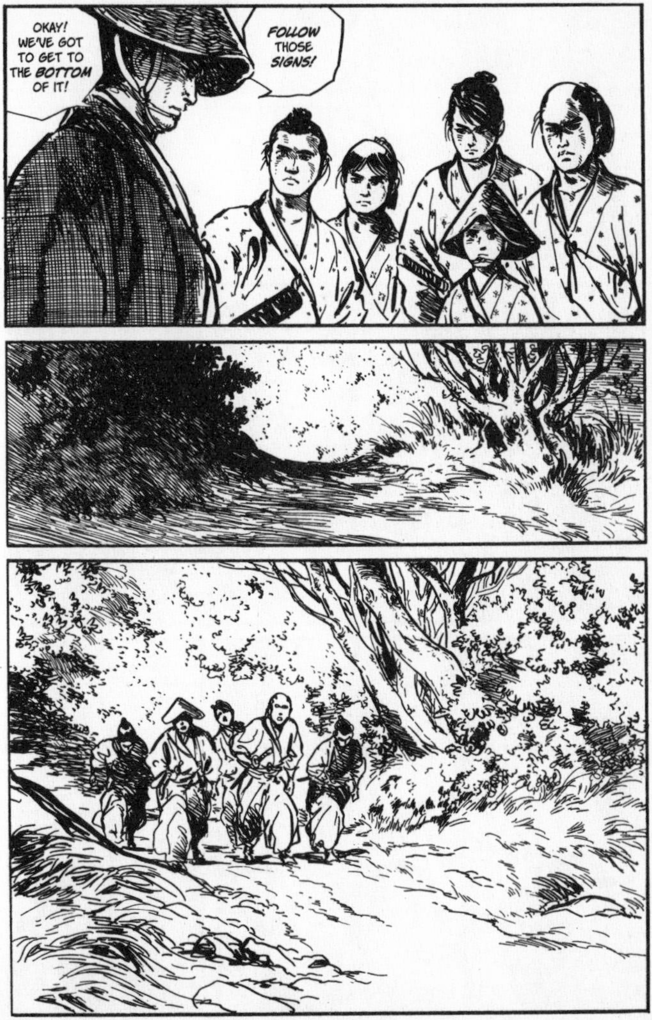
OKAY! WE'VE GOT TO GET TO THE *BOTTOM* OF IT!
FOLLOW THOSE *SIGNS!*

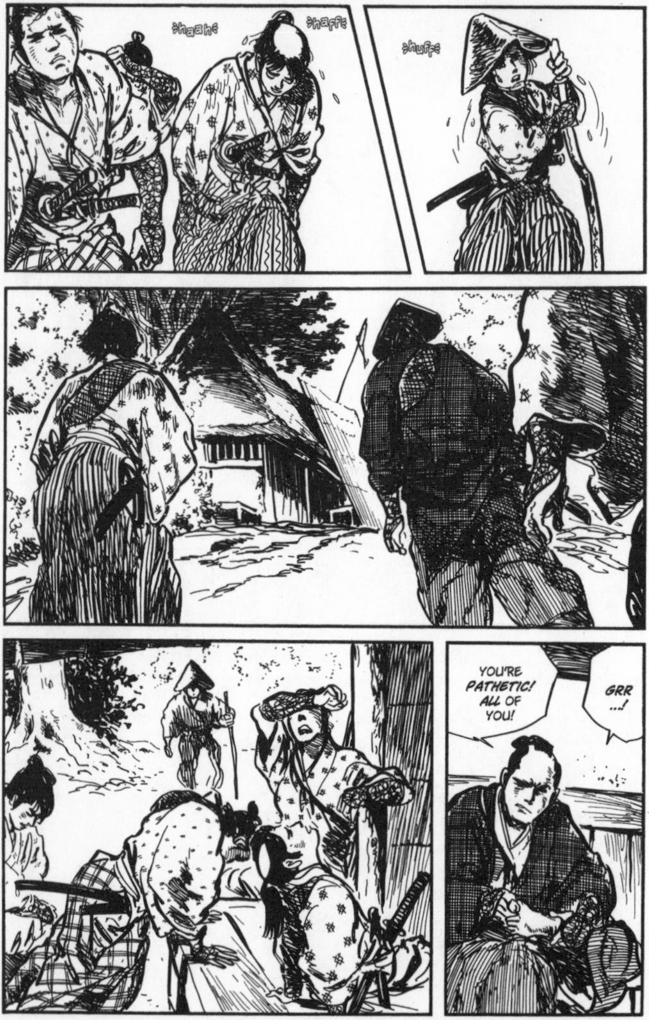
haah
haff
huff
YOU'RE PATHETIC! ALL OF YOU!
GRR ...!

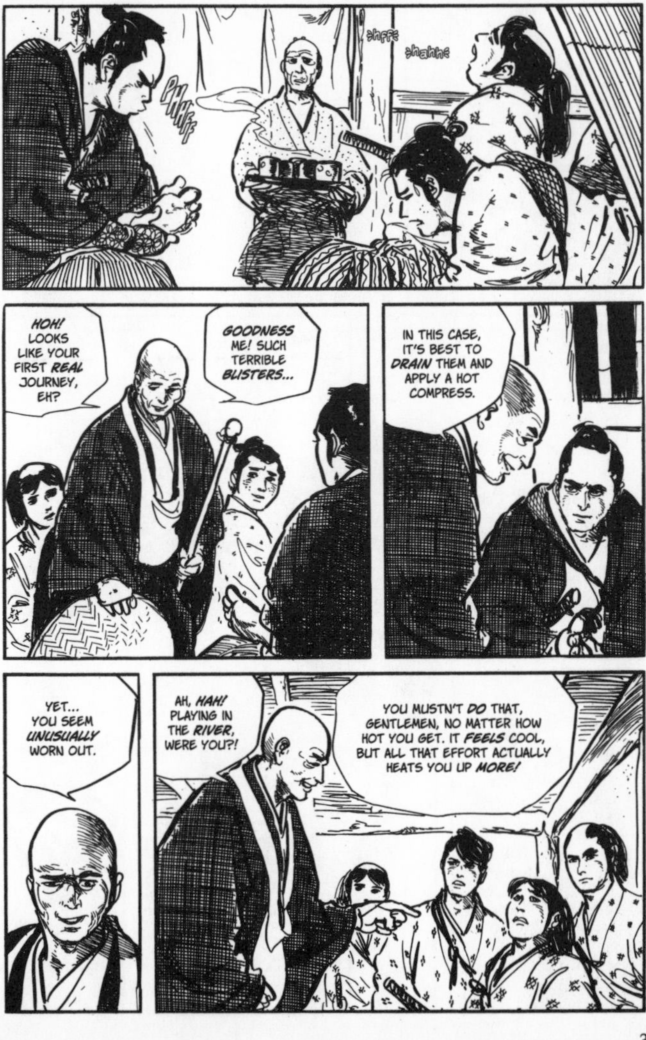
PHHFF
hff
hahh
HOH! LOOKS LIKE YOUR FIRST REAL JOURNEY, EH?
GOODNESS ME! SUCH TERRIBLE BLISTERS...
IN THIS CASE, IT'S BEST TO DRAIN THEM AND APPLY A HOT COMPRESS.
YET... YOU SEEM UNUSUALLY WORN OUT.
AH, HAH! PLAYING IN THE RIVER, WERE YOU?!
YOU MUSTN'T DO THAT, GENTLEMEN, NO MATTER HOW HOT YOU GET. IT FEELS COOL, BUT ALL THAT EFFORT ACTUALLY HEATS YOU UP MORE!

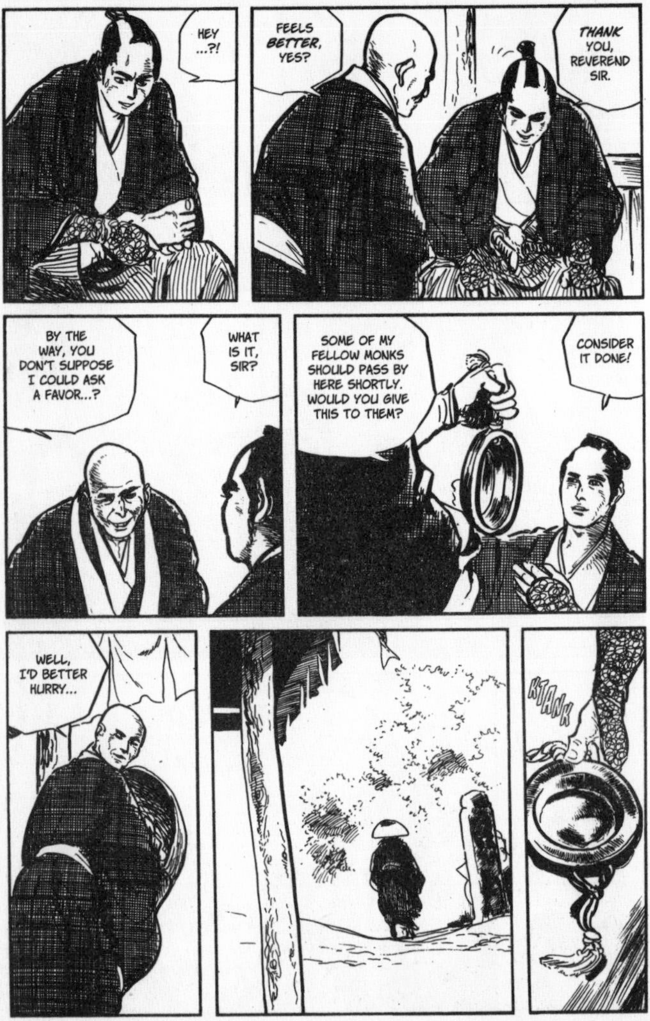
HEY ...?!
FEELS *BETTER,* YES?
THANK YOU, REVEREND SIR.
BY THE WAY, YOU DON'T SUPPOSE I COULD ASK A FAVOR...?
WHAT IS IT, SIR?
SOME OF MY FELLOW MONKS SHOULD PASS BY HERE SHORTLY. WOULD YOU GIVE THIS TO THEM?
CONSIDER IT DONE!
WELL, I'D BETTER HURRY...
KTANK

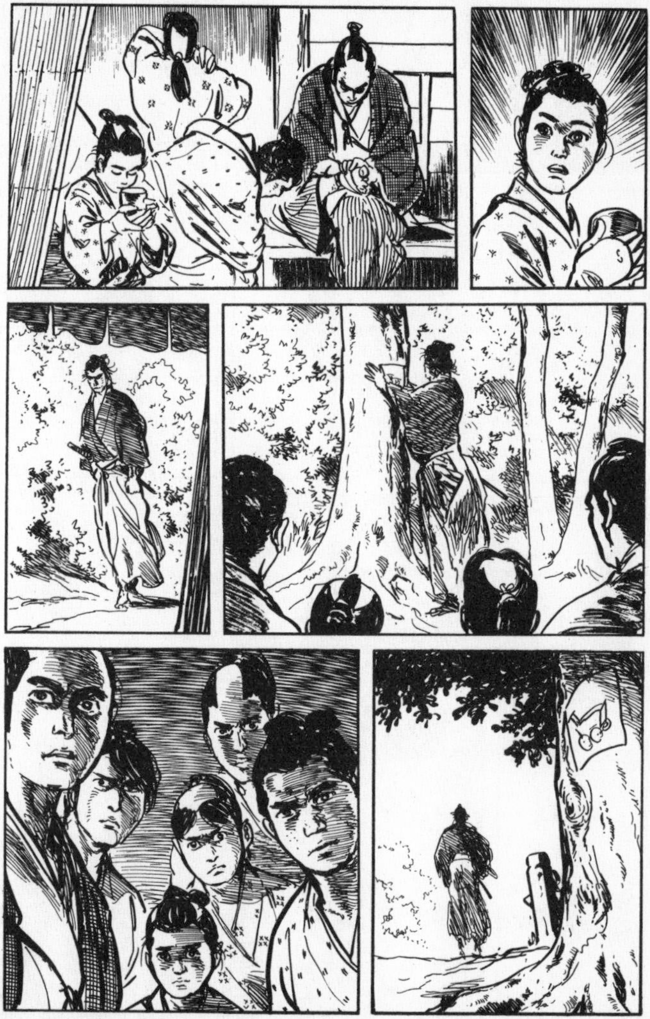

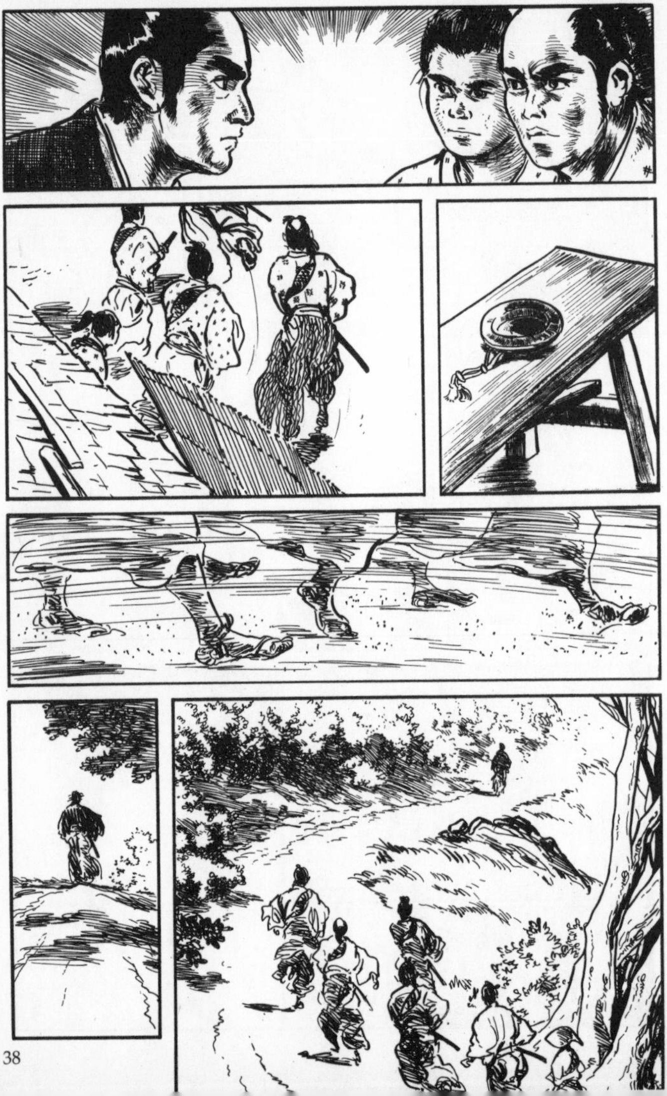

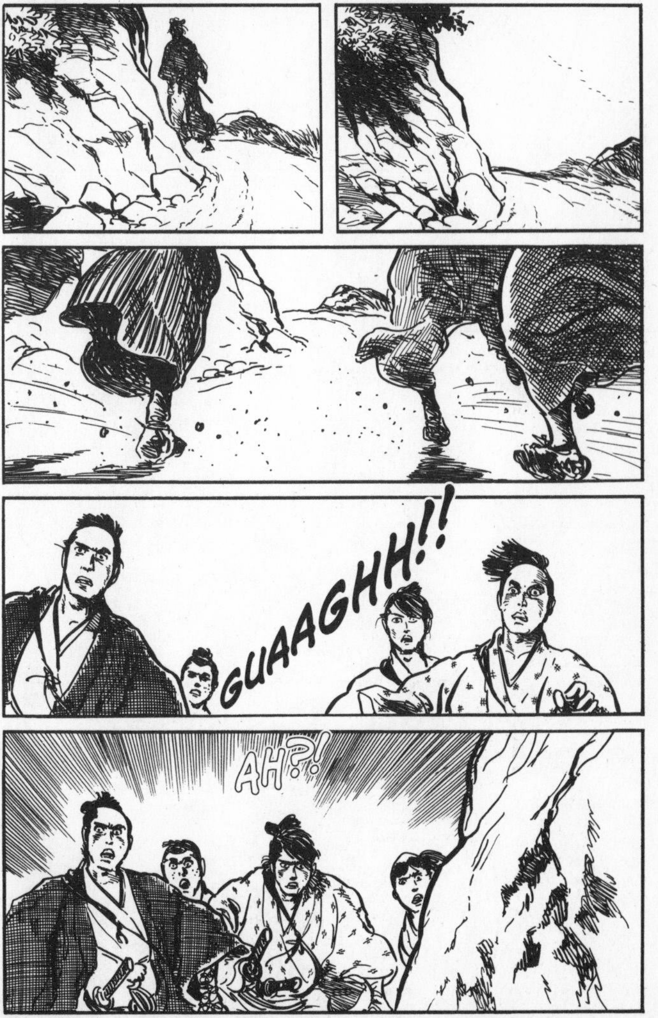
GUAAGHH!!
AH?!

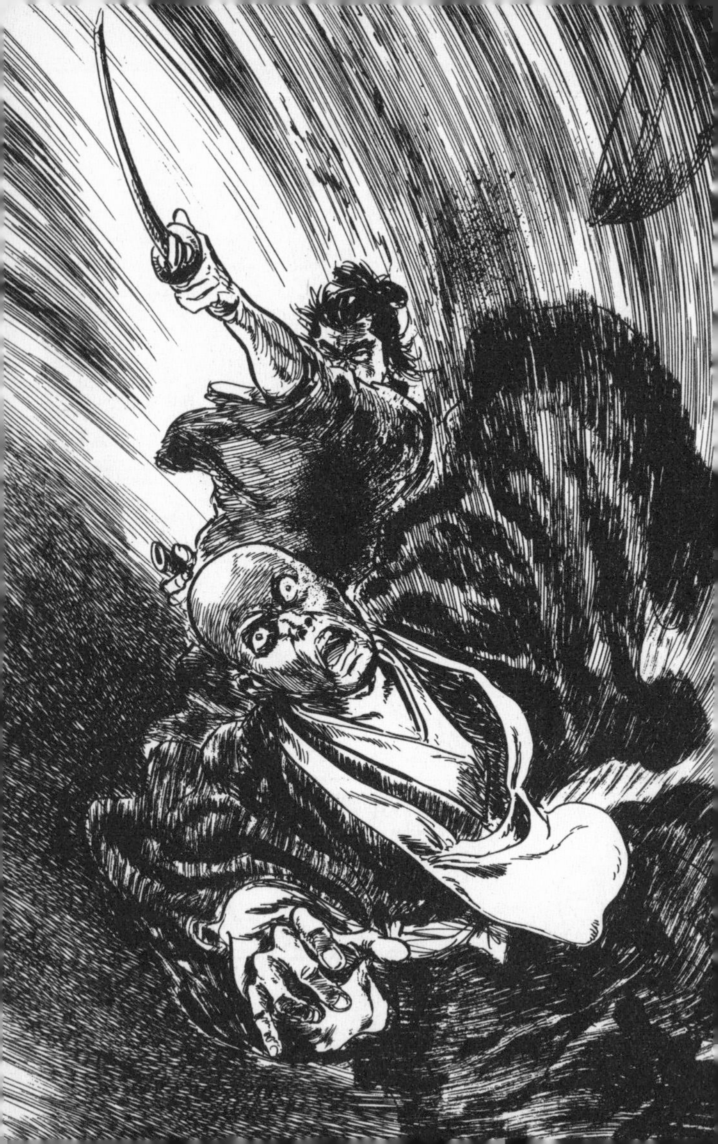

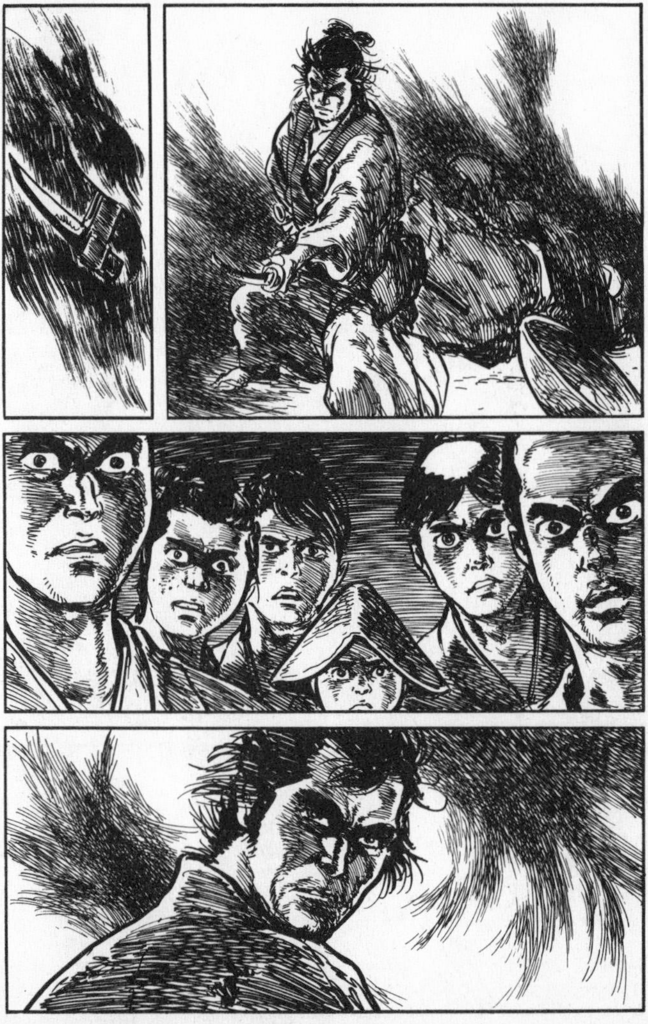

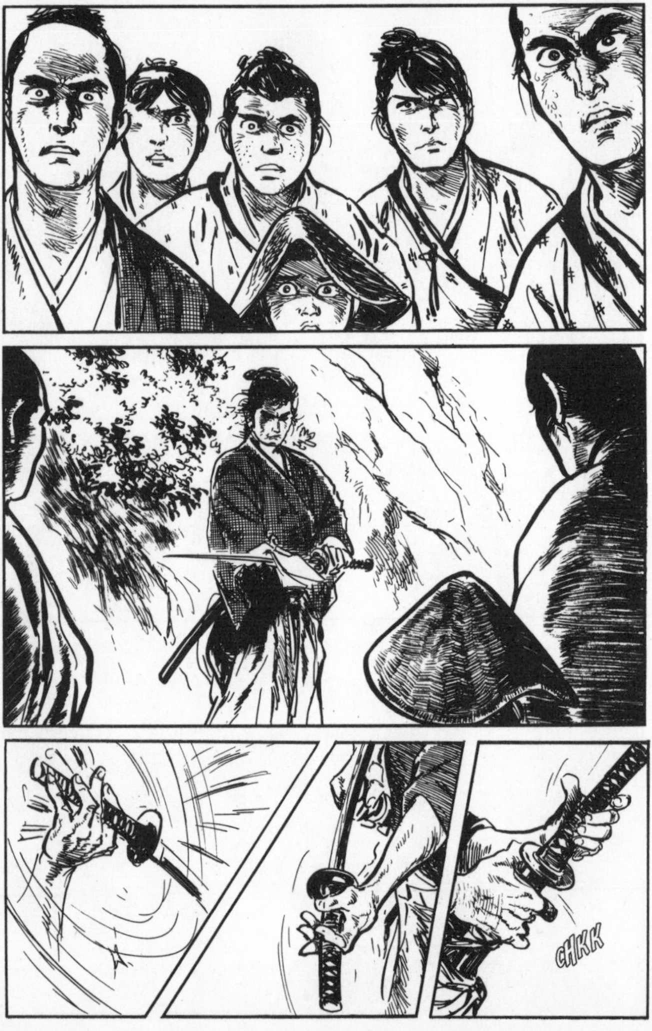
CHKK

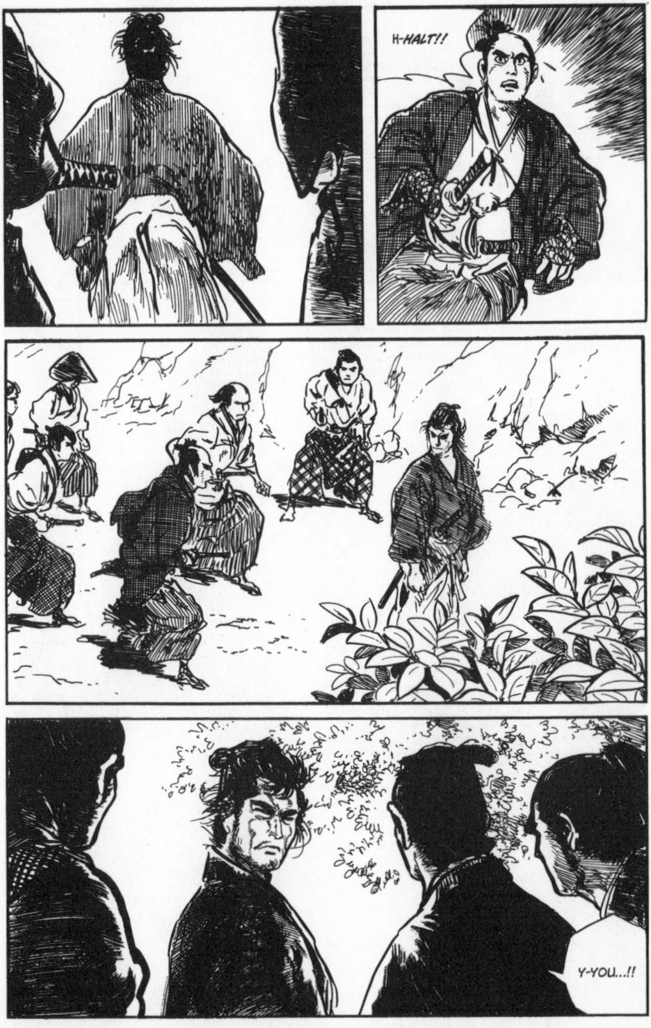
H-HALT!!
Y-YOU...!!

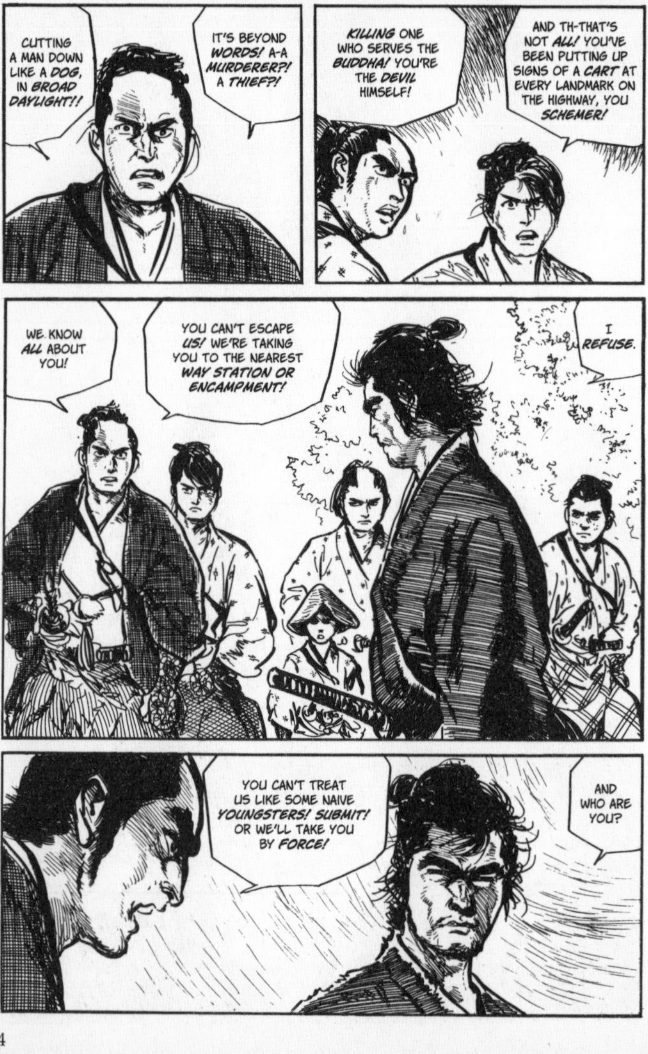
CUTTING A MAN DOWN LIKE A DOG, IN BROAD DAYLIGHT!!
IT'S BEYOND WORDS! A-A MURDERER?! A THIEF?!
KILLING ONE WHO SERVES THE BUDDHA! YOU'RE THE DEVIL HIMSELF!
AND TH-THAT'S NOT ALL! YOU'VE BEEN PUTTING UP SIGNS OF A CART AT EVERY LANDMARK ON THE HIGHWAY, YOU SCHEMER!
WE KNOW ALL ABOUT YOU!
YOU CAN'T ESCAPE US! WE'RE TAKING YOU TO THE NEAREST WAY STATION OR ENCAMPMENT!
I REFUSE.
YOU CAN'T TREAT US LIKE SOME NAIVE YOUNGSTERS! SUBMIT! OR WE'LL TAKE YOU BY FORCE!
AND WHO ARE YOU?

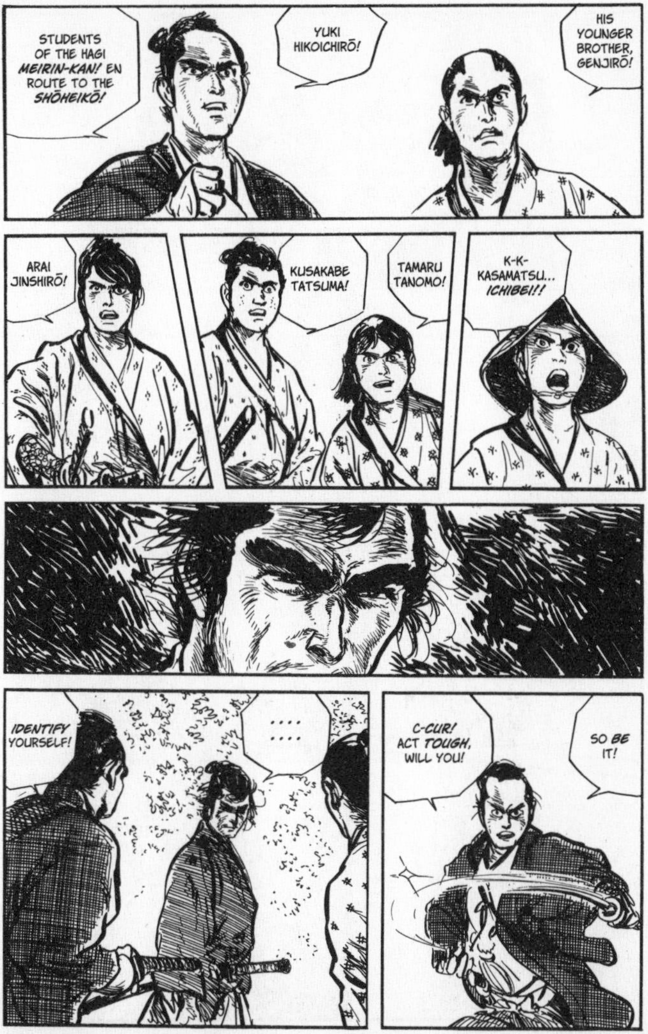
STUDENTS OF THE HAGI *MEIRIN-KAN!* EN ROUTE TO THE *SHŌHEIKŌ!*
YUKI HIKOICHIRŌ!
HIS YOUNGER BROTHER, GENJIRŌ!
ARAI JINSHIRŌ!
KUSAKABE TATSUMA!
TAMARU TANOMO!
K-K-KASAMATSU... *ICHIBEI!!*
IDENTIFY YOURSELF!
....
....
C-CUR! ACT *TOUGH,* WILL YOU!
SO *BE* IT!

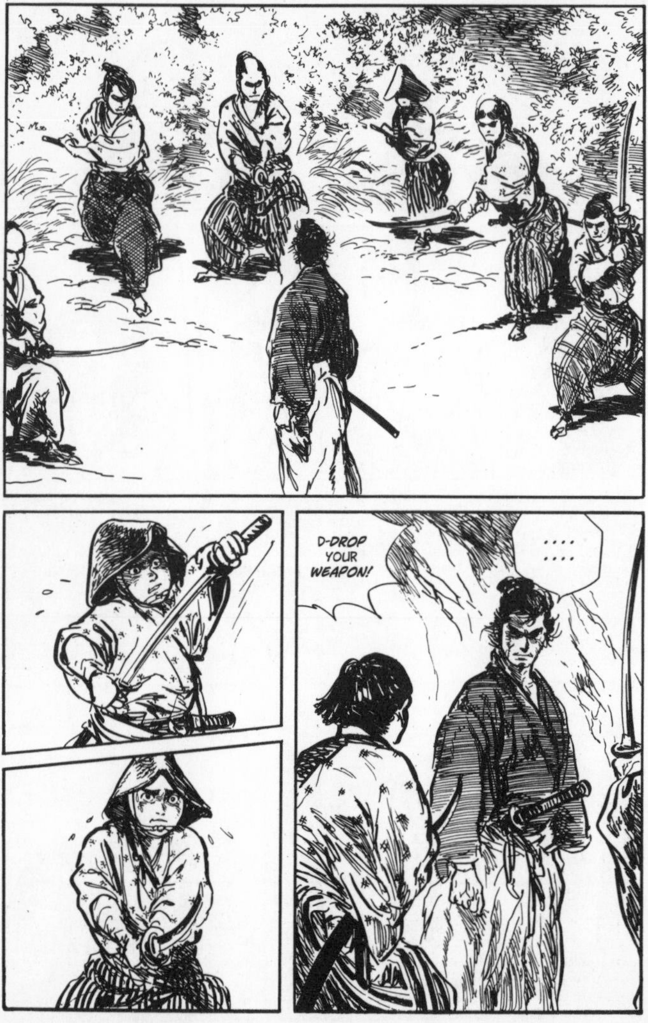
D-DROP YOUR WEAPON!
....
....

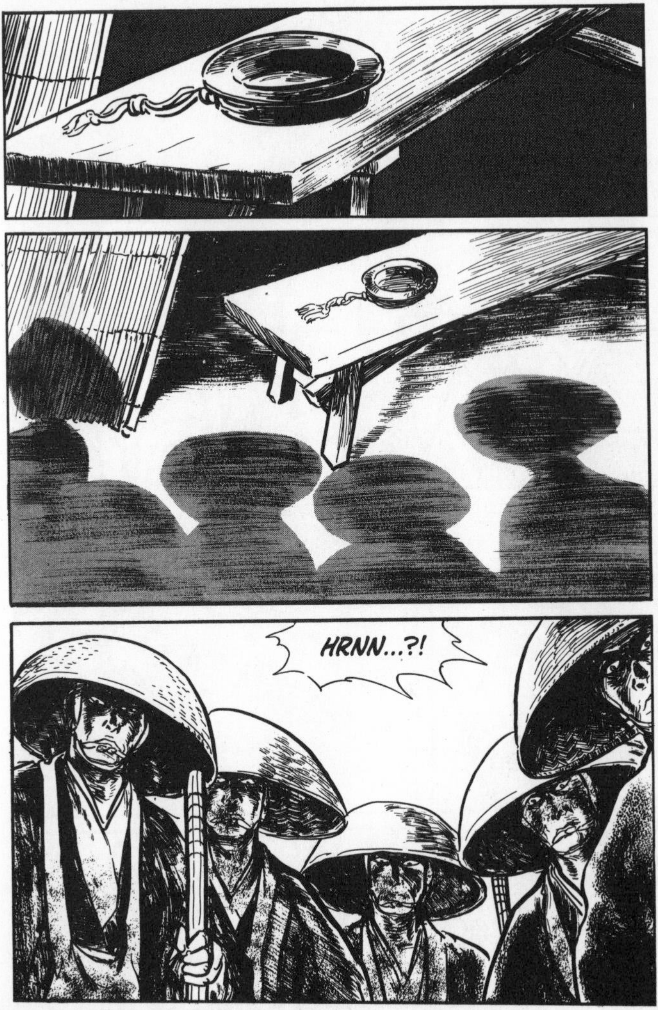
HRNN...?!

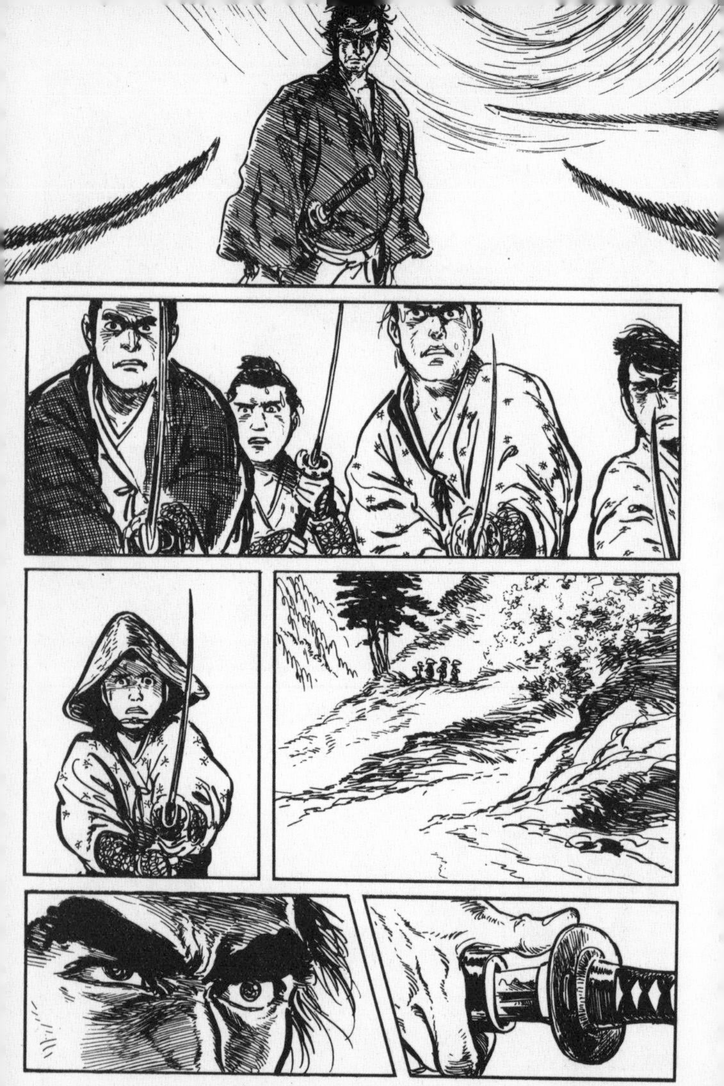

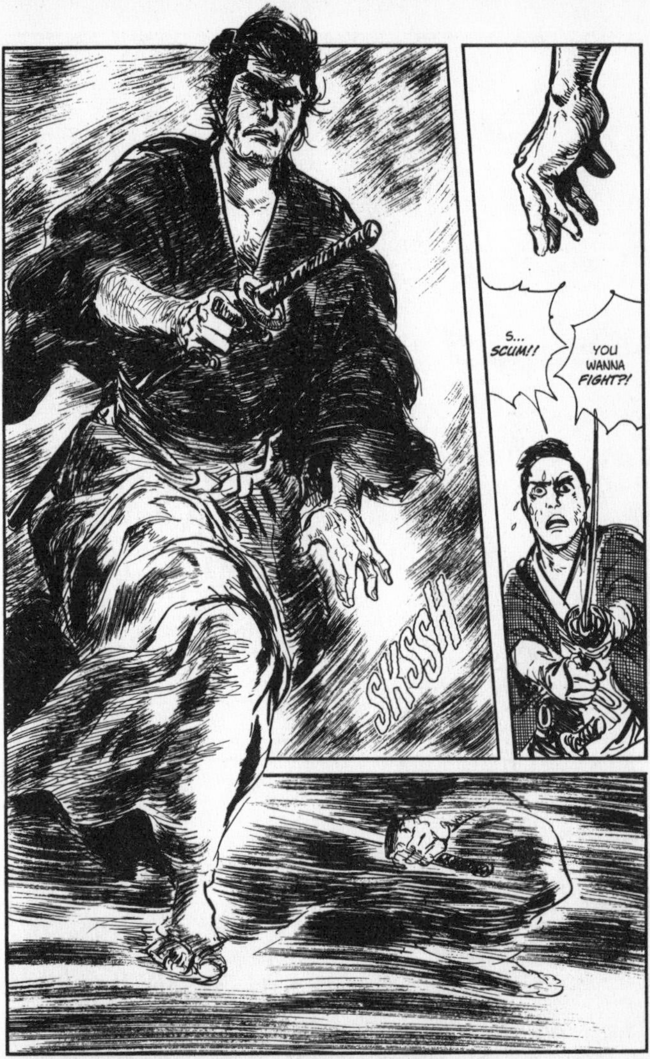
SKSSH
S... SCUM!!
YOU WANNA FIGHT?!

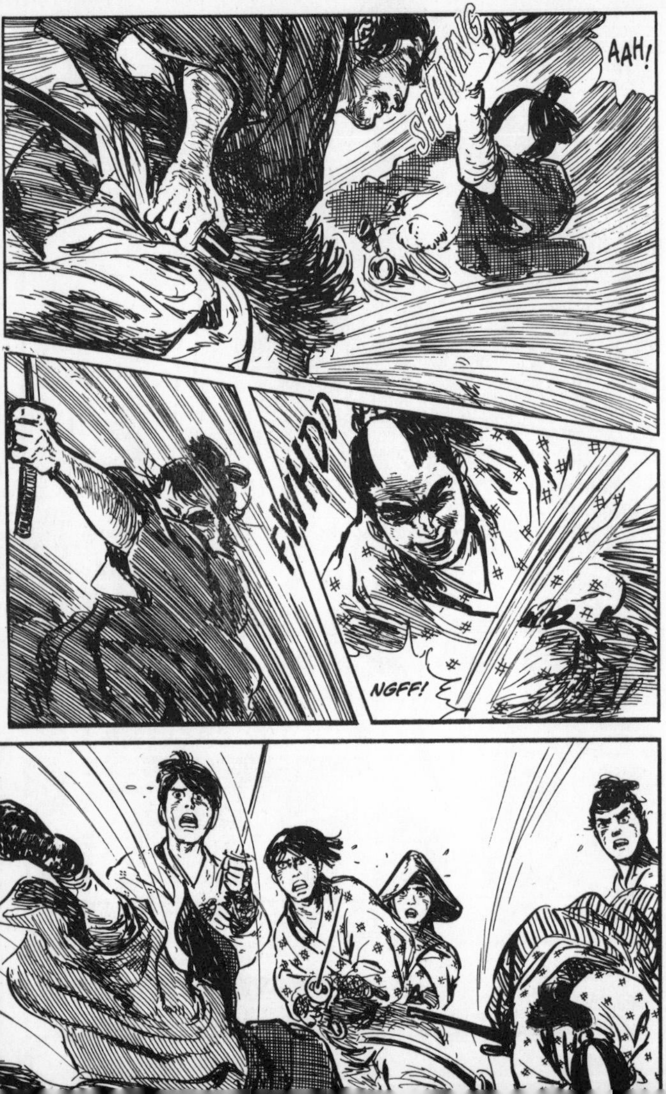
SHANG
AAH!
FWHOD
NGFF!

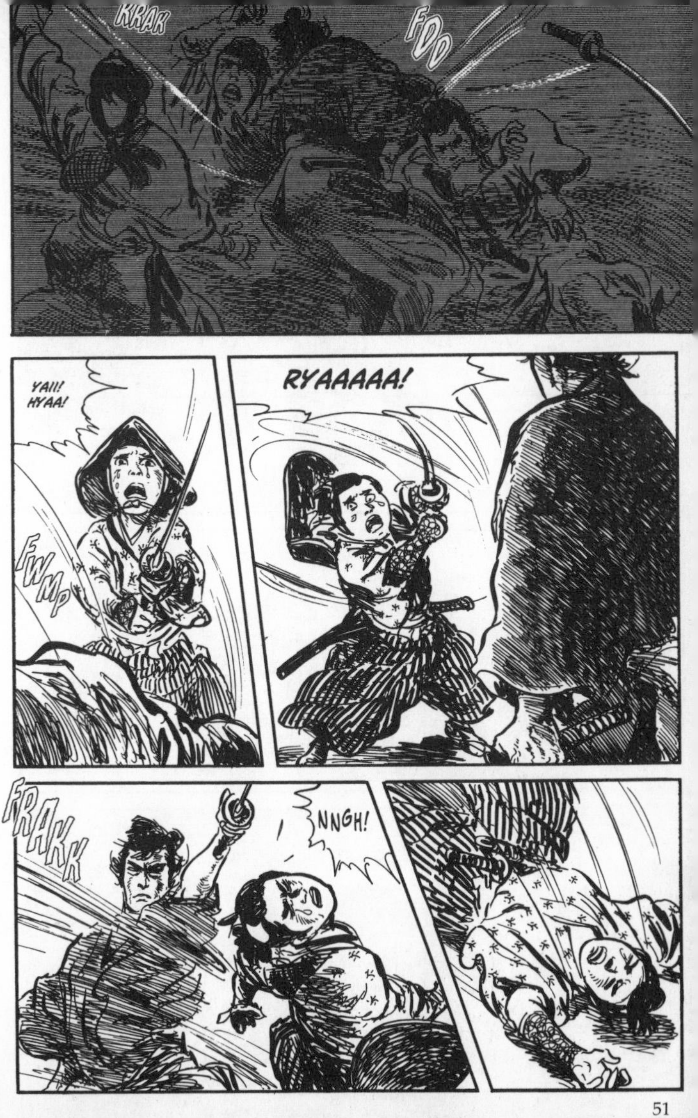
KRAK
FDD
YAII! HYAA!
FWMP
RYAAAAA!
FRAKK
NNGH!

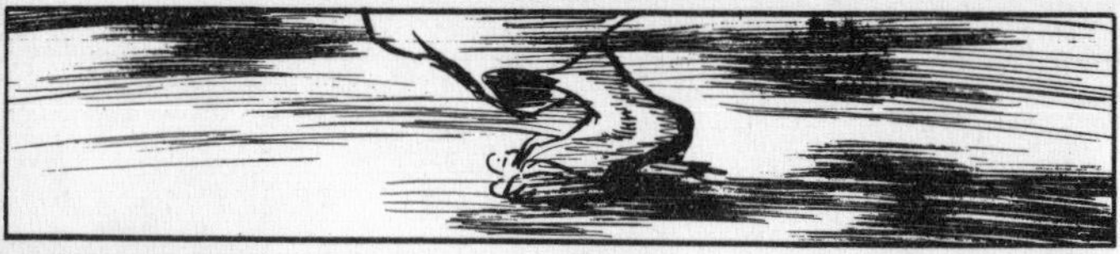

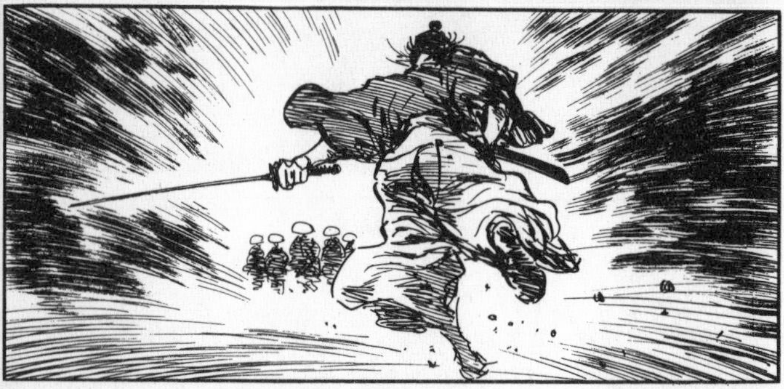

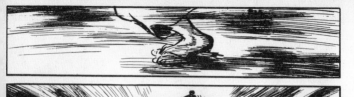

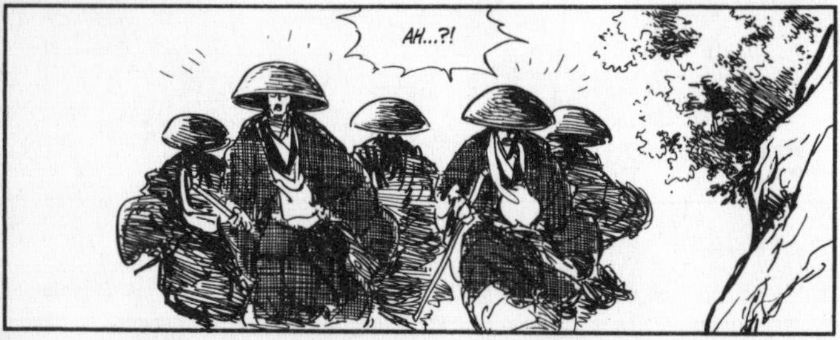
AH...?!

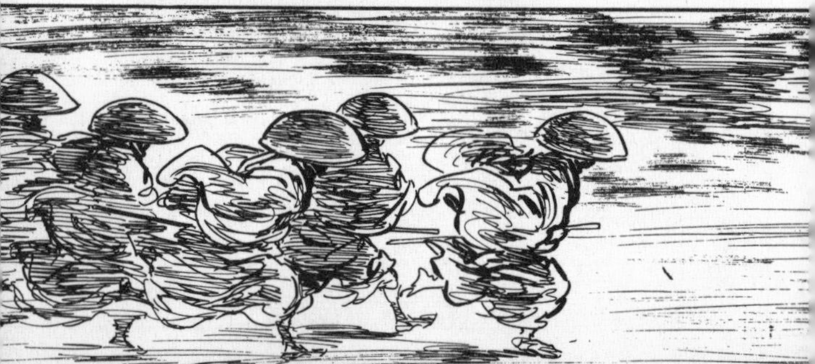

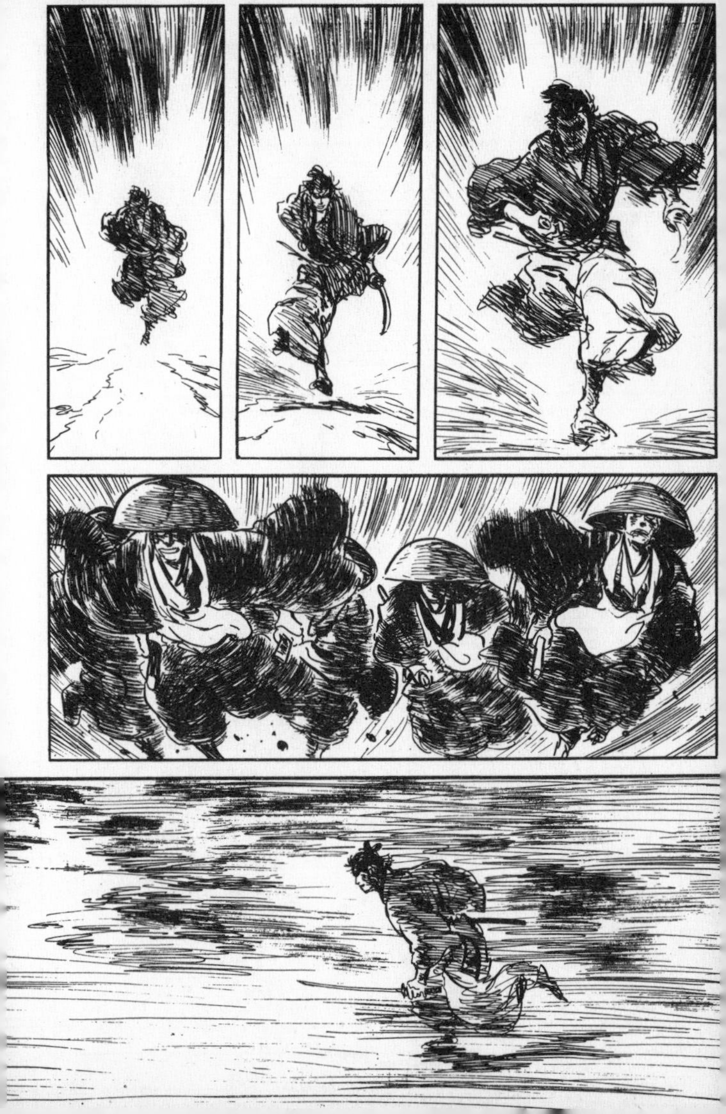

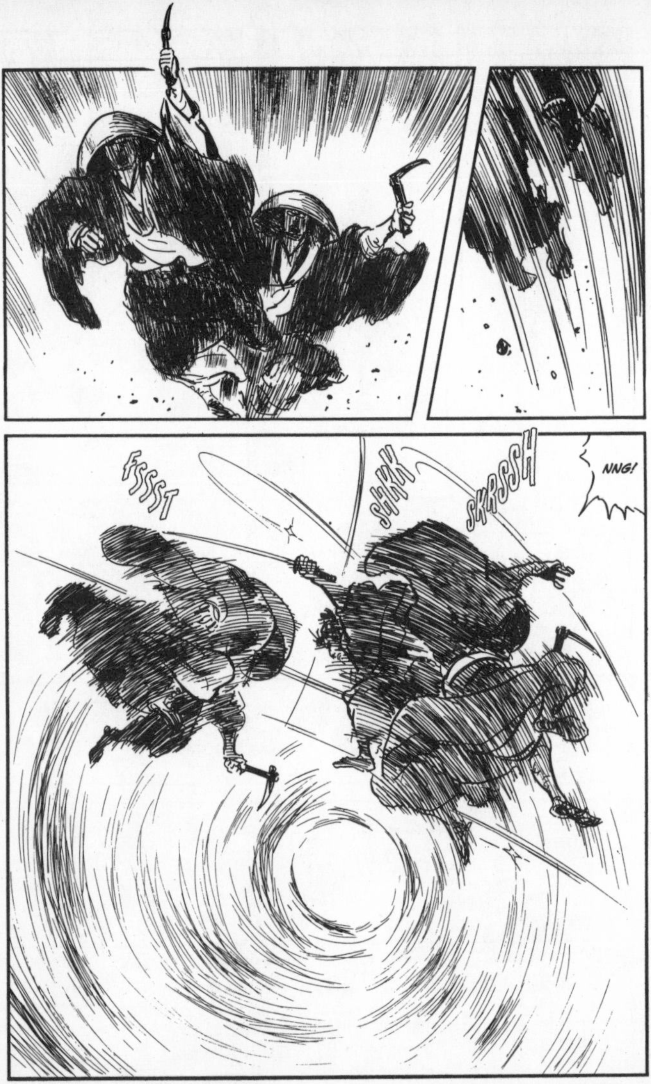
FSSST
SHKK
SKRSSH
NNG!

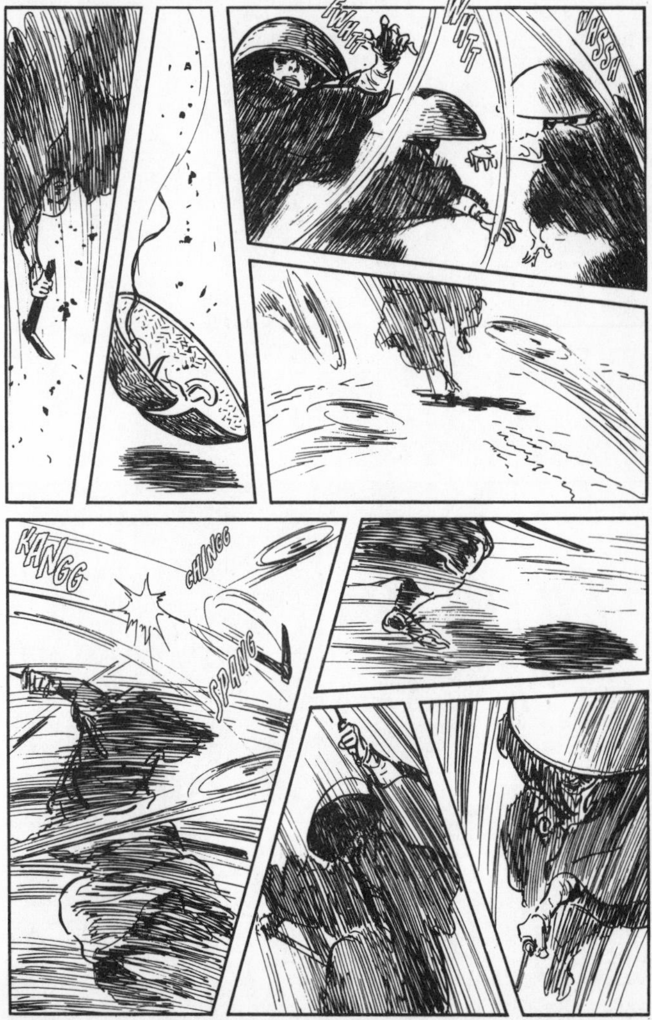
FWHTT
WHTT
WHSSH
KANGG
CHINGG
SPANG

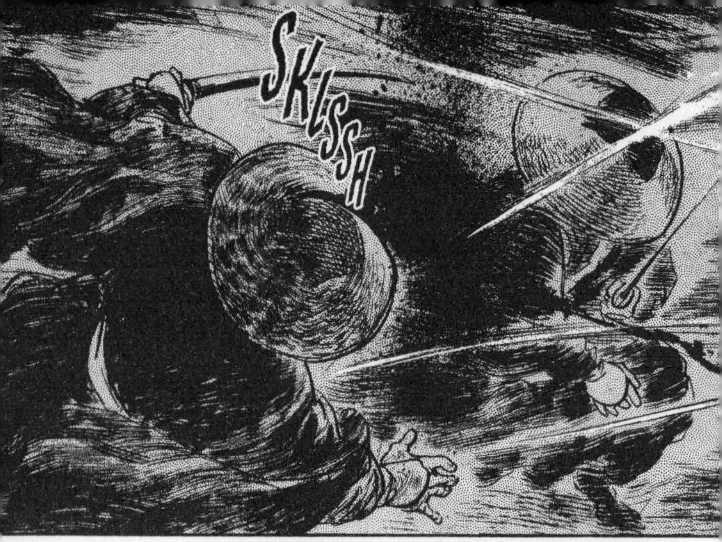
SKLSSH

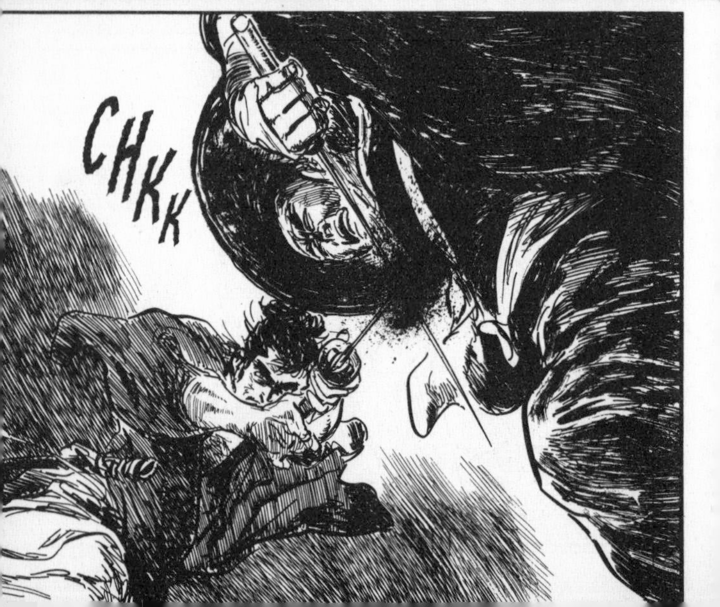
CHKK

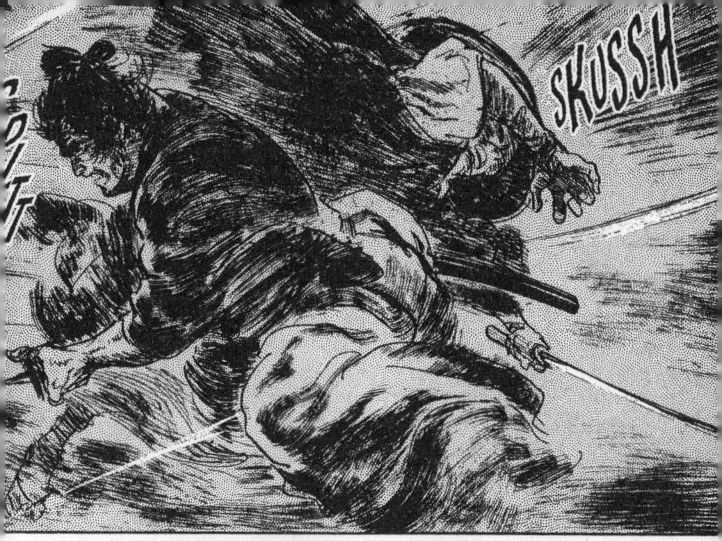
SKUSSH

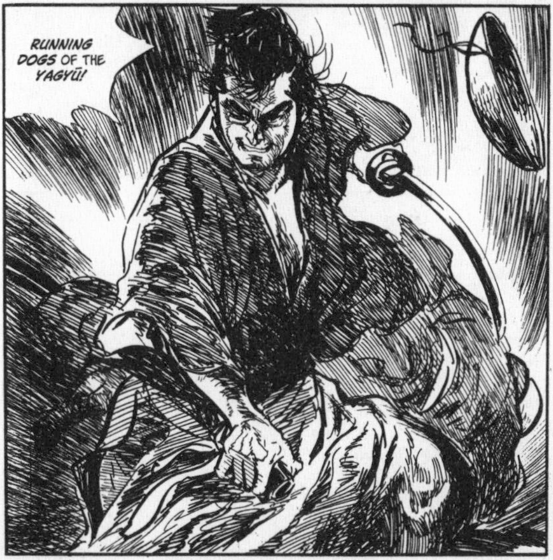
RUNNING DOGS OF THE YAGYŪ!

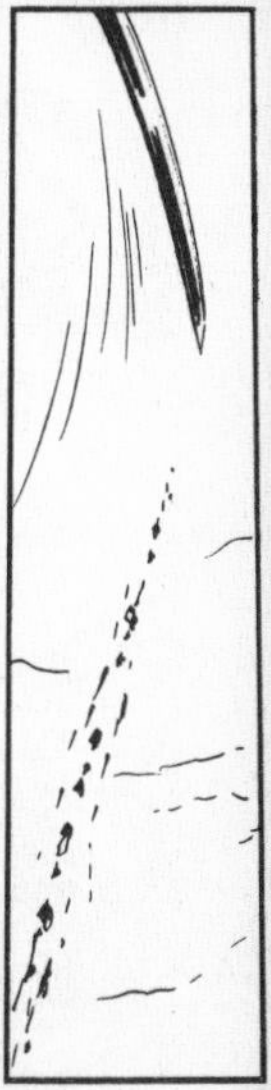

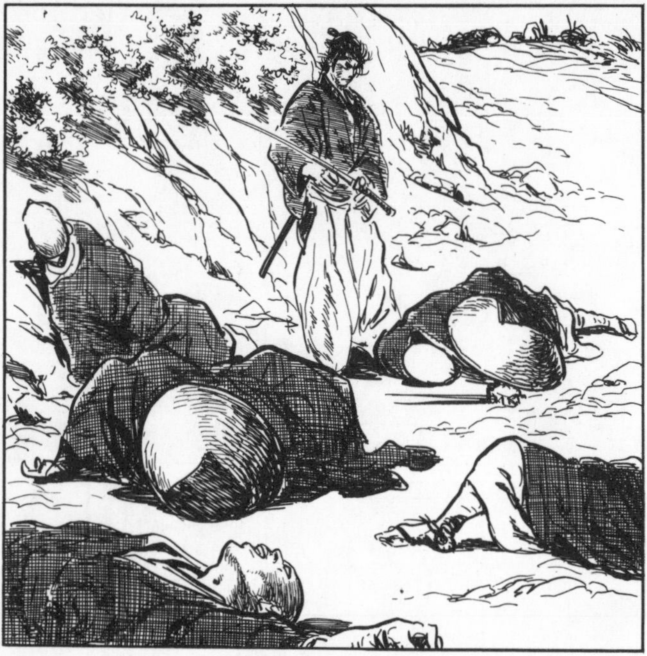

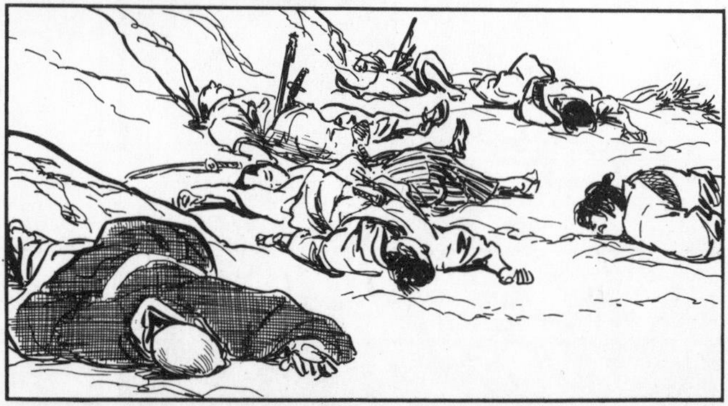

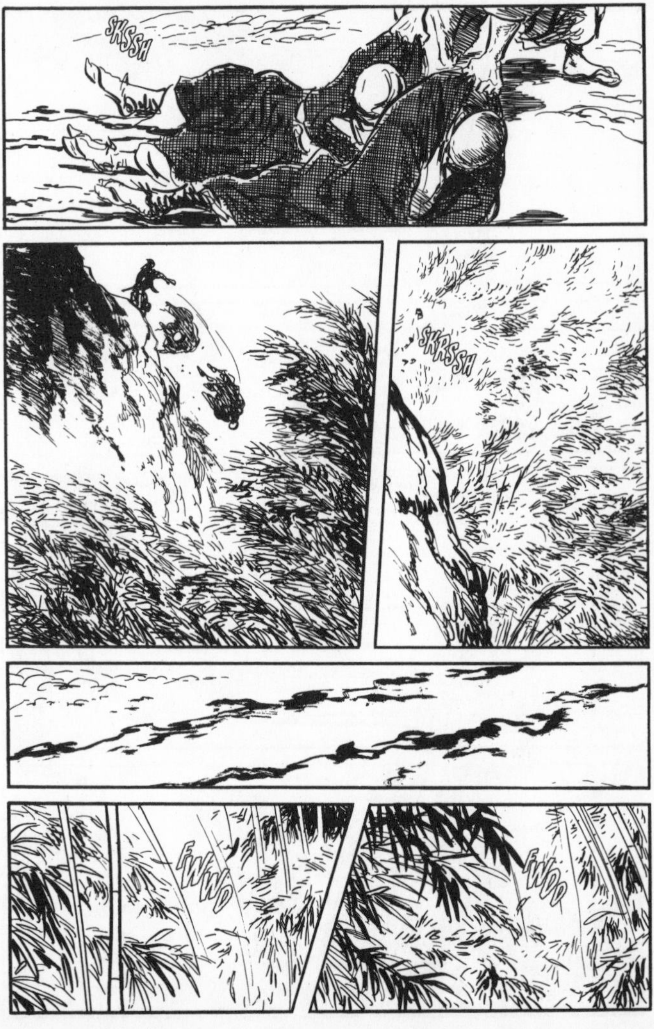
SKSSH
SKRSSH
FWWO
FWOO

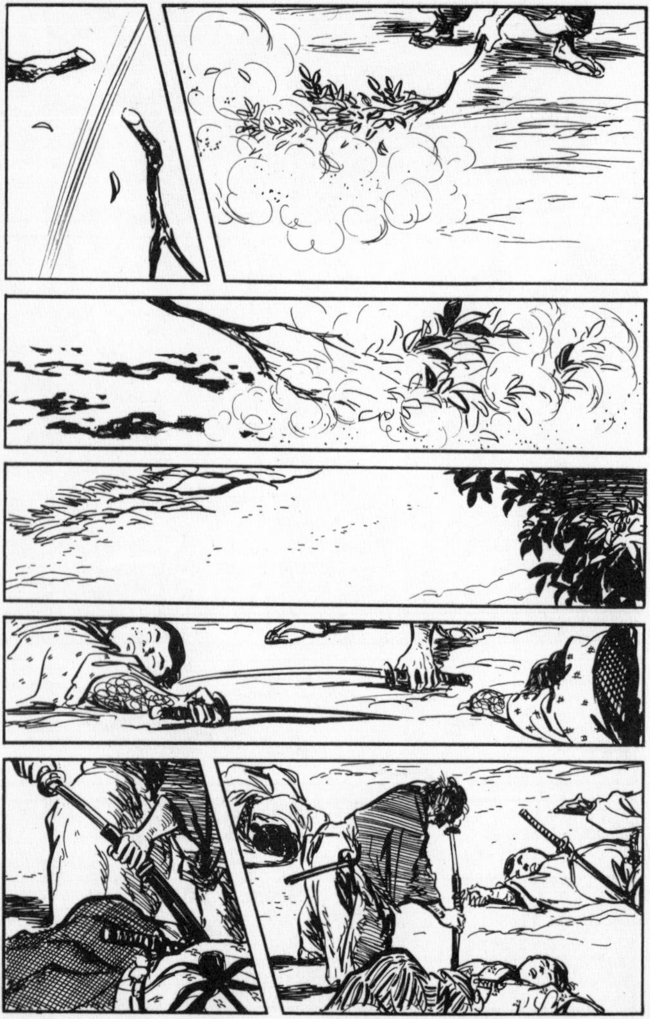

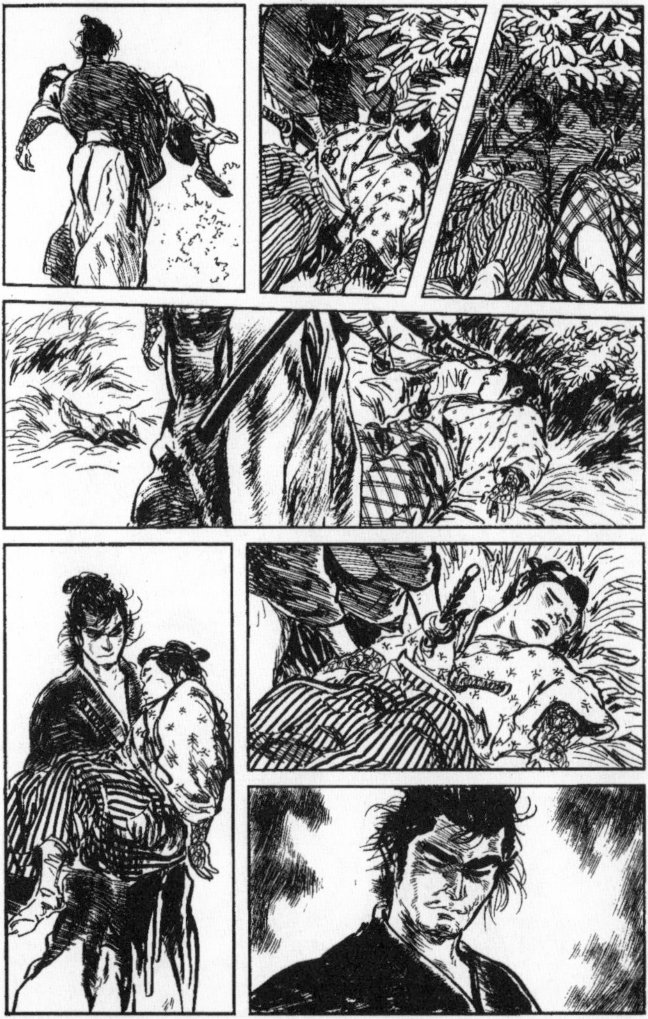

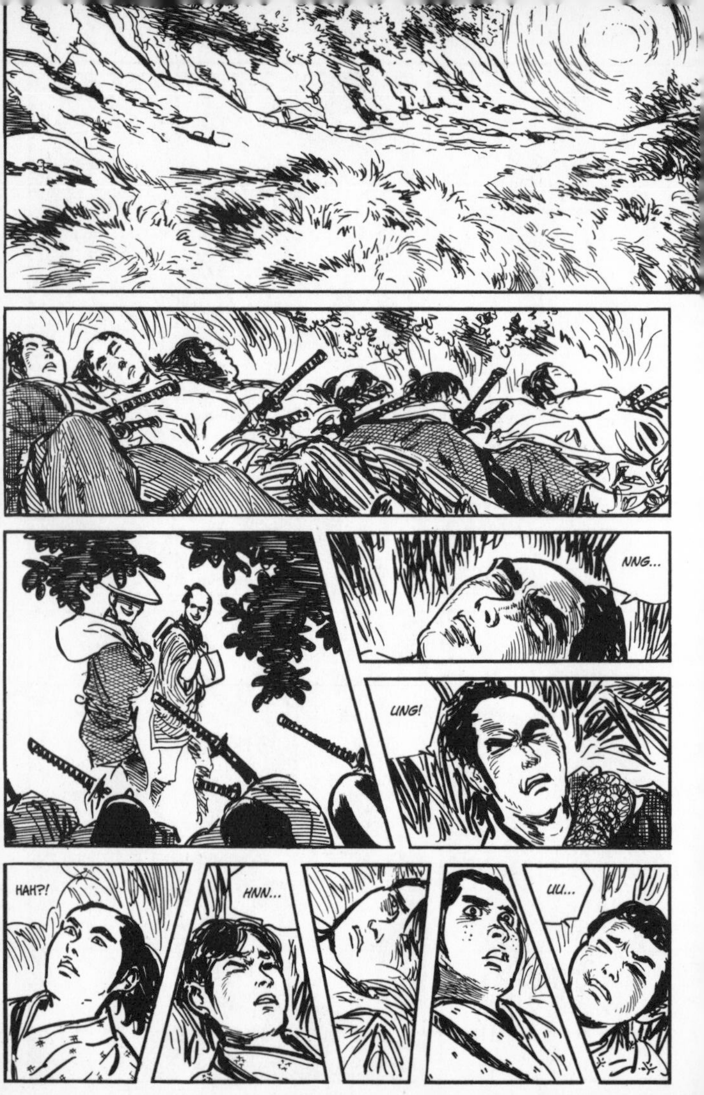
NNG...
UNG!
HAH?!
HNN...
UU...

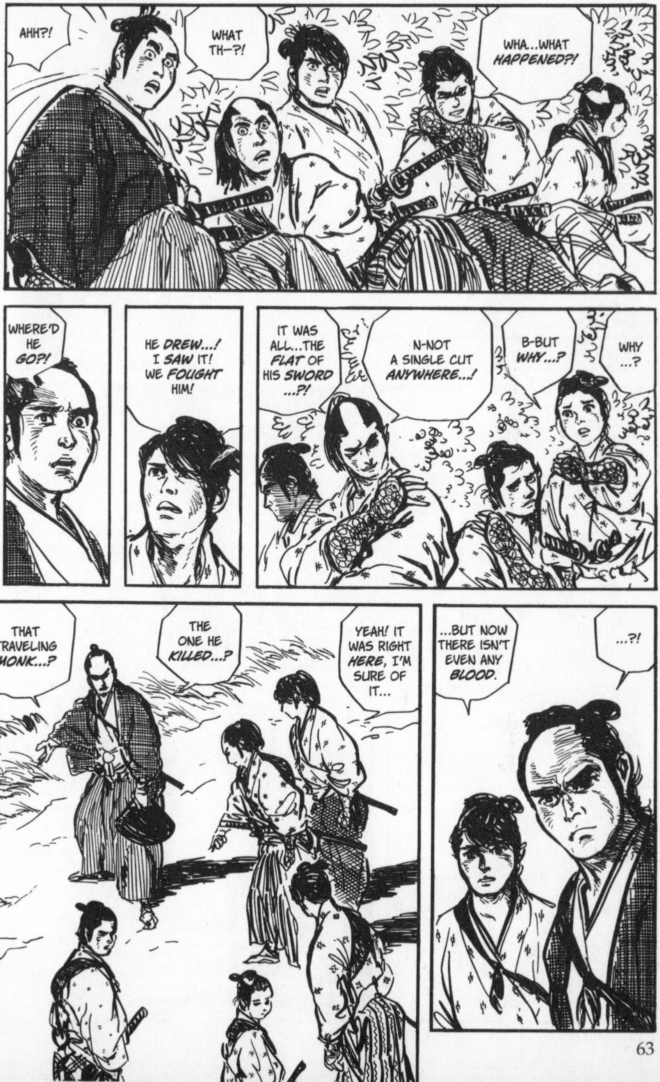
AHH?!
WHAT TH–?!
WHA...WHAT HAPPENED?!
WHERE'D HE GO?!
HE DREW...! I SAW IT! WE FOUGHT HIM!
IT WAS ALL...THE FLAT OF HIS SWORD ...?!
N-NOT A SINGLE CUT ANYWHERE...!
B-BUT WHY...?
WHY ...?
THAT TRAVELING MONK...?
THE ONE HE KILLED...?
YEAH! IT WAS RIGHT HERE, I'M SURE OF IT...
...BUT NOW THERE ISN'T EVEN ANY BLOOD.
...?!

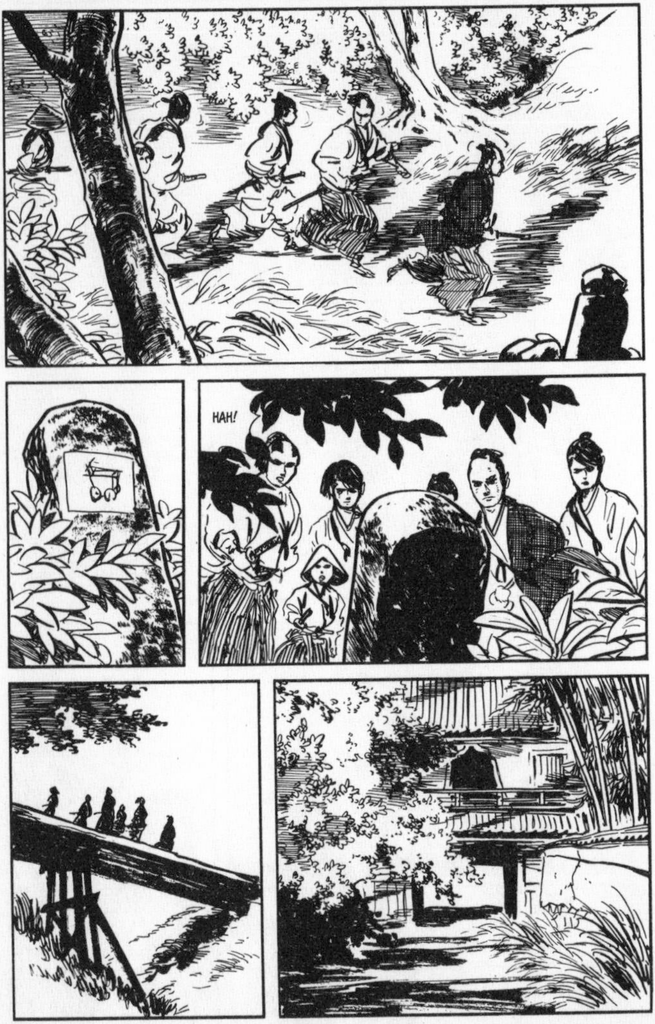
HAH!

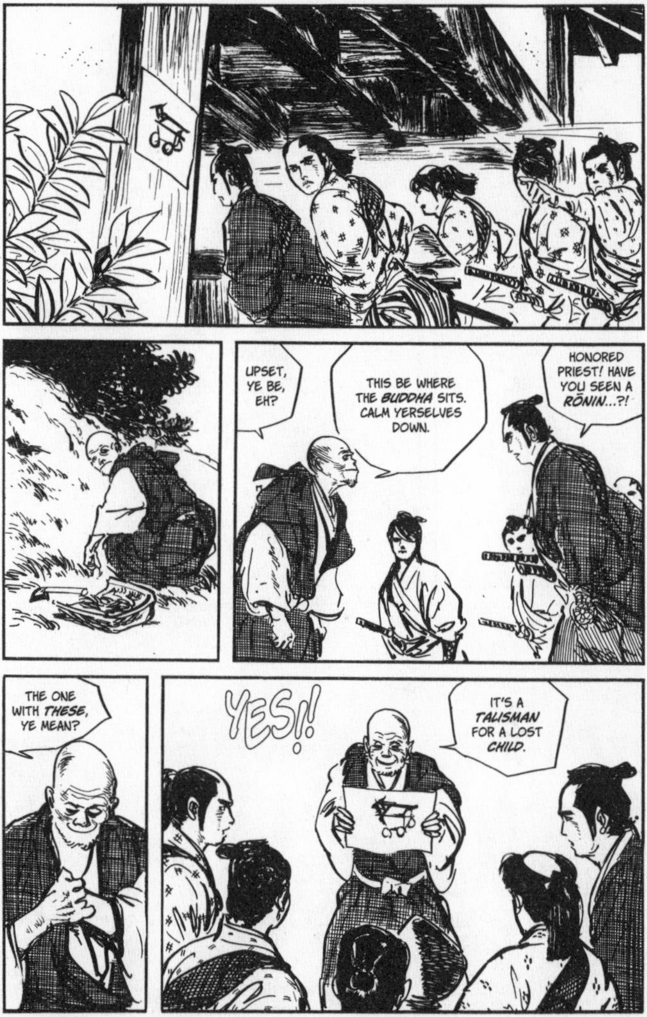
UPSET, YE BE, EH?
THIS BE WHERE THE *BUDDHA* SITS. CALM YERSELVES DOWN.
HONORED PRIEST! HAVE YOU SEEN A *RŌNIN*...?!
THE ONE WITH *THESE*, YE MEAN?
YES!!
IT'S A *TALISMAN* FOR A LOST *CHILD*.

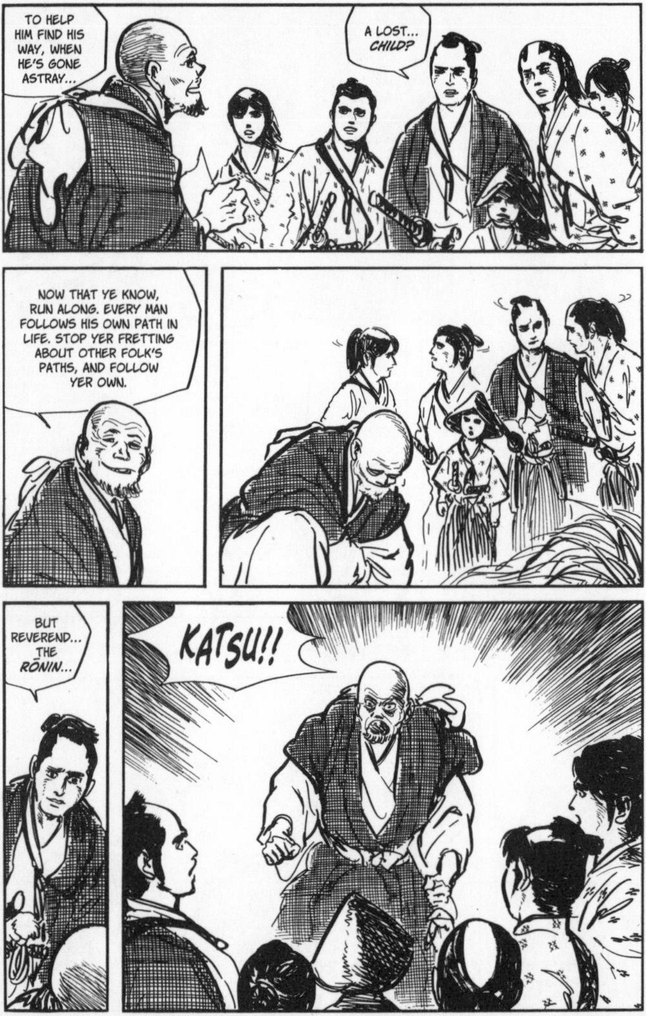
TO HELP HIM FIND HIS WAY, WHEN HE'S GONE ASTRAY...
A LOST... *CHILD?*
NOW THAT YE KNOW, RUN ALONG. EVERY MAN FOLLOWS HIS OWN PATH IN LIFE. STOP YER FRETTING ABOUT OTHER FOLK'S PATHS, AND FOLLOW YER OWN.
BUT REVEREND... THE *RŌNIN*...
KATSU!!

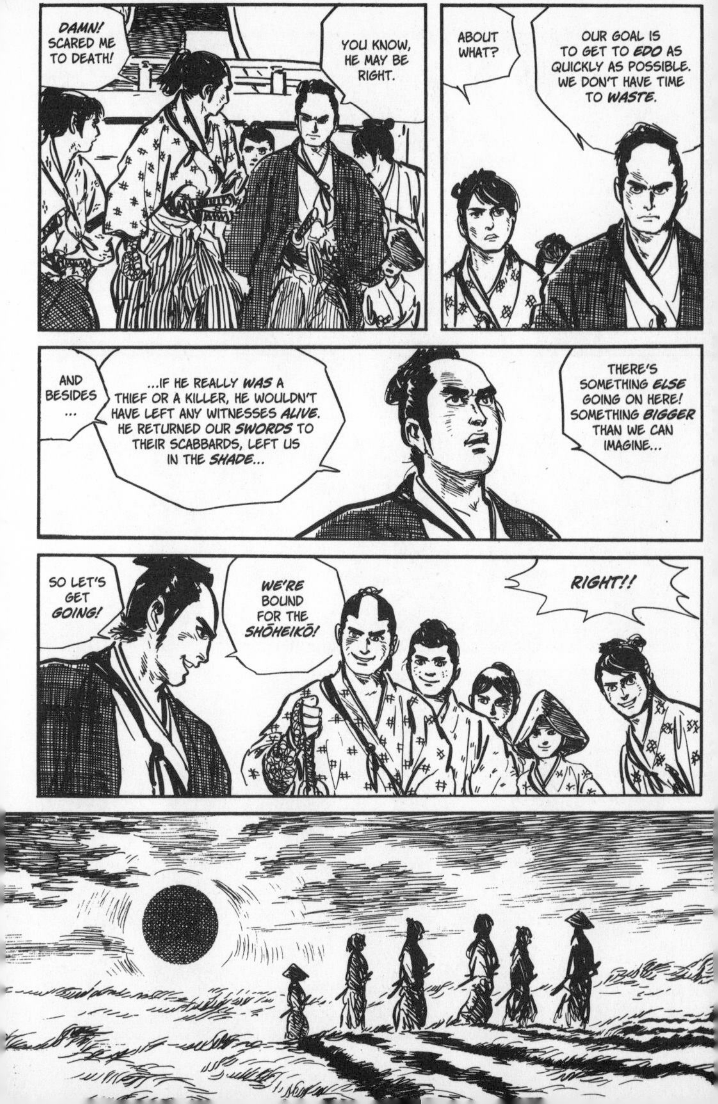
DAMN! SCARED ME TO DEATH!
YOU KNOW, HE MAY BE RIGHT.
ABOUT WHAT?
OUR GOAL IS TO GET TO EDO AS QUICKLY AS POSSIBLE. WE DON'T HAVE TIME TO WASTE.
AND BESIDES ...
...IF HE REALLY WAS A THIEF OR A KILLER, HE WOULDN'T HAVE LEFT ANY WITNESSES ALIVE. HE RETURNED OUR SWORDS TO THEIR SCABBARDS, LEFT US IN THE SHADE...
THERE'S SOMETHING ELSE GOING ON HERE! SOMETHING BIGGER THAN WE CAN IMAGINE...
SO LET'S GET GOING!
WE'RE BOUND FOR THE SHŌHEIKŌ!
RIGHT!!

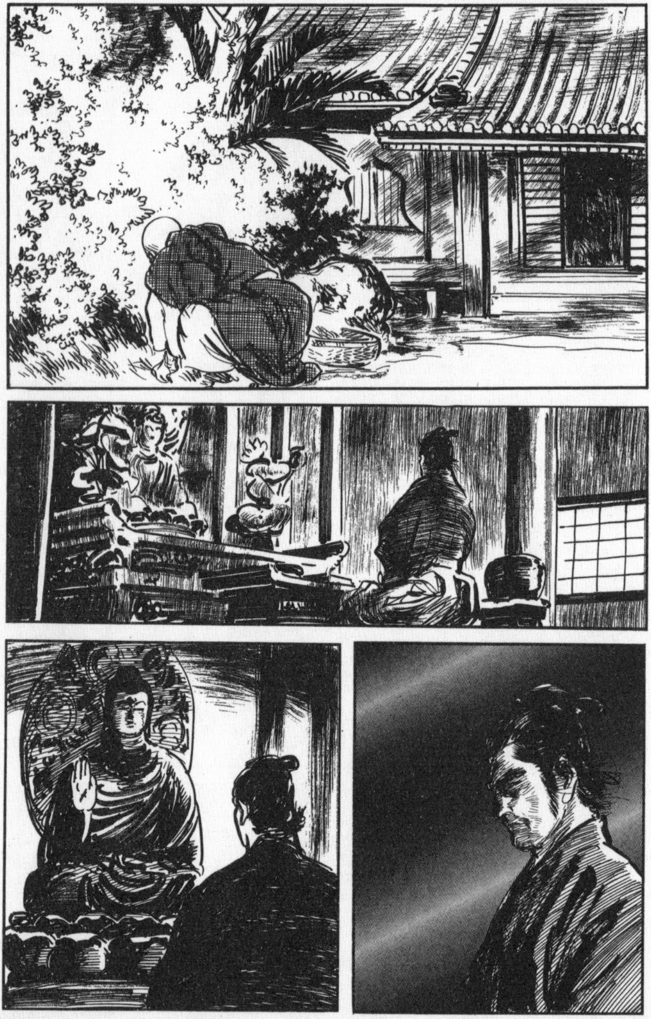

the fifty-sixth

Ailing Star

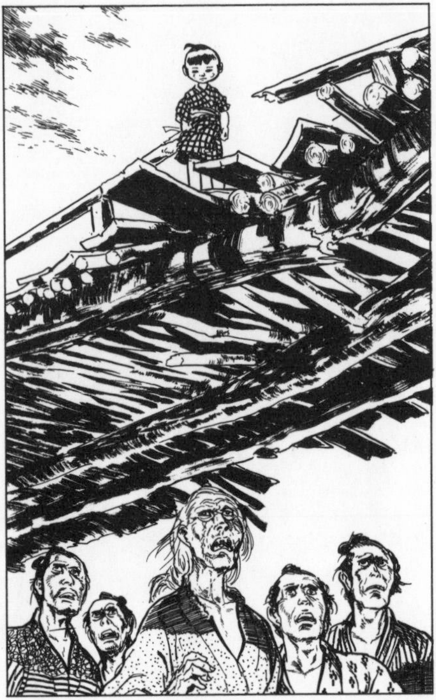

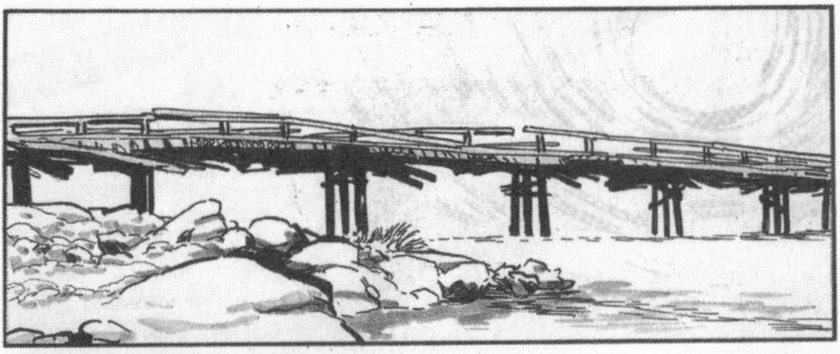

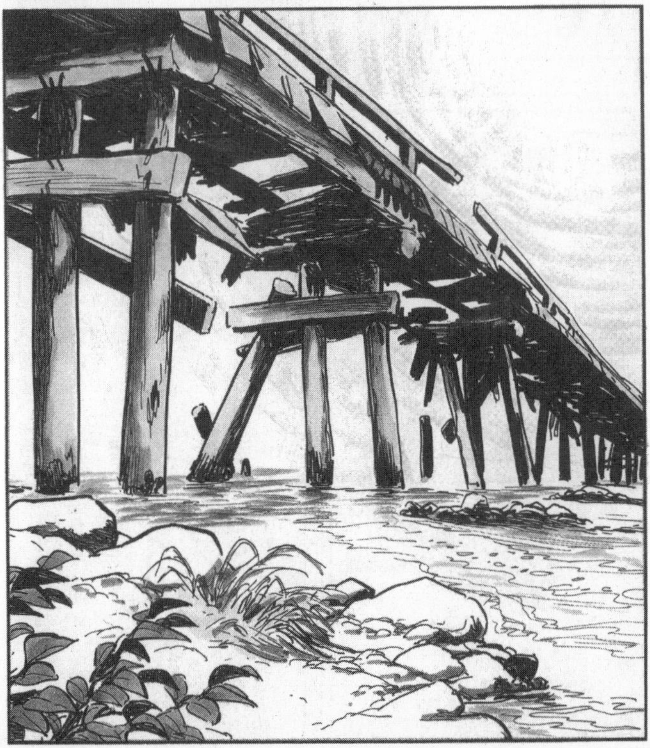

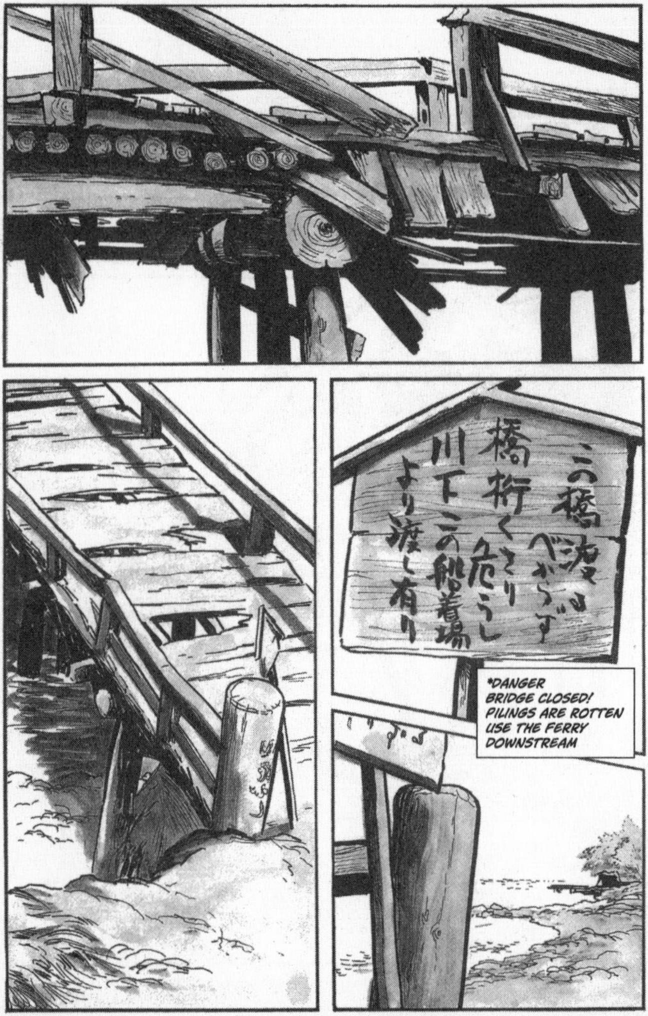
この橋渡るべからず
橋桁くさり危うし
川下この船着場
より渡し有り
*DANGER
BRIDGE CLOSED!
PILINGS ARE ROTTEN
USE THE FERRY
DOWNSTREAM

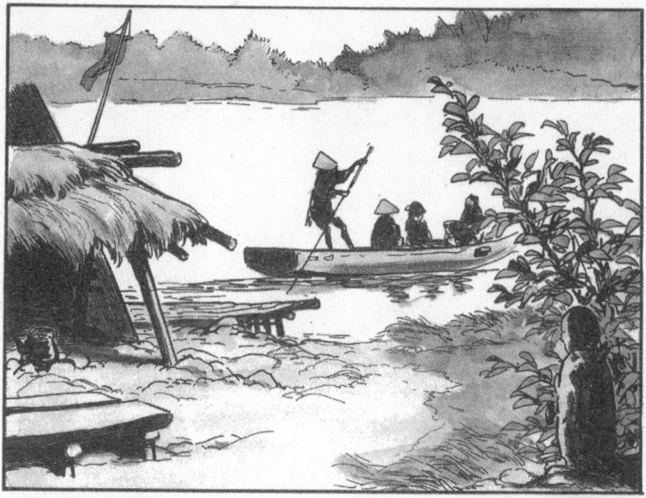
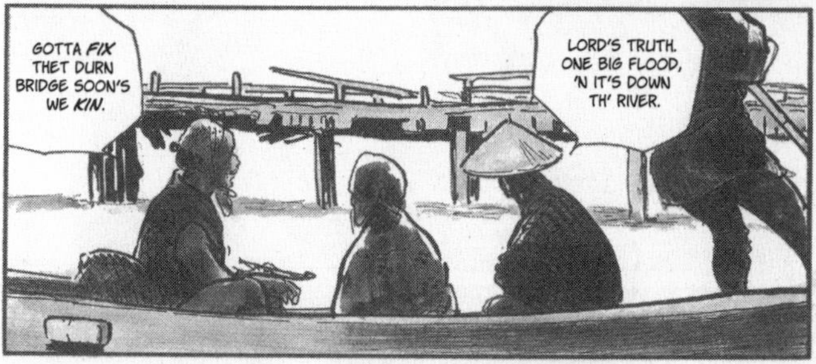
GOTTA *FIX* THET DURN BRIDGE SOON'S WE *KIN*.
LORD'S TRUTH. ONE BIG FLOOD, 'N IT'S DOWN TH' RIVER.
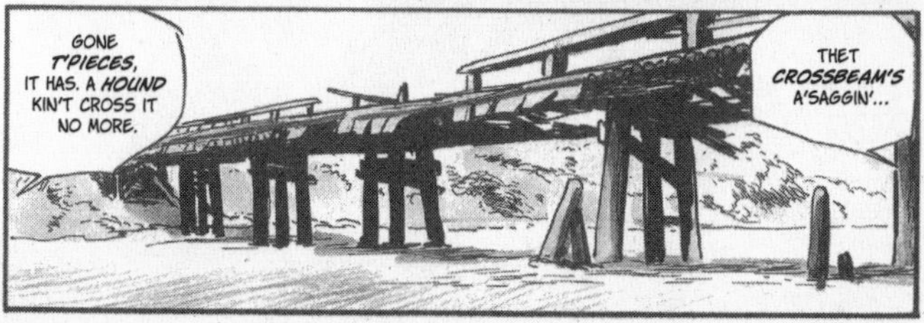
GONE *T'PIECES*, IT HAS. A *HOUND* KIN'T CROSS IT NO MORE.
THET *CROSSBEAM'S* A'SAGGIN'...

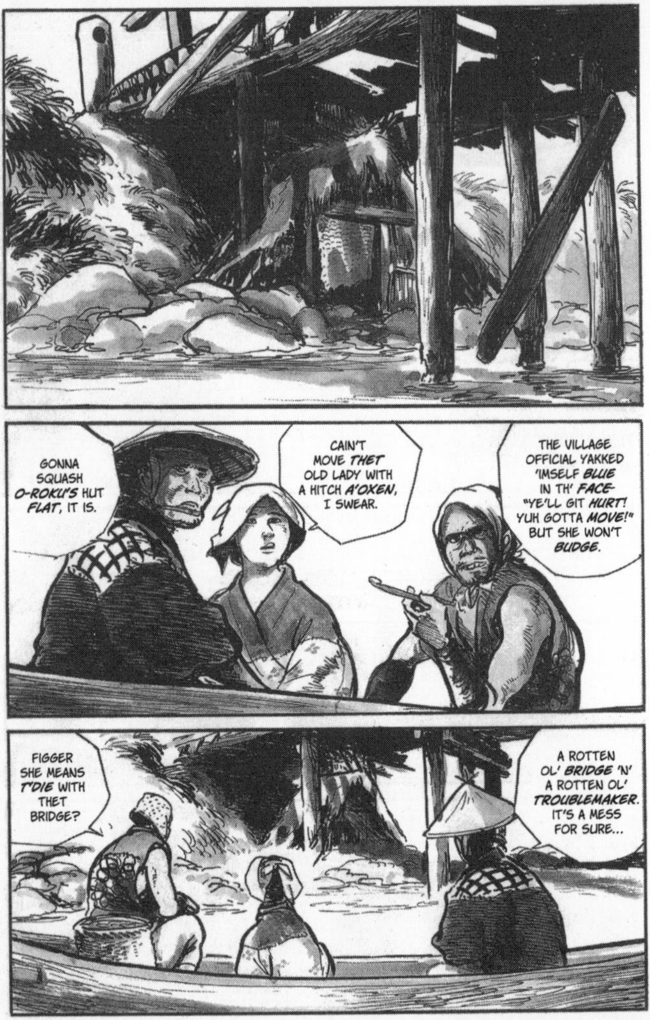
GONNA SQUASH O-ROKU'S HUT FLAT, IT IS.
CAIN'T MOVE THET OLD LADY WITH A HITCH A'OXEN, I SWEAR.
THE VILLAGE OFFICIAL YAKKED 'IMSELF BLUE IN TH' FACE- "YE'LL GIT HURT! YUH GOTTA MOVE!" BUT SHE WON'T BUDGE.
FIGGER SHE MEANS T'DIE WITH THET BRIDGE?
A ROTTEN OL' BRIDGE 'N' A ROTTEN OL' TROUBLEMAKER. IT'S A MESS FOR SURE...

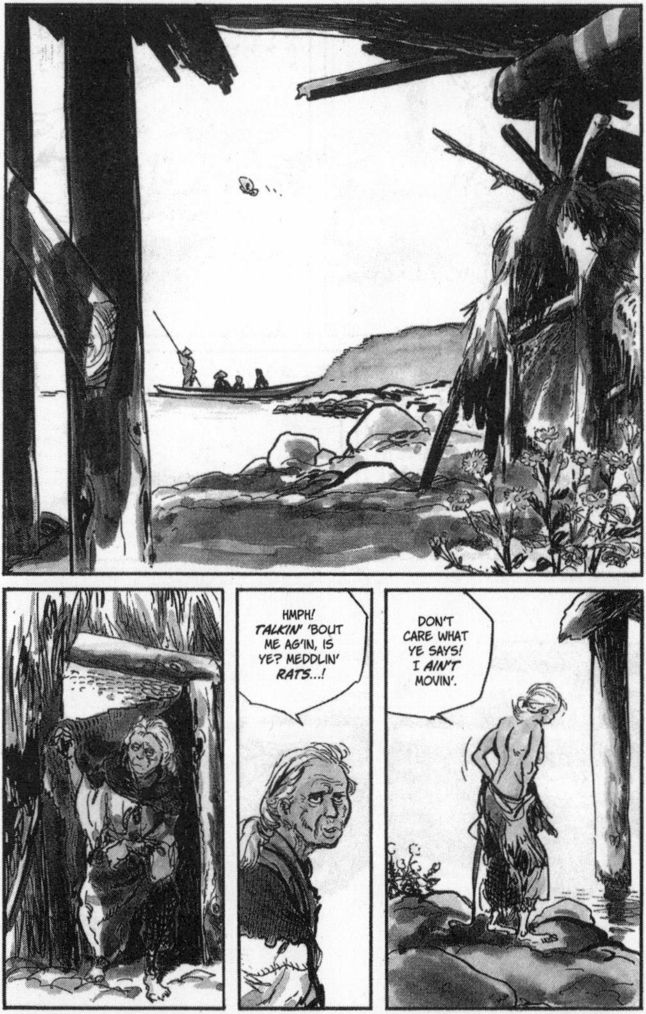
HMPH! TALKIN' 'BOUT ME AG'IN, IS YE? MEDDLIN' RATS...!
DON'T CARE WHAT YE SAYS! I AIN'T MOVIN'.

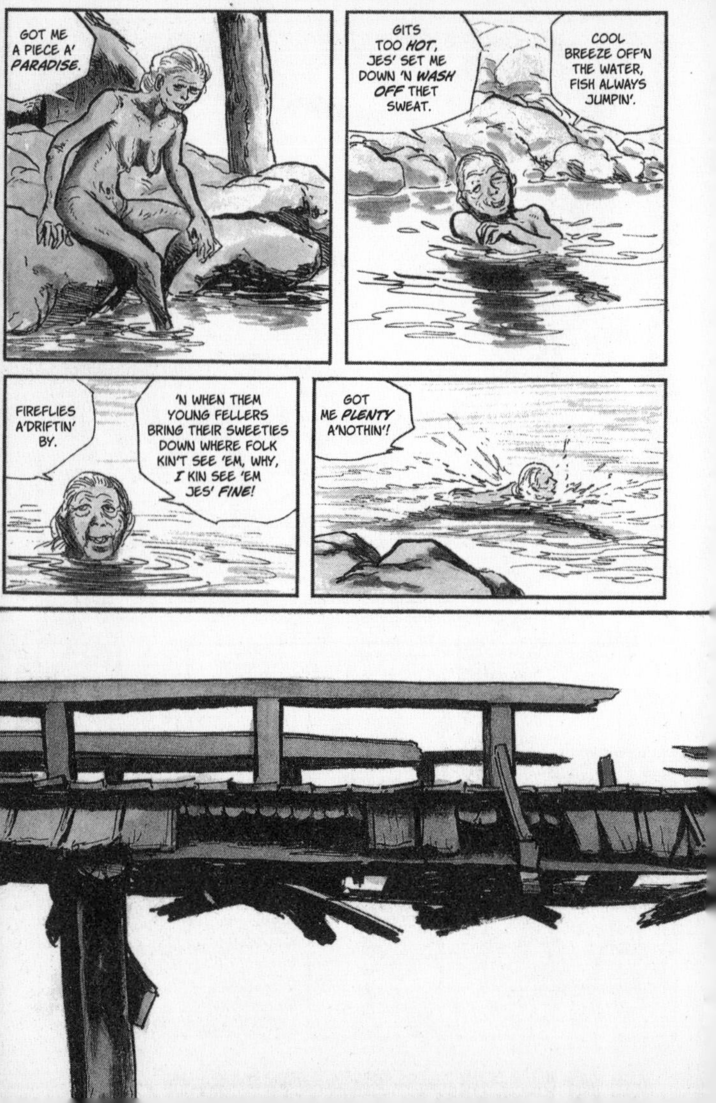
GOT ME A PIECE A' *PARADISE.*
GITS TOO *HOT*, JES' SET ME DOWN 'N *WASH OFF* THET SWEAT.
COOL BREEZE OFF'N THE WATER, FISH ALWAYS JUMPIN'.
FIREFLIES A'DRIFTIN' BY.
'N WHEN THEM YOUNG FELLERS BRING THEIR SWEETIES DOWN WHERE FOLK KIN'T SEE 'EM, WHY, *I* KIN SEE 'EM JES' *FINE!*
GOT ME *PLENTY* A'NOTHIN'!

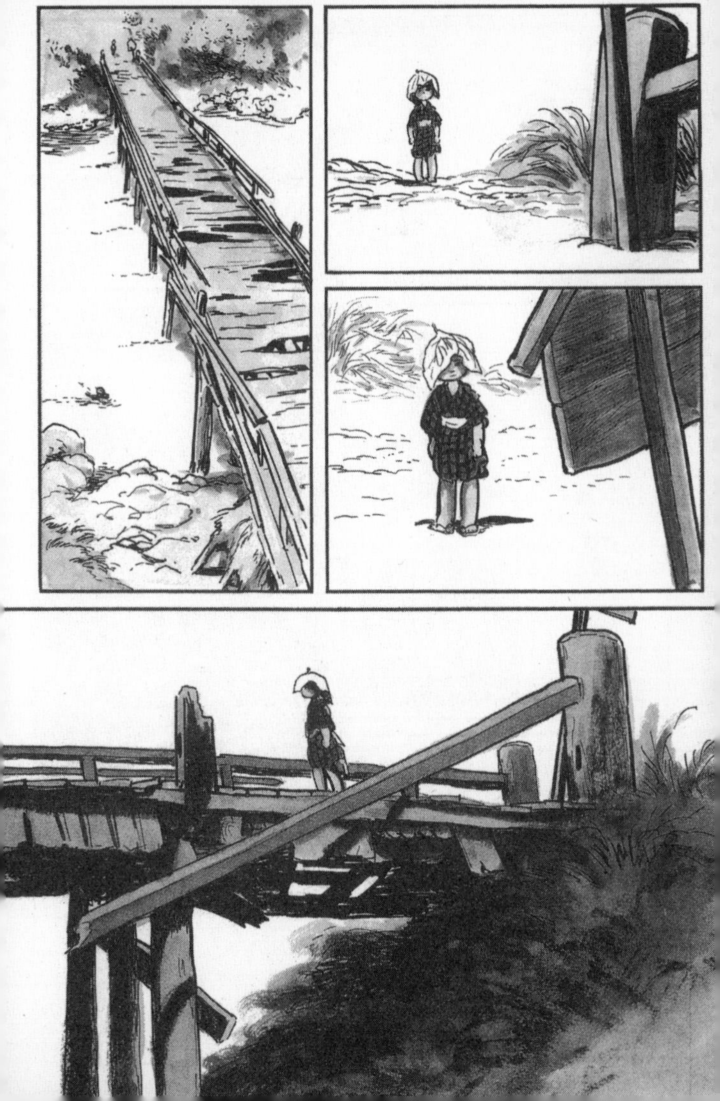

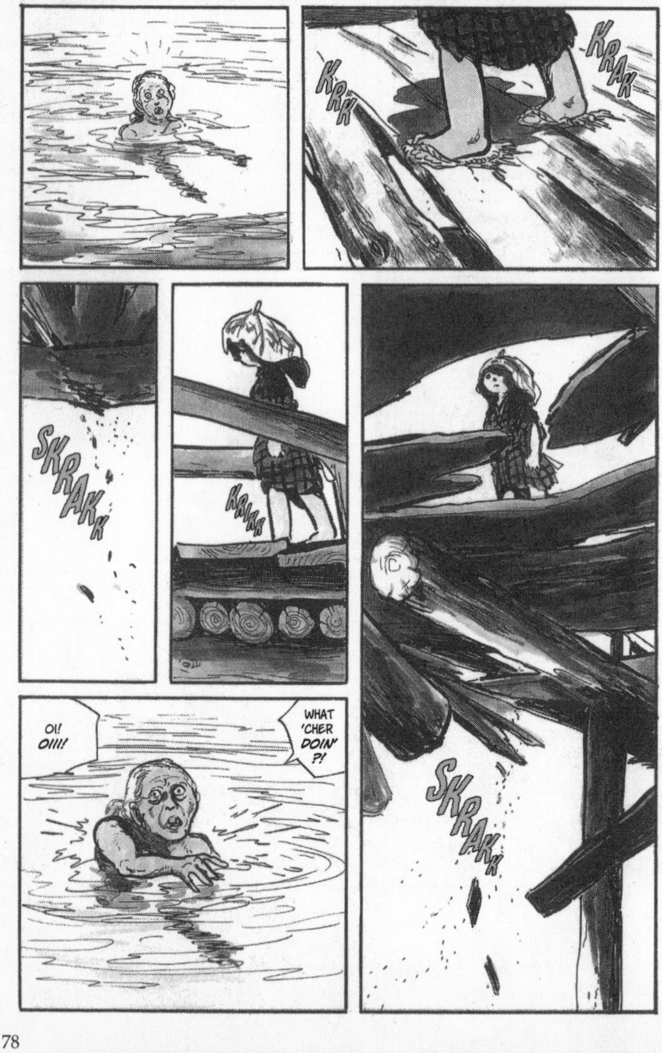
KRK
KRAK
SKRAKK
KRIKK
OI! OIII!
WHAT 'CHER DOIN' ?!
SKRAKK

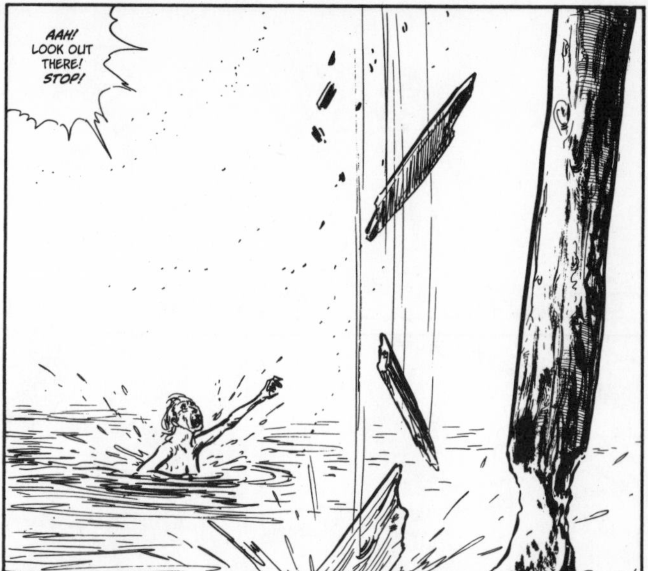
AAH! LOOK OUT THERE! STOP!
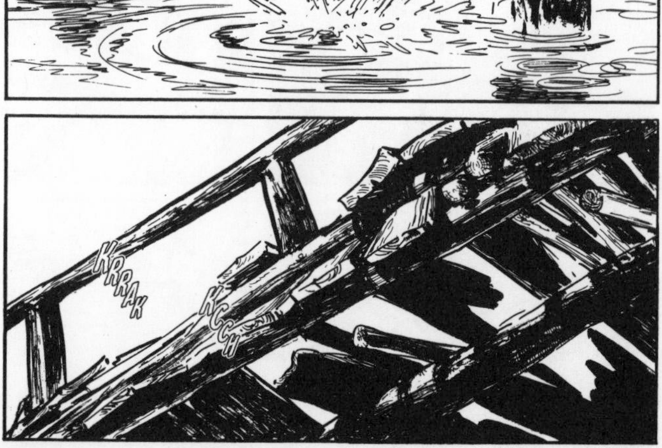
KRRAK
KCCH

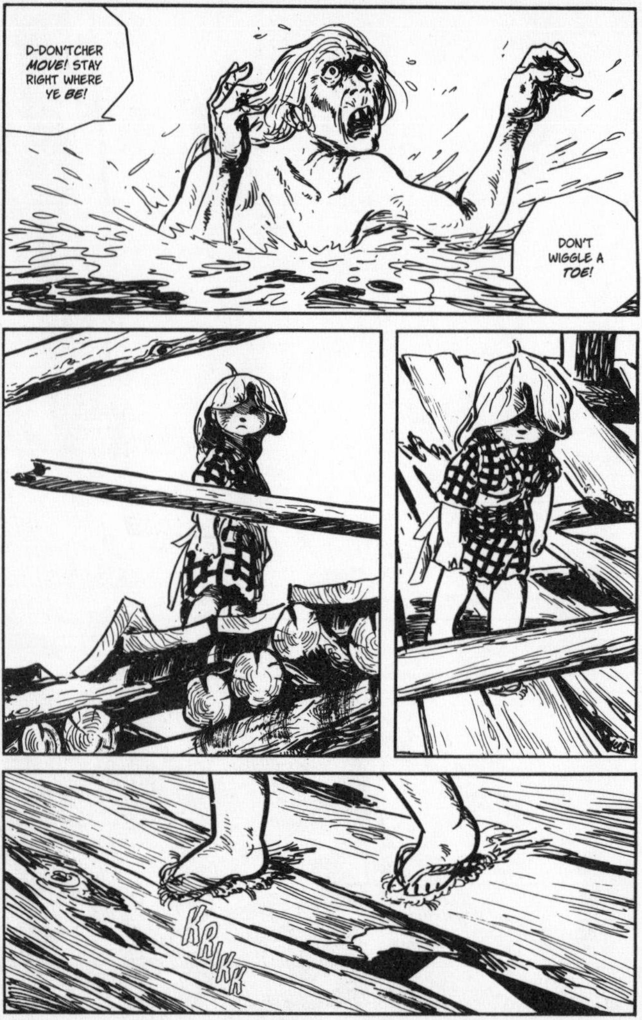
D-DON'TCHER MOVE! STAY RIGHT WHERE YE BE!
DON'T WIGGLE A TOE!
KRIKK

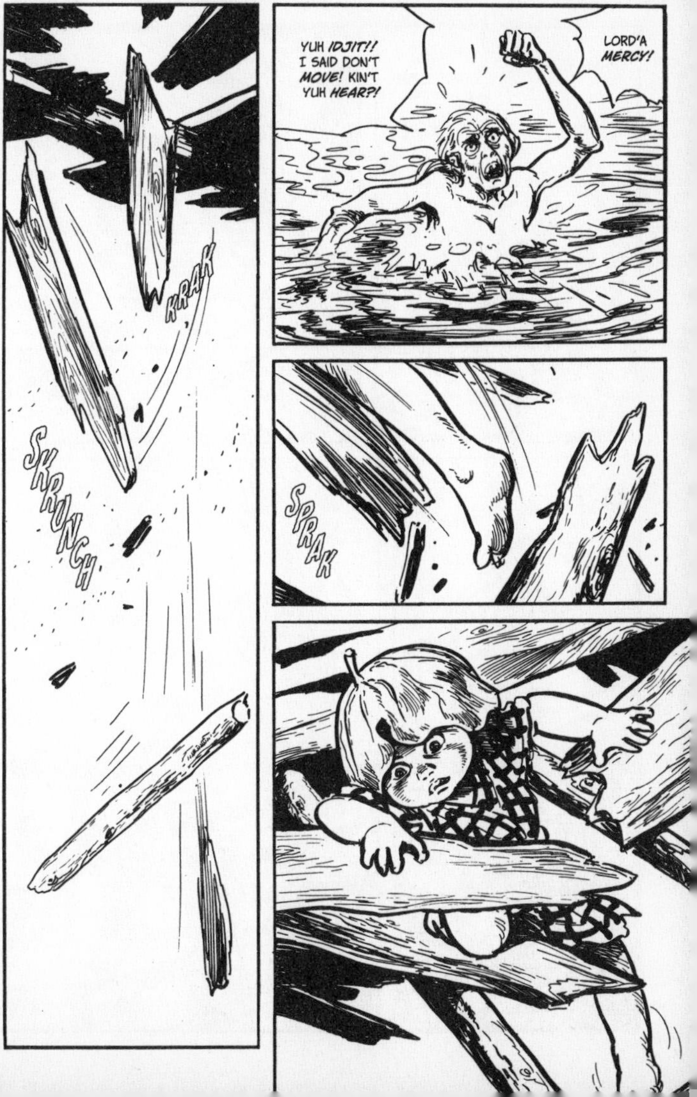
KRAK
SKRUNCH
YUH IDJIT!! I SAID DON'T MOVE! KIN'T YUH HEAR?!
LORD'A MERCY!
SPRAK

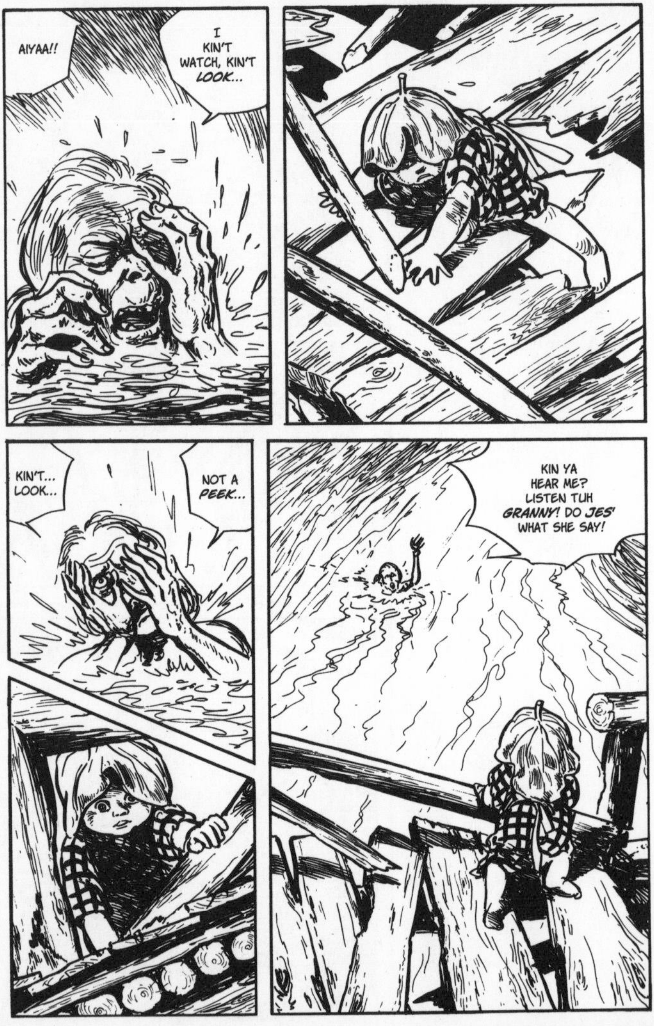
AIYAA!!
I KIN'T WATCH, KIN'T *LOOK*...
KIN'T... LOOK...
NOT A *PEEK*...
KIN YA HEAR ME? LISTEN TUH *GRANNY*! DO *JES'* WHAT SHE SAY!

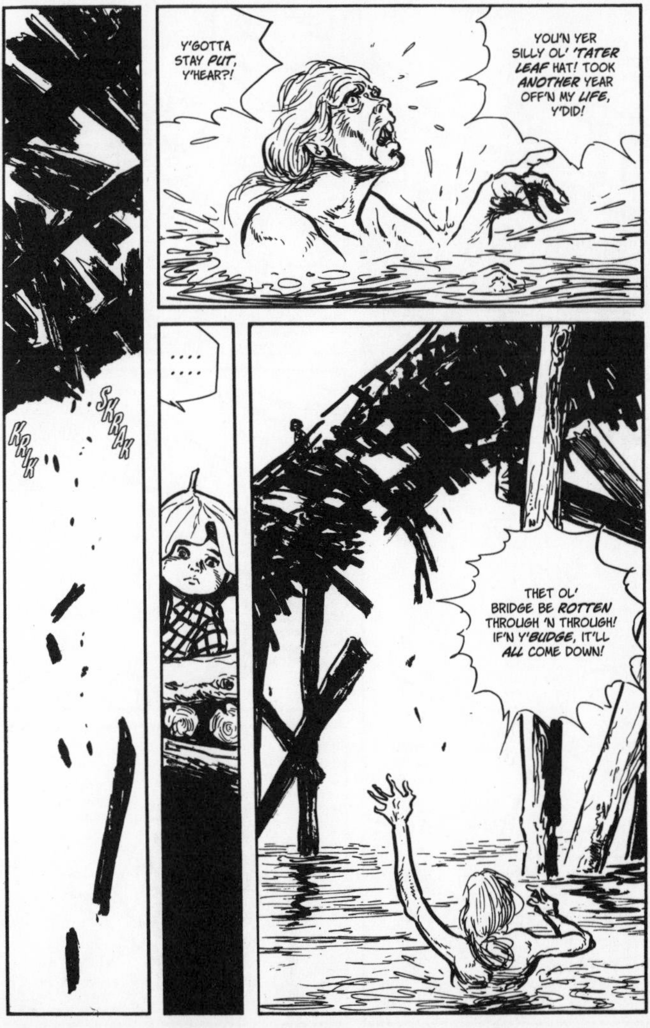
Y'GOTTA STAY *PUT*, Y'HEAR?!
YOU'N YER SILLY OL' *'TATER LEAF* HAT! TOOK *ANOTHER* YEAR OFF'N MY *LIFE*, Y'DID!
SKRAK
KRIK
....
....
THET OL' BRIDGE BE *ROTTEN* THROUGH 'N THROUGH! IF'N Y'*BUDGE*, IT'LL *ALL* COME DOWN!

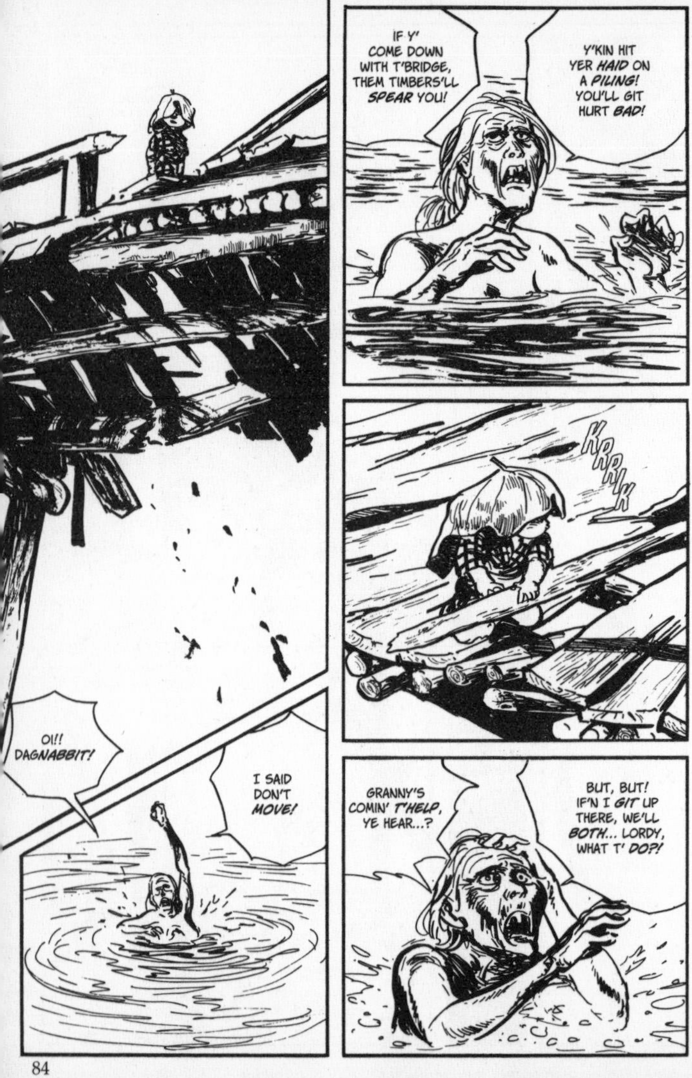
OI!! DAGNABBIT!
I SAID DON'T MOVE!
IF Y' COME DOWN WITH T'BRIDGE, THEM TIMBERS'LL SPEAR YOU!
Y'KIN HIT YER HAID ON A PILING! YOU'LL GIT HURT BAD!
KRRIK
GRANNY'S COMIN' T'HELP, YE HEAR...?
BUT, BUT! IF'N I GIT UP THERE, WE'LL BOTH... LORDY, WHAT T' DO?!

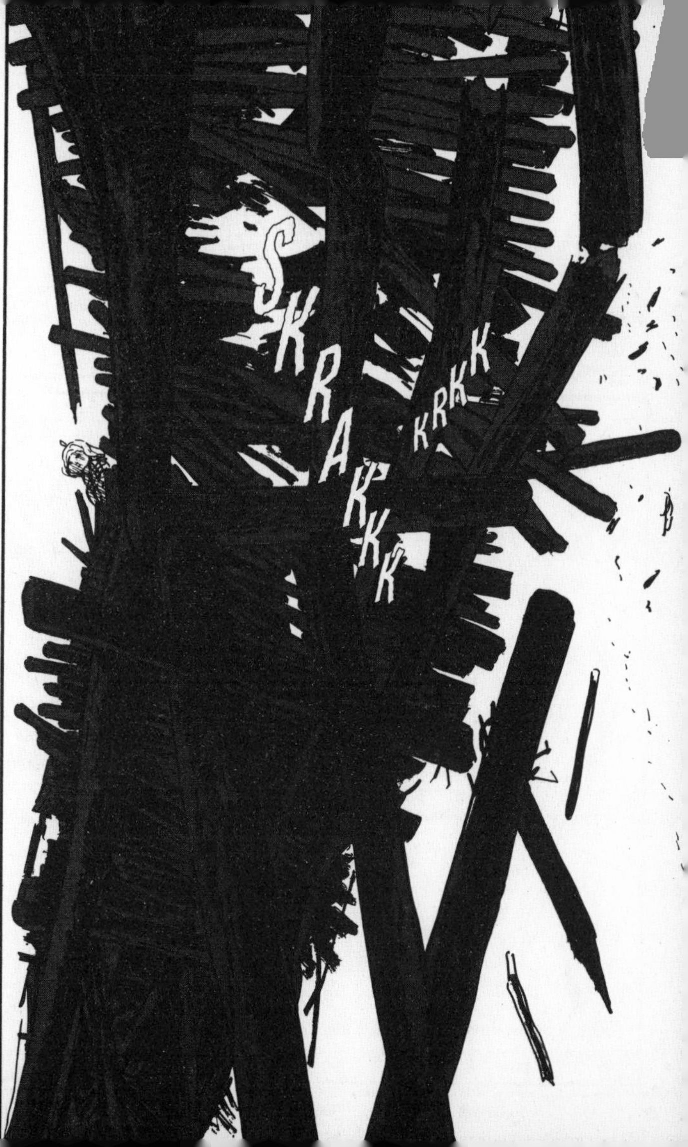
SKRAKKK
KRKK

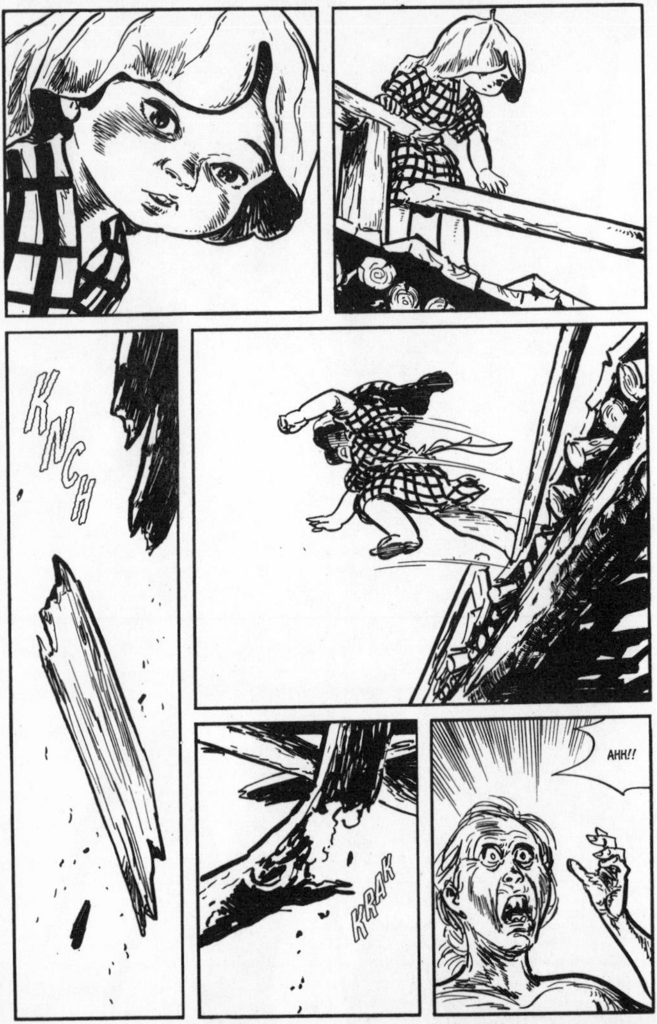
KNCH
KRAK
AHH!!

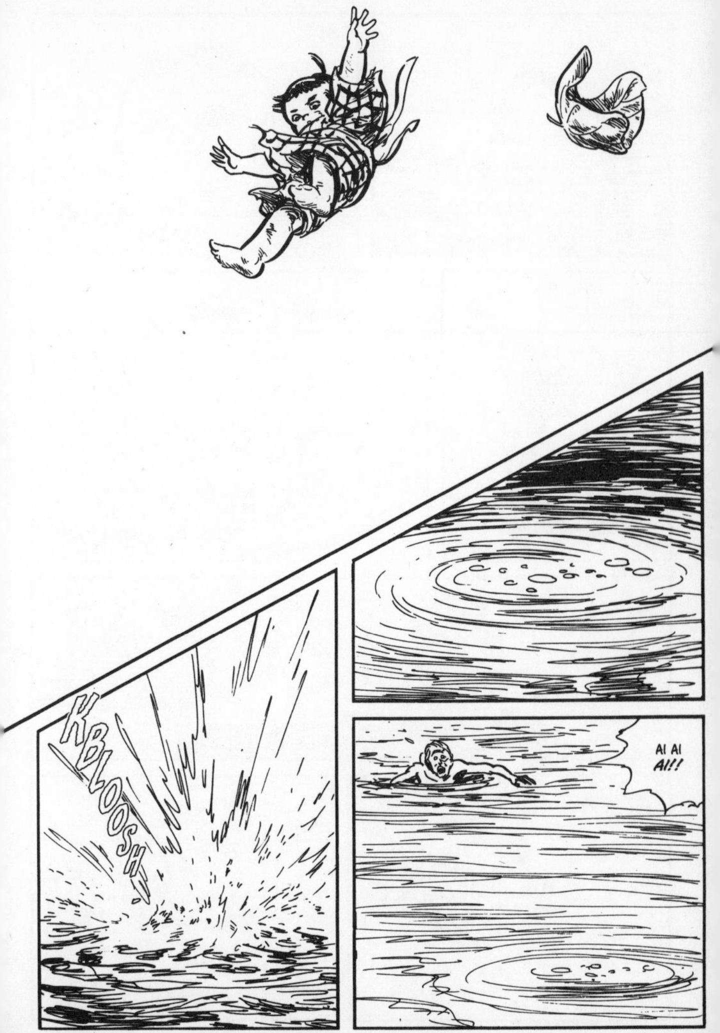
KBLOOSH
AI AI
AI!!

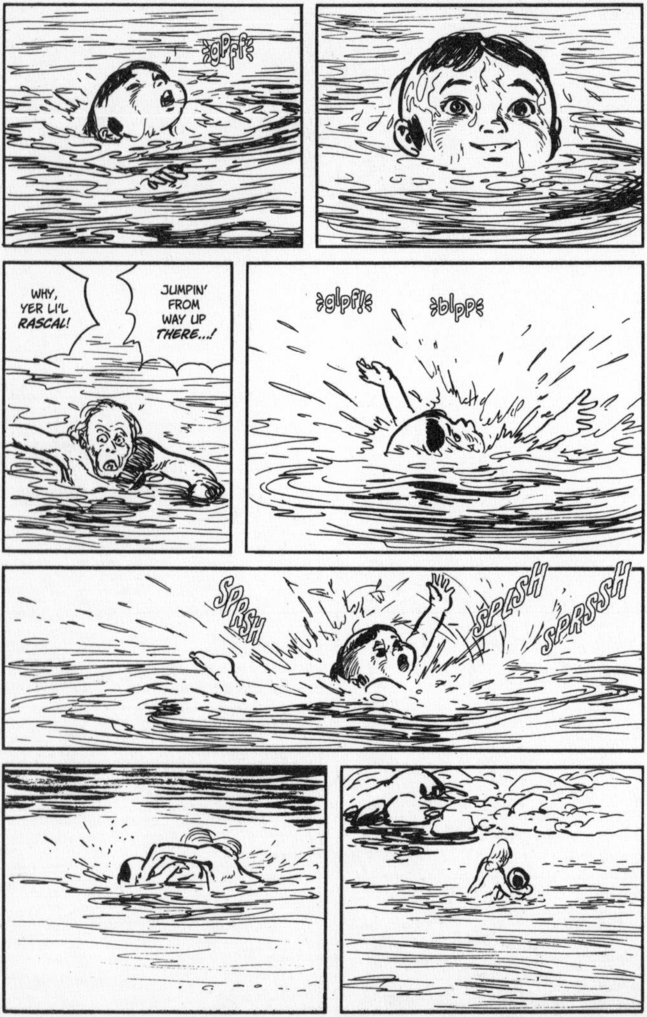
gpff
WHY, YER LI'L RASCAL!
JUMPIN' FROM WAY UP THERE...!
glpf!
blpp
SPRSH
SPLSH
SPRSSH

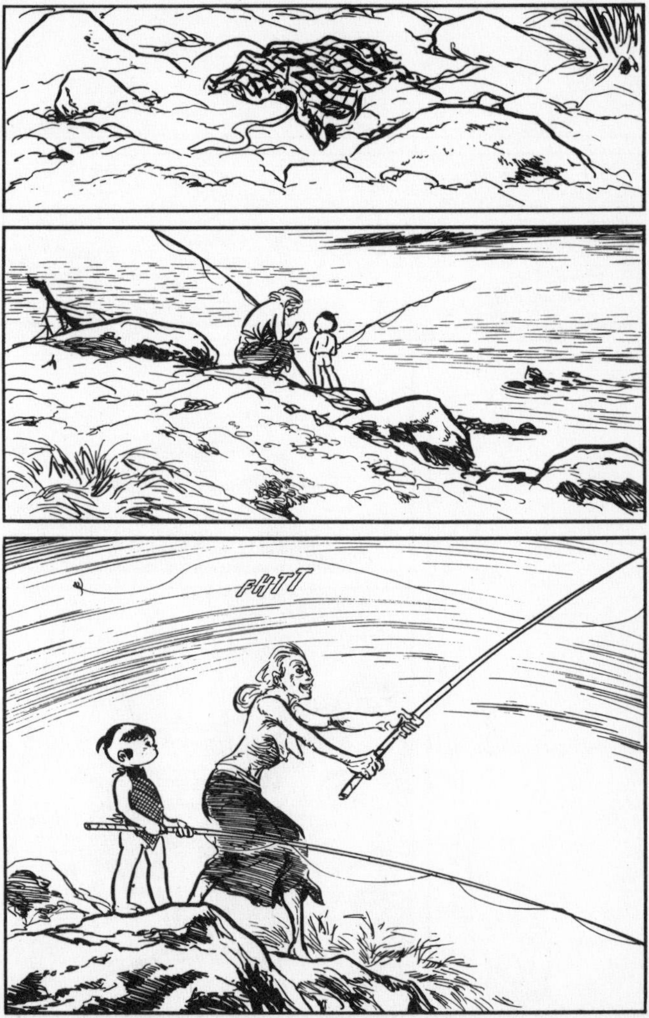
FHTT

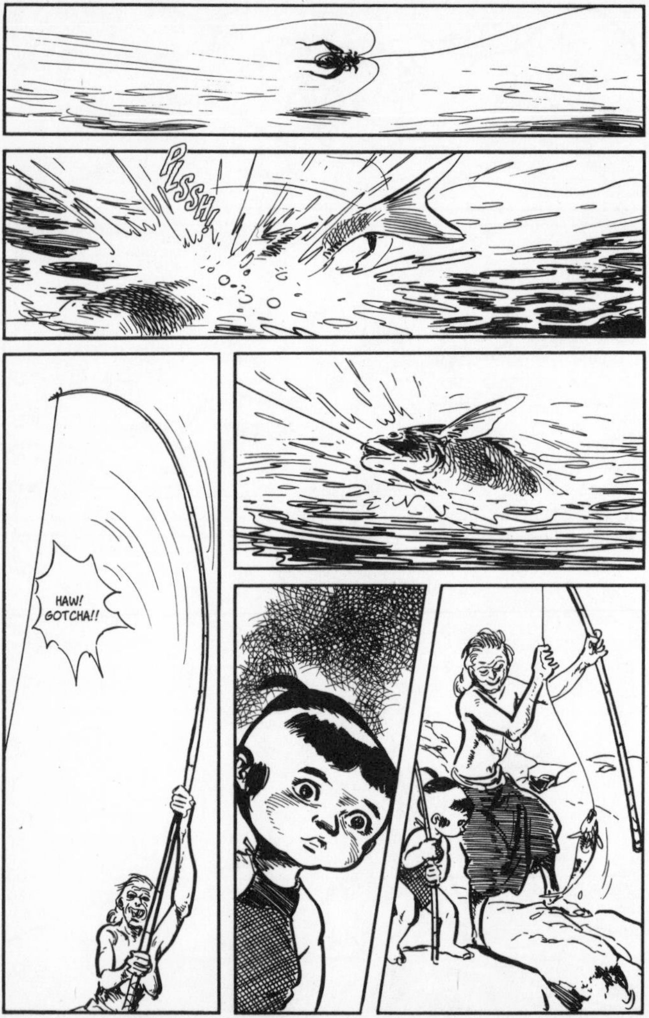
PLSSH!
HAW! GOTCHA!!

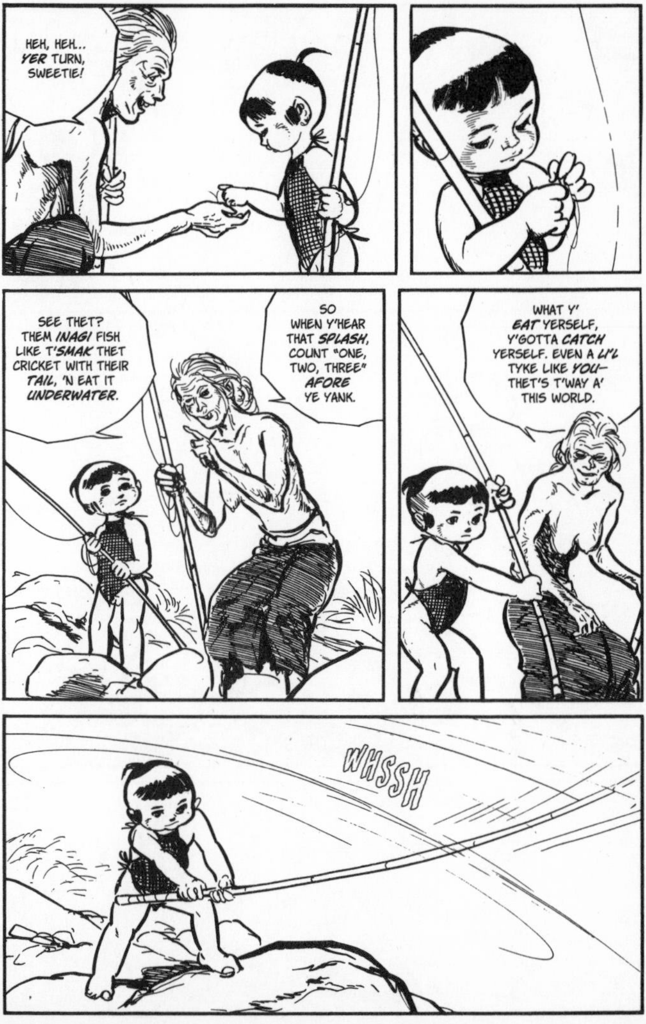
HEH, HEH... YER TURN, SWEETIE!
SEE THET? THEM INAGI FISH LIKE T'SMAK THET CRICKET WITH THEIR TAIL, 'N EAT IT UNDERWATER.
SO WHEN Y'HEAR THAT SPLASH, COUNT "ONE, TWO, THREE" AFORE YE YANK.
WHAT Y' EAT YERSELF, Y'GOTTA CATCH YERSELF. EVEN A LI'L TYKE LIKE YOU— THET'S T'WAY A' THIS WORLD.
WHSSH

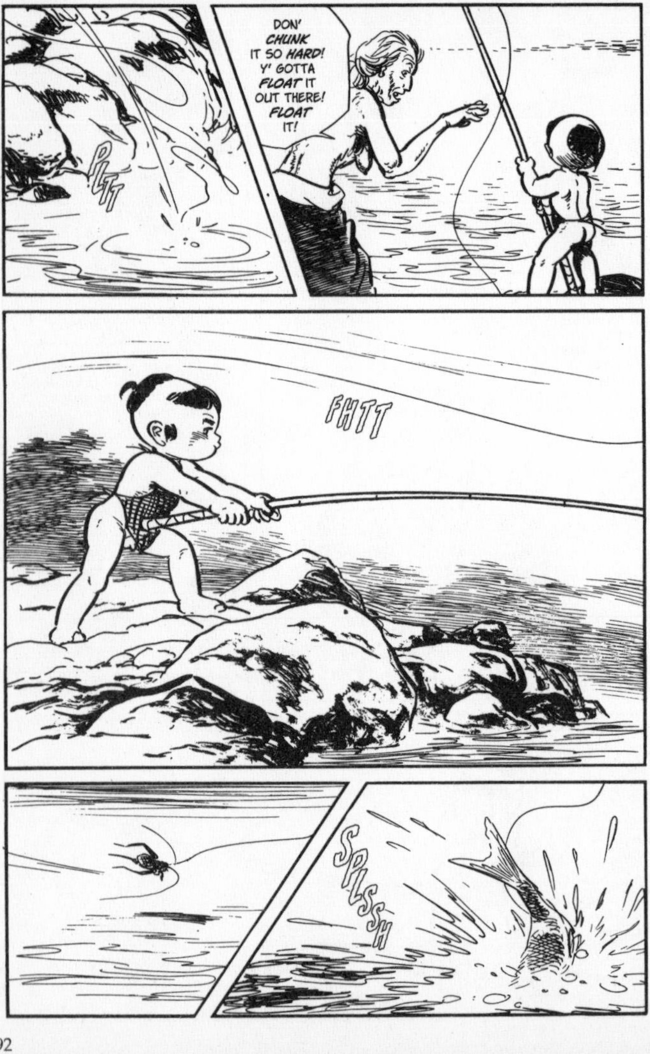
PLTT
DON' CHUNK IT SO HARD! Y' GOTTA FLOAT IT OUT THERE! FLOAT IT!
FHTT
SPLSSH

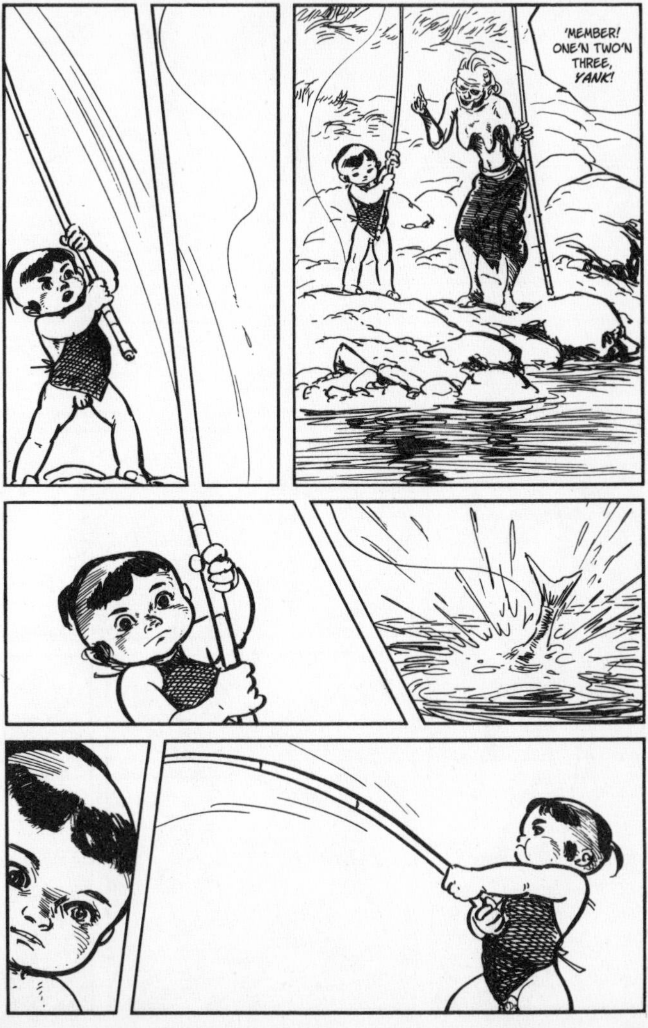
'MEMBER! ONE'N TWO'N THREE, *YANK!*

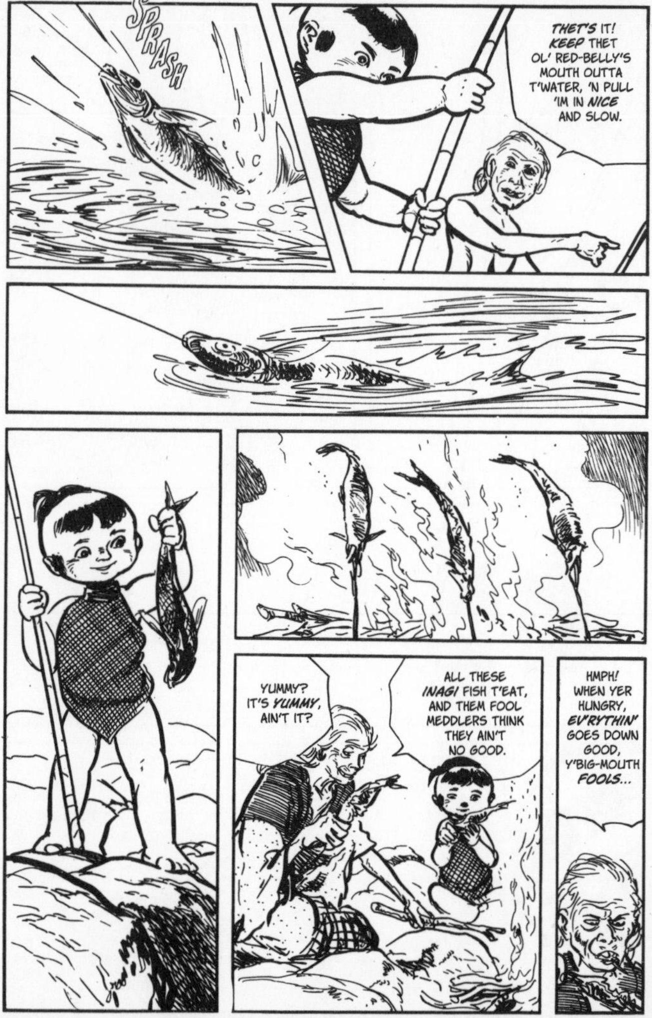
SPRASH
THET'S IT! KEEP THET OL' RED-BELLY'S MOUTH OUTTA T'WATER, 'N PULL 'IM IN NICE AND SLOW.
YUMMY? IT'S YUMMY, AIN'T IT?
ALL THESE INAGI FISH T'EAT, AND THEM FOOL MEDDLERS THINK THEY AIN'T NO GOOD.
HMPH! WHEN YER HUNGRY, EV'RYTHIN' GOES DOWN GOOD, Y'BIG-MOUTH FOOLS...

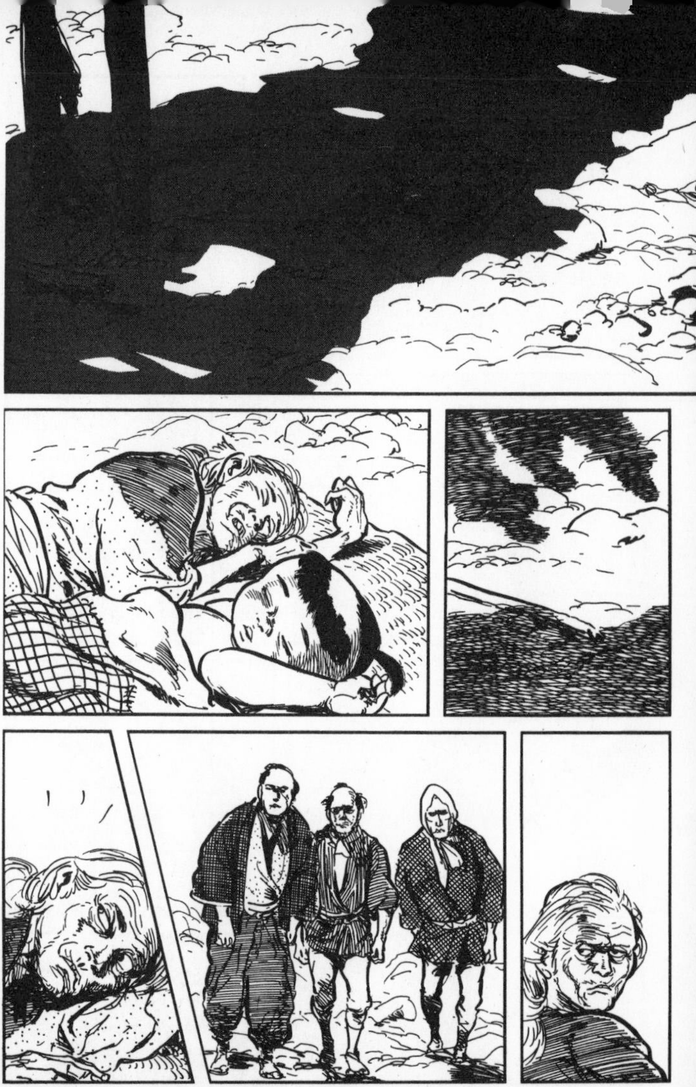

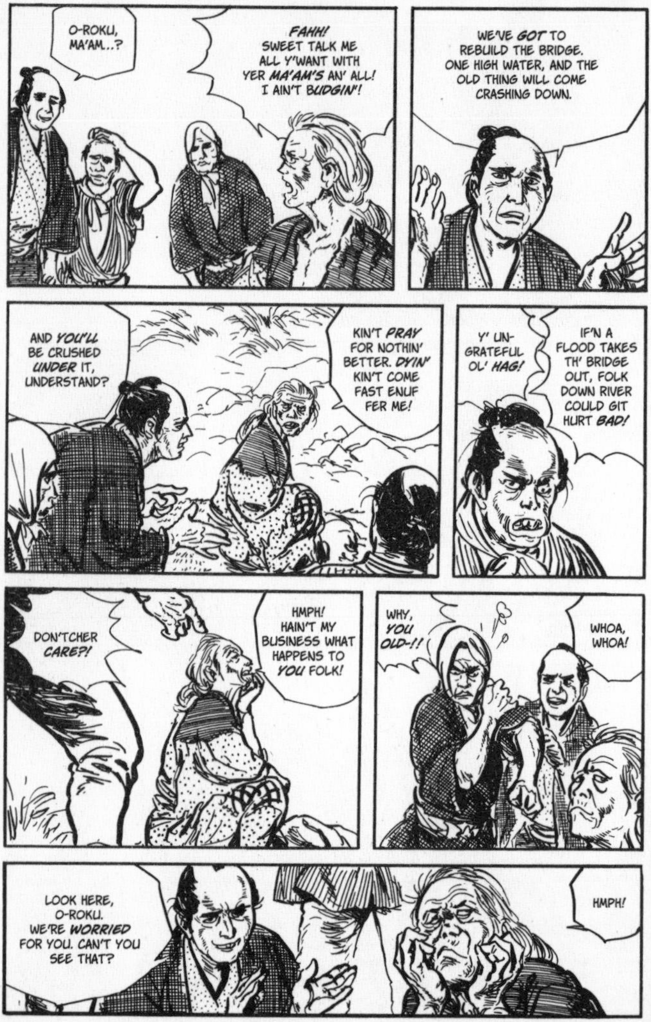
O-ROKU, MA'AM..?
FAHH! SWEET TALK ME ALL Y'WANT WITH YER MA'AM'S AN' ALL! I AIN'T BUDGIN'!
WE'VE GOT TO REBUILD THE BRIDGE. ONE HIGH WATER, AND THE OLD THING WILL COME CRASHING DOWN.
AND YOU'LL BE CRUSHED UNDER IT, UNDERSTAND?
KIN'T PRAY FOR NOTHIN' BETTER. DYIN' KIN'T COME FAST ENUF FER ME!
Y' UNGRATEFUL OL' HAG!
IF'N A FLOOD TAKES TH' BRIDGE OUT, FOLK DOWN RIVER COULD GIT HURT BAD!
DON'TCHER CARE?!
HMPH! HAIN'T MY BUSINESS WHAT HAPPENS TO YOU FOLK!
WHY, YOU OLD-!!
WHOA, WHOA!
LOOK HERE, O-ROKU. WE'RE WORRIED FOR YOU. CAN'T YOU SEE THAT?
HMPH!

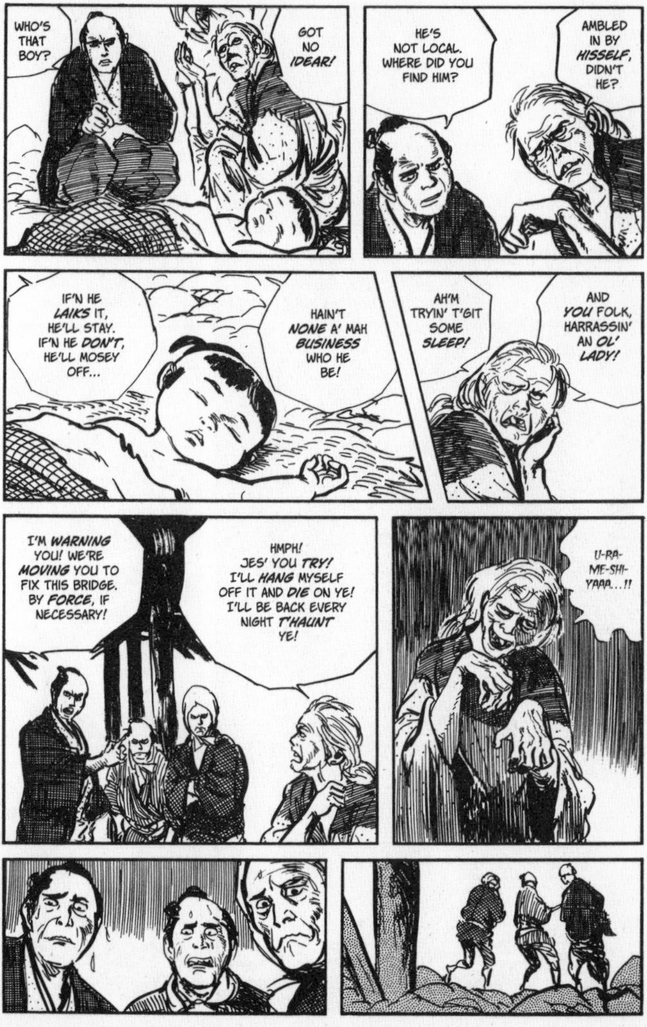

WHO'S THAT BOY?
GOT NO IDEAR!
HE'S NOT LOCAL. WHERE DID YOU FIND HIM?
AMBLED IN BY HISSELF, DIDN'T HE?
IF'N HE LAIKS IT, HE'LL STAY. IF'N HE DON'T, HE'LL MOSEY OFF...
HAIN'T NONE A' MAH BUSINESS WHO HE BE!
AH'M TRYIN' T'GIT SOME SLEEP!
AND YOU FOLK, HARRASSIN' AN OL' LADY!
I'M WARNING YOU! WE'RE MOVING YOU TO FIX THIS BRIDGE. BY FORCE, IF NECESSARY!
HMPH! JES' YOU TRY! I'LL HANG MYSELF OFF IT AND DIE ON YE! I'LL BE BACK EVERY NIGHT T'HAUNT YE!
U-RA-ME-SHI-YAAA...!!

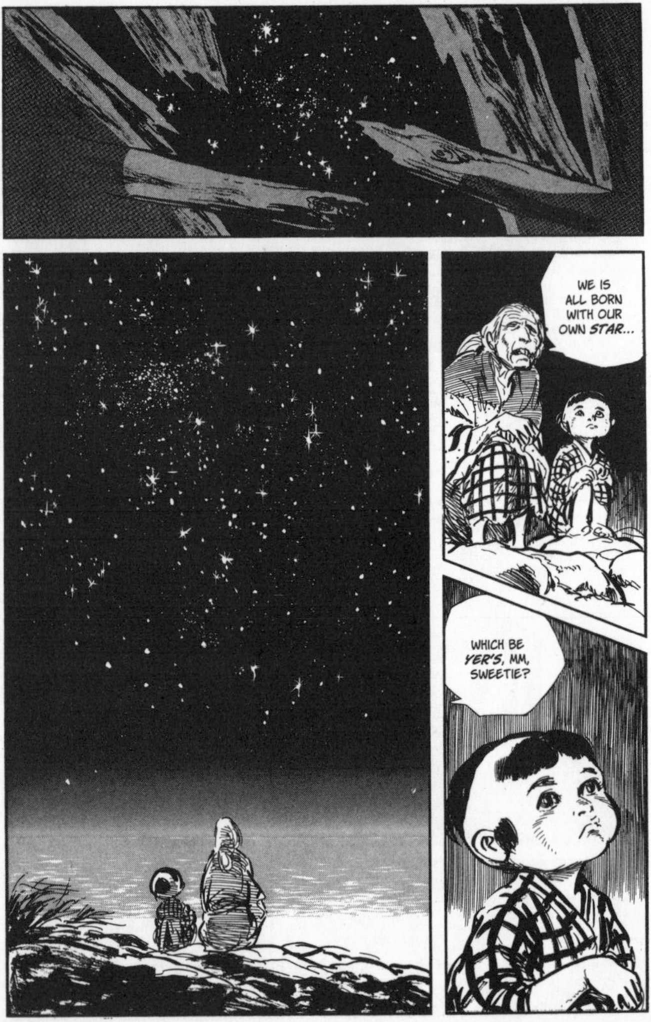
WE IS ALL BORN WITH OUR OWN *STAR*...
WHICH BE *YER'S*, MM, SWEETIE?

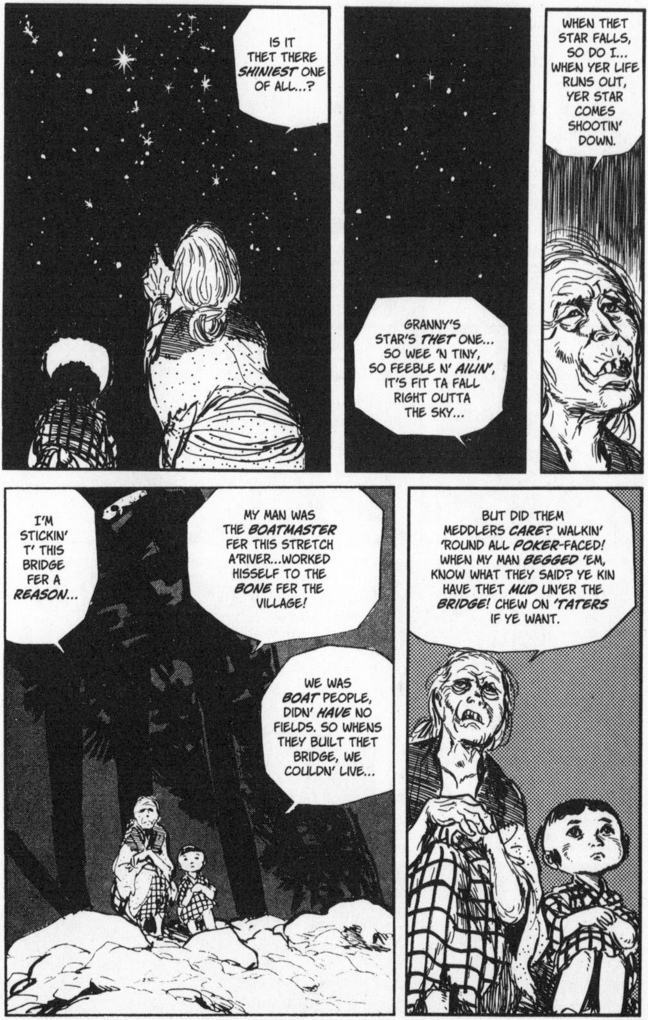
IS IT THET THERE *SHINIEST* ONE OF ALL...?
GRANNY'S STAR'S *THET* ONE... SO WEE 'N TINY, SO FEEBLE N' *AILIN'*, IT'S FIT TA FALL RIGHT OUTTA THE SKY...
WHEN THET STAR FALLS, SO DO I... WHEN YER LIFE RUNS OUT, YER STAR COMES SHOOTIN' DOWN.
I'M STICKIN' T' THIS BRIDGE FER A *REASON*...
MY MAN WAS THE *BOATMASTER* FER THIS STRETCH A'RIVER...WORKED HISSELF TO THE *BONE* FER THE VILLAGE!
WE WAS *BOAT* PEOPLE, DIDN' *HAVE* NO FIELDS. SO WHENS THEY BUILT THET BRIDGE, WE COULDN' LIVE...
BUT DID THEM MEDDLERS *CARE*? WALKIN' 'ROUND ALL *POKER*-FACED! WHEN MY MAN *BEGGED* 'EM, KNOW WHAT THEY SAID? YE KIN HAVE THET *MUD* UN'ER THE *BRIDGE*! CHEW ON *'TATERS* IF YE WANT.

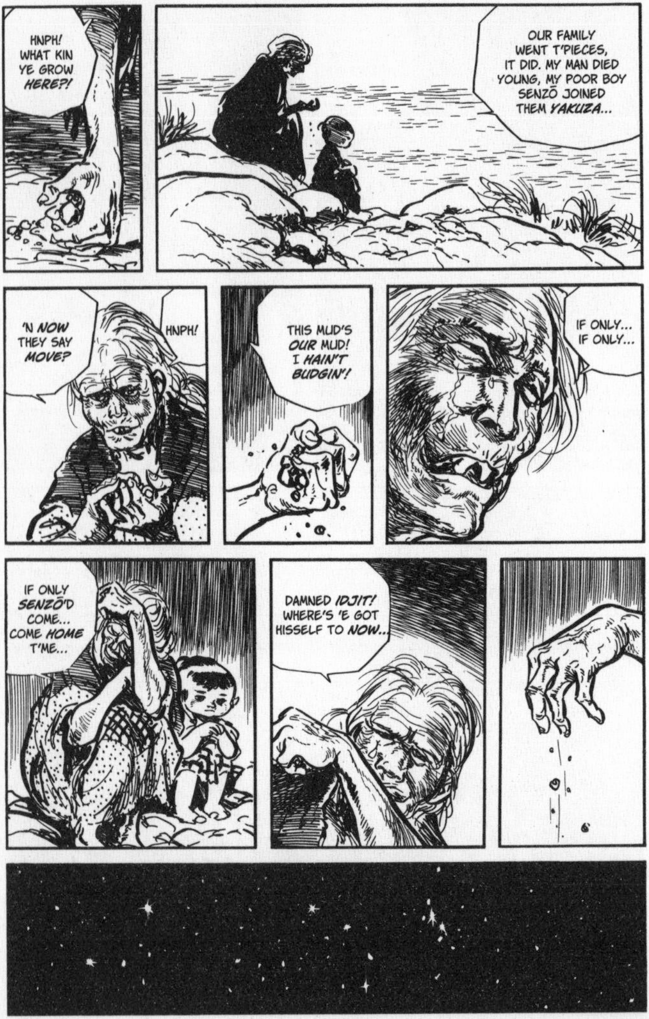
HNPH! WHAT KIN YE GROW HERE?!
OUR FAMILY WENT T'PIECES, IT DID. MY MAN DIED YOUNG, MY POOR BOY SENZŌ JOINED THEM YAKUZA...
'N NOW THEY SAY MOVE?
HNPH!
THIS MUD'S OUR MUD! I HAIN'T BUDGIN'!
IF ONLY... IF ONLY...
IF ONLY SENZŌ'D COME... COME HOME T'ME...
DAMNED IDJIT! WHERE'S 'E GOT HISSELF TO NOW...

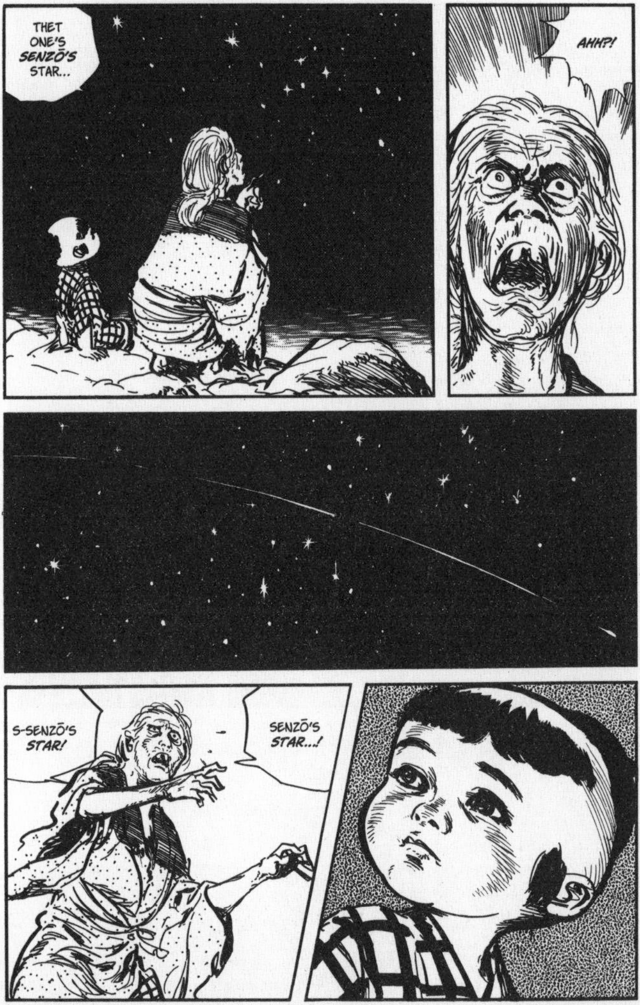
THET ONE'S SENZŌ'S STAR...
AHH?!
S-SENZŌ'S STAR!
SENZŌ'S STAR...!

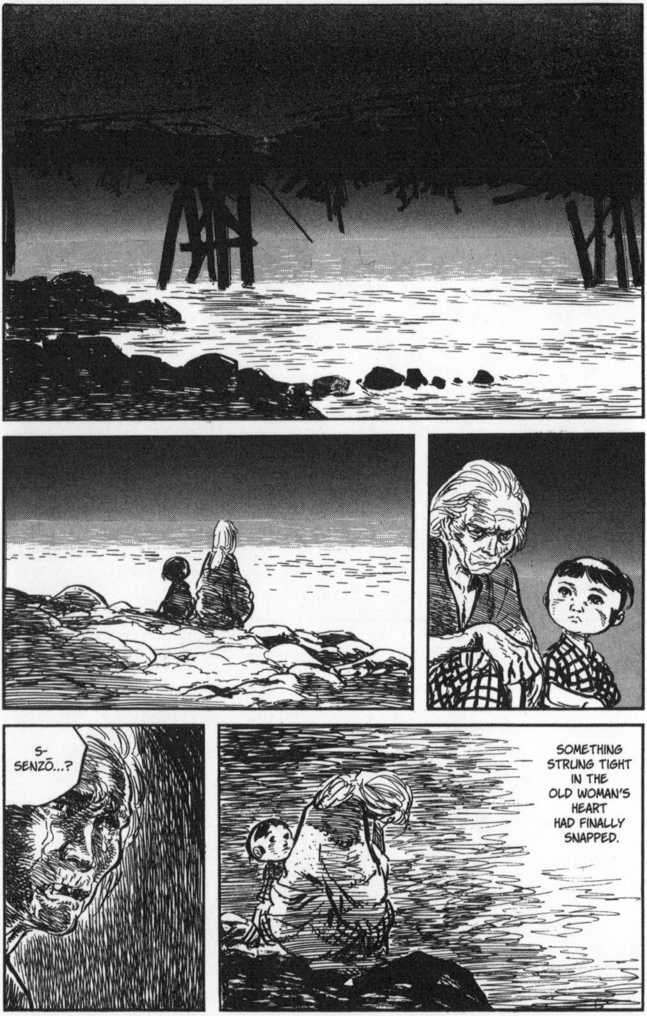
S-
SENZŌ...?
SOMETHING STRUNG TIGHT IN THE OLD WOMAN'S HEART HAD FINALLY SNAPPED.

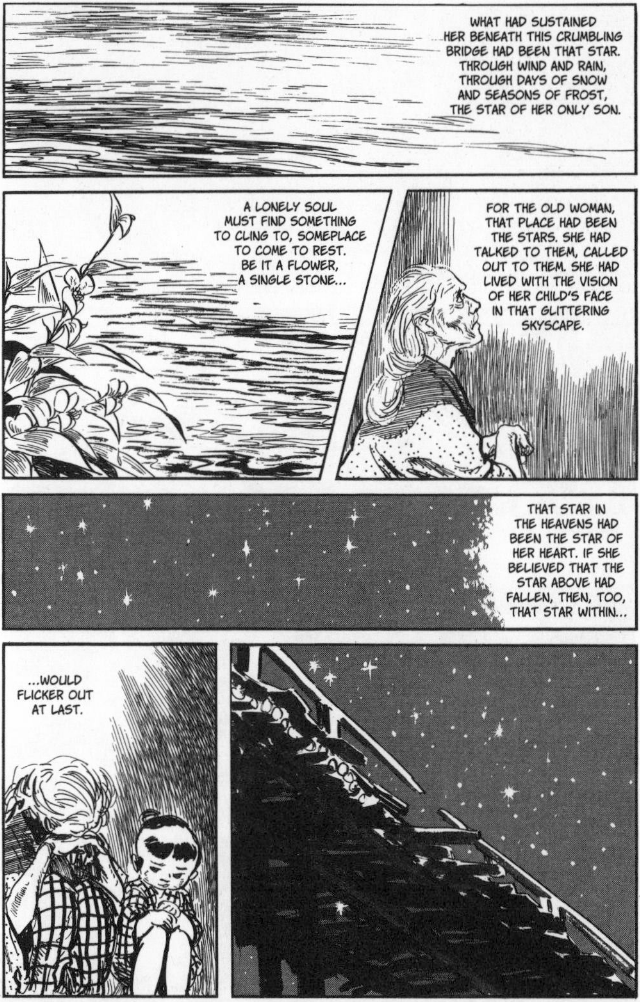
WHAT HAD SUSTAINED HER BENEATH THIS CRUMBLING BRIDGE HAD BEEN THAT STAR. THROUGH WIND AND RAIN, THROUGH DAYS OF SNOW AND SEASONS OF FROST, THE STAR OF HER ONLY SON.
A LONELY SOUL MUST FIND SOMETHING TO CLING TO, SOMEPLACE TO COME TO REST. BE IT A FLOWER, A SINGLE STONE...
FOR THE OLD WOMAN, THAT PLACE HAD BEEN THE STARS. SHE HAD TALKED TO THEM, CALLED OUT TO THEM. SHE HAD LIVED WITH THE VISION OF HER CHILD'S FACE IN THAT GLITTERING SKYSCAPE.
THAT STAR IN THE HEAVENS HAD BEEN THE STAR OF HER HEART. IF SHE BELIEVED THAT THE STAR ABOVE HAD FALLEN, THEN, TOO, THAT STAR WITHIN...
...WOULD FLICKER OUT AT LAST.

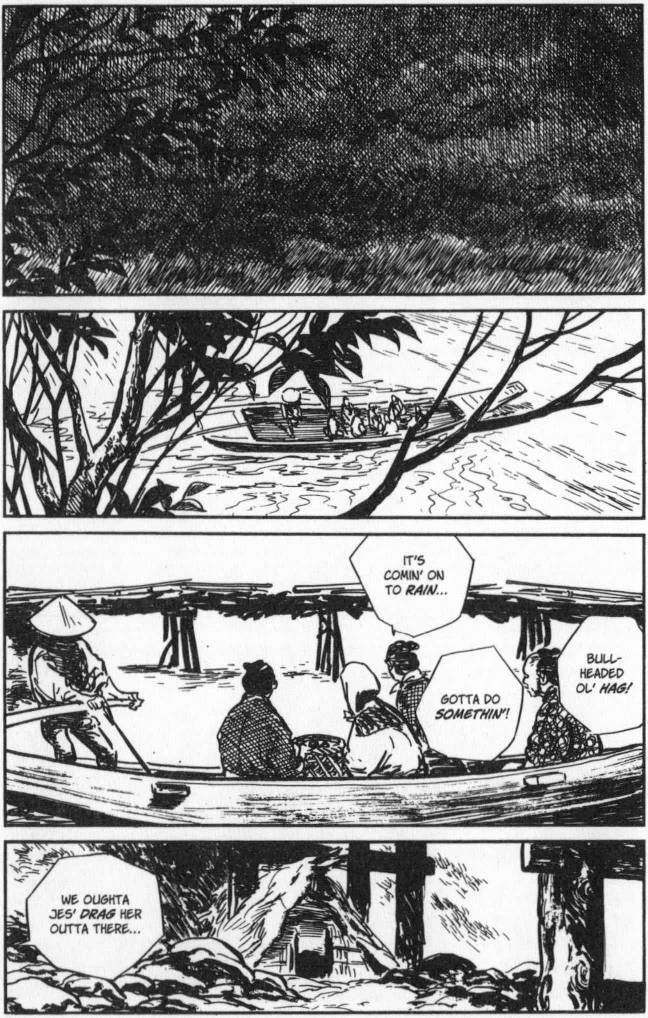
IT'S COMIN' ON TO RAIN...
GOTTA DO SOMETHIN'!
BULL-HEADED OL' HAG!
WE OUGHTA JES' DRAG HER OUTTA THERE...

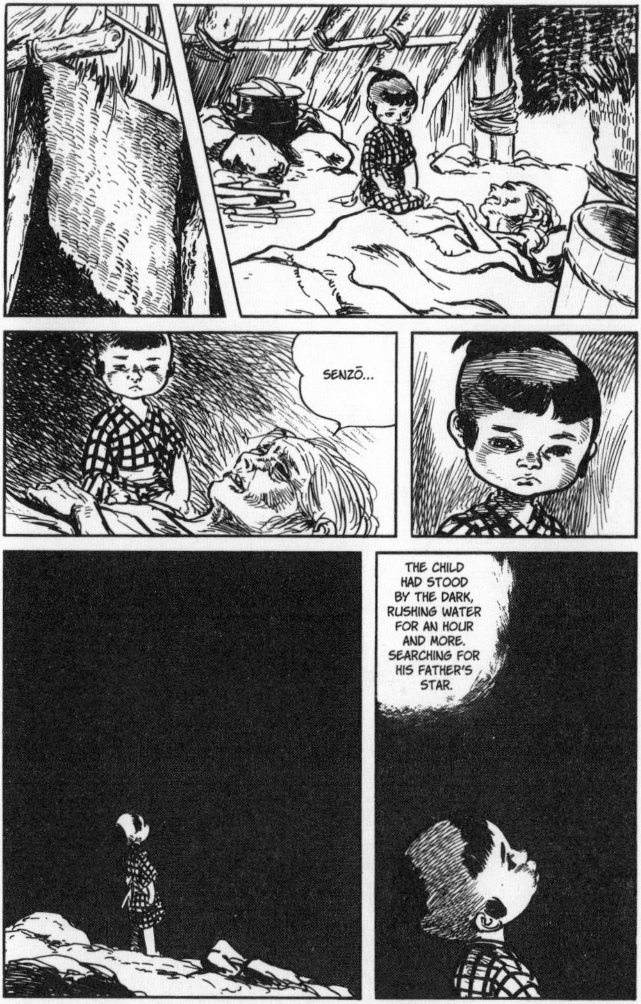
SENZŌ...
THE CHILD HAD STOOD BY THE DARK, RUSHING WATER FOR AN HOUR AND MORE. SEARCHING FOR HIS FATHER'S STAR.

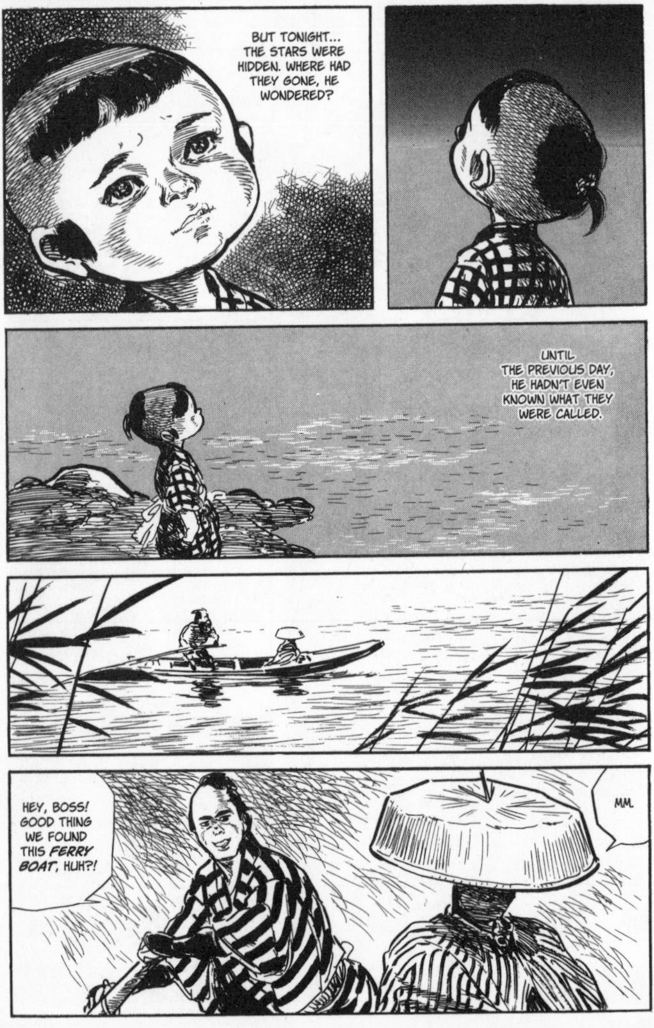
BUT TONIGHT... THE STARS WERE HIDDEN. WHERE HAD THEY GONE, HE WONDERED?
UNTIL THE PREVIOUS DAY, HE HADN'T EVEN KNOWN WHAT THEY WERE CALLED.
HEY, BOSS! GOOD THING WE FOUND THIS *FERRY BOAT*, HUH?!
MM.

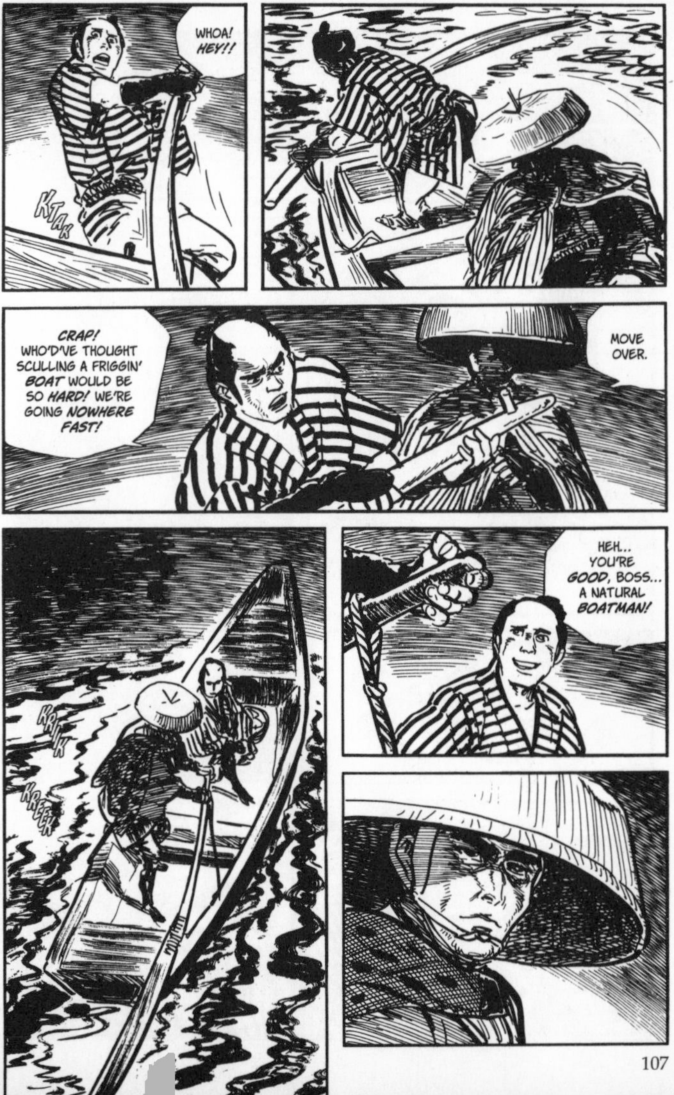
WHOA! HEY!!
KTAK
CRAP! WHO'D'VE THOUGHT SCULLING A FRIGGIN' BOAT WOULD BE SO HARD! WE'RE GOING NOWHERE FAST!
MOVE OVER.
KRIIIK
KREEK
HEH... YOU'RE GOOD, BOSS... A NATURAL BOATMAN!

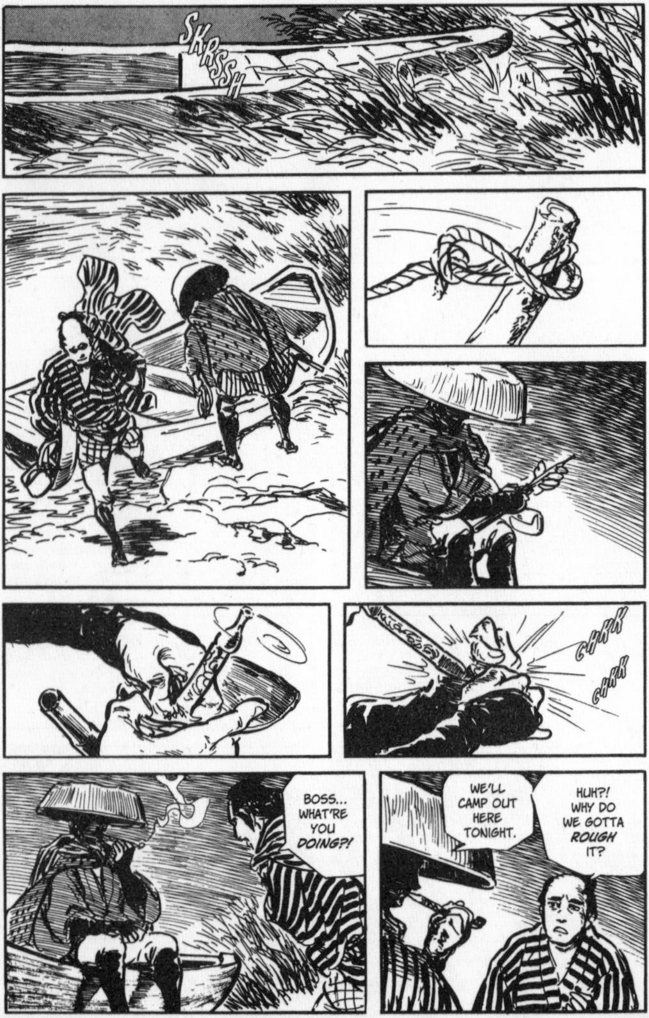
SKRSSH
CHKK
CHKK
BOSS... WHAT'RE YOU DOING?!
WE'LL CAMP OUT HERE TONIGHT.
HUH?! WHY DO WE GOTTA ROUGH IT?

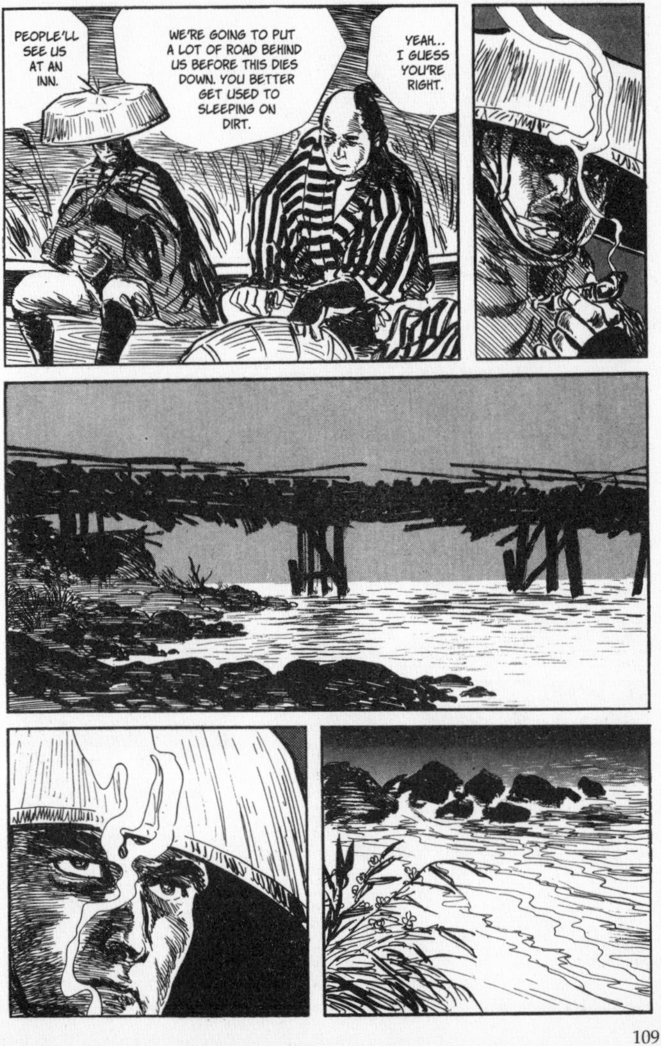
PEOPLE'LL SEE US AT AN INN.
WE'RE GOING TO PUT A LOT OF ROAD BEHIND US BEFORE THIS DIES DOWN. YOU BETTER GET USED TO SLEEPING ON DIRT.
YEAH... I GUESS YOU'RE RIGHT.

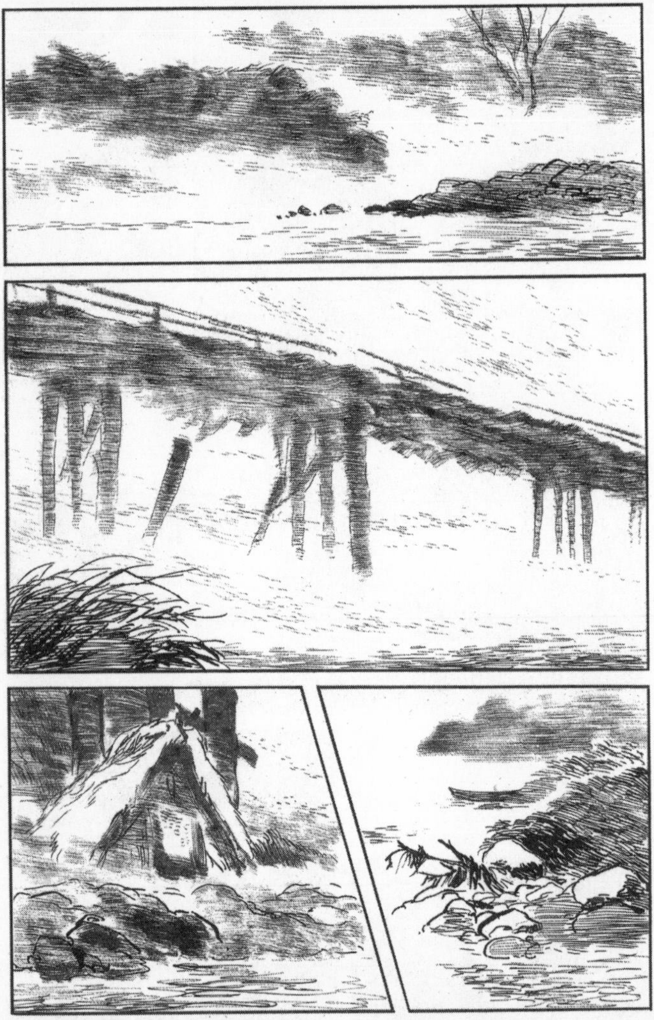

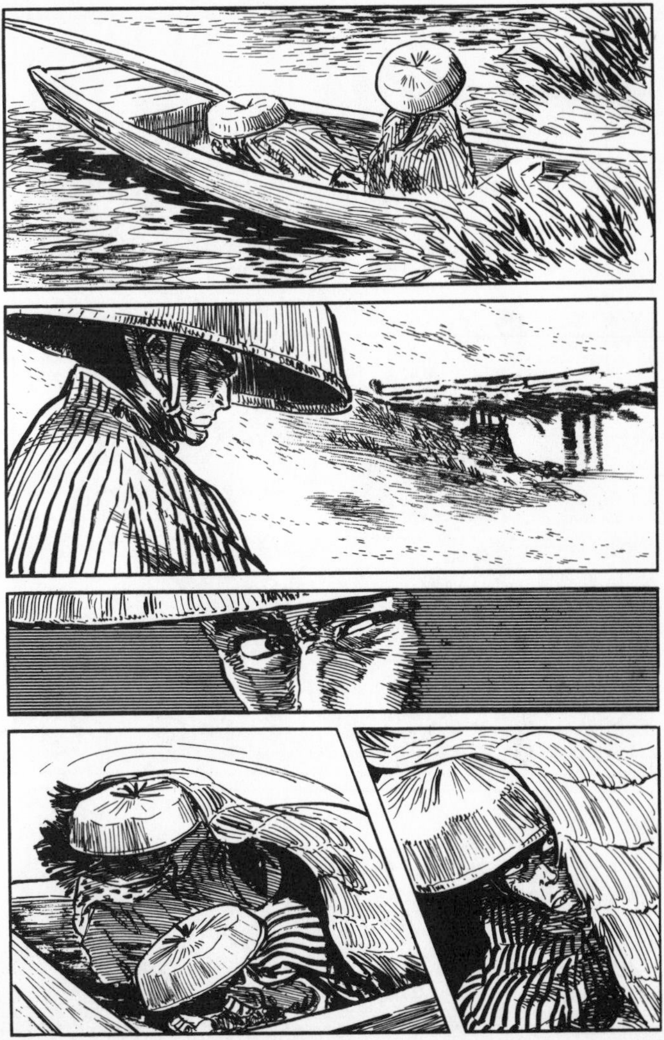

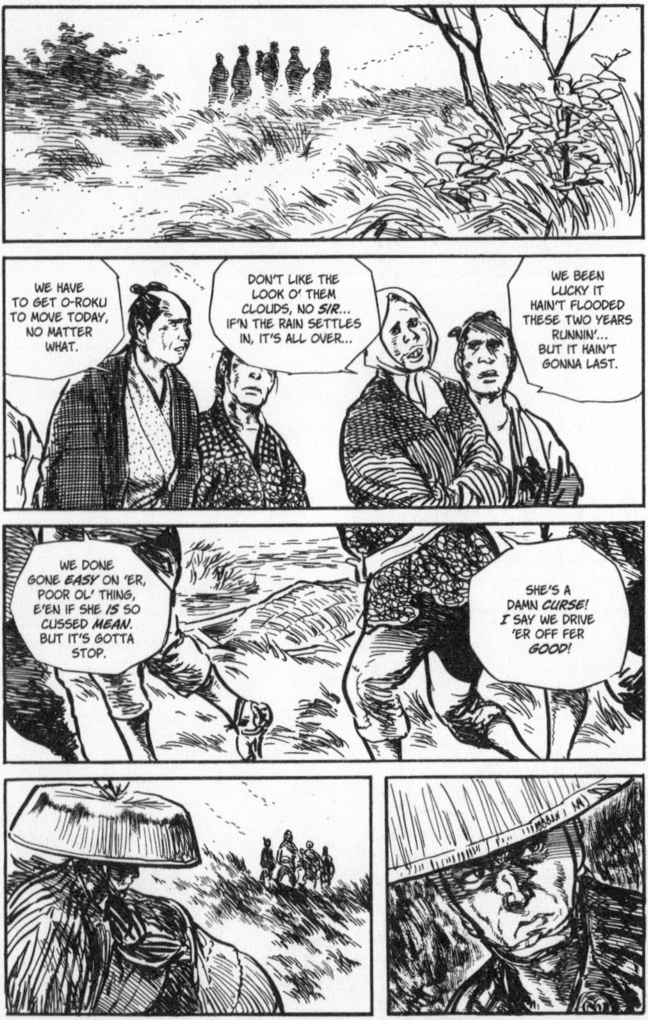
WE HAVE TO GET O-ROKU TO MOVE TODAY, NO MATTER WHAT.
DON'T LIKE THE LOOK O' THEM CLOUDS, NO *SIR*... IF'N THE RAIN SETTLES IN, IT'S ALL OVER...
WE BEEN LUCKY IT HAIN'T FLOODED THESE TWO YEARS RUNNIN'... BUT IT HAIN'T GONNA LAST.
WE DONE GONE *EASY* ON 'ER, POOR OL' THING, E'EN IF SHE *IS* SO CUSSED *MEAN*. BUT IT'S GOTTA STOP.
SHE'S A DAMN *CURSE*! *I* SAY WE DRIVE 'ER OFF FER *GOOD*!

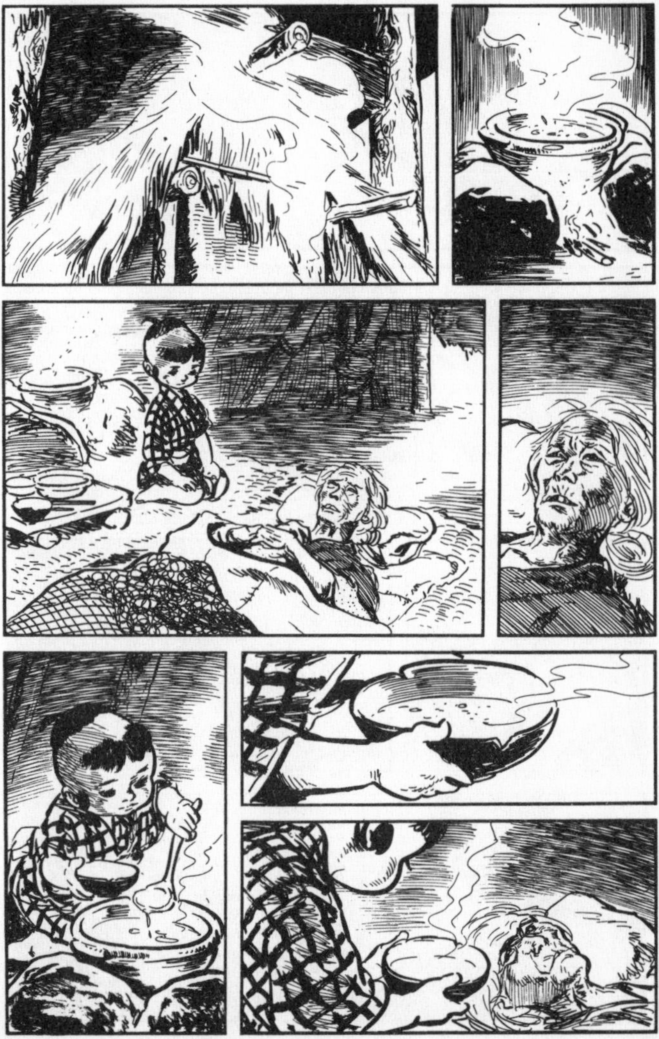

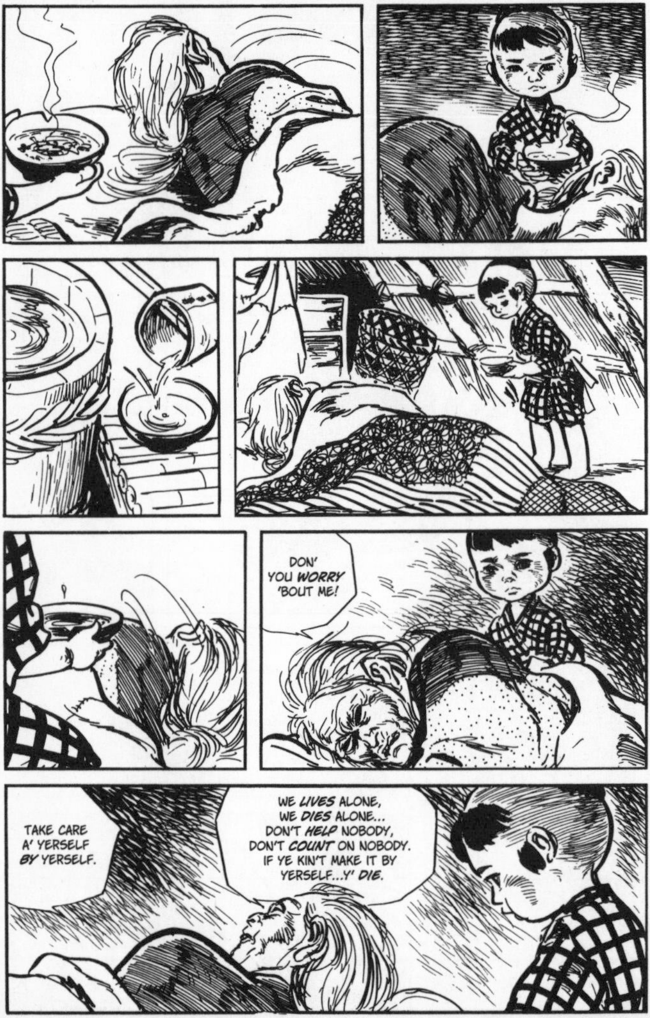
DON' YOU WORRY 'BOUT ME!
TAKE CARE A' YERSELF BY YERSELF.
WE LIVES ALONE, WE DIES ALONE... DON'T HELP NOBODY, DON'T COUNT ON NOBODY. IF YE KIN'T MAKE IT BY YERSELF...Y' DIE.

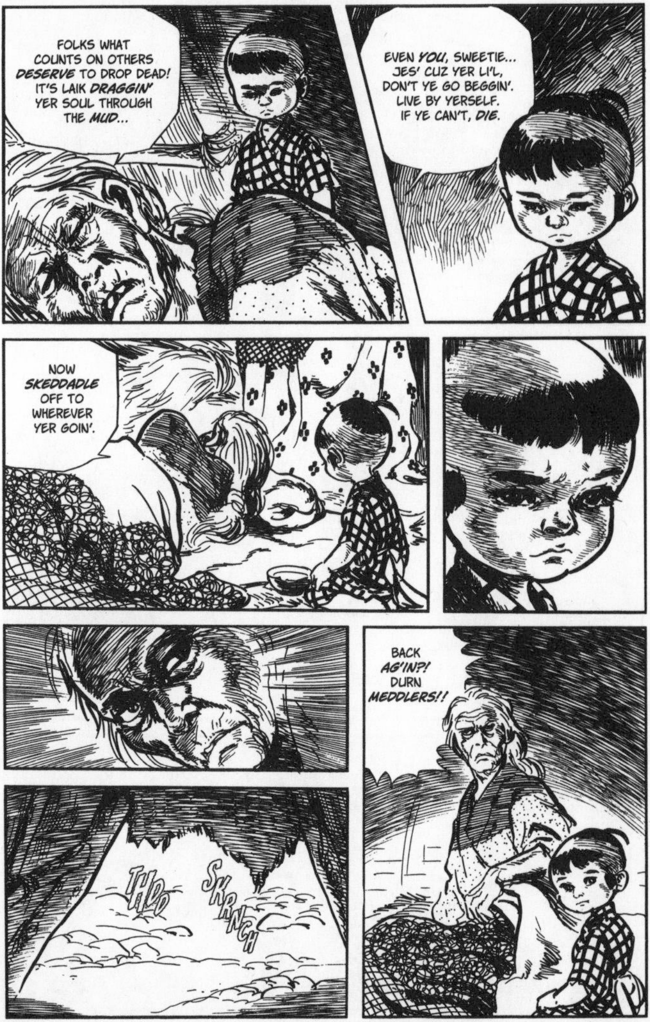
FOLKS WHAT COUNTS ON OTHERS DESERVE TO DROP DEAD! IT'S LAIK DRAGGIN' YER SOUL THROUGH THE MUD...
EVEN YOU, SWEETIE... JES' CUZ YER LI'L, DON'T YE GO BEGGIN'. LIVE BY YERSELF. IF YE CAN'T, DIE.
NOW SKEDDADLE OFF TO WHEREVER YER GOIN'.
THDD
SKRNCH
BACK AG'IN?! DURN MEDDLERS!!

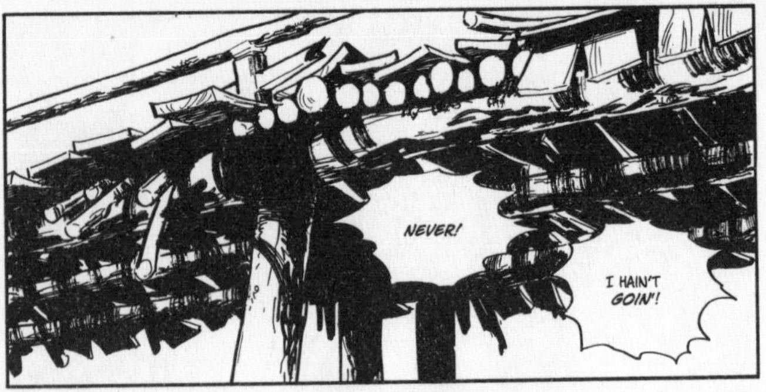
NEVER!
I HAIN'T *GOIN'*!

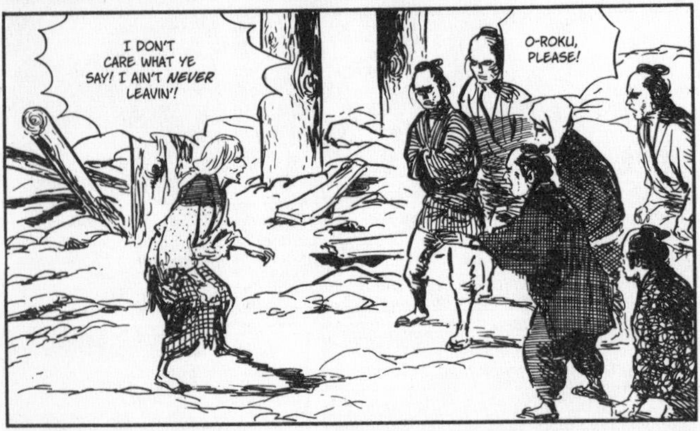
I DON'T CARE WHAT YE SAY! I AIN'T *NEVER* LEAVIN'!
O-ROKU, PLEASE!

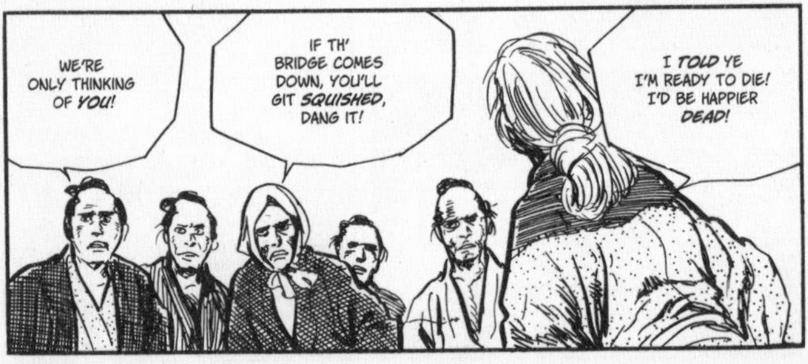
WE'RE ONLY THINKING OF *YOU*!
IF TH' BRIDGE COMES DOWN, YOU'LL GIT *SQUISHED*, DANG IT!
I *TOLD* YE I'M READY TO DIE! I'D BE HAPPIER *DEAD*!

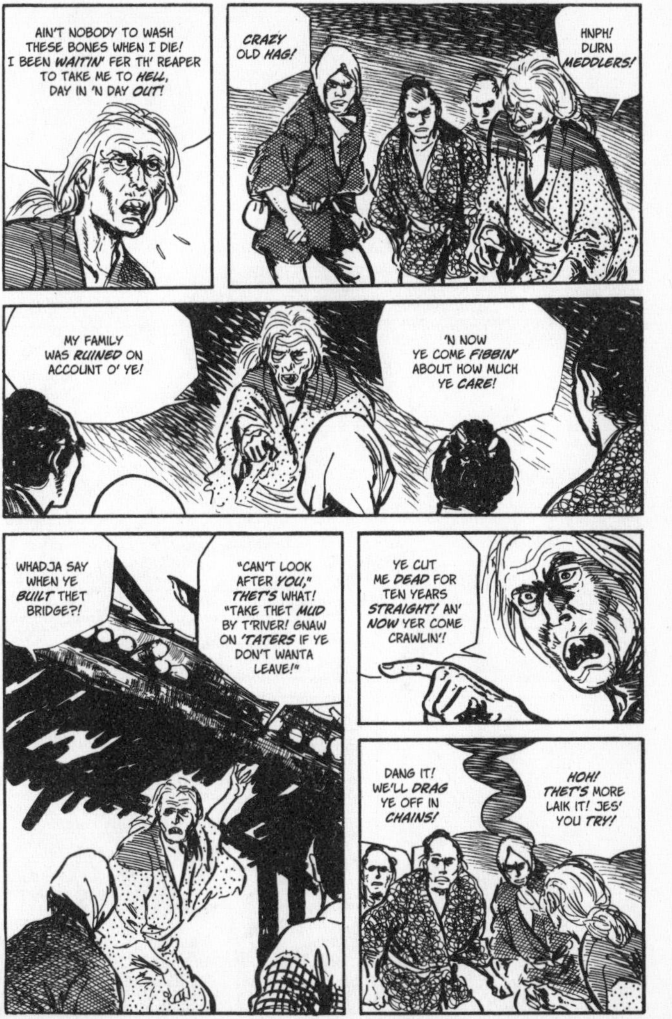
AIN'T NOBODY TO WASH THESE BONES WHEN I DIE! I BEEN WAITIN' FER TH' REAPER TO TAKE ME TO HELL, DAY IN 'N DAY OUT!
CRAZY OLD HAG!
HNPH! DURN MEDDLERS!
MY FAMILY WAS RUINED ON ACCOUNT O' YE!
'N NOW YE COME FIBBIN' ABOUT HOW MUCH YE CARE!
WHADJA SAY WHEN YE BUILT THET BRIDGE?!
"CAN'T LOOK AFTER YOU," THET'S WHAT! "TAKE THET MUD BY T'RIVER! GNAW ON 'TATERS IF YE DON'T WANTA LEAVE!"
YE CUT ME DEAD FOR TEN YEARS STRAIGHT! AN' NOW YER COME CRAWLIN'!
DANG IT! WE'LL DRAG YE OFF IN CHAINS!
HOH! THET'S MORE LAIK IT! JES' YOU TRY!

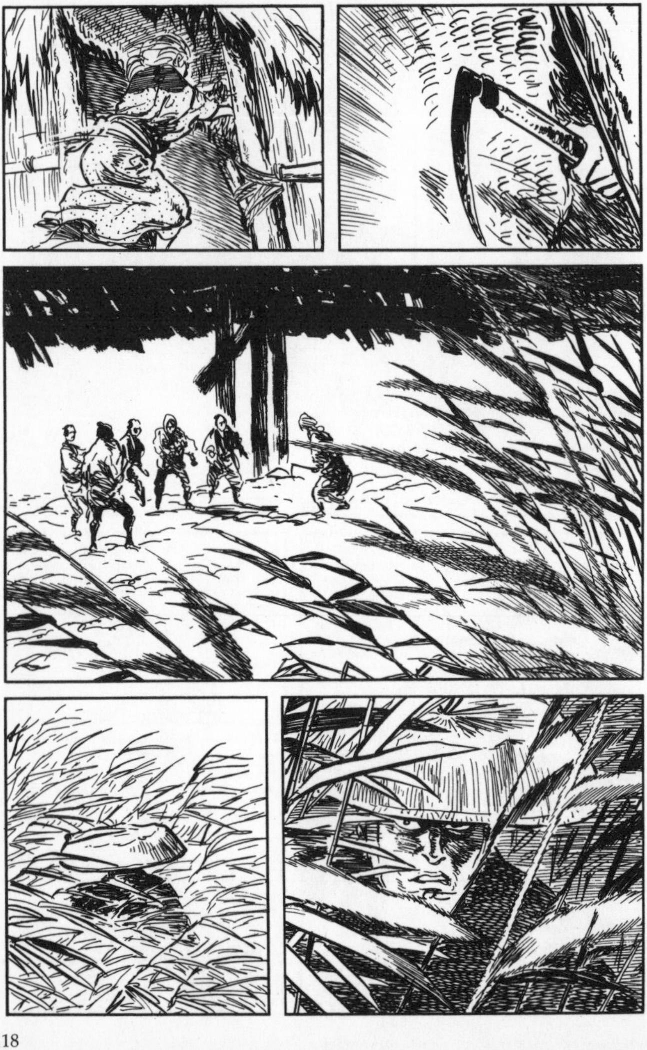

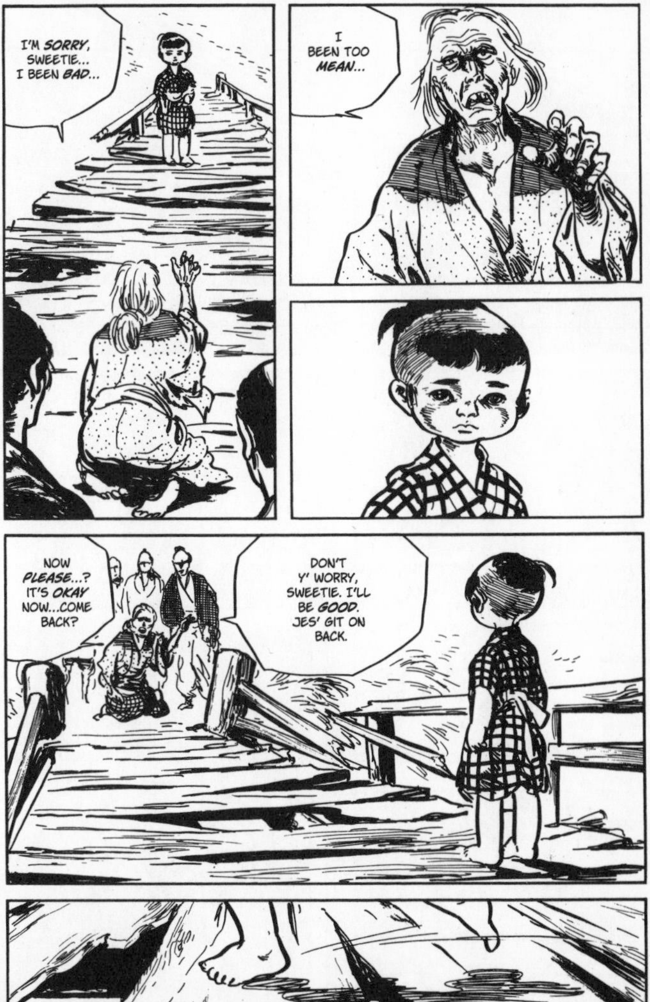
I'M SORRY, SWEETIE... I BEEN BAD...
I BEEN TOO MEAN...
NOW PLEASE...? IT'S OKAY NOW...COME BACK?
DON'T Y' WORRY, SWEETIE. I'LL BE GOOD. JES' GIT ON BACK.

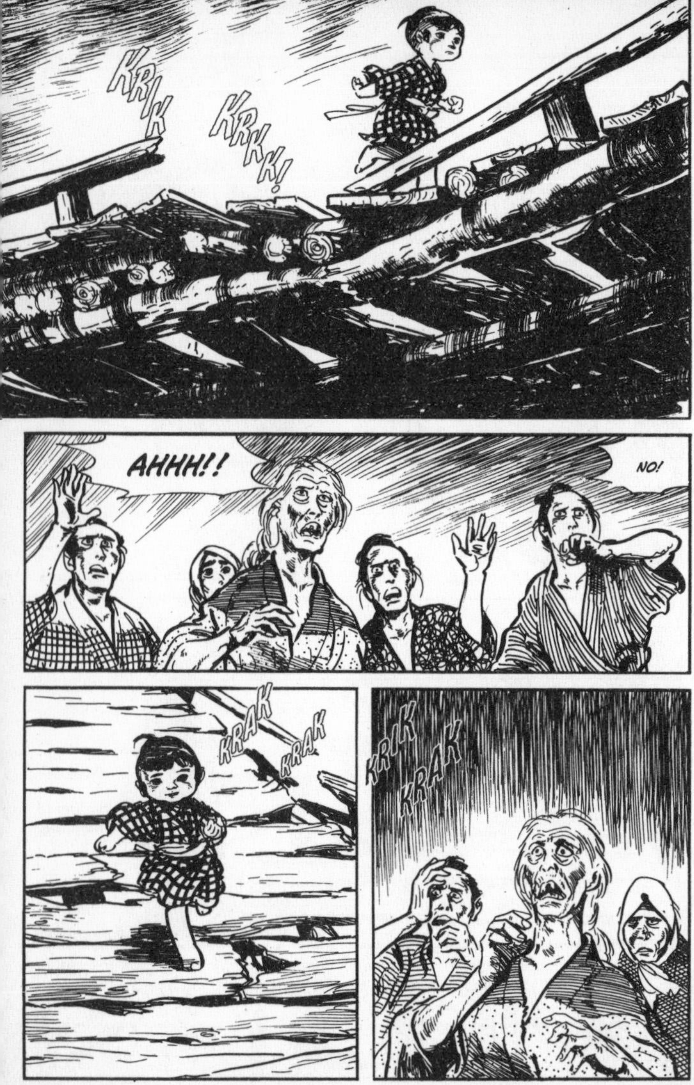
KRIK
KRKKK!
AHHH!!
NO!
KRAK
KRAK
KRIK
KRAK

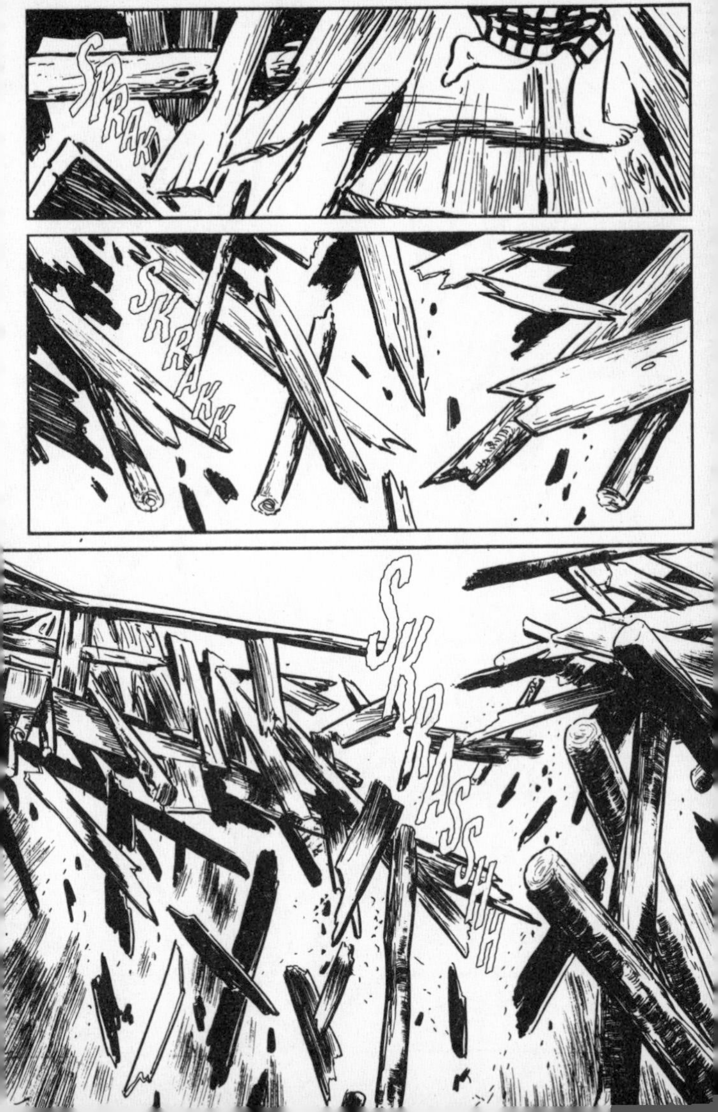
SPRAKK
SKRAKK
SKRASSHH

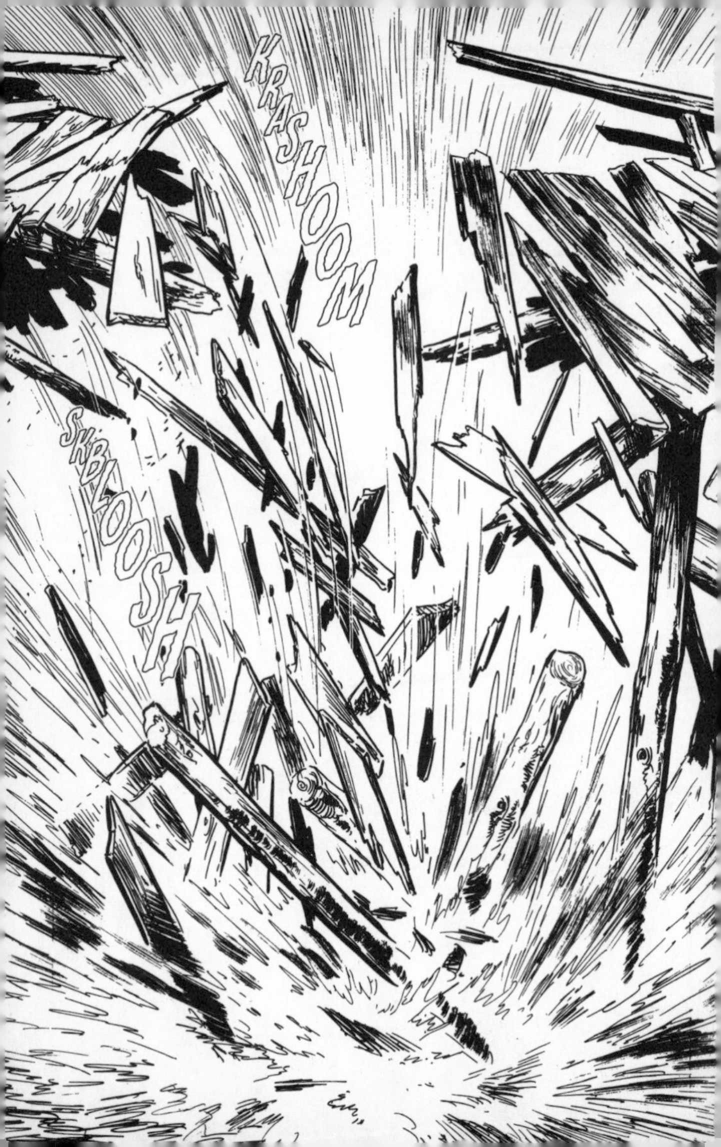
KRASHOOM
SKBLOOSH

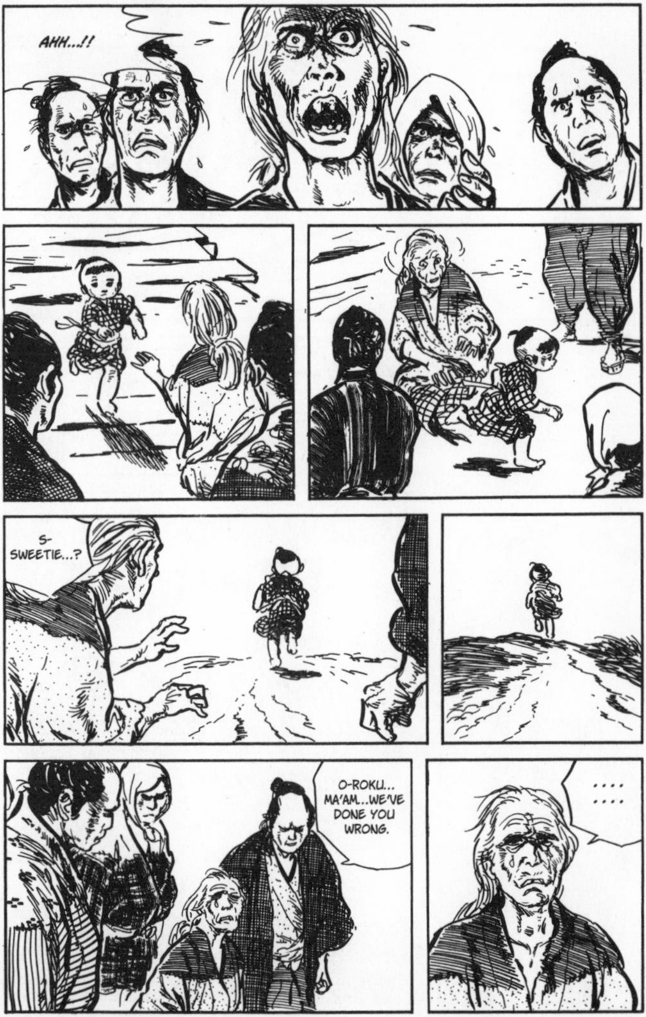
AHH...!!
S-SWEETIE...?
O-ROKU... MA'AM...WE'VE DONE YOU WRONG.
....
....

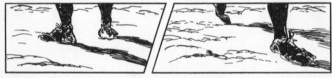

B-BOSS...?
WHERE YA
GOING...?

BACK.
I'M TURNING
MYSELF IN.

WH-
WHAT?!

128

the fifty-seventh

Thirteen Strings

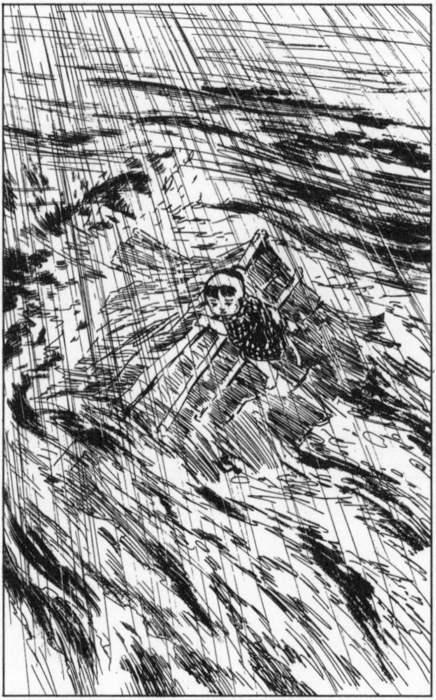

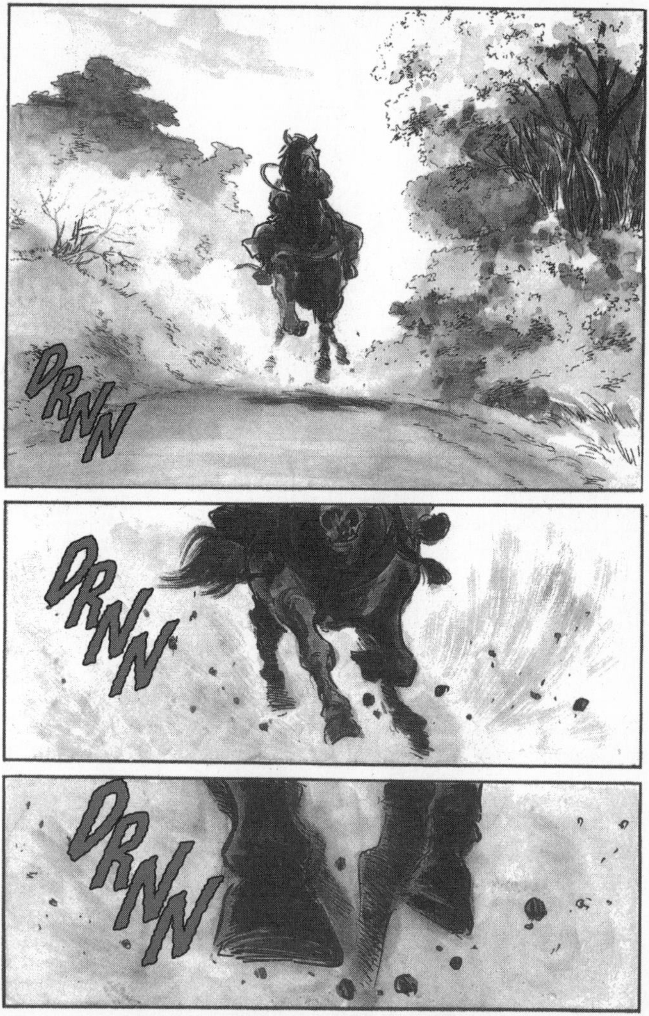
DRNN
DRNN
DRNN

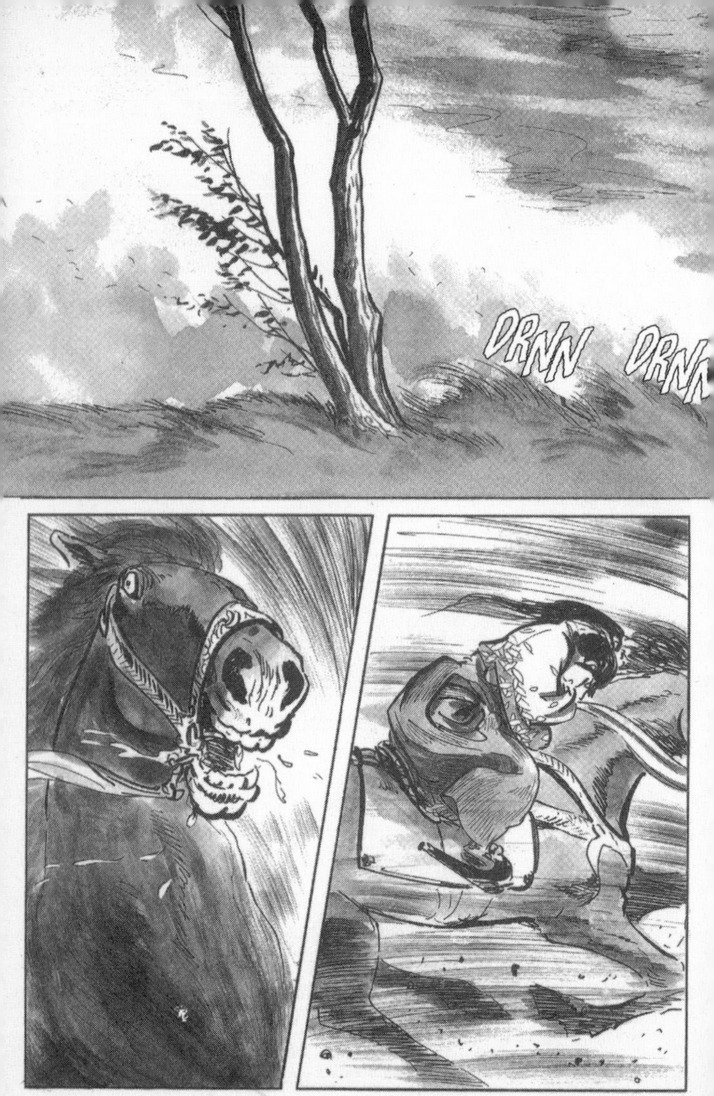
DRNN DRNN

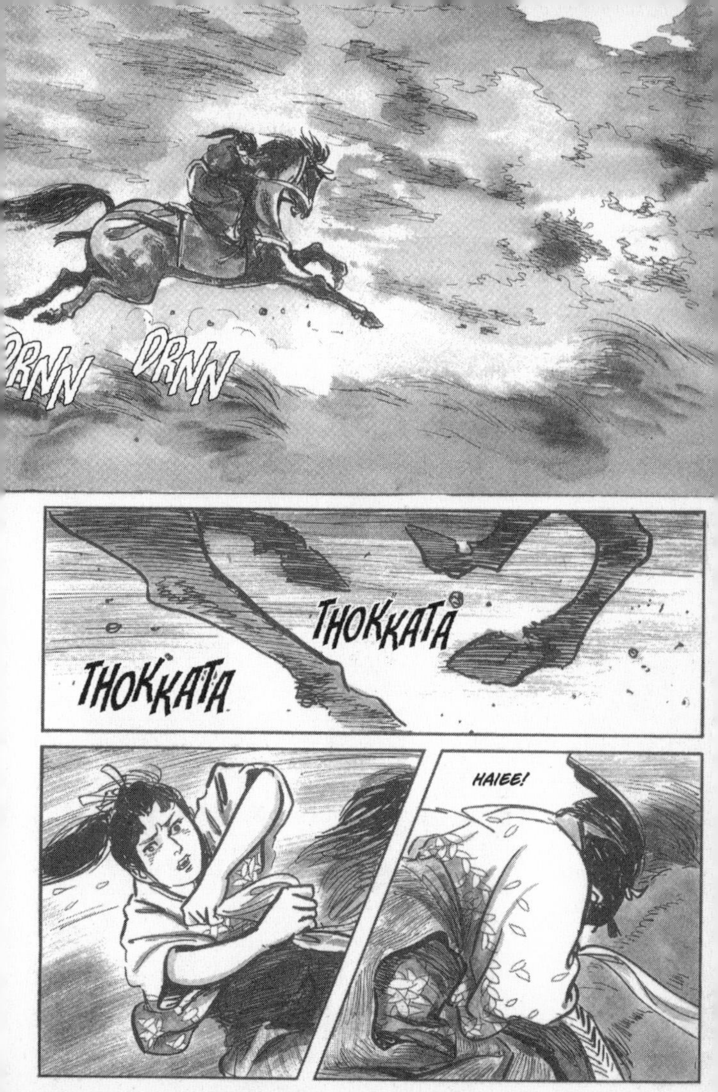
DRNN
DRNN
THOKKATA
THOKKATA
HAIEE!

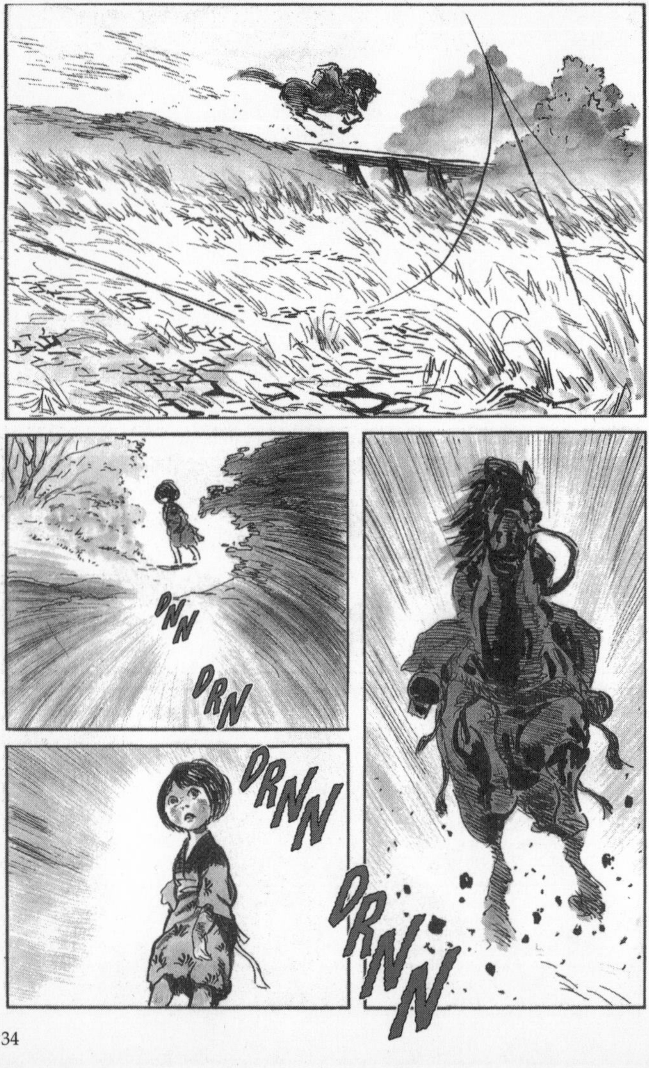
DNN
DRN
DRNN
DRNN

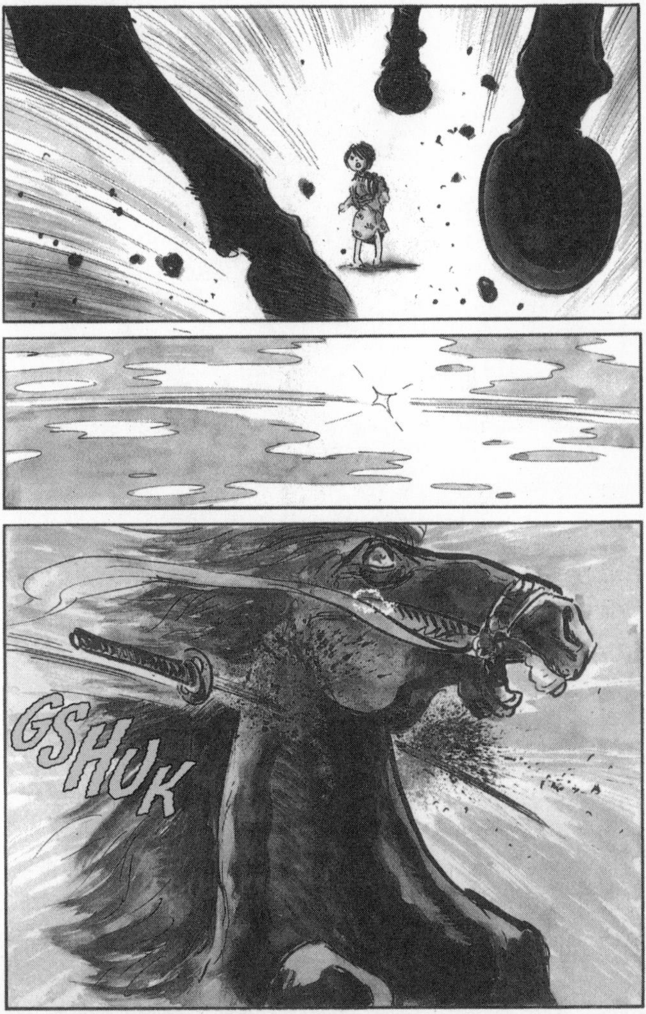
GSHUK

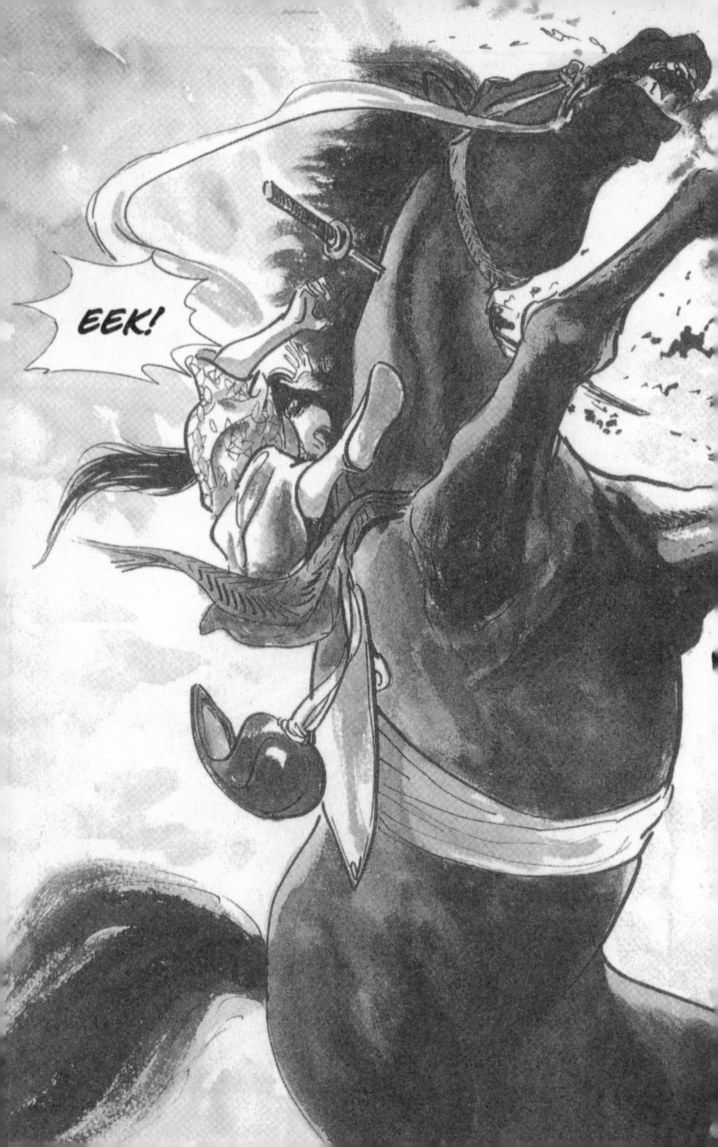
EEK!

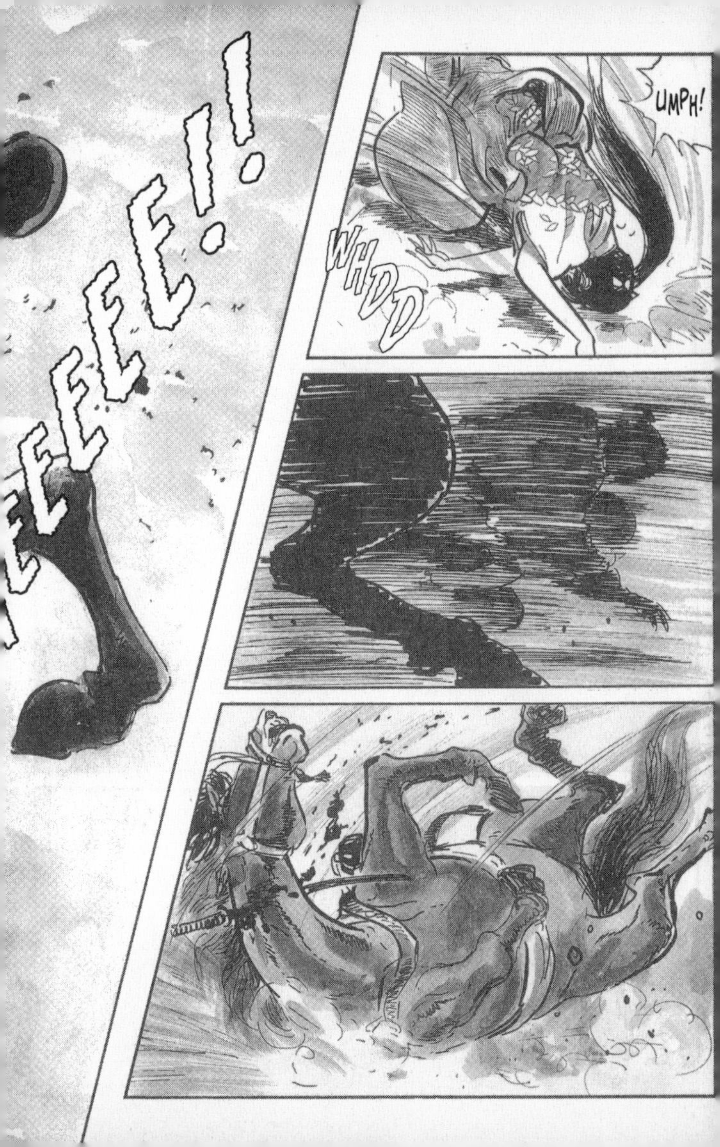
EEEEEE!!
UMPH!
WHDD

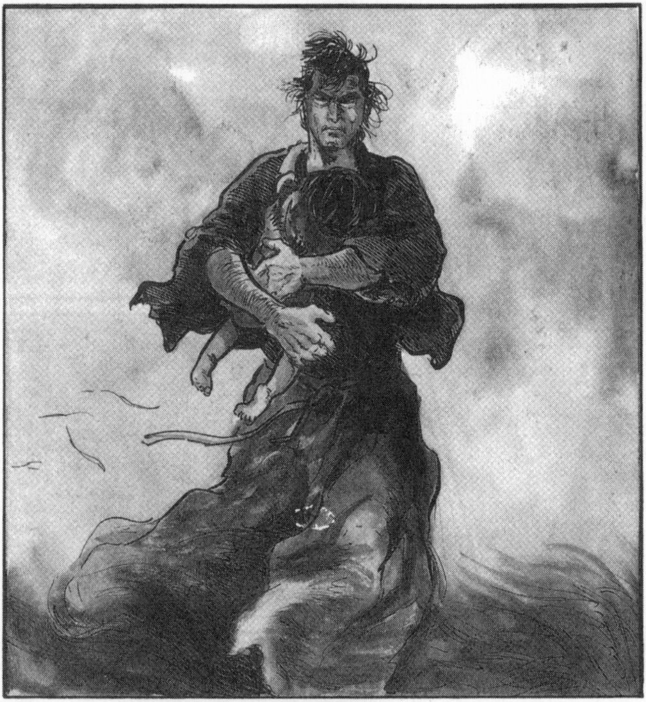

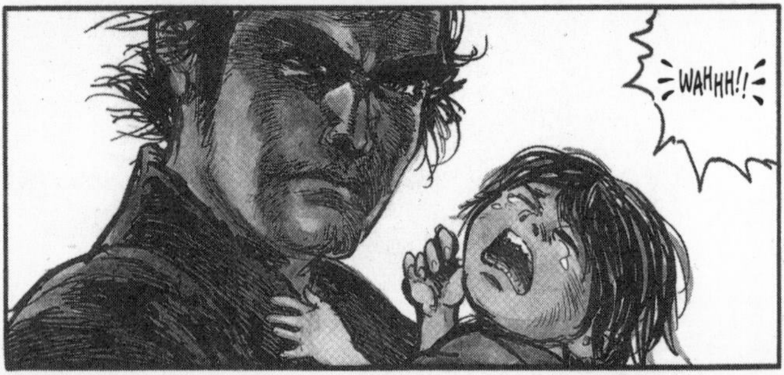
WAHHH!!

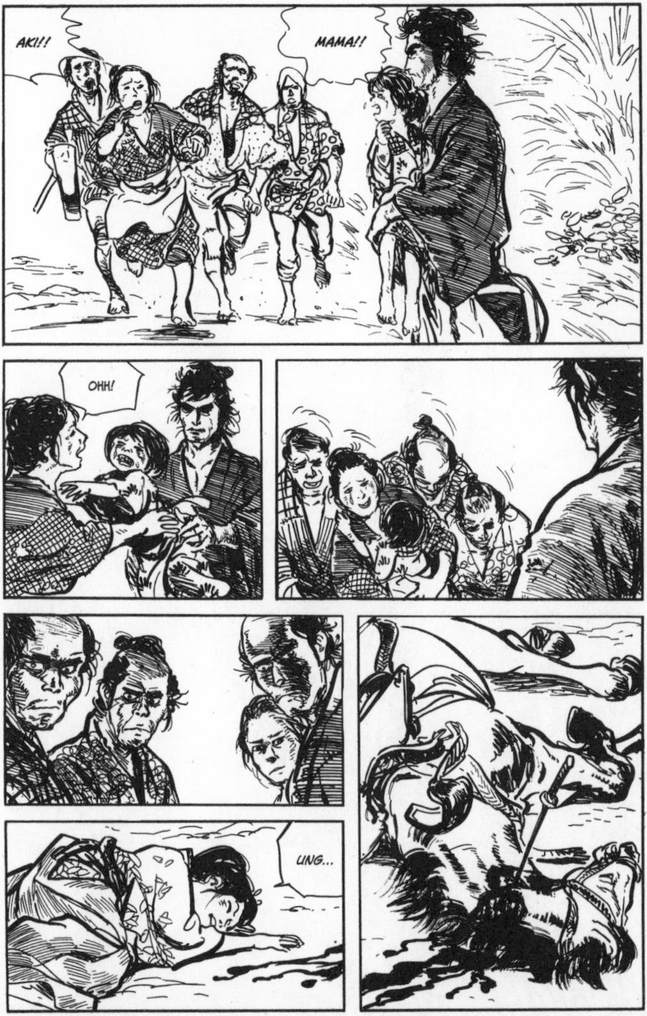
AKI!!
MAMA!!
OHH!
UNG...

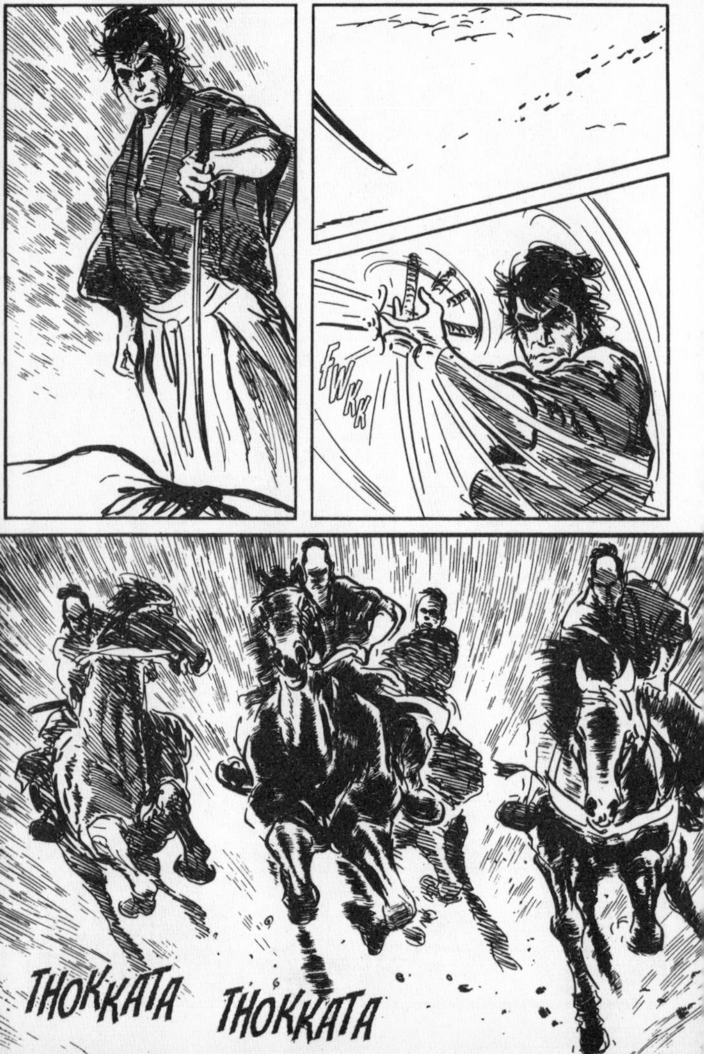
FWKK
THOKKATA
THOKKATA

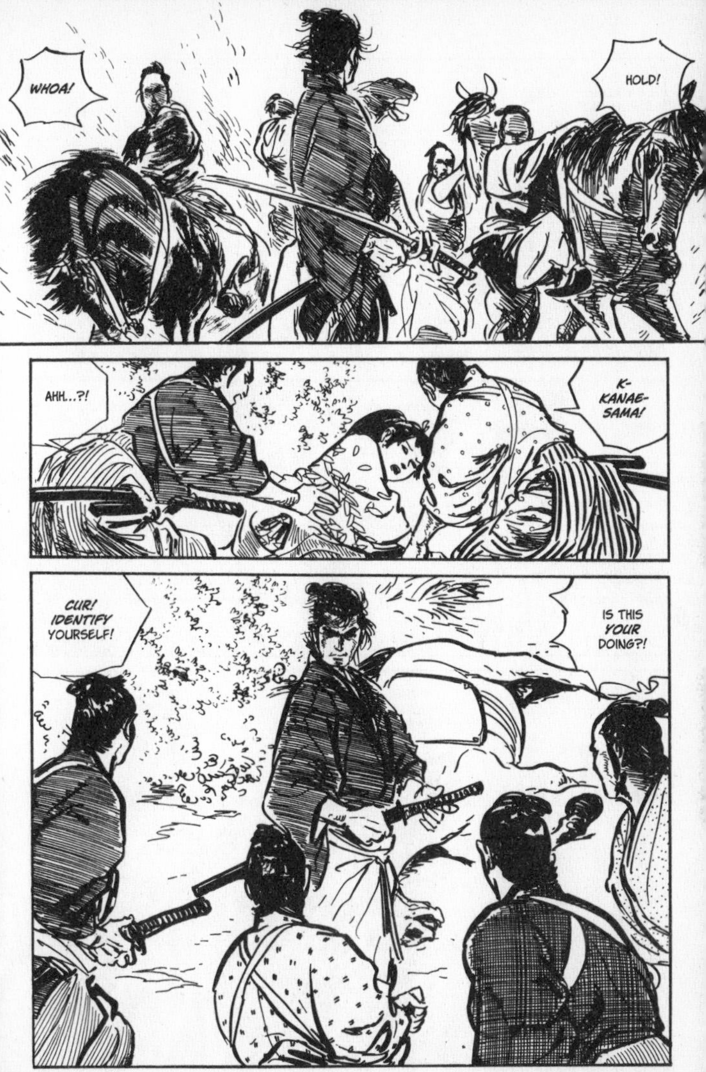

WHOA!
HOLD!
AHH...?!
K-KANAE-SAMA!
CUR! IDENTIFY YOURSELF!
IS THIS YOUR DOING?!

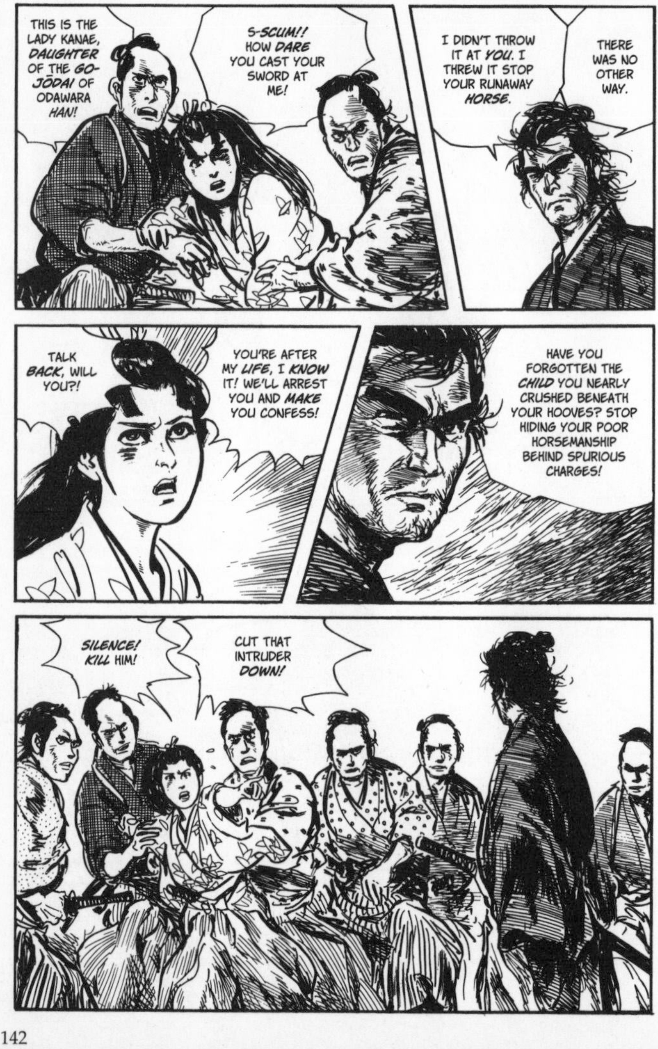
THIS IS THE LADY KANAE, DAUGHTER OF THE GO-JŌDAI OF ODAWARA HAN!
S-SCUM!! HOW DARE YOU CAST YOUR SWORD AT ME!
I DIDN'T THROW IT AT YOU. I THREW IT STOP YOUR RUNAWAY HORSE.
THERE WAS NO OTHER WAY.
TALK BACK, WILL YOU?!
YOU'RE AFTER MY LIFE, I KNOW IT! WE'LL ARREST YOU AND MAKE YOU CONFESS!
HAVE YOU FORGOTTEN THE CHILD YOU NEARLY CRUSHED BENEATH YOUR HOOVES? STOP HIDING YOUR POOR HORSEMANSHIP BEHIND SPURIOUS CHARGES!
SILENCE! KILL HIM!
CUT THAT INTRUDER DOWN!

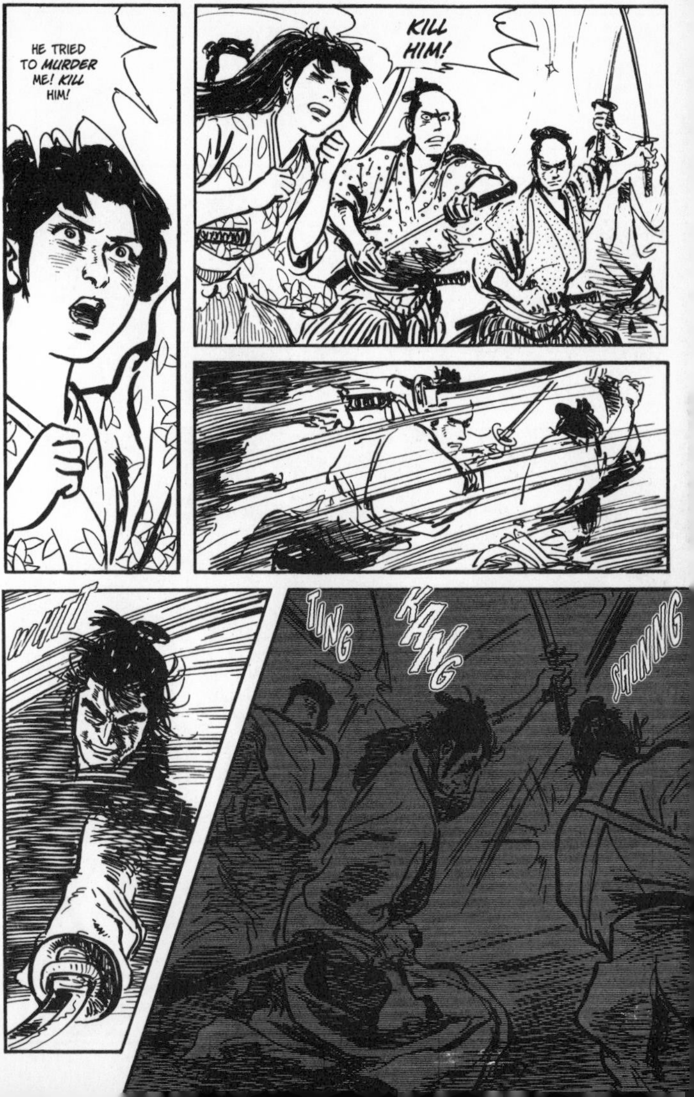
HE TRIED TO *MURDER* ME! *KILL* HIM!
KILL HIM!
WHITT
TING
KANG
SHINNG

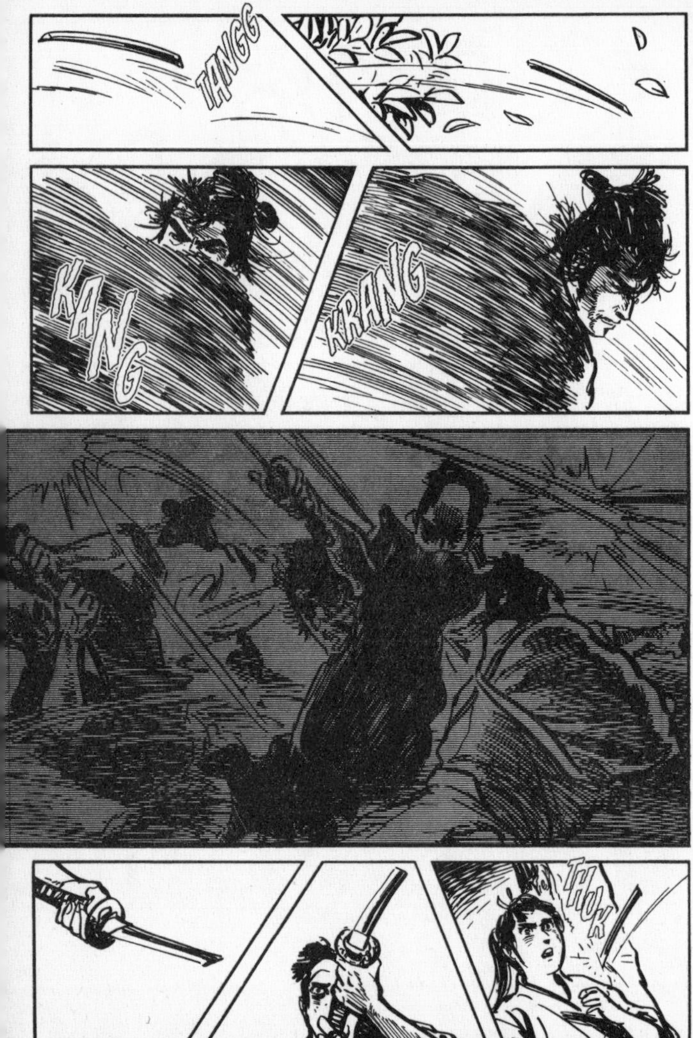
TANGG
KANG
KRANG
THUK

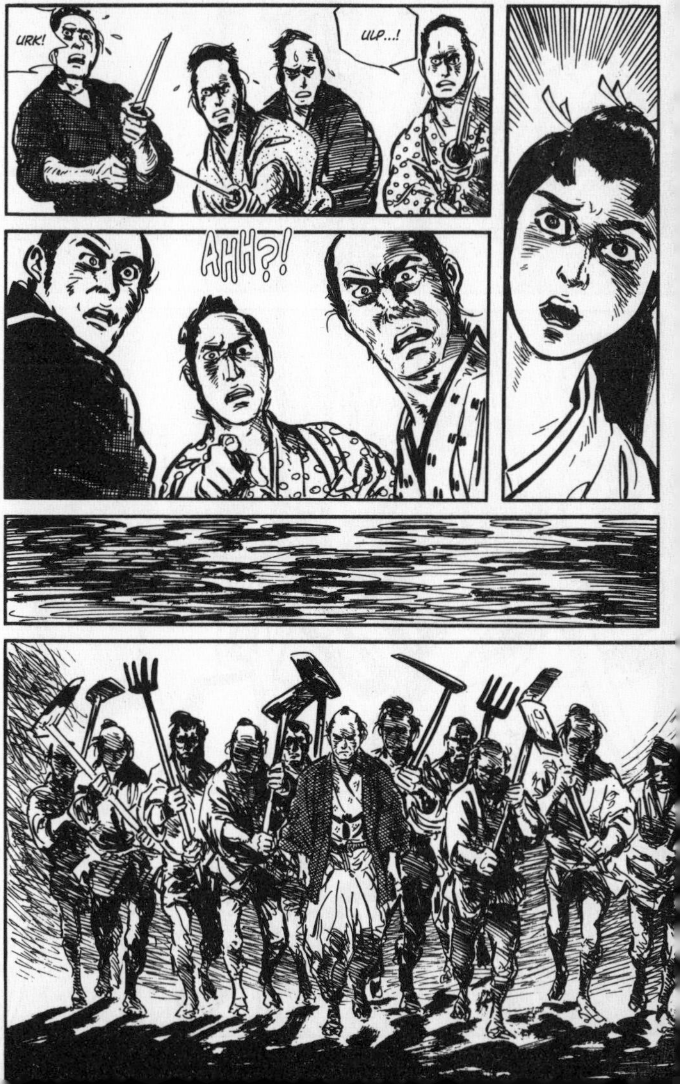
URK!
ULP...!
AHH?!

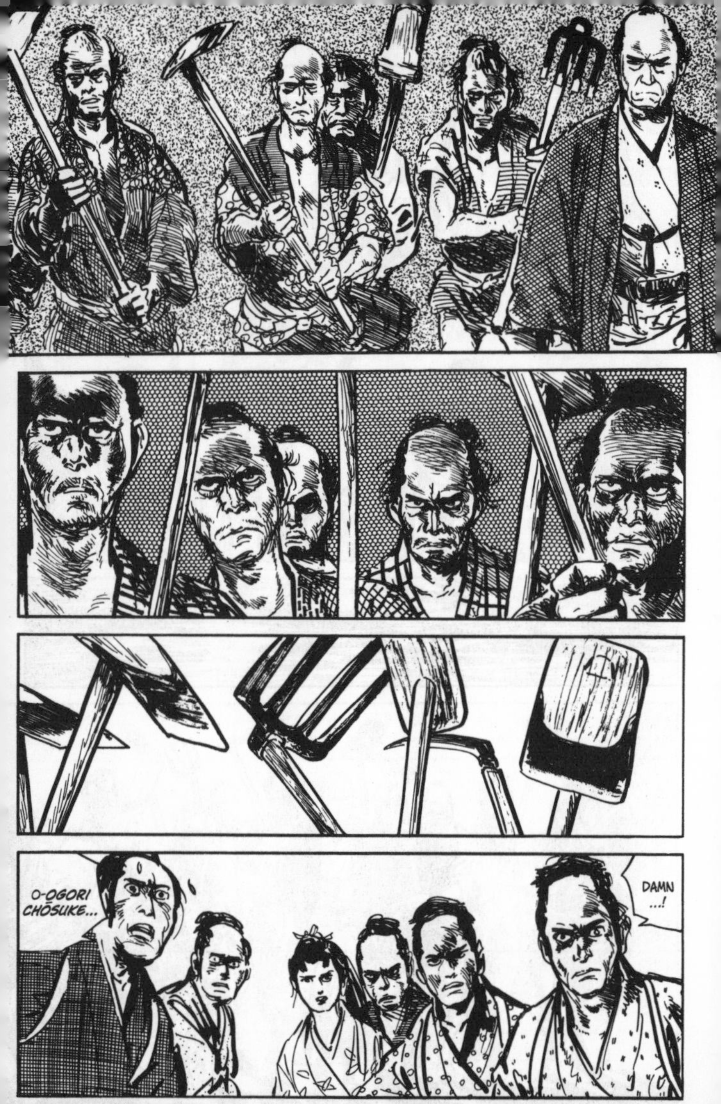
O-OGORI CHŌSUKE...
DAMN ...!

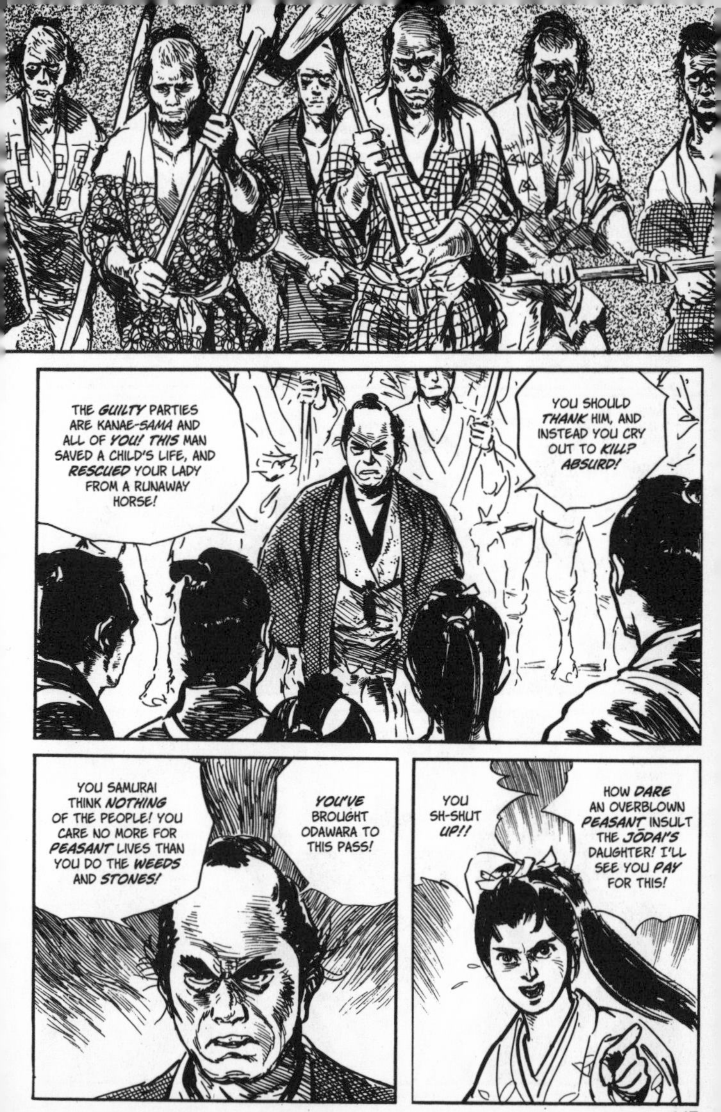
THE GUILTY PARTIES ARE KANAE-SAMA AND ALL OF YOU! THIS MAN SAVED A CHILD'S LIFE, AND RESCUED YOUR LADY FROM A RUNAWAY HORSE!
YOU SHOULD THANK HIM, AND INSTEAD YOU CRY OUT TO KILL? ABSURD!
YOU SAMURAI THINK NOTHING OF THE PEOPLE! YOU CARE NO MORE FOR PEASANT LIVES THAN YOU DO THE WEEDS AND STONES!
YOU'VE BROUGHT ODAWARA TO THIS PASS!
YOU SH-SHUT UP!!
HOW DARE AN OVERBLOWN PEASANT INSULT THE JŌDAI'S DAUGHTER! I'LL SEE YOU PAY FOR THIS!

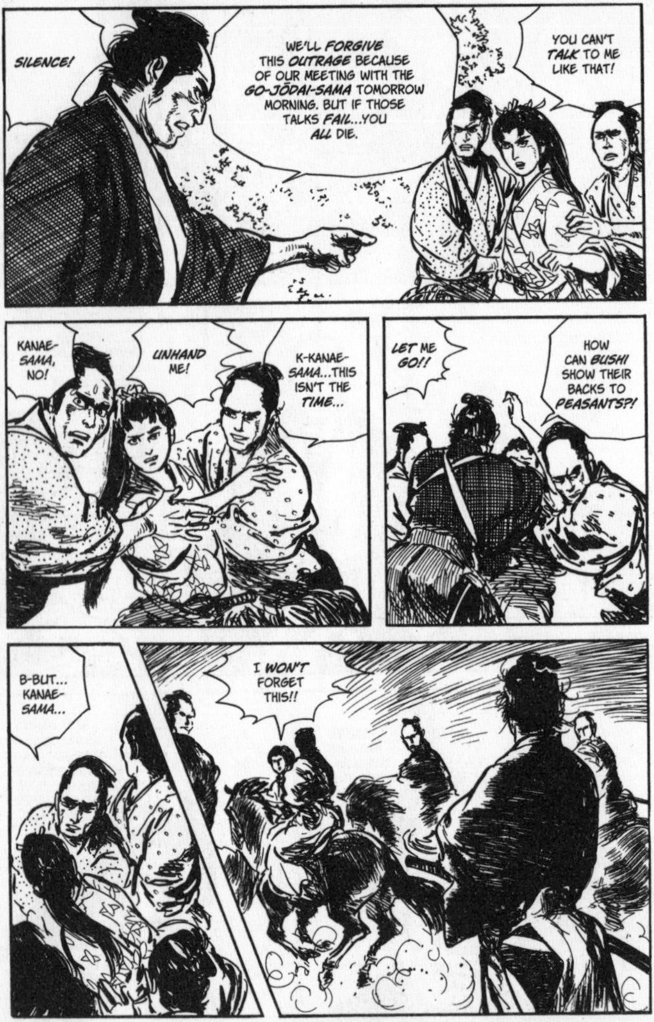
SILENCE!
WE'LL FORGIVE THIS OUTRAGE BECAUSE OF OUR MEETING WITH THE GO-JŌDAI-SAMA TOMORROW MORNING. BUT IF THOSE TALKS FAIL...YOU ALL DIE.
YOU CAN'T TALK TO ME LIKE THAT!
KANAE-SAMA, NO!
UNHAND ME!
K-KANAE-SAMA...THIS ISN'T THE TIME...
LET ME GO!!
HOW CAN BUSHI SHOW THEIR BACKS TO PEASANTS?!
B-BUT... KANAE-SAMA...
I WON'T FORGET THIS!!

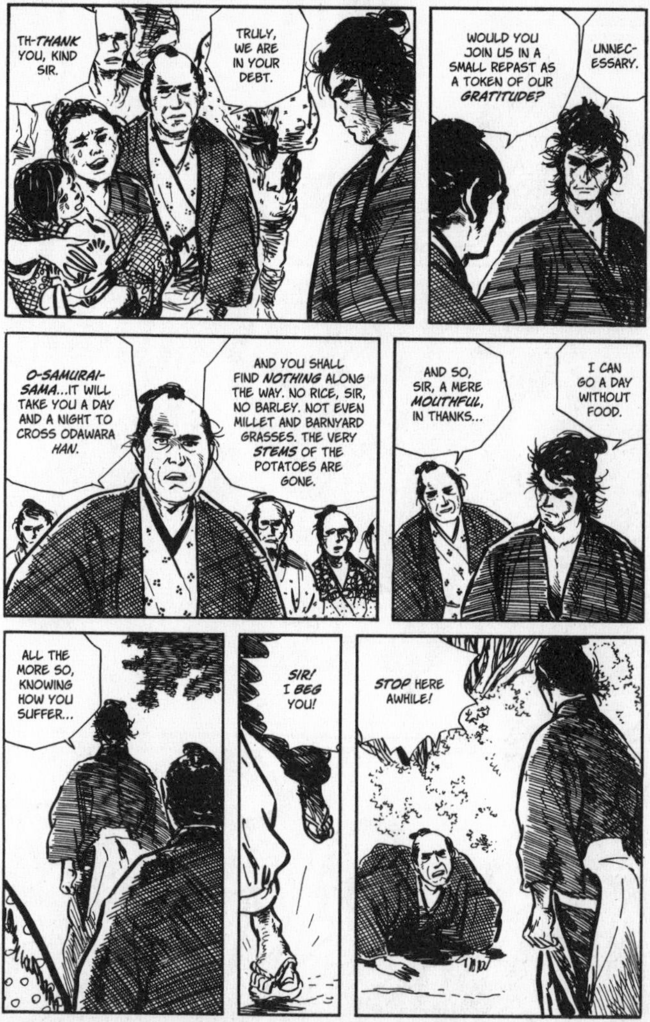

TH-*THANK* YOU, KIND SIR.
TRULY, WE ARE IN YOUR DEBT.
WOULD YOU JOIN US IN A SMALL REPAST AS A TOKEN OF OUR *GRATITUDE?*
UNNEC-ESSARY.
O-SAMURAI-SAMA...IT WILL TAKE YOU A DAY AND A NIGHT TO CROSS ODAWARA *HAN*.
AND YOU SHALL FIND *NOTHING* ALONG THE WAY. NO RICE, SIR, NO BARLEY. NOT EVEN MILLET AND BARNYARD GRASSES. THE VERY *STEMS* OF THE POTATOES ARE GONE.
AND SO, SIR, A MERE *MOUTHFUL*, IN THANKS...
I CAN GO A DAY WITHOUT FOOD.
ALL THE MORE SO, KNOWING HOW YOU SUFFER...
SIR! I *BEG* YOU!
STOP HERE AWHILE!

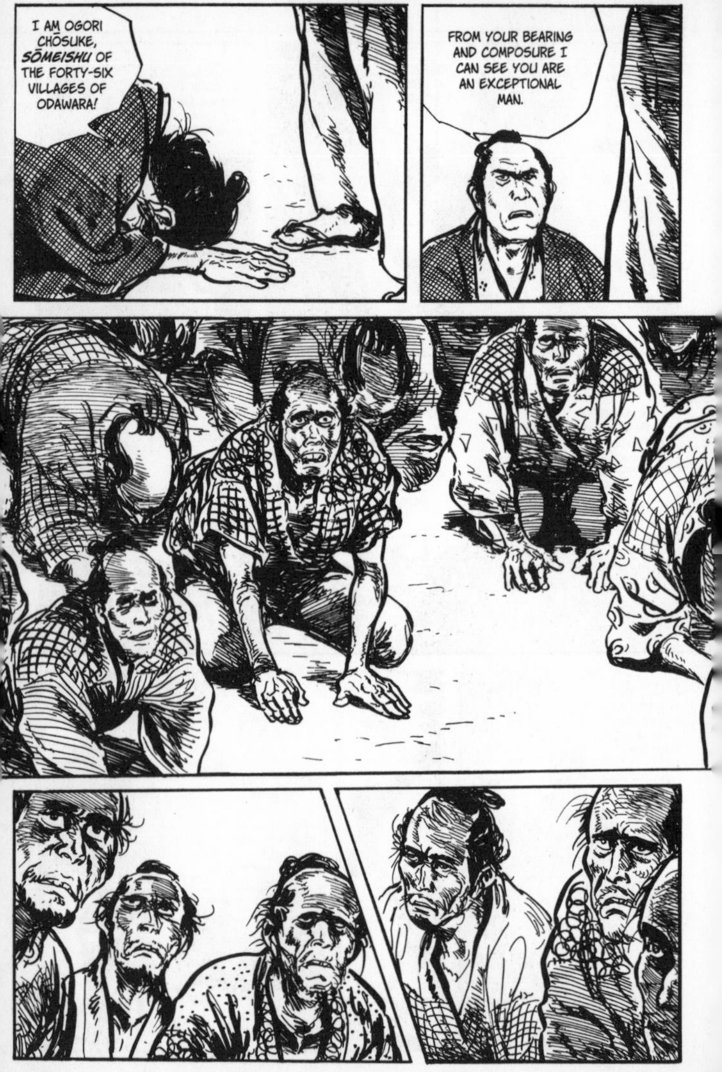
I AM OGORI CHŌSUKE, *SŌMEISHU* OF THE FORTY-SIX VILLAGES OF ODAWARA!
FROM YOUR BEARING AND COMPOSURE I CAN SEE YOU ARE AN EXCEPTIONAL MAN.

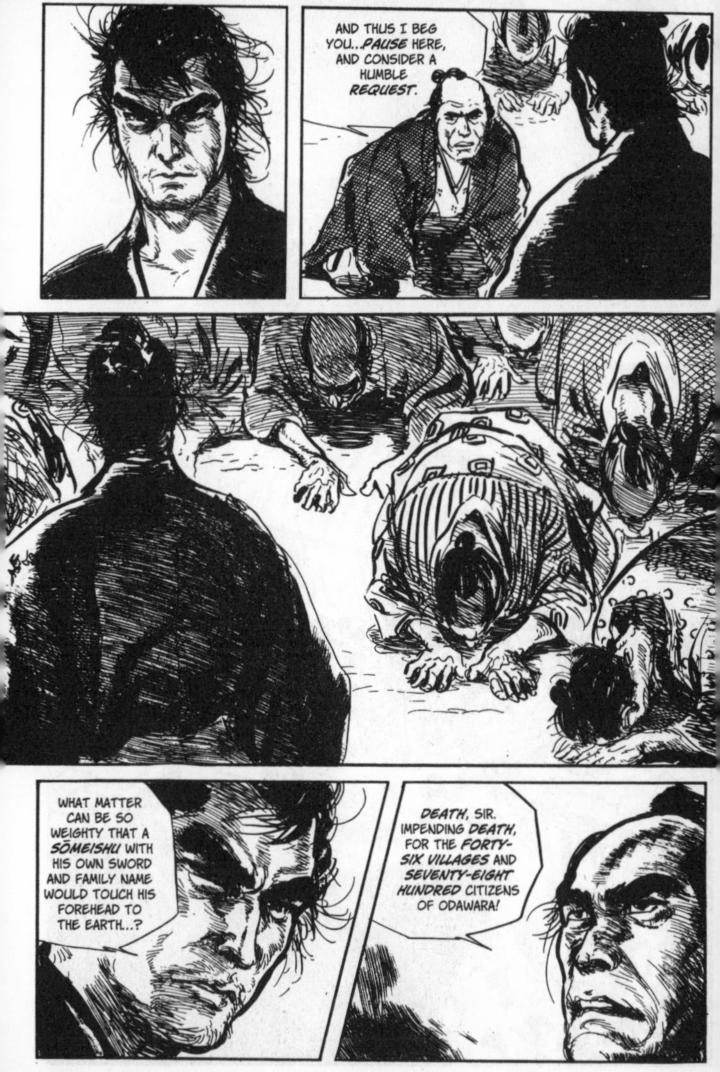
AND THUS I BEG YOU...*PAUSE* HERE, AND CONSIDER A HUMBLE *REQUEST*.
WHAT MATTER CAN BE SO WEIGHTY THAT A *SŌMEISHU* WITH HIS OWN SWORD AND FAMILY NAME WOULD TOUCH HIS FOREHEAD TO THE EARTH...?
DEATH, SIR. IMPENDING *DEATH*, FOR THE *FORTY-SIX VILLAGES* AND *SEVENTY-EIGHT HUNDRED* CITIZENS OF ODAWARA!

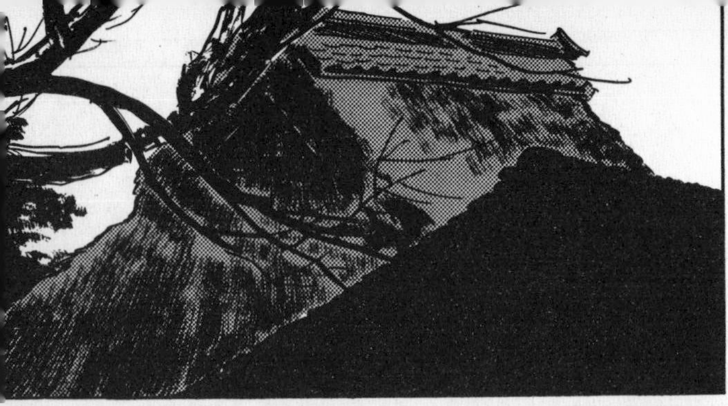

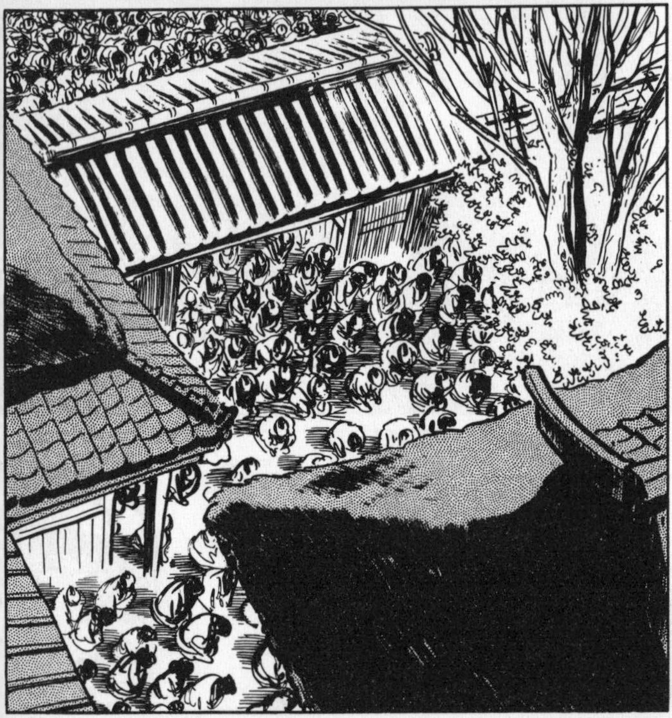

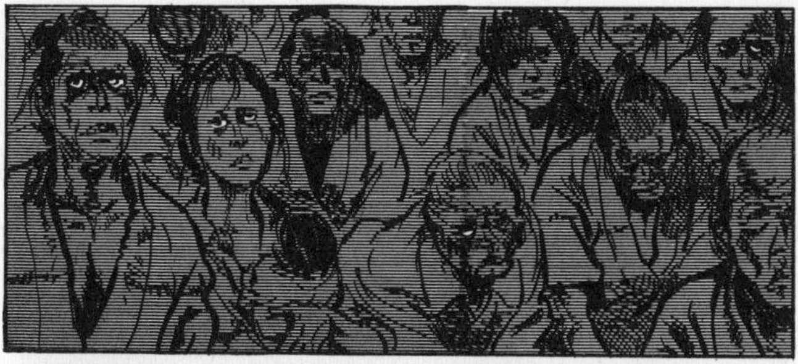

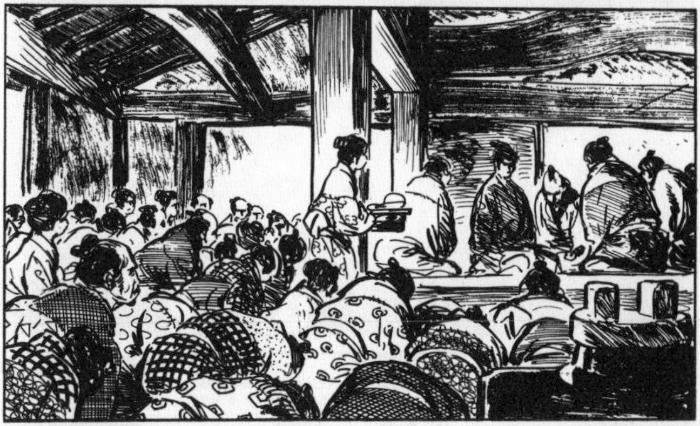

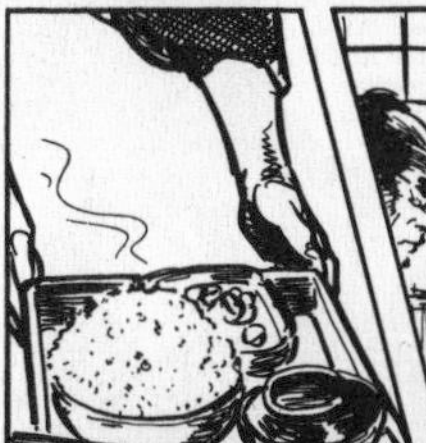

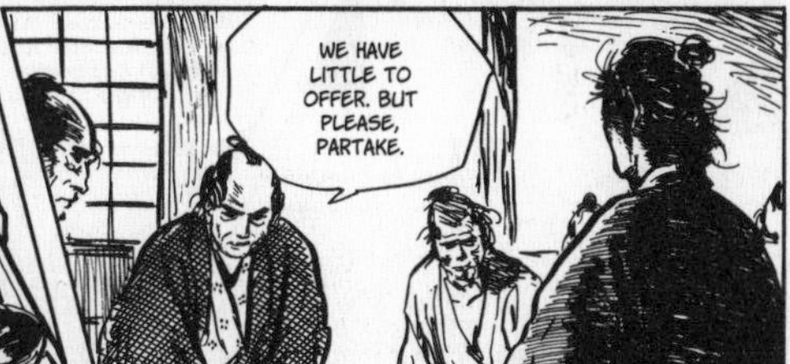
WE HAVE LITTLE TO OFFER. BUT PLEASE, PARTAKE.

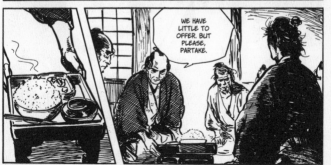

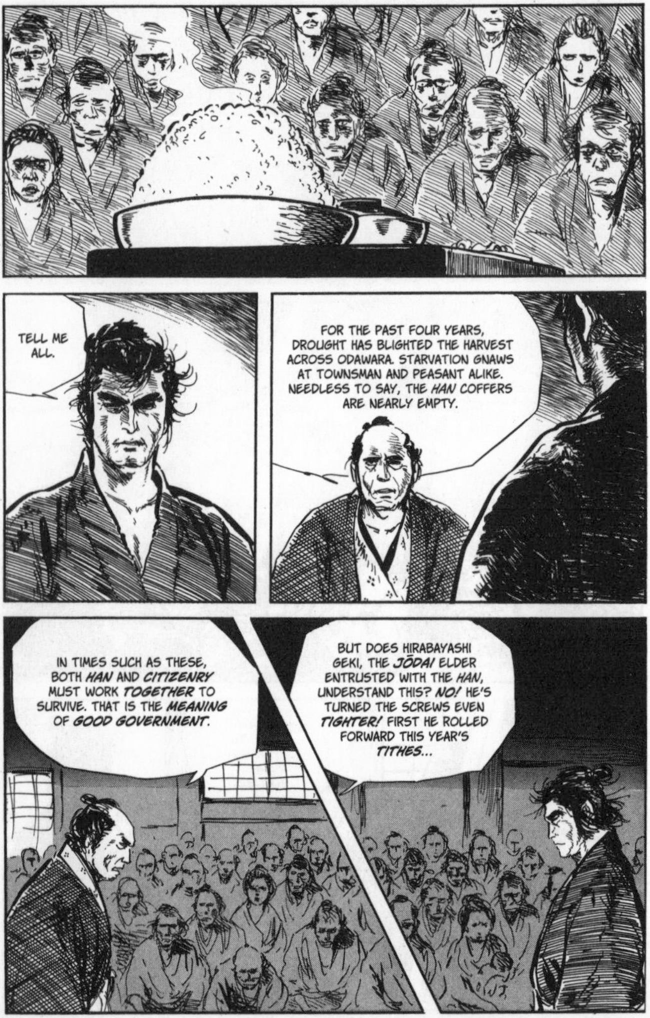
TELL ME ALL.
FOR THE PAST FOUR YEARS, DROUGHT HAS BLIGHTED THE HARVEST ACROSS ODAWARA. STARVATION GNAWS AT TOWNSMAN AND PEASANT ALIKE. NEEDLESS TO SAY, THE *HAN* COFFERS ARE NEARLY EMPTY.
IN TIMES SUCH AS THESE, BOTH *HAN* AND *CITIZENRY* MUST WORK *TOGETHER* TO SURVIVE. THAT IS THE *MEANING* OF *GOOD GOVERNMENT*.
BUT DOES HIRABAYASHI GEKI, THE *JŌDAI* ELDER ENTRUSTED WITH THE *HAN*, UNDERSTAND THIS? *NO!* HE'S TURNED THE SCREWS EVEN *TIGHTER!* FIRST HE ROLLED FORWARD THIS YEAR'S *TITHES*...

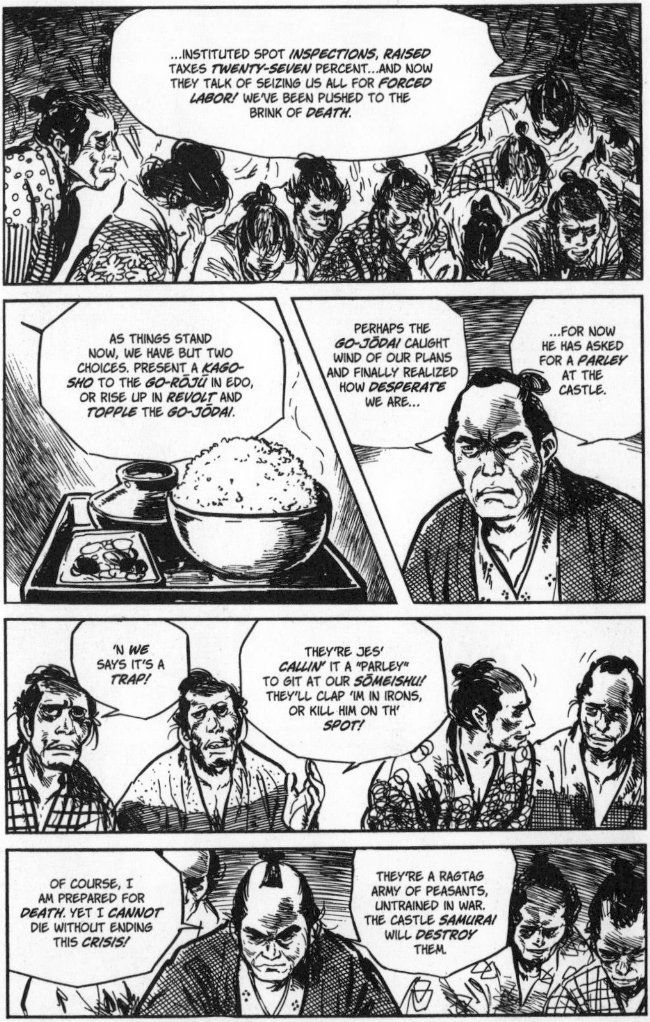
...INSTITUTED SPOT INSPECTIONS, RAISED TAXES TWENTY-SEVEN PERCENT...AND NOW THEY TALK OF SEIZING US ALL FOR FORCED LABOR! WE'VE BEEN PUSHED TO THE BRINK OF DEATH.
AS THINGS STAND NOW, WE HAVE BUT TWO CHOICES. PRESENT A KAGO-SHO TO THE GO-RŌJŪ IN EDO, OR RISE UP IN REVOLT AND TOPPLE THE GO-JŌDAI.
PERHAPS THE GO-JŌDAI CAUGHT WIND OF OUR PLANS AND FINALLY REALIZED HOW DESPERATE WE ARE...
...FOR NOW HE HAS ASKED FOR A PARLEY AT THE CASTLE.
'N WE SAYS IT'S A TRAP!
THEY'RE JES' CALLIN' IT A "PARLEY" TO GIT AT OUR SŌMEISHU! THEY'LL CLAP 'IM IN IRONS, OR KILL HIM ON TH' SPOT!
OF COURSE, I AM PREPARED FOR DEATH. YET I CANNOT DIE WITHOUT ENDING THIS CRISIS!
THEY'RE A RAGTAG ARMY OF PEASANTS, UNTRAINED IN WAR. THE CASTLE SAMURAI WILL DESTROY THEM.

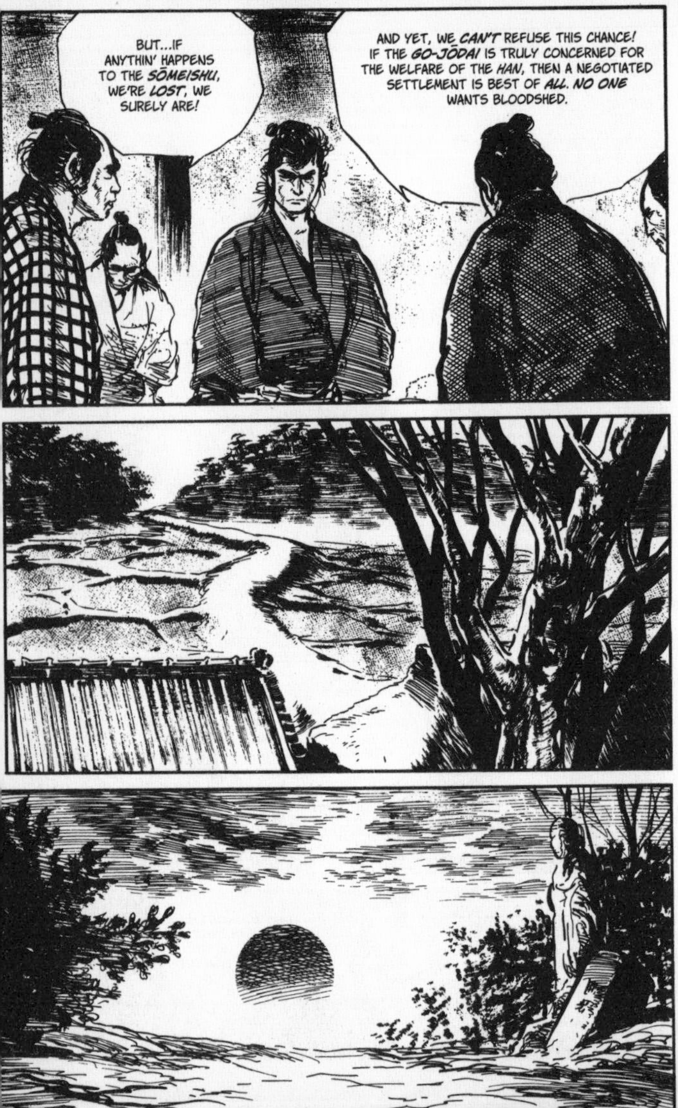
BUT...IF ANYTHIN' HAPPENS TO THE *SŌMEISHU*, WE'RE *LOST*, WE SURELY ARE!
AND YET, WE *CAN'T* REFUSE THIS CHANCE! IF THE *GO-JŌDAI* IS TRULY CONCERNED FOR THE WELFARE OF THE *HAN*, THEN A NEGOTIATED SETTLEMENT IS BEST OF *ALL*. *NO ONE* WANTS BLOODSHED.

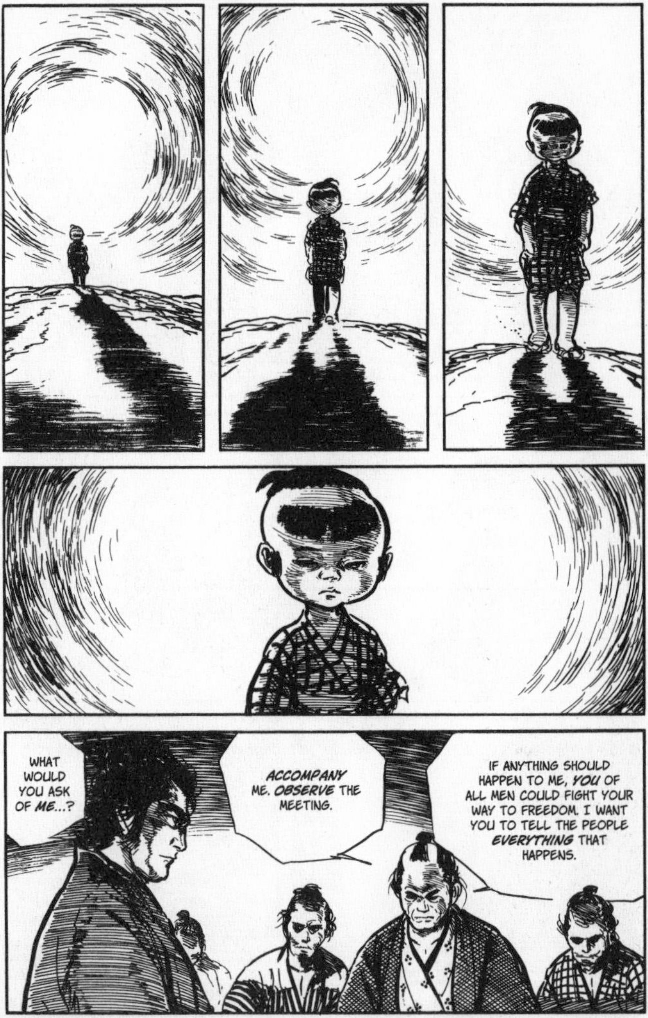
WHAT WOULD YOU ASK OF *ME*...?
ACCOMPANY ME. *OBSERVE* THE MEETING.
IF ANYTHING SHOULD HAPPEN TO ME, *YOU* OF ALL MEN COULD FIGHT YOUR WAY TO FREEDOM. I WANT YOU TO TELL THE PEOPLE *EVERYTHING* THAT HAPPENS.

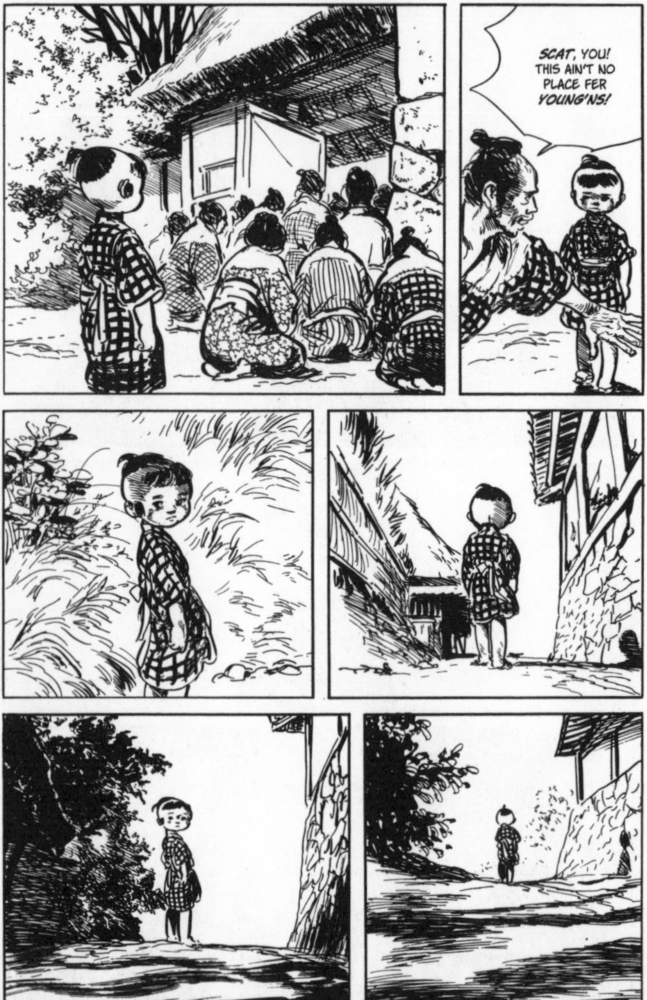
SCAT, YOU! THIS AIN'T NO PLACE FER YOUNG'NS!

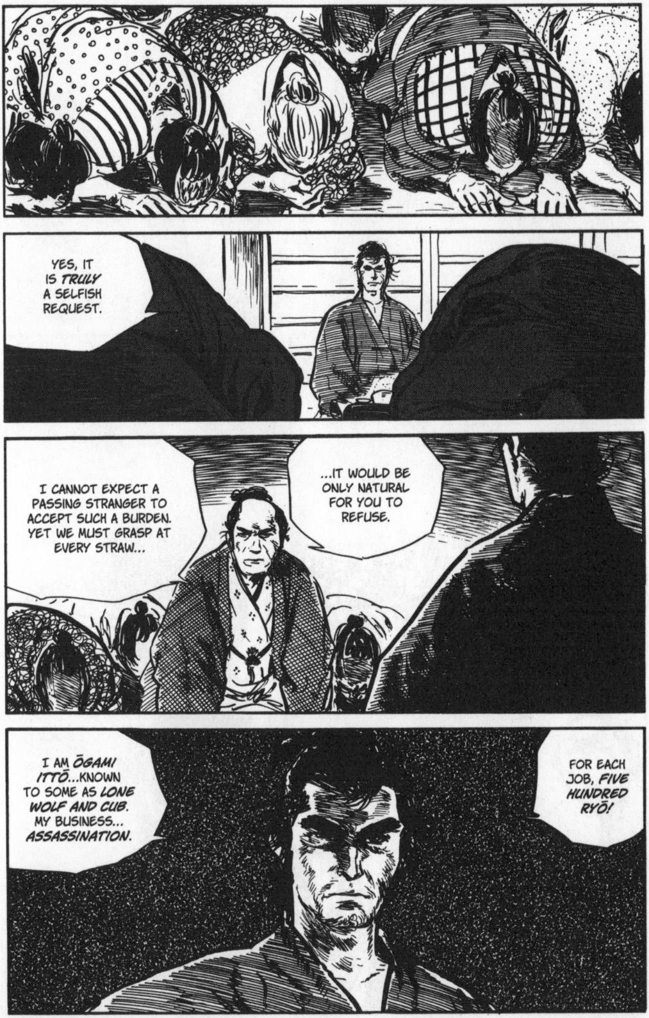
YES, IT IS *TRULY* A SELFISH REQUEST.
I CANNOT EXPECT A PASSING STRANGER TO ACCEPT SUCH A BURDEN. YET WE MUST GRASP AT EVERY STRAW...
...IT WOULD BE ONLY NATURAL FOR YOU TO REFUSE.
I AM *ŌGAMI ITTŌ*...KNOWN TO SOME AS *LONE WOLF AND CUB*. MY BUSINESS... *ASSASSINATION*.
FOR EACH JOB, *FIVE HUNDRED RYŌ!*

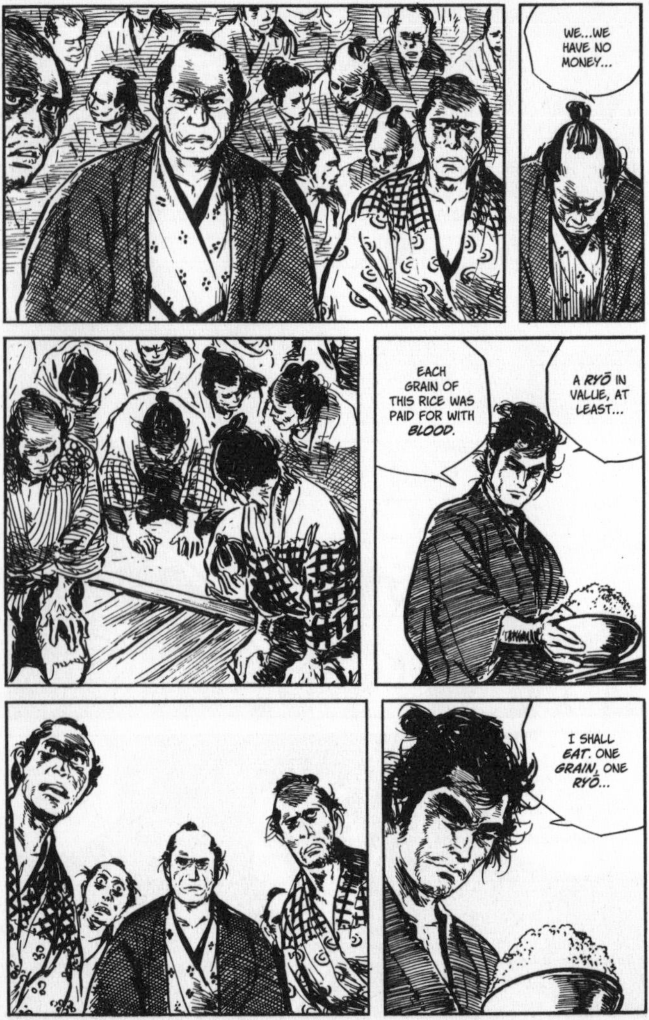
WE...WE HAVE NO MONEY...
EACH GRAIN OF THIS RICE WAS PAID FOR WITH *BLOOD.*
A *RYŌ* IN VALUE, AT LEAST...
I SHALL *EAT.* ONE *GRAIN,* ONE *RYŌ*...

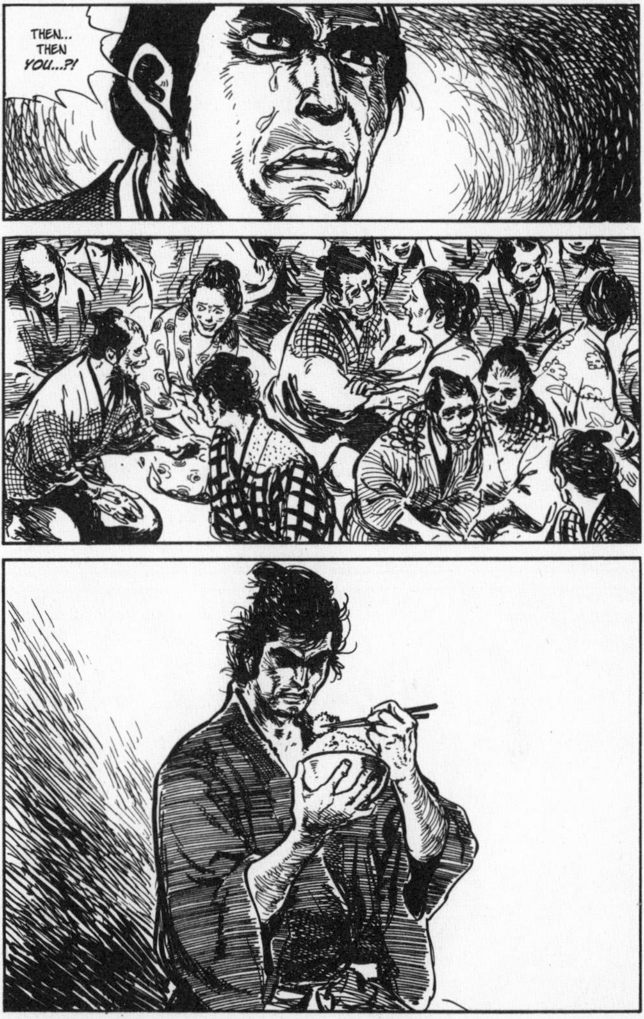
THEN... THEN YOU...?!

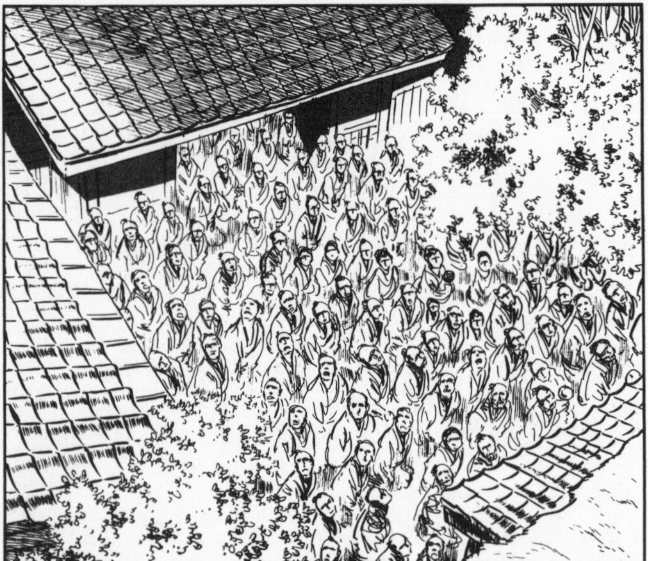

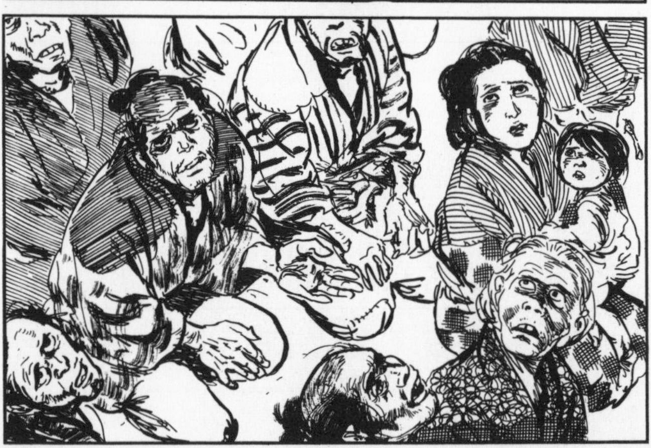

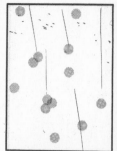

RAIN! IT'S RAININ'!

NOW, OF ALL TIMES...

163

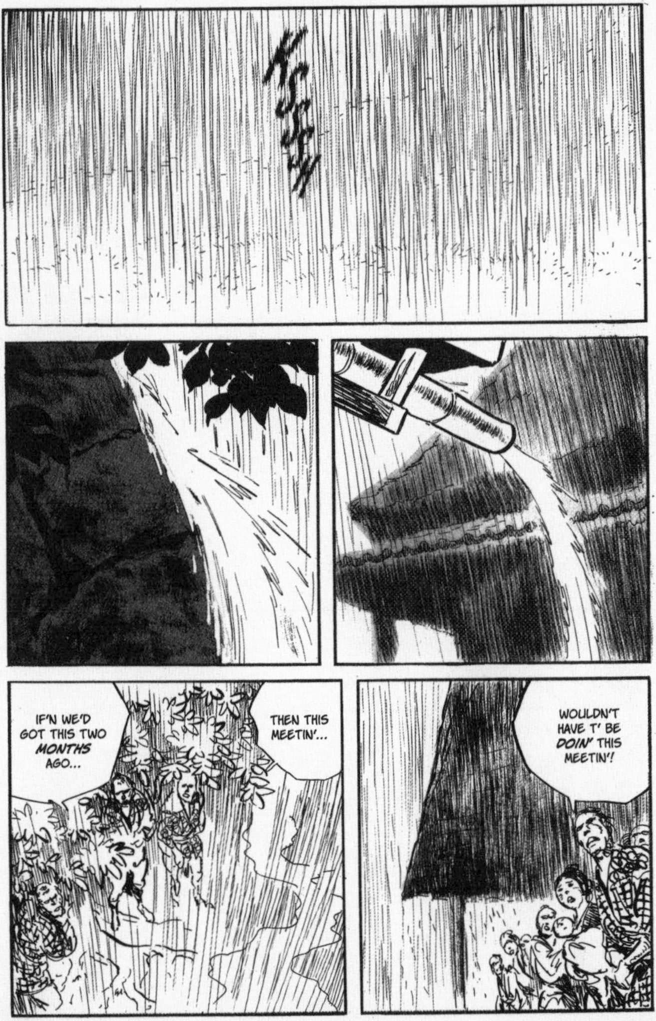
KSSSH
IF'N WE'D GOT THIS TWO *MONTHS* AGO...
THEN THIS MEETIN'...
WOULDN'T HAVE T' BE *DOIN'* THIS MEETIN'!

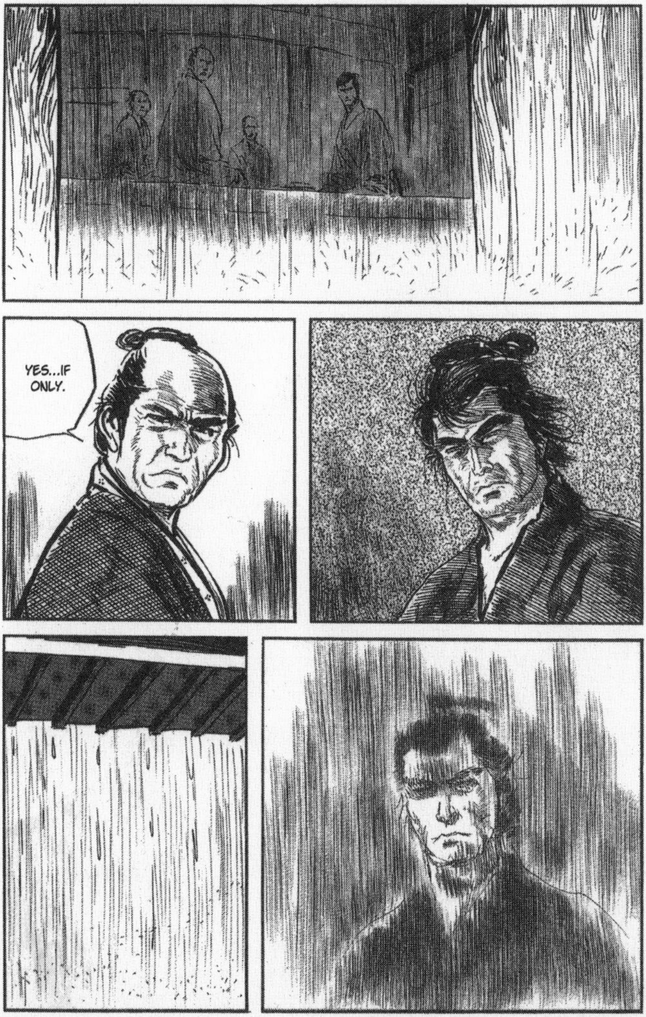
YES...IF ONLY.

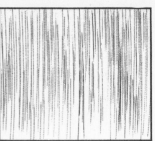

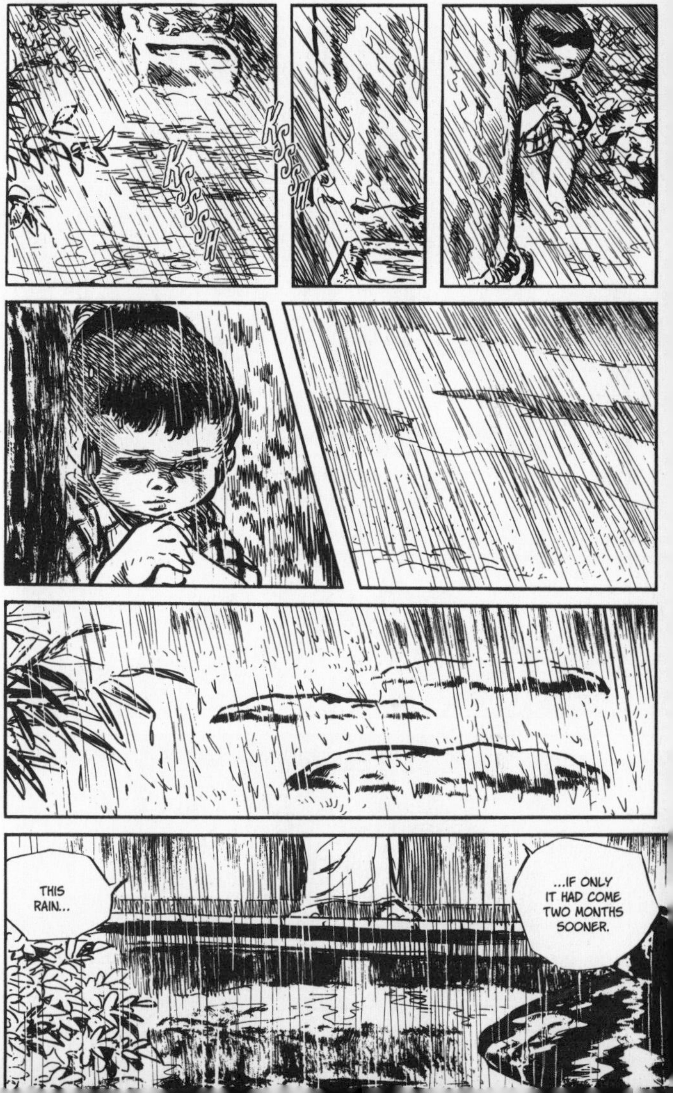
KSSSSH
KSSSH
THIS RAIN...
...IF ONLY IT HAD COME TWO MONTHS SOONER.

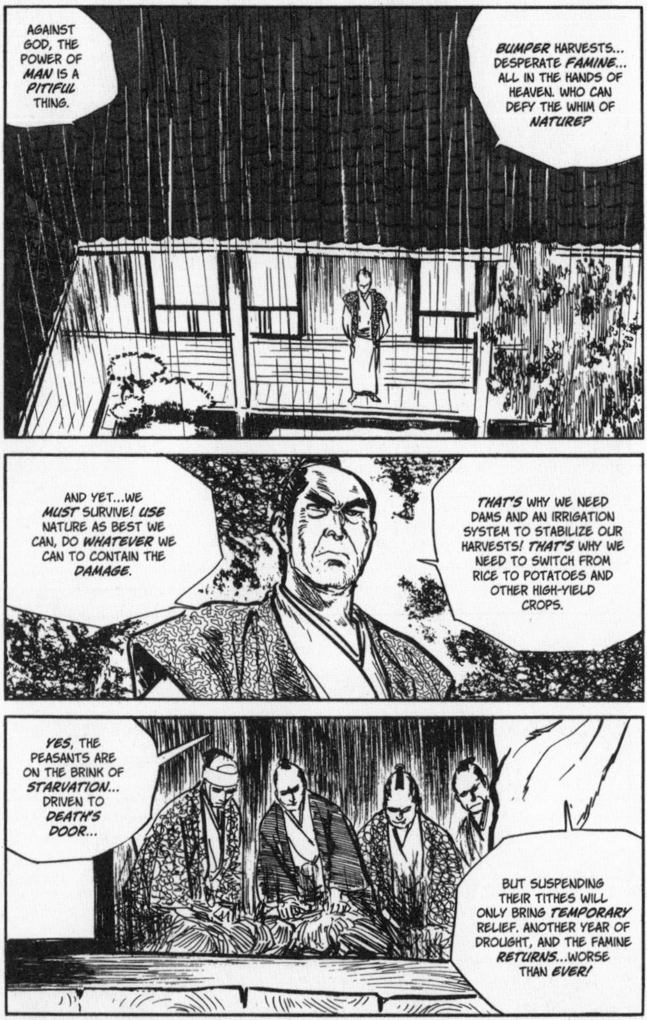
AGAINST GOD, THE POWER OF MAN IS A PITIFUL THING.
BUMPER HARVESTS... DESPERATE FAMINE... ALL IN THE HANDS OF HEAVEN. WHO CAN DEFY THE WHIM OF NATURE?
AND YET...WE MUST SURVIVE! USE NATURE AS BEST WE CAN, DO WHATEVER WE CAN TO CONTAIN THE DAMAGE.
THAT'S WHY WE NEED DAMS AND AN IRRIGATION SYSTEM TO STABILIZE OUR HARVESTS! THAT'S WHY WE NEED TO SWITCH FROM RICE TO POTATOES AND OTHER HIGH-YIELD CROPS.
YES, THE PEASANTS ARE ON THE BRINK OF STARVATION... DRIVEN TO DEATH'S DOOR...
BUT SUSPENDING THEIR TITHES WILL ONLY BRING TEMPORARY RELIEF. ANOTHER YEAR OF DROUGHT, AND THE FAMINE RETURNS...WORSE THAN EVER!

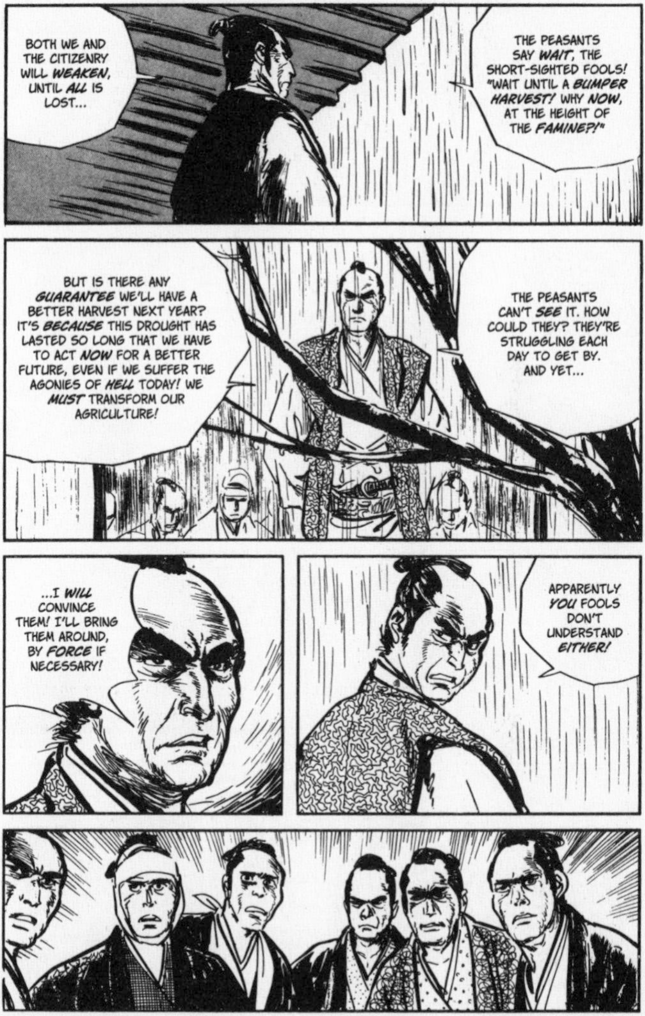
BOTH WE AND THE CITIZENRY WILL WEAKEN, UNTIL ALL IS LOST...
THE PEASANTS SAY WAIT, THE SHORT-SIGHTED FOOLS! "WAIT UNTIL A BUMPER HARVEST! WHY NOW, AT THE HEIGHT OF THE FAMINE?!"
BUT IS THERE ANY GUARANTEE WE'LL HAVE A BETTER HARVEST NEXT YEAR? IT'S BECAUSE THIS DROUGHT HAS LASTED SO LONG THAT WE HAVE TO ACT NOW FOR A BETTER FUTURE, EVEN IF WE SUFFER THE AGONIES OF HELL TODAY! WE MUST TRANSFORM OUR AGRICULTURE!
THE PEASANTS CAN'T SEE IT. HOW COULD THEY? THEY'RE STRUGGLING EACH DAY TO GET BY. AND YET...
...I WILL CONVINCE THEM! I'LL BRING THEM AROUND, BY FORCE IF NECESSARY!
APPARENTLY YOU FOOLS DON'T UNDERSTAND EITHER!

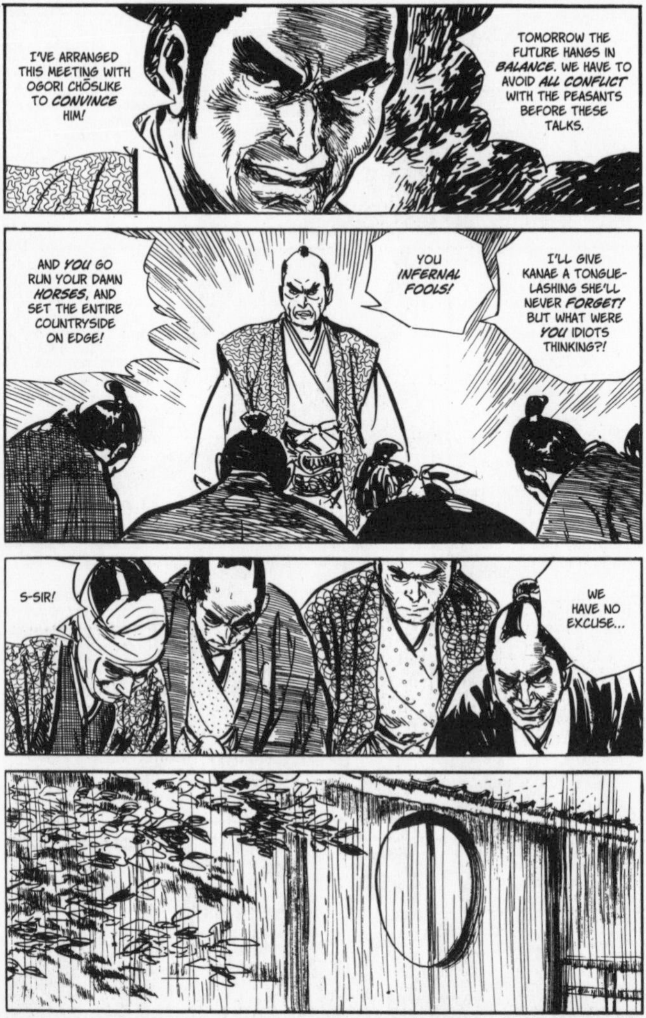
I'VE ARRANGED THIS MEETING WITH OGORI CHŌSUKE TO CONVINCE HIM!
TOMORROW THE FUTURE HANGS IN BALANCE. WE HAVE TO AVOID ALL CONFLICT WITH THE PEASANTS BEFORE THESE TALKS.
AND YOU GO RUN YOUR DAMN HORSES, AND SET THE ENTIRE COUNTRYSIDE ON EDGE!
YOU INFERNAL FOOLS!
I'LL GIVE KANAE A TONGUE-LASHING SHE'LL NEVER FORGET! BUT WHAT WERE YOU IDIOTS THINKING?!
S-SIR!
WE HAVE NO EXCUSE...

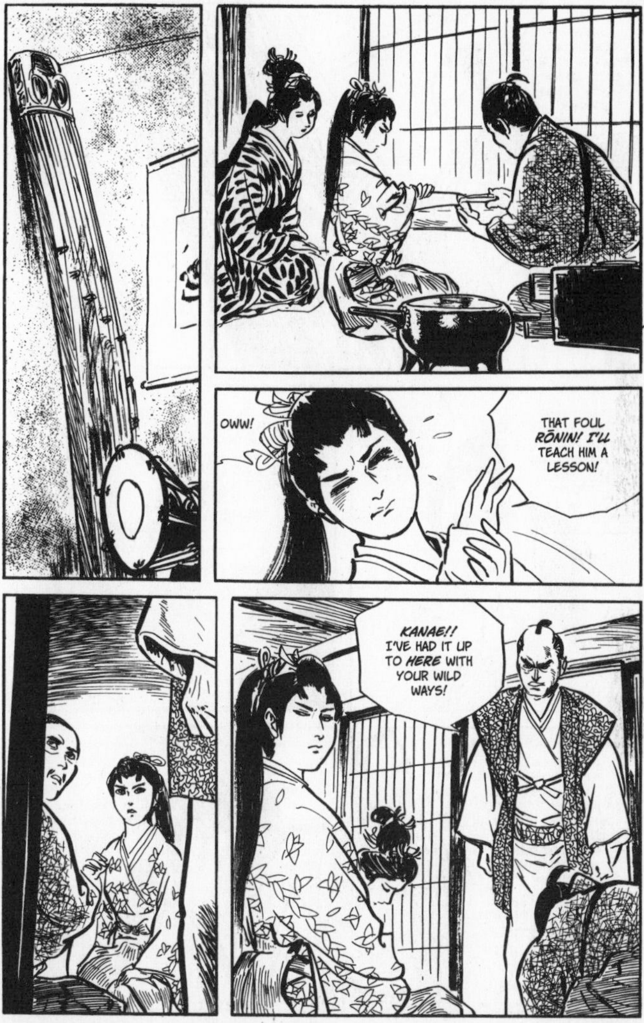

OWW!
THAT FOUL *RŌNIN!* *I'LL* TEACH HIM A LESSON!
KANAE!! I'VE HAD IT UP TO *HERE* WITH YOUR WILD WAYS!

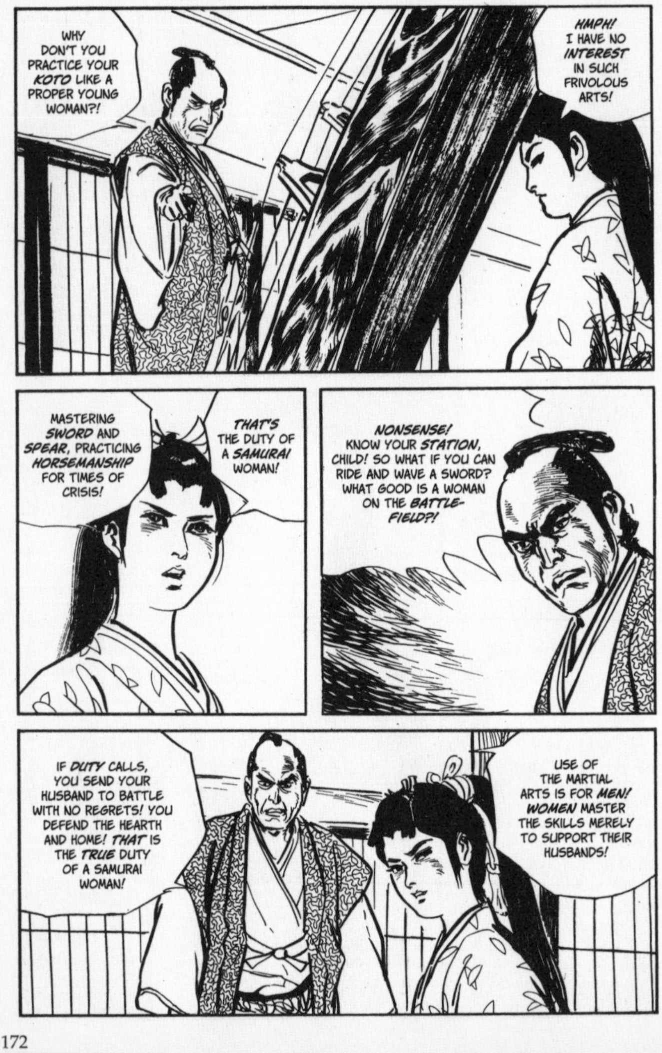
WHY DON'T YOU PRACTICE YOUR *KOTO* LIKE A PROPER YOUNG WOMAN?!
HMPH! I HAVE NO *INTEREST* IN SUCH FRIVOLOUS ARTS!
MASTERING *SWORD* AND *SPEAR*, PRACTICING *HORSEMANSHIP* FOR TIMES OF CRISIS!
THAT'S THE DUTY OF A *SAMURAI* WOMAN!
NONSENSE! KNOW YOUR *STATION*, CHILD! SO WHAT IF YOU CAN RIDE AND WAVE A SWORD? WHAT GOOD IS A WOMAN ON THE *BATTLE-FIELD?!*
IF *DUTY* CALLS, YOU SEND YOUR HUSBAND TO BATTLE WITH NO REGRETS! YOU DEFEND THE HEARTH AND HOME! *THAT* IS THE *TRUE* DUTY OF A SAMURAI WOMAN!
USE OF THE MARTIAL ARTS IS FOR *MEN! WOMEN* MASTER THE SKILLS MERELY TO SUPPORT THEIR HUSBANDS!

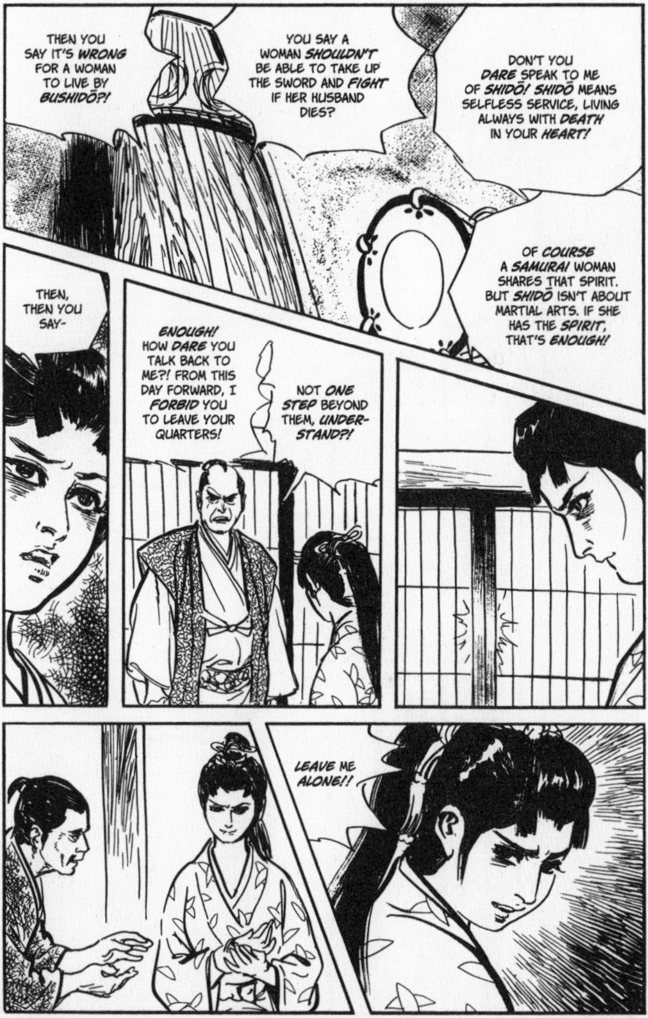
THEN YOU SAY IT'S *WRONG* FOR A WOMAN TO LIVE BY *BUSHIDŌ?!*
YOU SAY A WOMAN *SHOULDN'T* BE ABLE TO TAKE UP THE SWORD AND *FIGHT* IF HER HUSBAND DIES?
DON'T YOU *DARE* SPEAK TO ME OF *SHIDŌ! SHIDŌ* MEANS SELFLESS SERVICE, LIVING ALWAYS WITH *DEATH* IN YOUR *HEART!*
OF *COURSE* A *SAMURAI* WOMAN SHARES THAT SPIRIT. BUT *SHIDŌ* ISN'T ABOUT MARTIAL ARTS. IF SHE HAS THE *SPIRIT*, THAT'S *ENOUGH!*
THEN, THEN YOU SAY-
ENOUGH! HOW *DARE* YOU TALK BACK TO ME?! FROM THIS DAY FORWARD, I *FORBID* YOU TO LEAVE YOUR QUARTERS!
NOT *ONE STEP* BEYOND THEM, *UNDER-STAND?!*
LEAVE ME ALONE!!

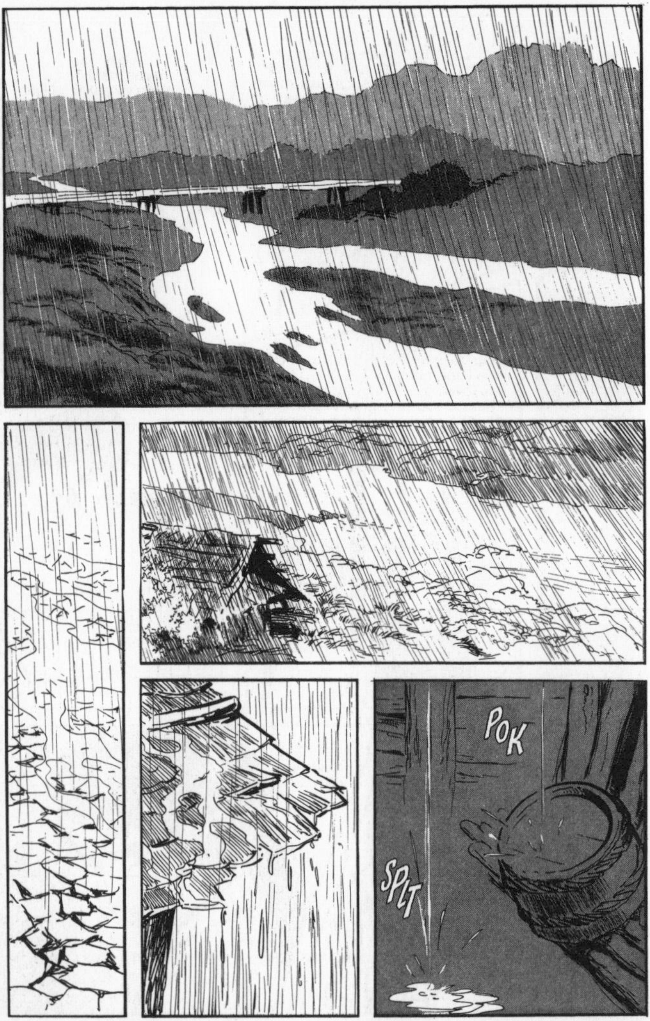
POK
SPLT

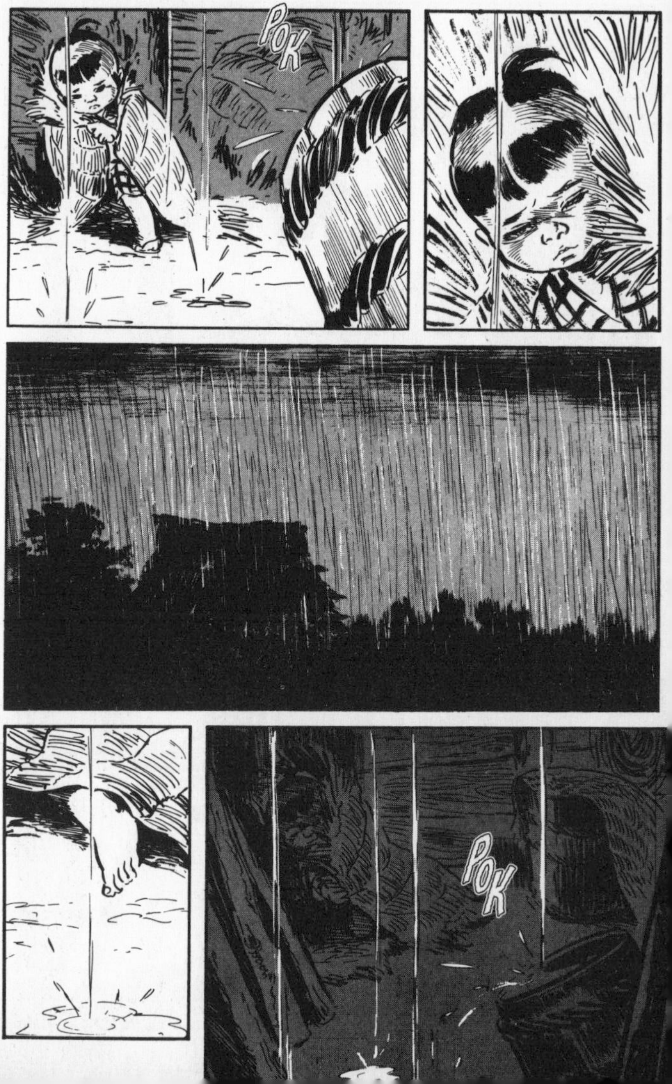
POK
POK

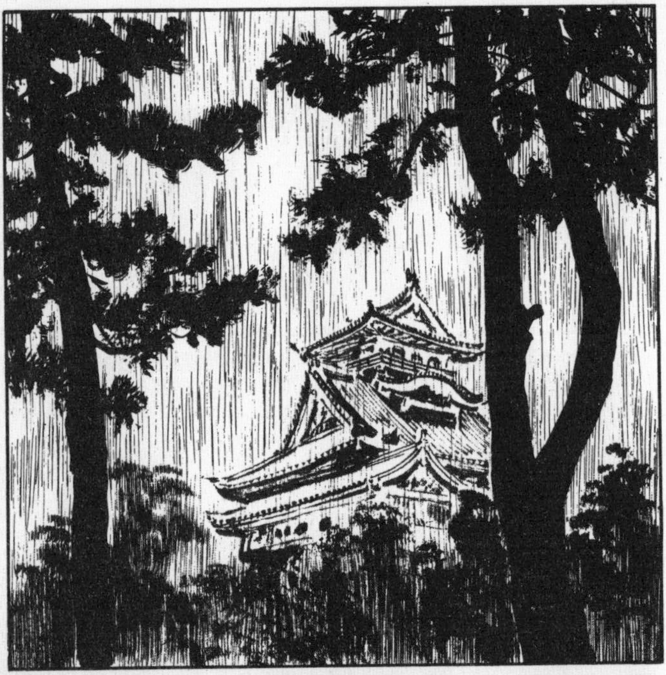
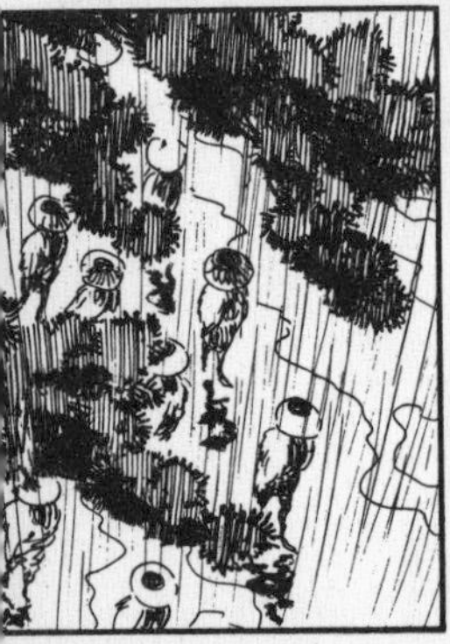
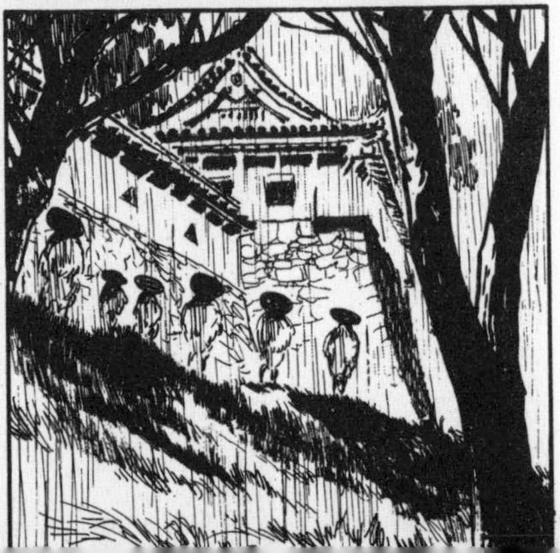

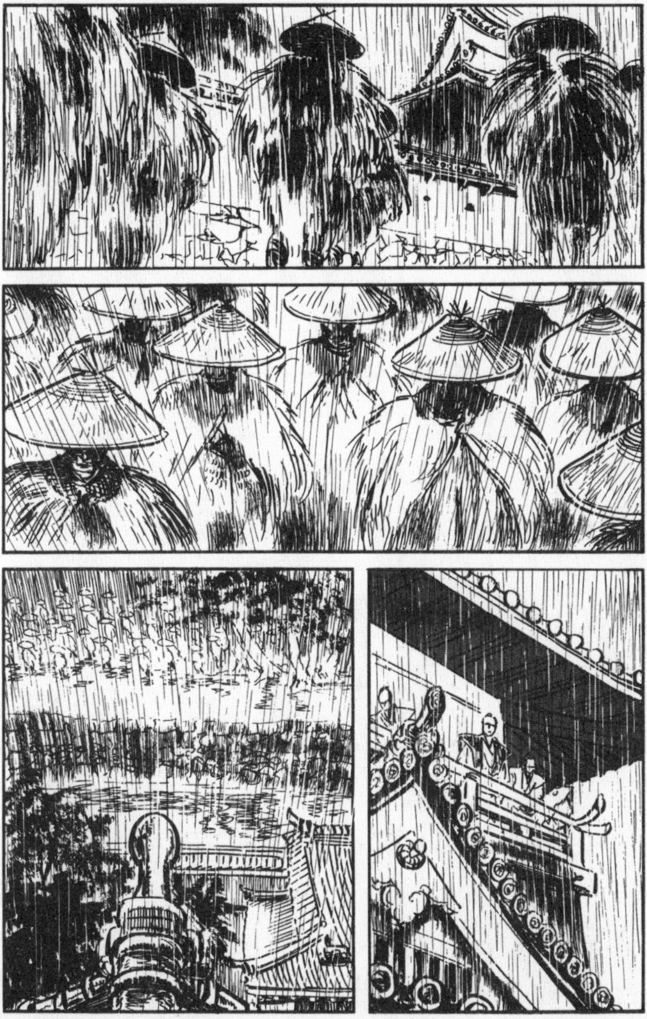

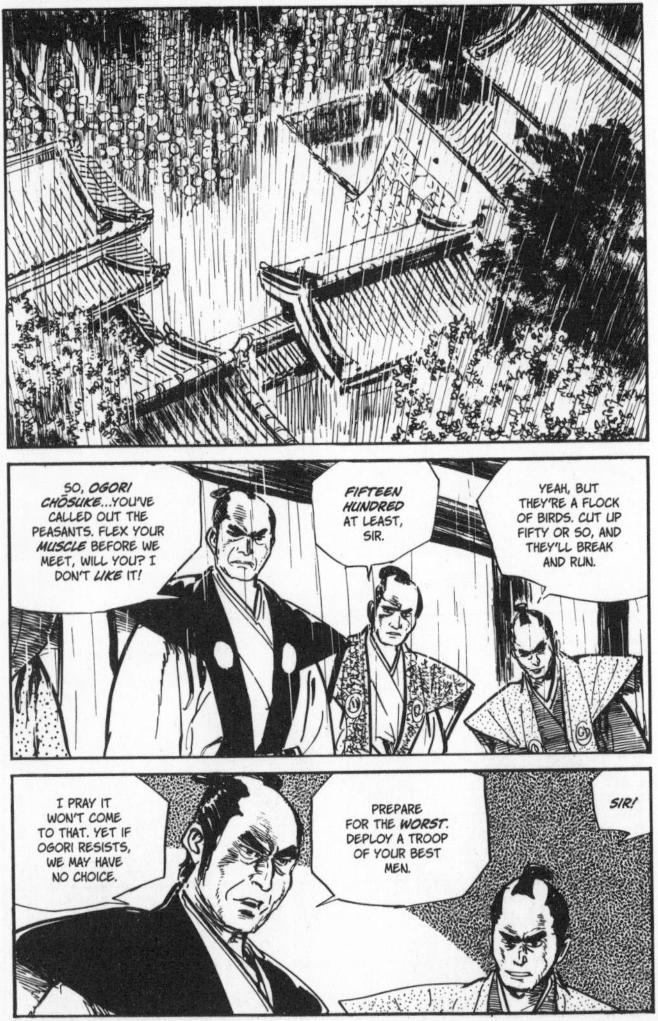
SO, *OGORI CHŌSUKE*...YOU'VE CALLED OUT THE PEASANTS. FLEX YOUR *MUSCLE* BEFORE WE MEET, WILL YOU? I DON'T *LIKE* IT!
FIFTEEN HUNDRED AT LEAST, SIR.
YEAH, BUT THEY'RE A FLOCK OF BIRDS. CUT UP FIFTY OR SO, AND THEY'LL BREAK AND RUN.
I PRAY IT WON'T COME TO THAT. YET IF OGORI RESISTS, WE MAY HAVE NO CHOICE.
PREPARE FOR THE *WORST*. DEPLOY A TROOP OF YOUR BEST MEN.
SIR!

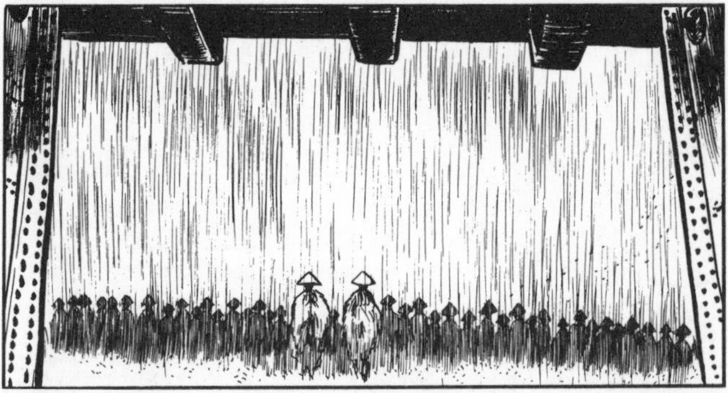
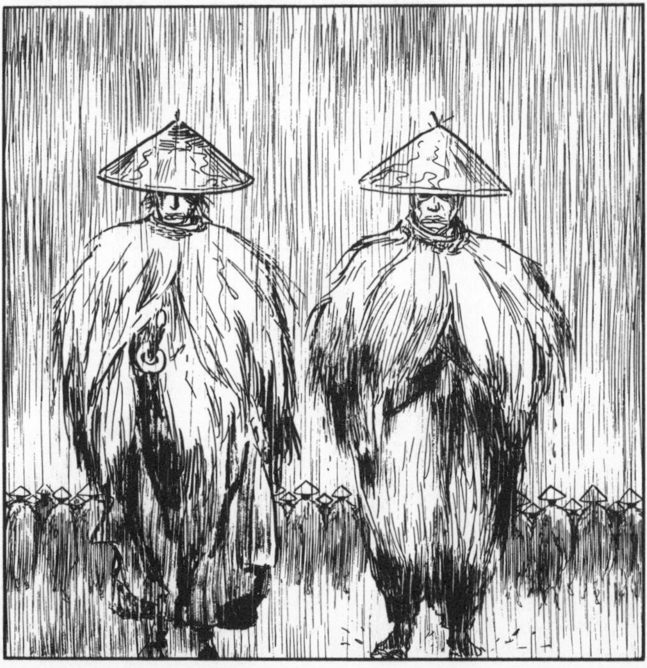

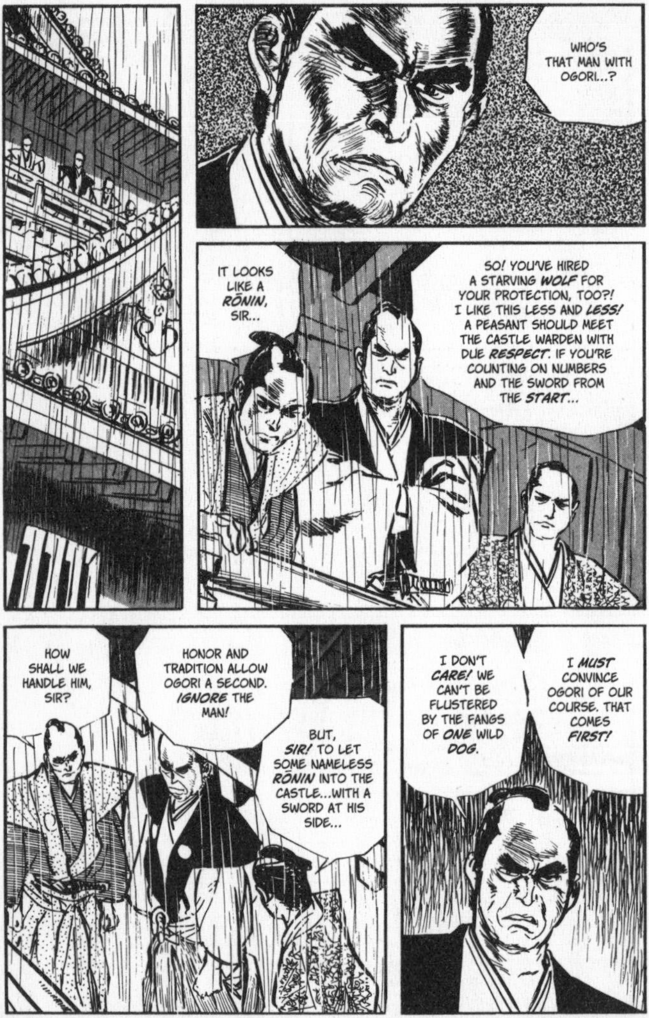

WHO'S THAT MAN WITH OGORI...?
IT LOOKS LIKE A *RŌNIN*, SIR...
SO! YOU'VE HIRED A STARVING *WOLF* FOR YOUR PROTECTION, TOO?! I LIKE THIS LESS AND *LESS!* A PEASANT SHOULD MEET THE CASTLE WARDEN WITH DUE *RESPECT*. IF YOU'RE COUNTING ON NUMBERS AND THE SWORD FROM THE *START*...
HOW SHALL WE HANDLE HIM, SIR?
HONOR AND TRADITION ALLOW OGORI A SECOND. *IGNORE* THE MAN!
BUT, *SIR!* TO LET SOME NAMELESS *RŌNIN* INTO THE CASTLE...WITH A SWORD AT HIS SIDE...
I DON'T *CARE!* WE CAN'T BE FLUSTERED BY THE FANGS OF *ONE* WILD *DOG*.
I *MUST* CONVINCE OGORI OF OUR COURSE. THAT COMES *FIRST!*

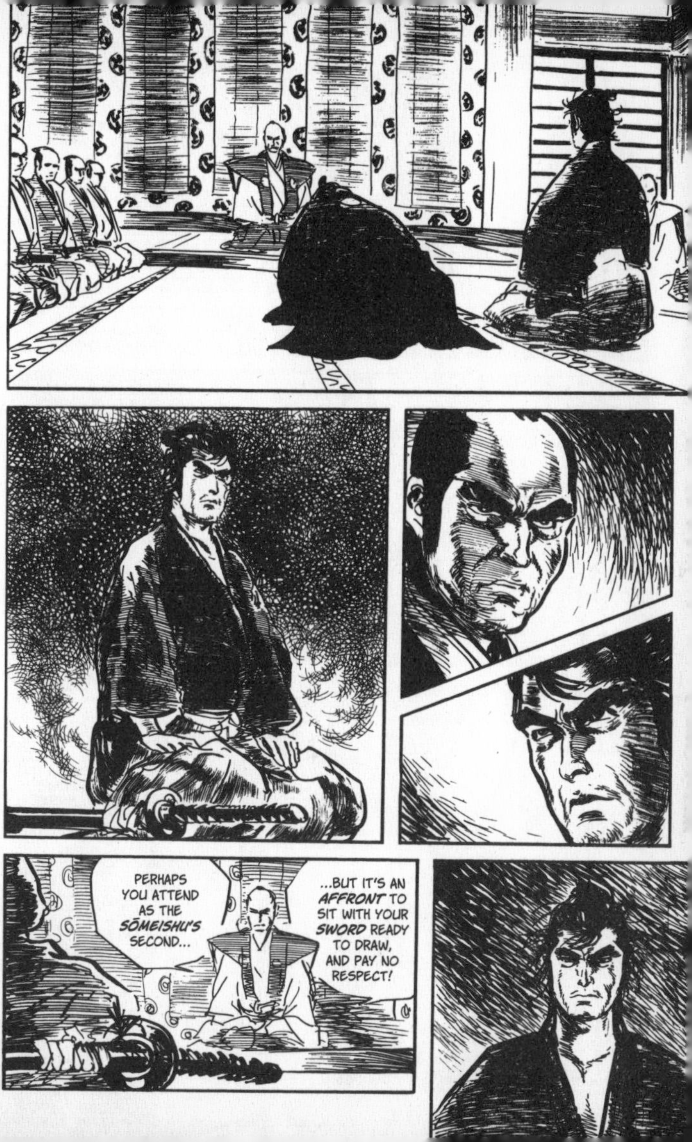
PERHAPS YOU ATTEND AS THE SŌMEISHU'S SECOND...
...BUT IT'S AN AFFRONT TO SIT WITH YOUR SWORD READY TO DRAW, AND PAY NO RESPECT!

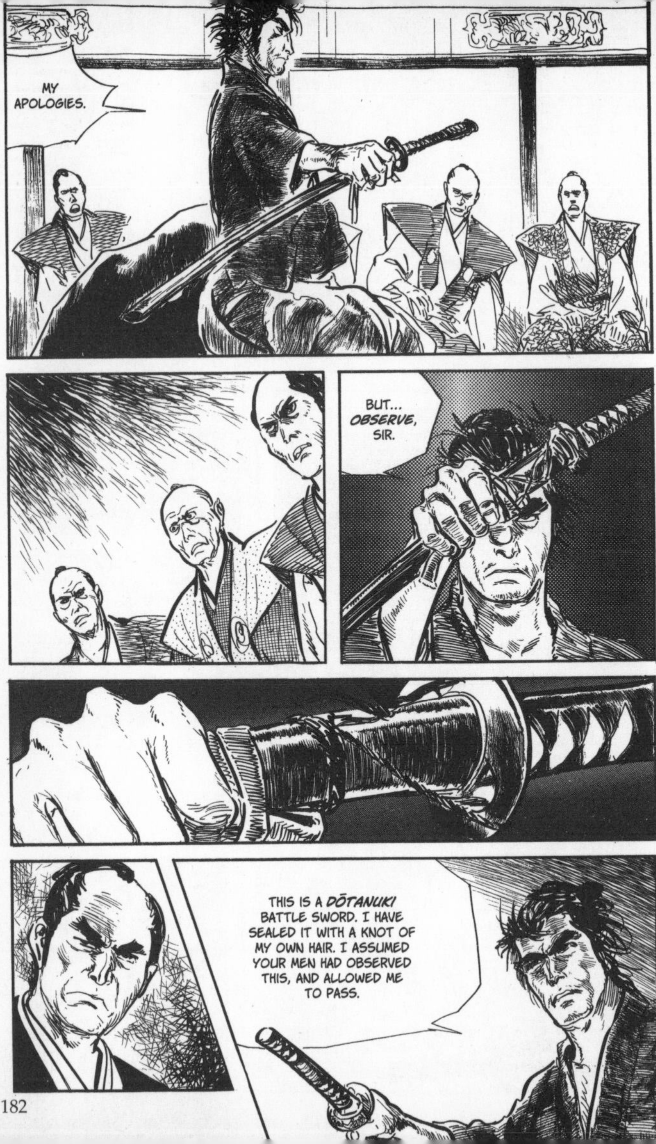
MY APOLOGIES.
BUT... *OBSERVE*, SIR.
THIS IS A *DŌTANUKI* BATTLE SWORD. I HAVE SEALED IT WITH A KNOT OF MY OWN HAIR. I ASSUMED YOUR MEN HAD OBSERVED THIS, AND ALLOWED ME TO PASS.

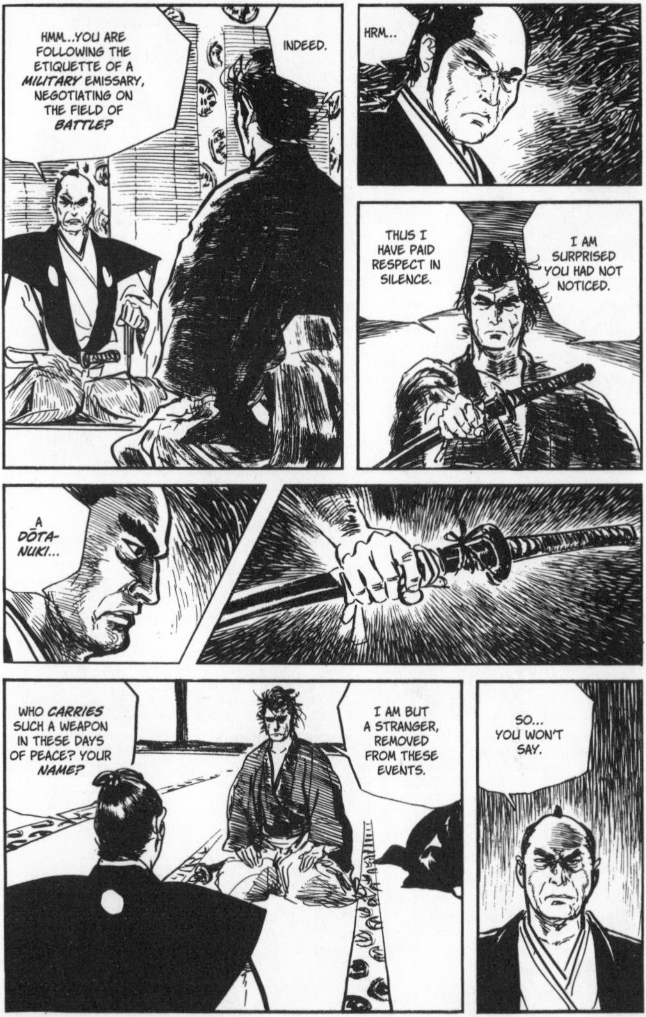

HMM...YOU ARE FOLLOWING THE ETIQUETTE OF A *MILITARY* EMISSARY, NEGOTIATING ON THE FIELD OF *BATTLE?*
INDEED.
HRM...
THUS I HAVE PAID RESPECT IN SILENCE.
I AM SURPRISED YOU HAD NOT NOTICED.
A *DŌTA-NUKI...*
WHO *CARRIES* SUCH A WEAPON IN THESE DAYS OF PEACE? YOUR *NAME?*
I AM BUT A STRANGER, REMOVED FROM THESE EVENTS.
SO... YOU WON'T SAY.

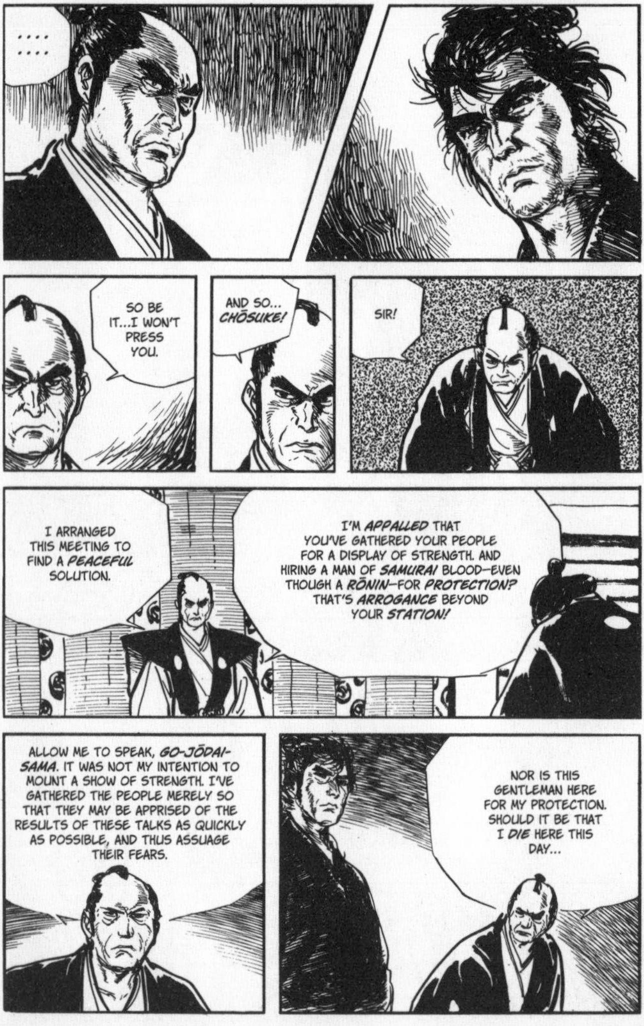
....
....
SO BE IT...I WON'T PRESS YOU.
AND SO... *CHŌSUKE!*
SIR!
I ARRANGED THIS MEETING TO FIND A *PEACEFUL* SOLUTION.
I'M *APPALLED* THAT YOU'VE GATHERED YOUR PEOPLE FOR A DISPLAY OF STRENGTH. AND HIRING A MAN OF *SAMURAI* BLOOD—EVEN THOUGH A *RŌNIN*—FOR *PROTECTION?* THAT'S *ARROGANCE* BEYOND YOUR *STATION!*
ALLOW ME TO SPEAK, *GO-JŌDAI-SAMA*. IT WAS NOT MY INTENTION TO MOUNT A SHOW OF STRENGTH. I'VE GATHERED THE PEOPLE MERELY SO THAT THEY MAY BE APPRISED OF THE RESULTS OF THESE TALKS AS QUICKLY AS POSSIBLE, AND THUS ASSUAGE THEIR FEARS.
NOR IS THIS GENTLEMAN HERE FOR MY PROTECTION. SHOULD IT BE THAT I *DIE* HERE THIS DAY...

I HAVE MERELY ASKED HIM TO *OBSERVE* ALL THAT HAPPENS...

...AND *REPORT* IN *FULL* TO THE PEOPLE.

THE GENTLEMAN HAS NO INTEREST IN OUR DISPUTE. AND THUS I CONSIDERED HIM SUITABLE TO REPORT IMPARTIALLY ON ALL THAT HAPPENS.

MY PEOPLE ARE FEARFUL. I WORRY THAT THEY WILL NOT TAKE THINGS CALMLY, AND COULD FLY INTO A PANIC. THUS I REQUESTED HIS PRESENCE.

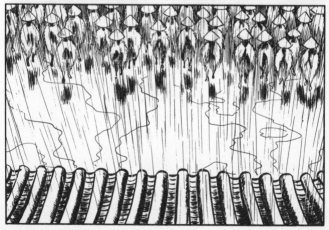

185

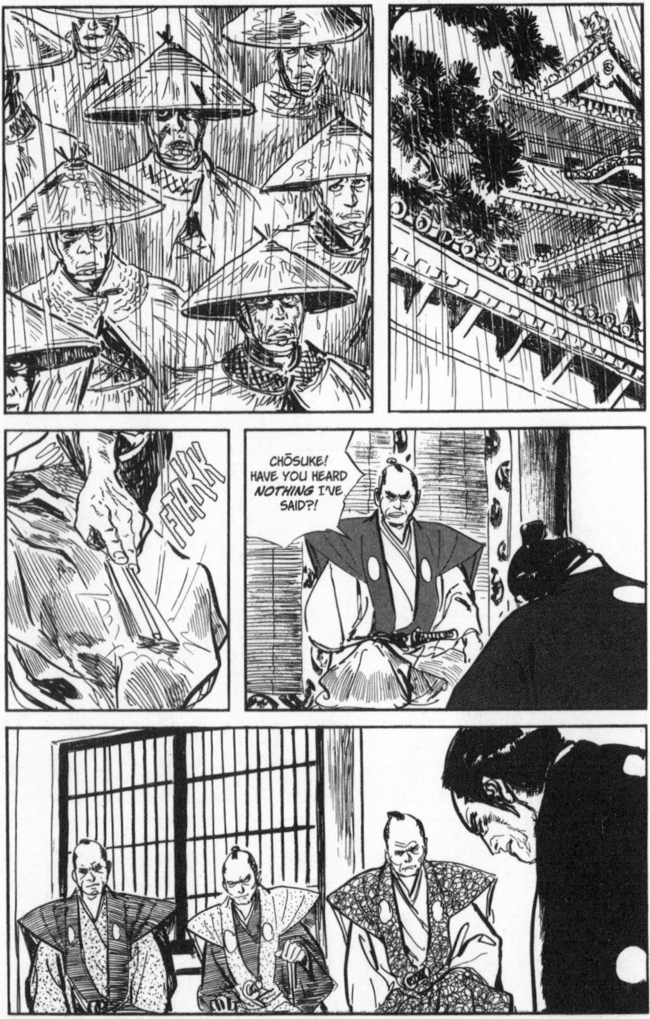
FTAKK
CHŌSUKE! HAVE YOU HEARD *NOTHING* I'VE SAID?!

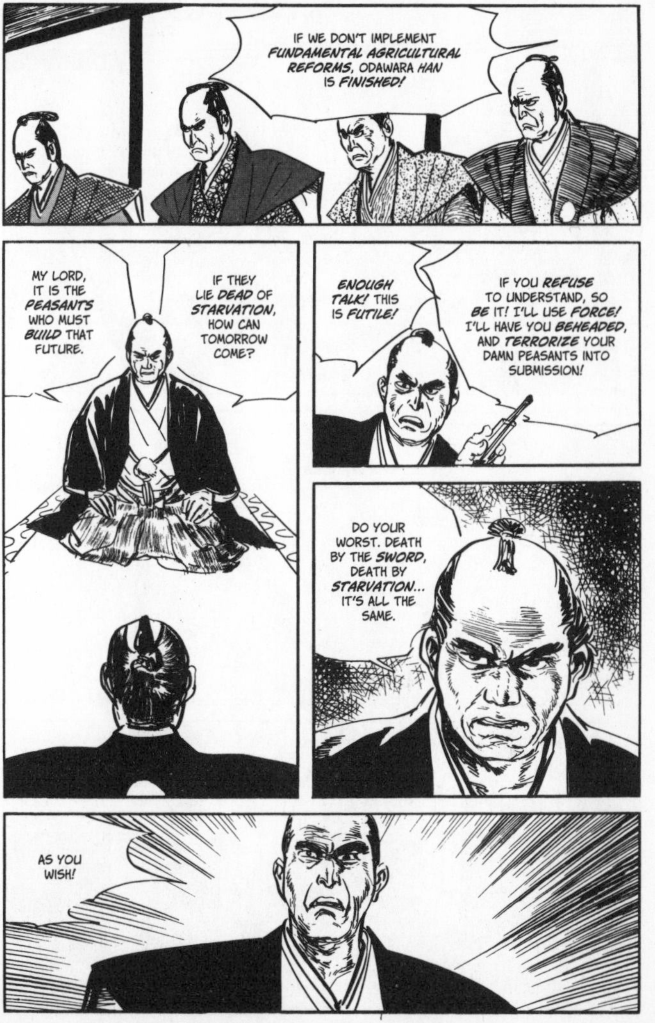
IF WE DON'T IMPLEMENT FUNDAMENTAL AGRICULTURAL REFORMS, ODAWARA HAN IS FINISHED!
MY LORD, IT IS THE PEASANTS WHO MUST BUILD THAT FUTURE.
IF THEY LIE DEAD OF STARVATION, HOW CAN TOMORROW COME?
ENOUGH TALK! THIS IS FUTILE!
IF YOU REFUSE TO UNDERSTAND, SO BE IT! I'LL USE FORCE! I'LL HAVE YOU BEHEADED, AND TERRORIZE YOUR DAMN PEASANTS INTO SUBMISSION!
DO YOUR WORST. DEATH BY THE SWORD, DEATH BY STARVATION... IT'S ALL THE SAME.
AS YOU WISH!

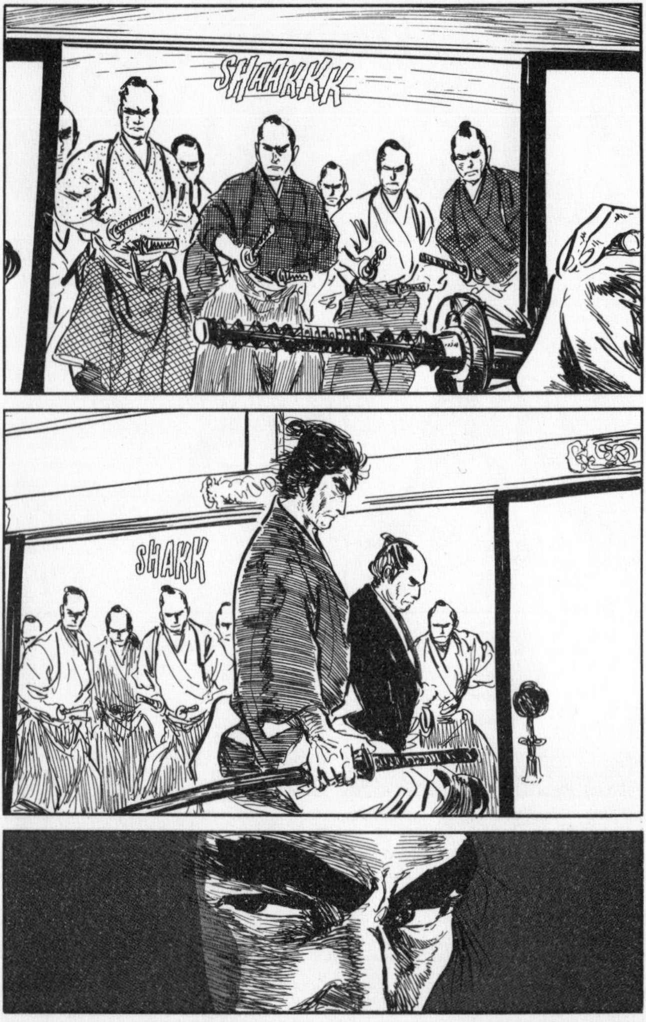
SHAAKKK
SHAKK

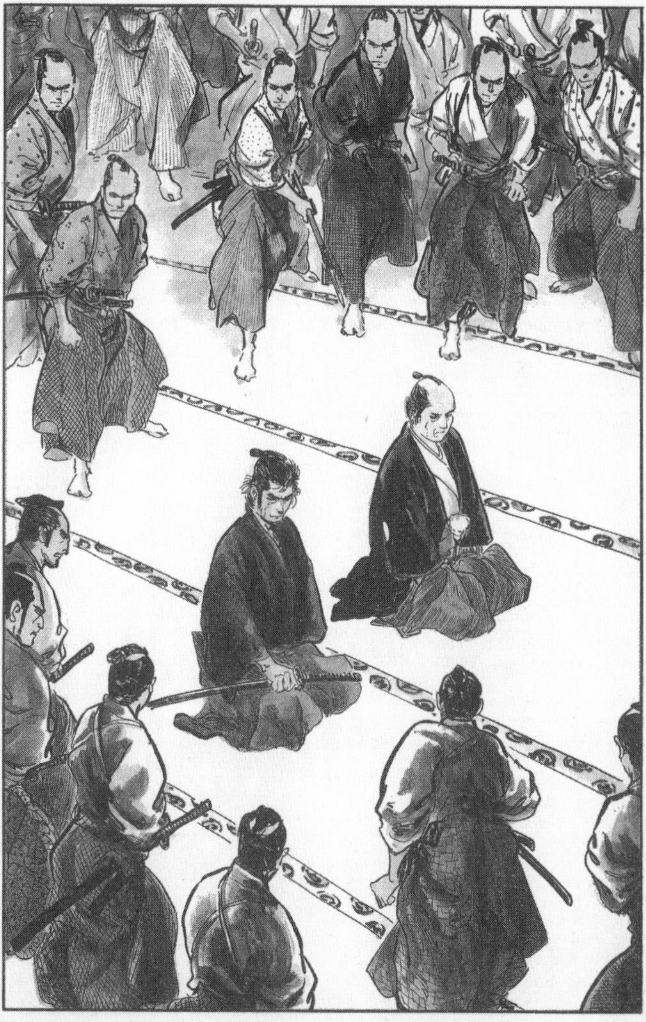

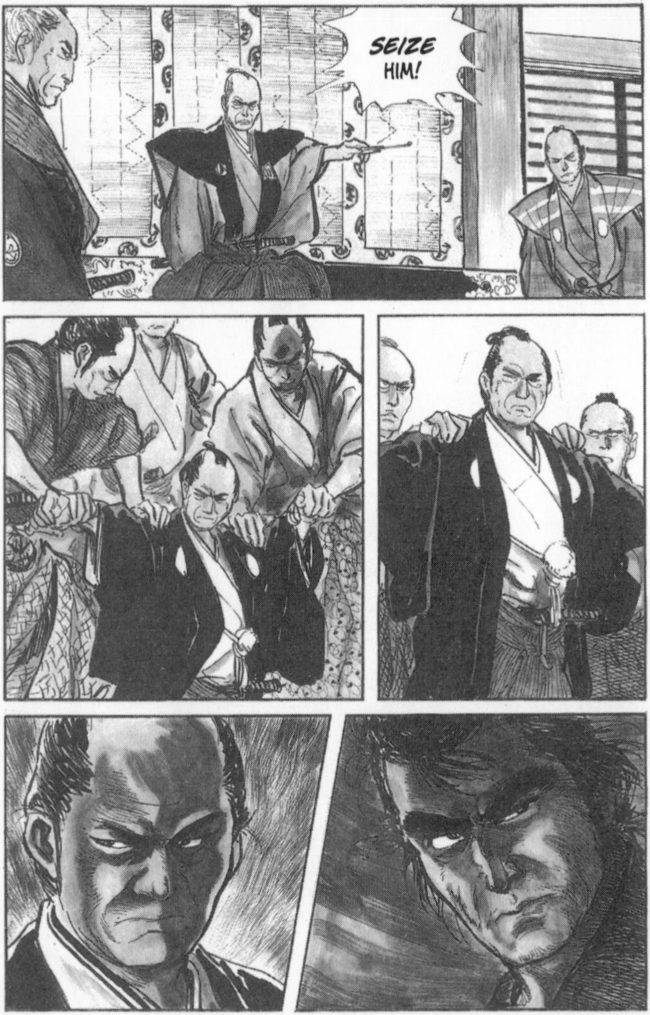
SEIZE HIM!

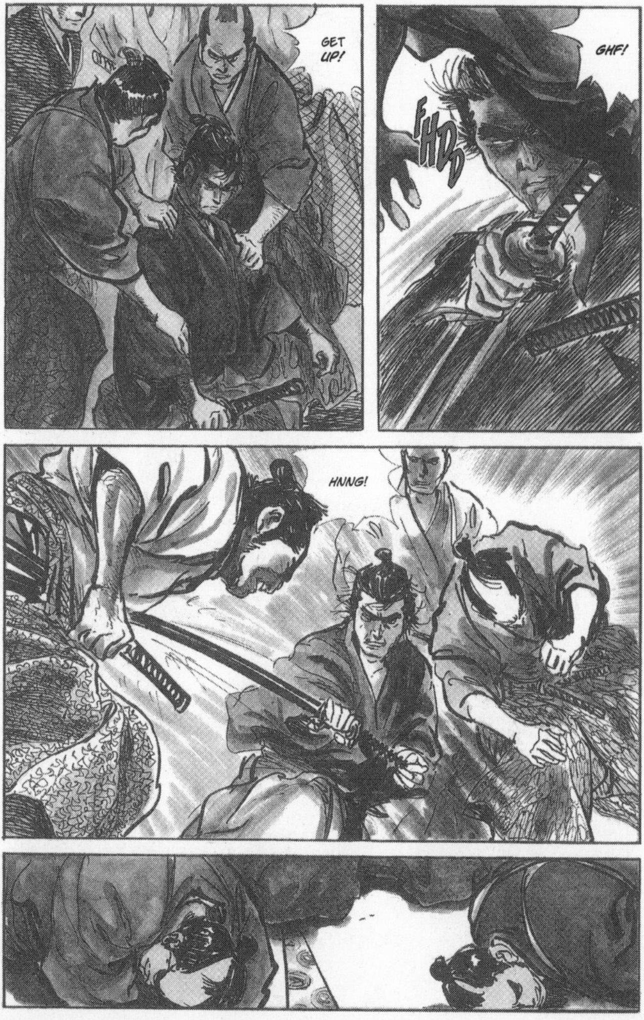
GET UP!
GHF!
FHDD
HNNG!

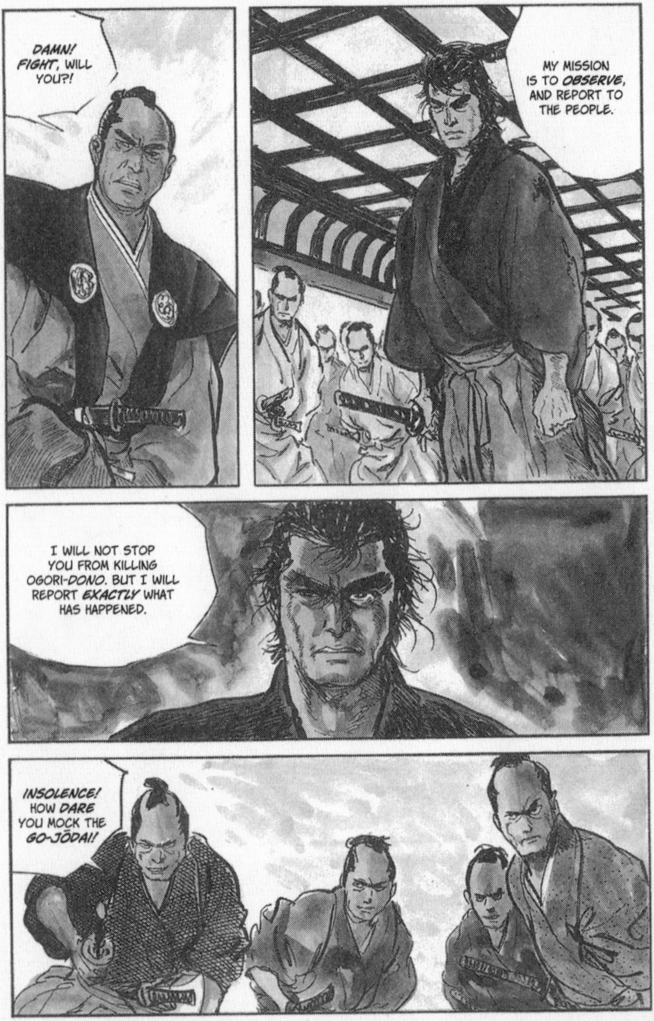
DAMN! FIGHT, WILL YOU?!
MY MISSION IS TO OBSERVE, AND REPORT TO THE PEOPLE.
I WILL NOT STOP YOU FROM KILLING OGORI-DONO. BUT I WILL REPORT EXACTLY WHAT HAS HAPPENED.
INSOLENCE! HOW DARE YOU MOCK THE GO-JŌDAI!

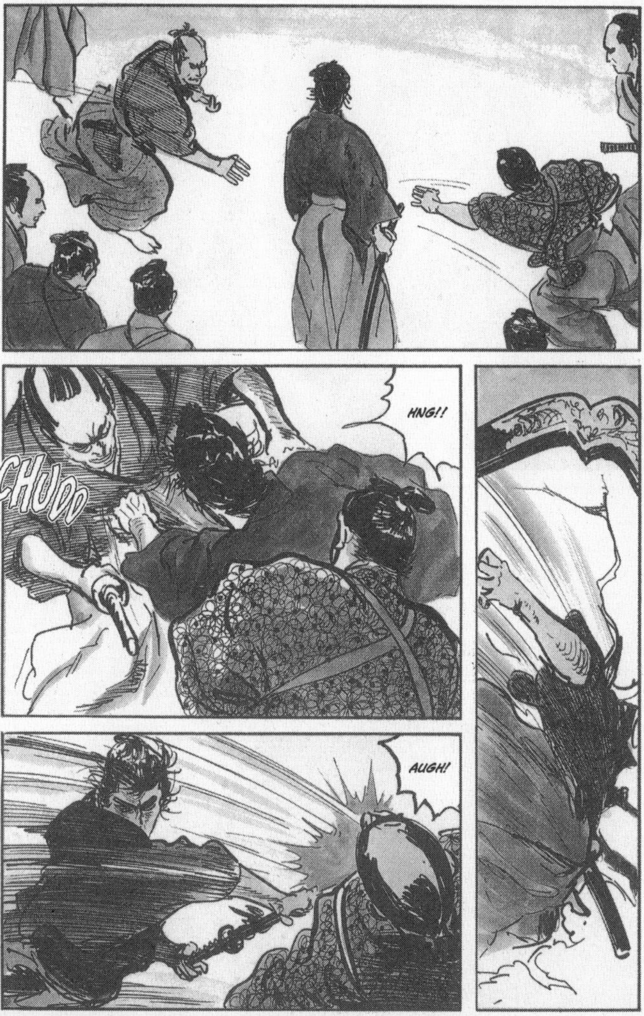
HNG!!
CHUDD
AUGH!

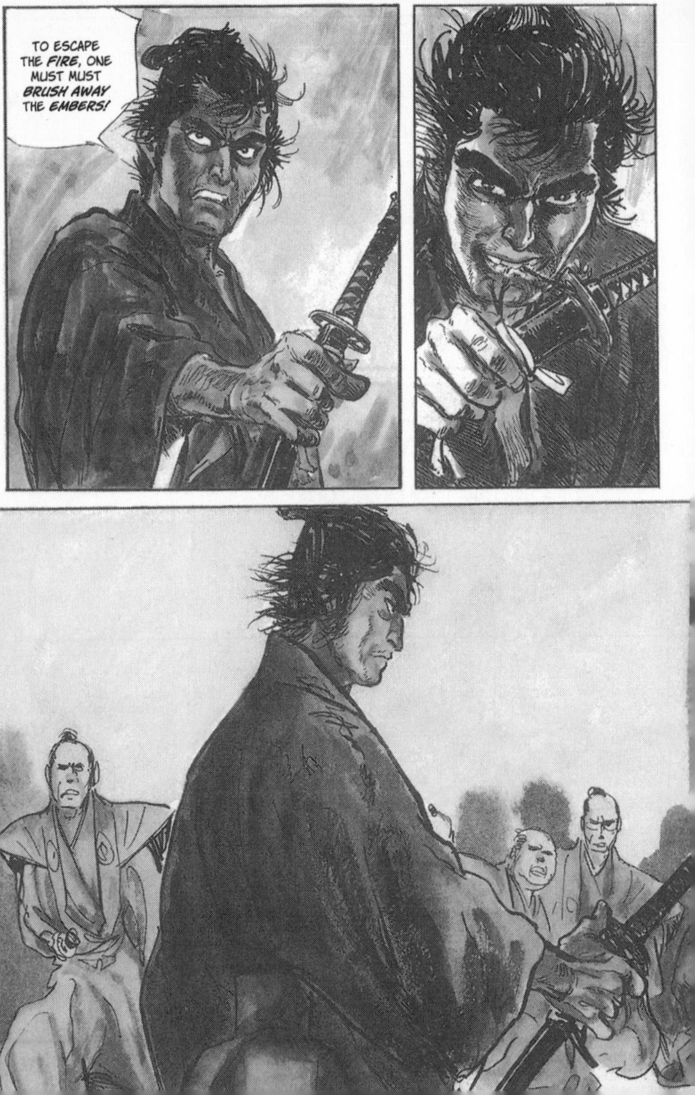
TO ESCAPE THE *FIRE*, ONE MUST MUST ***BRUSH AWAY*** THE ***EMBERS!***

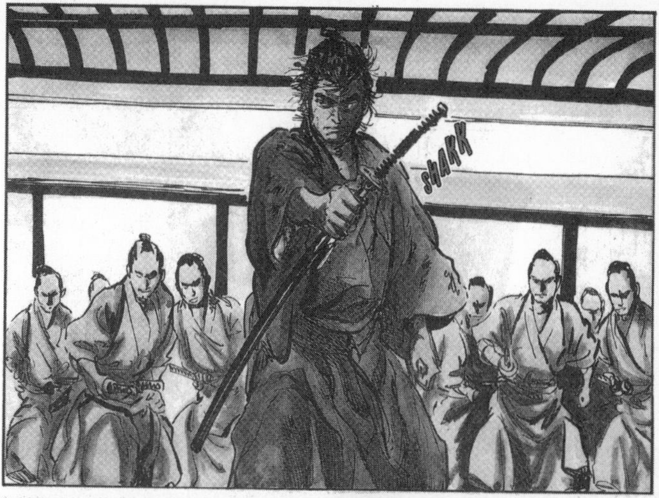
SHARK

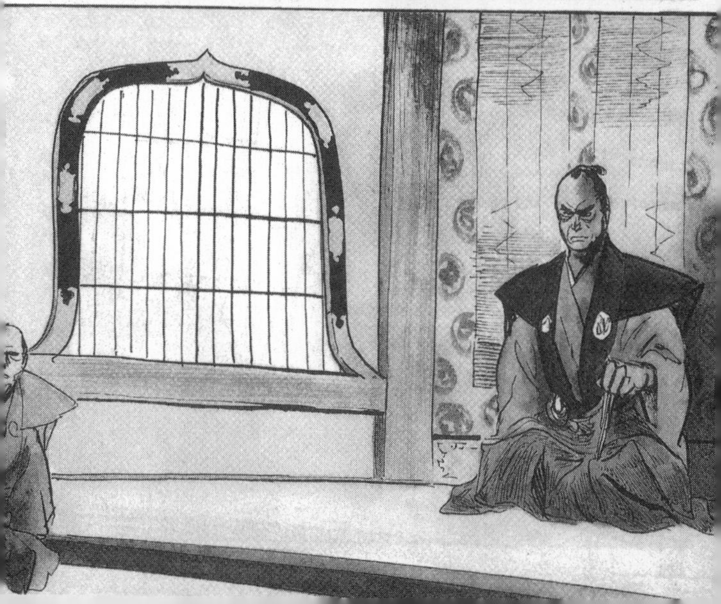

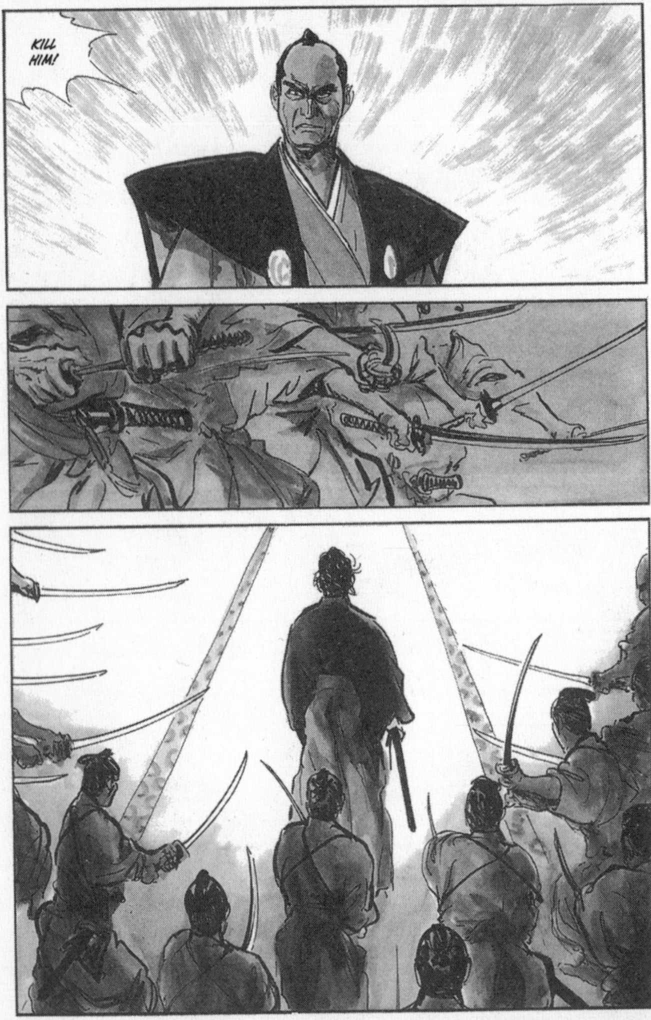
KILL HIM!

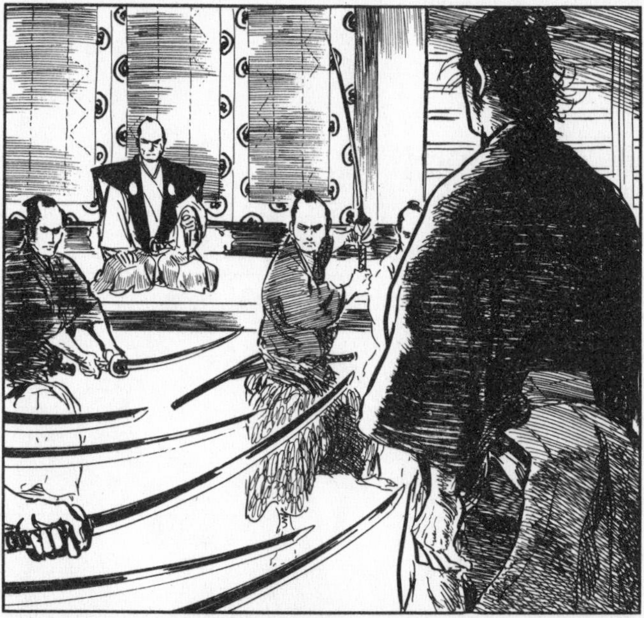

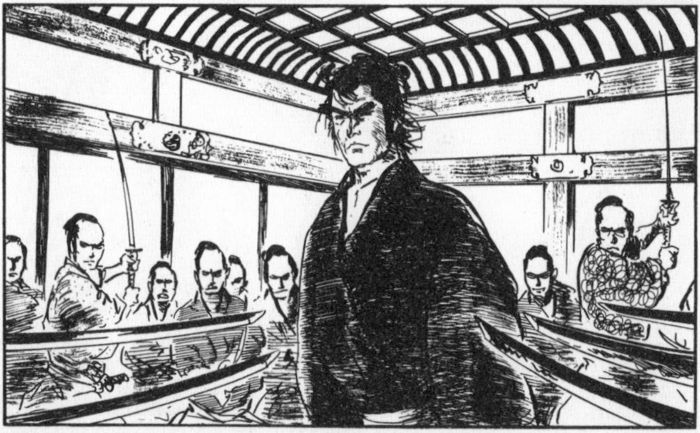

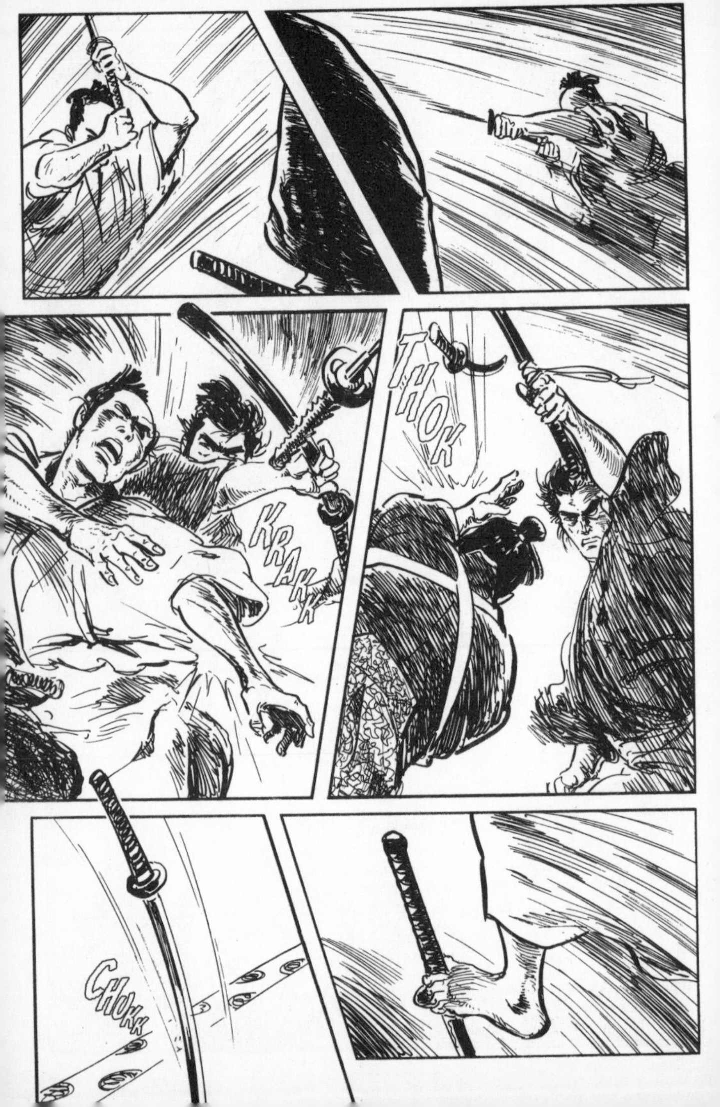
KRAKK
THOK
CHOKK

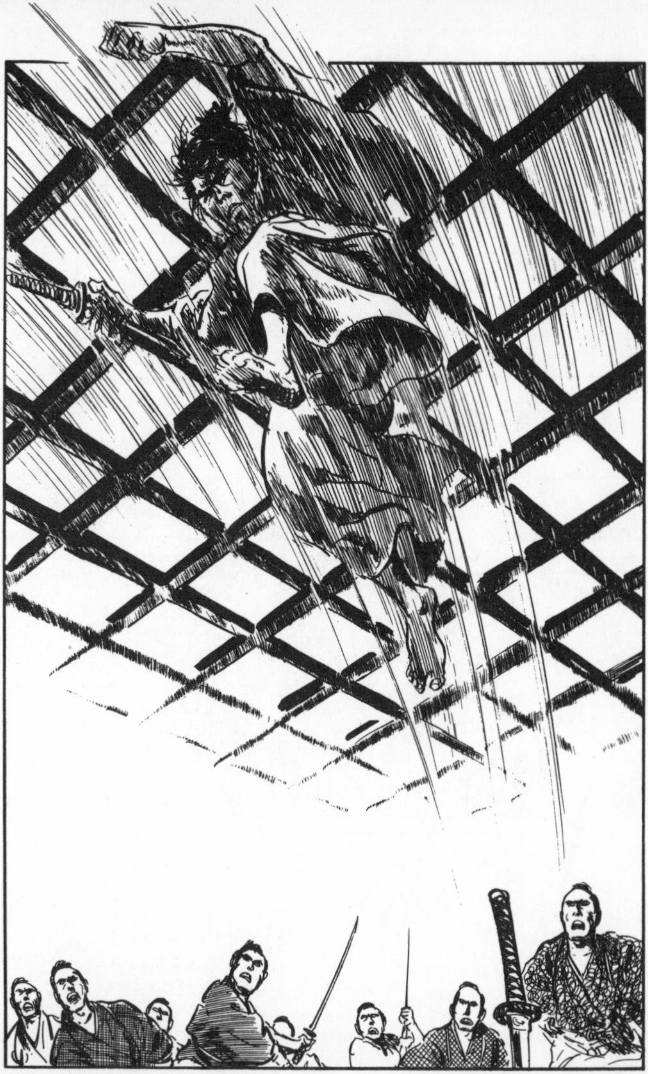

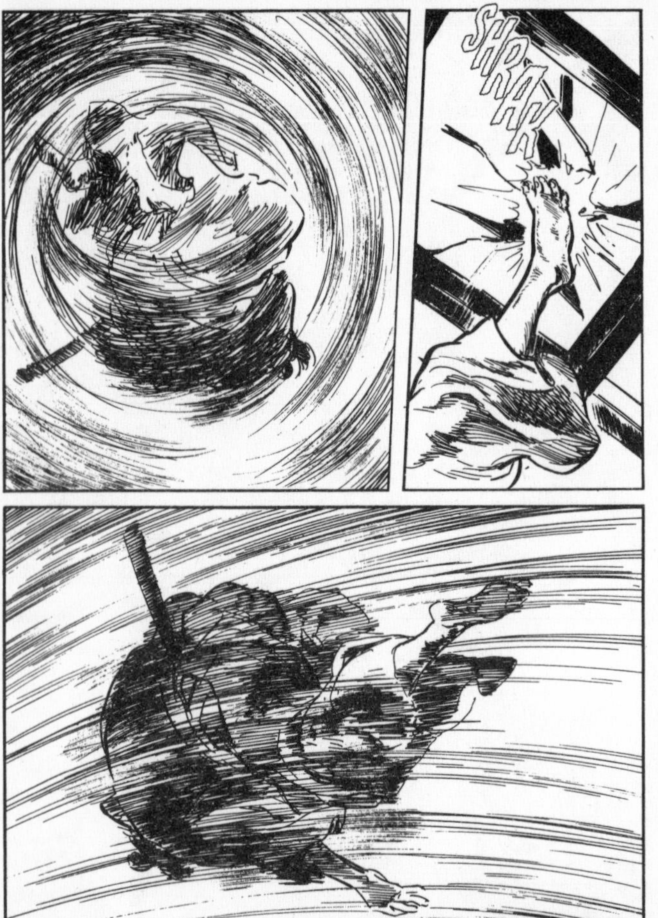
SHRAK

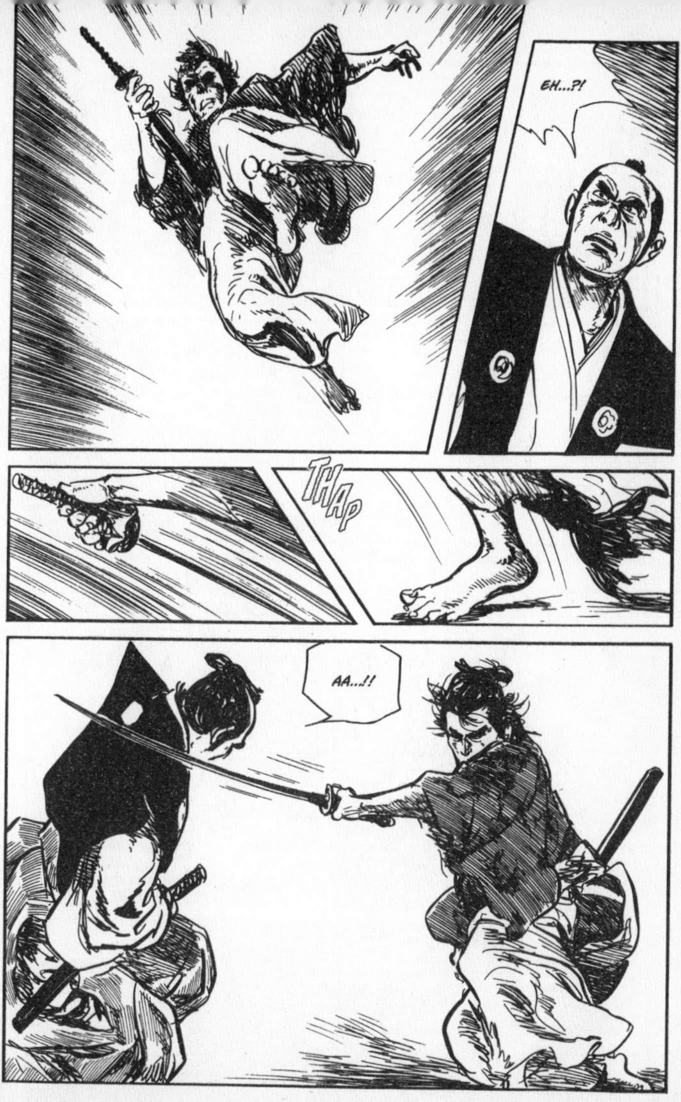
EH...?!
THAP
AA...!!

WHA...?!?

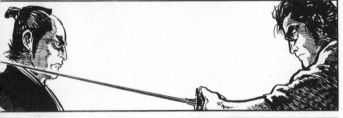

RGG!

YOU *BASTARD!* LOWER YOUR *SWORD*, OR OGORI CHŌSUKE *DIES!*

AS I SAID... I'M NOT HERE TO *PROTECT* OGORI-DONO.

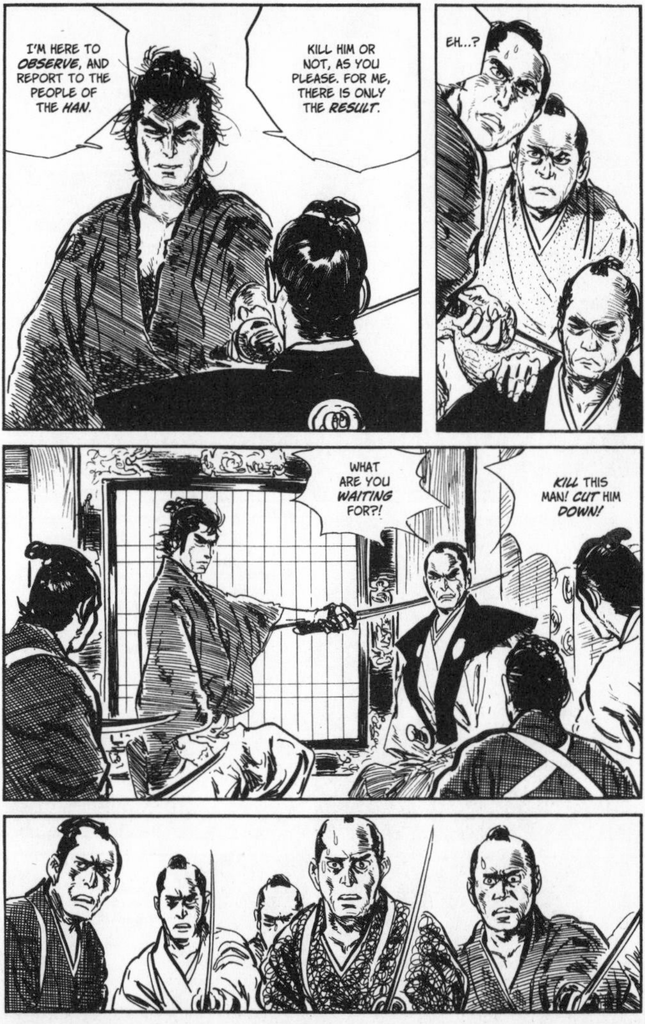

I'M HERE TO OBSERVE, AND REPORT TO THE PEOPLE OF THE HAN.
KILL HIM OR NOT, AS YOU PLEASE. FOR ME, THERE IS ONLY THE RESULT.
EH...?
WHAT ARE YOU WAITING FOR?!
KILL THIS MAN! CUT HIM DOWN!

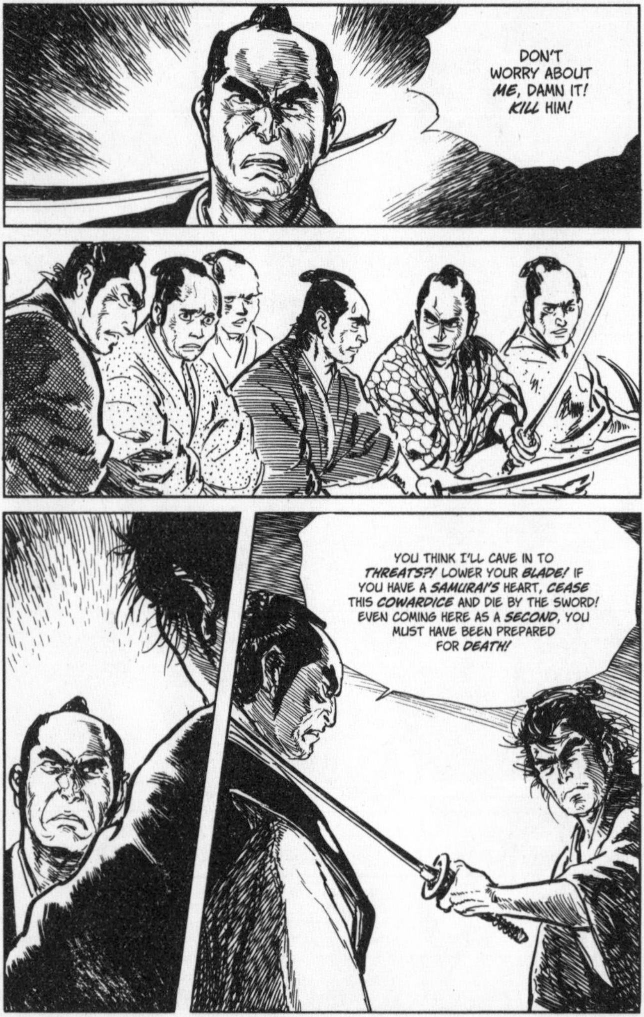
DON'T WORRY ABOUT *ME*, DAMN IT! *KILL* HIM!
YOU THINK I'LL CAVE IN TO *THREATS?!* LOWER YOUR *BLADE!* IF YOU HAVE A *SAMURAI'S* HEART, *CEASE* THIS *COWARDICE* AND DIE BY THE SWORD! EVEN COMING HERE AS A *SECOND*, YOU MUST HAVE BEEN PREPARED FOR *DEATH!*

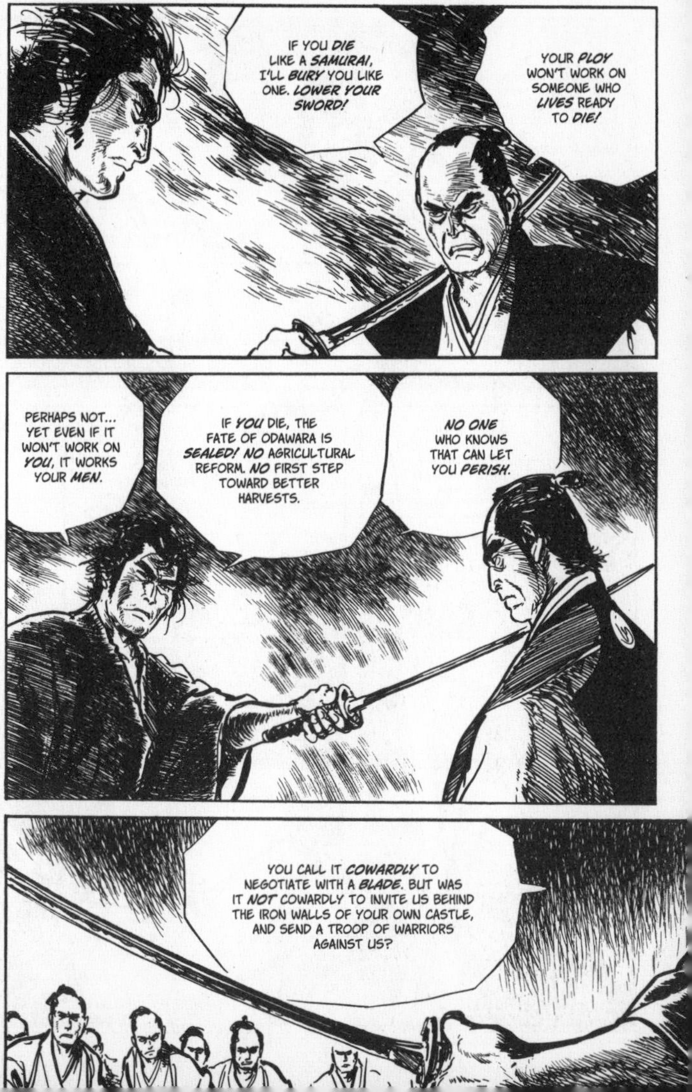
IF YOU DIE LIKE A SAMURAI, I'LL BURY YOU LIKE ONE. LOWER YOUR SWORD!
YOUR PLOY WON'T WORK ON SOMEONE WHO LIVES READY TO DIE!
PERHAPS NOT... YET EVEN IF IT WON'T WORK ON YOU, IT WORKS YOUR MEN.
IF YOU DIE, THE FATE OF ODAWARA IS SEALED! NO AGRICULTURAL REFORM. NO FIRST STEP TOWARD BETTER HARVESTS.
NO ONE WHO KNOWS THAT CAN LET YOU PERISH.
YOU CALL IT COWARDLY TO NEGOTIATE WITH A BLADE. BUT WAS IT NOT COWARDLY TO INVITE US BEHIND THE IRON WALLS OF YOUR OWN CASTLE, AND SEND A TROOP OF WARRIORS AGAINST US?

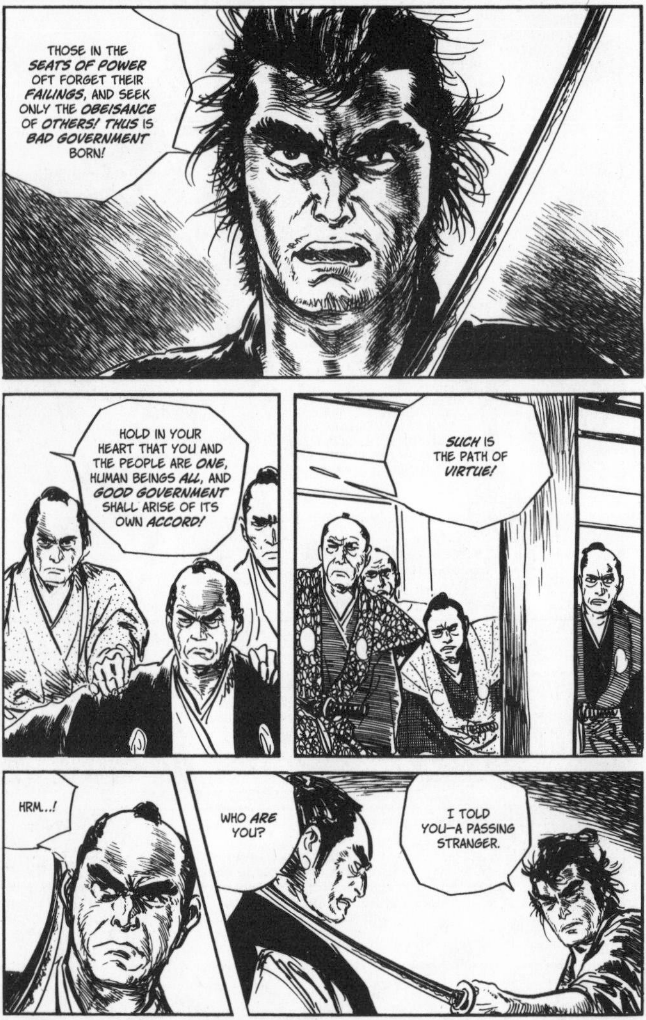
THOSE IN THE *SEATS OF POWER* OFT FORGET THEIR *FAILINGS*, AND SEEK ONLY THE *OBEISANCE* OF *OTHERS! THUS* IS *BAD GOVERNMENT* BORN!
HOLD IN YOUR HEART THAT YOU AND THE PEOPLE ARE *ONE*, HUMAN BEINGS *ALL*, AND *GOOD GOVERNMENT* SHALL ARISE OF ITS OWN *ACCORD!*
SUCH IS THE PATH OF *VIRTUE!*
HRM...!
WHO *ARE* YOU?
I TOLD YOU—A PASSING STRANGER.

THUS I UNDERSTAND THE SUFFERING OF THE *PEOPLE*, AND THE THINKING OF THE *CASTLE*.

AND AS THINGS STAND NOW, IT IS AS CLEAR AS A *FIRE* IN THE *NIGHT*. *NEITHER* OF YOU WILL GIVE GROUND, AND ALL WILL END IN *BLOODSHED*.

THEN... WHAT DO *YOU* SUGGEST WE DO?!

IF YOU WISH TO PLUCK THE *ROASTED CHESTNUTS*, YOU MUST STEP INTO THE *FIRE*.

MUST NOT YOU *BOTH* STAND IN THE OTHER'S SHOES?

TO PLUCK THE CHESTNUTS, STEP INTO THE *FIRE*...

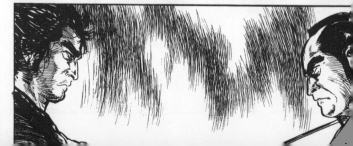

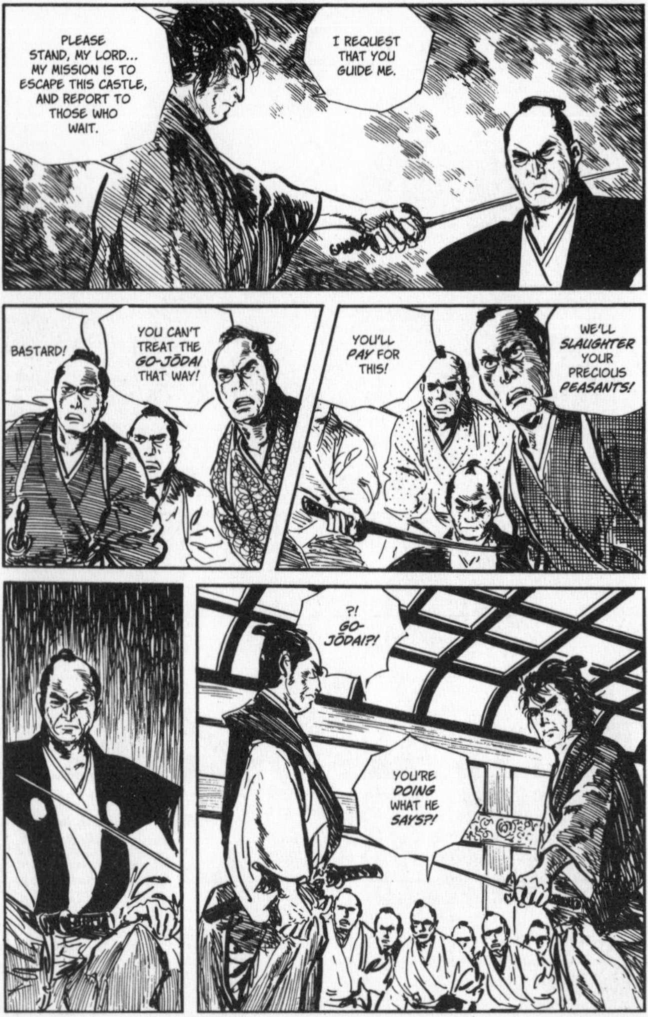
PLEASE STAND, MY LORD... MY MISSION IS TO ESCAPE THIS CASTLE, AND REPORT TO THOSE WHO WAIT.
I REQUEST THAT YOU GUIDE ME.
BASTARD!
YOU CAN'T TREAT THE GO-JŌDAI THAT WAY!
YOU'LL PAY FOR THIS!
WE'LL SLAUGHTER YOUR PRECIOUS PEASANTS!
?! GO-JŌDAI?!
YOU'RE DOING WHAT HE SAYS?!

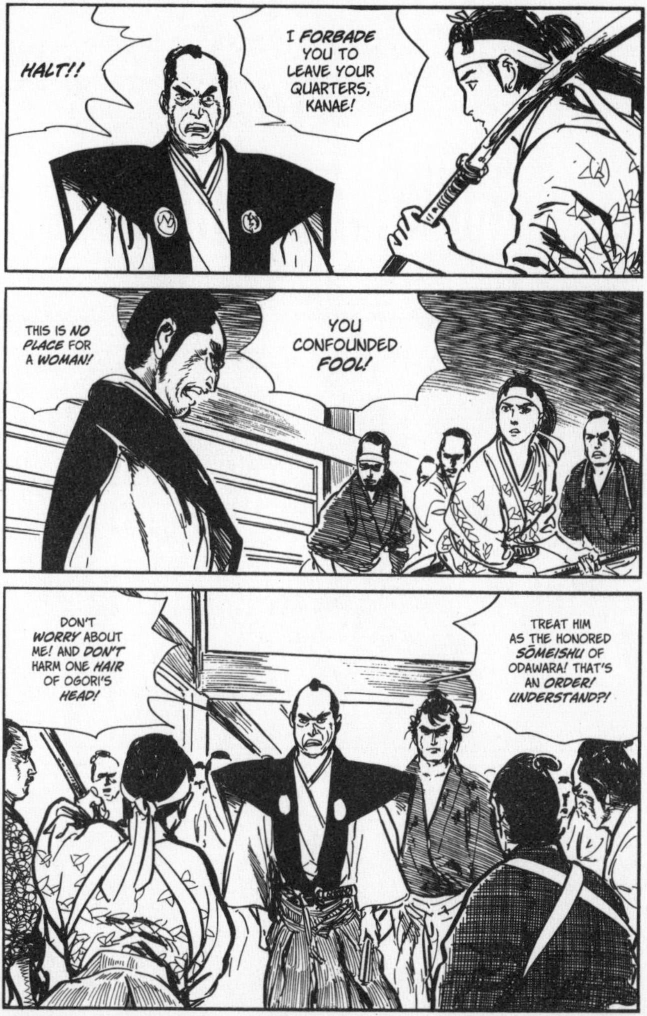

HALT!!
I FORBADE YOU TO LEAVE YOUR QUARTERS, KANAE!
THIS IS NO PLACE FOR A WOMAN!
YOU CONFOUNDED FOOL!
DON'T WORRY ABOUT ME! AND DON'T HARM ONE HAIR OF OGORI'S HEAD!
TREAT HIM AS THE HONORED SŌMEISHU OF ODAWARA! THAT'S AN ORDER! UNDERSTAND?!

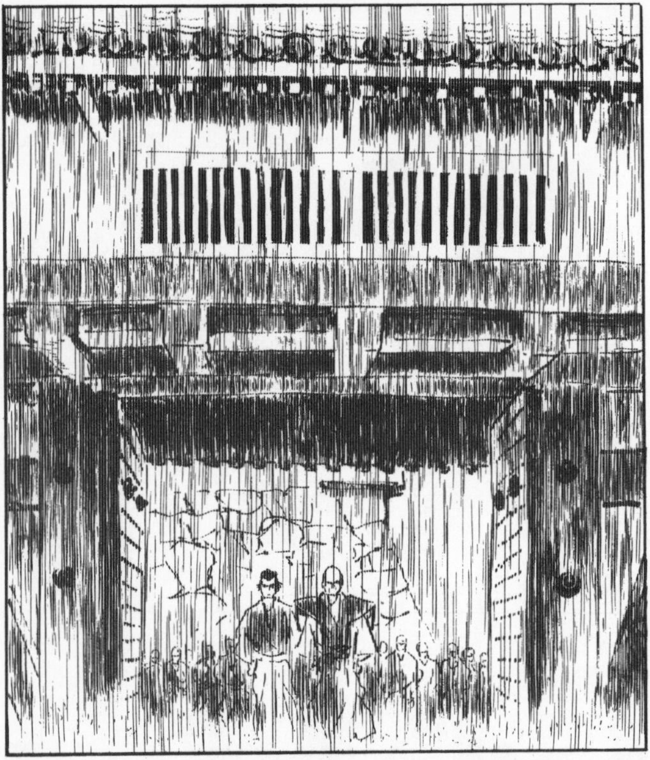

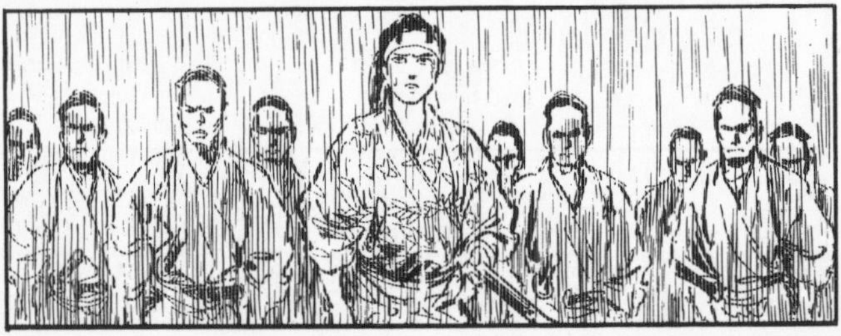

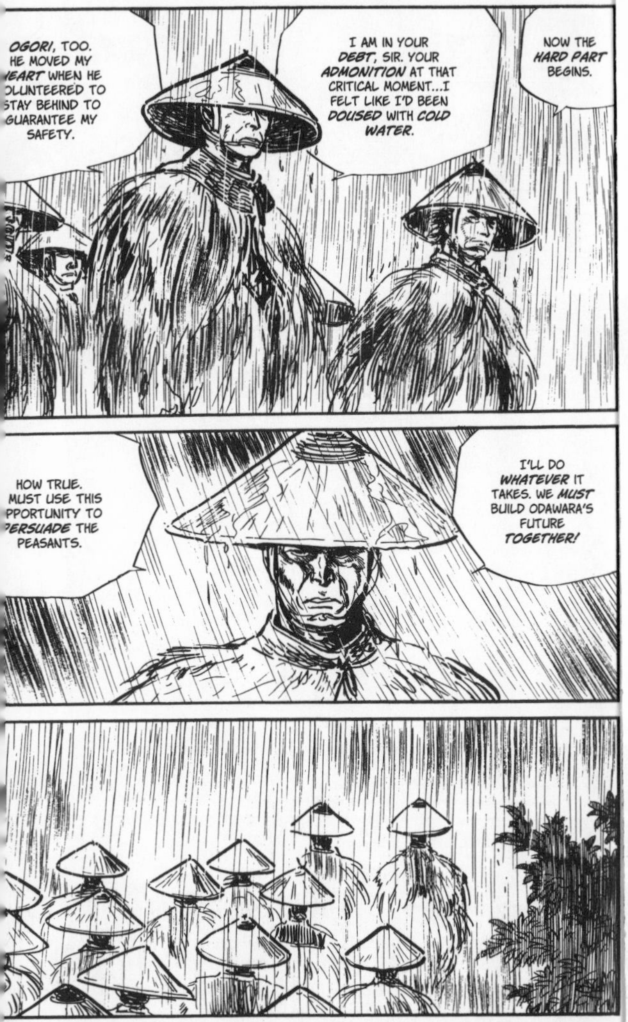
OGORI, TOO. HE MOVED MY HEART WHEN HE VOLUNTEERED TO STAY BEHIND TO GUARANTEE MY SAFETY.
I AM IN YOUR DEBT, SIR. YOUR ADMONITION AT THAT CRITICAL MOMENT...I FELT LIKE I'D BEEN DOUSED WITH COLD WATER.
NOW THE HARD PART BEGINS.
HOW TRUE. I MUST USE THIS OPPORTUNITY TO PERSUADE THE PEASANTS.
I'LL DO WHATEVER IT TAKES. WE MUST BUILD ODAWARA'S FUTURE TOGETHER!

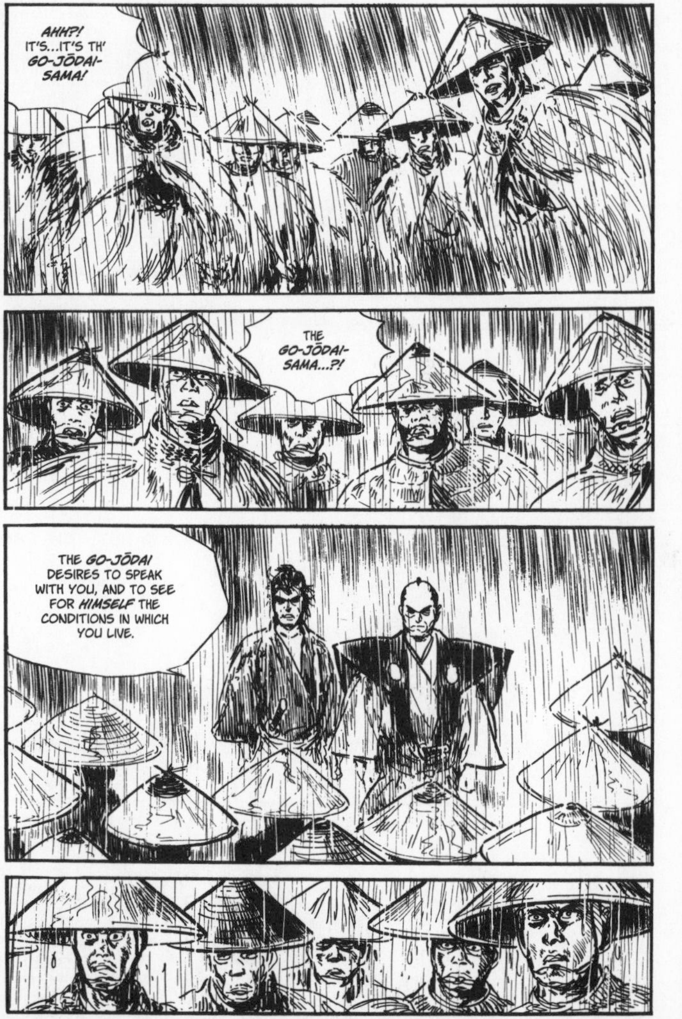
AHH?! IT'S...IT'S TH' GO-JŌDAI-SAMA!
THE GO-JŌDAI-SAMA...?!
THE GO-JŌDAI DESIRES TO SPEAK WITH YOU, AND TO SEE FOR HIMSELF THE CONDITIONS IN WHICH YOU LIVE.

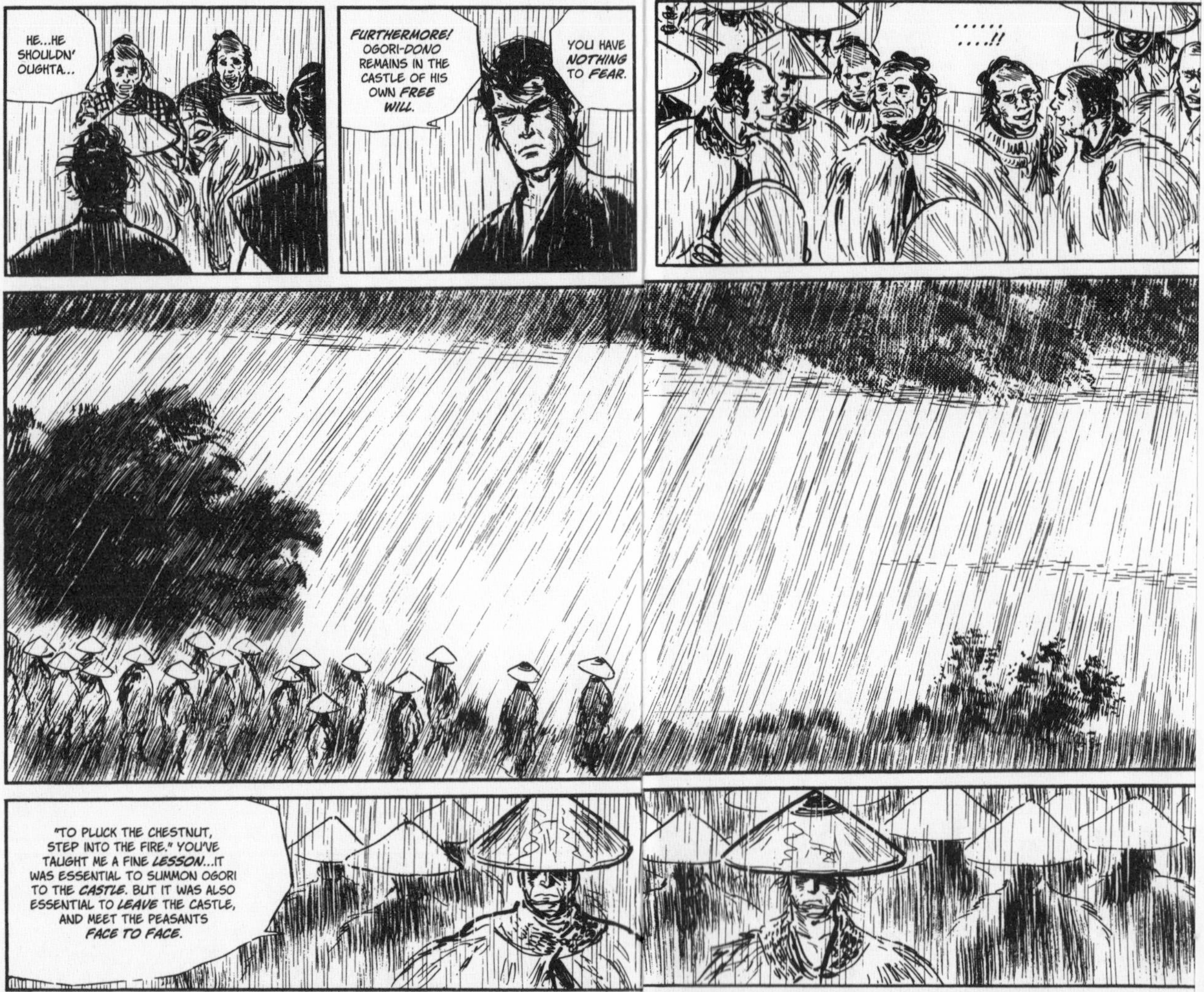
HE...HE SHOULDN' OUGHTA...
FURTHERMORE! OGORI-DONO REMAINS IN THE CASTLE OF HIS OWN *FREE WILL.*
YOU HAVE *NOTHING* TO *FEAR.*
......
....!!
"TO PLUCK THE CHESTNUT, STEP INTO THE FIRE." YOU'VE TAUGHT ME A FINE *LESSON*...IT WAS ESSENTIAL TO SUMMON OGORI TO THE *CASTLE*. BUT IT WAS ALSO ESSENTIAL TO *LEAVE* THE CASTLE, AND MEET THE PEASANTS *FACE TO FACE*.

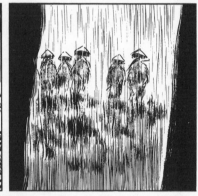

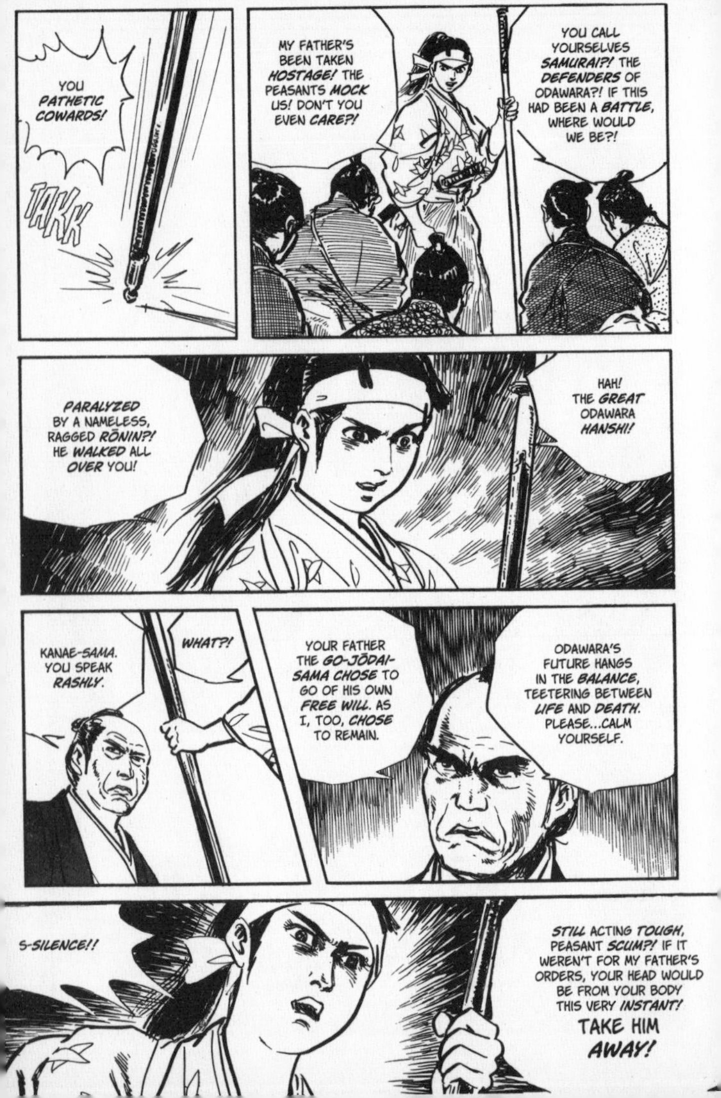
YOU PATHETIC COWARDS!
TAKK
MY FATHER'S BEEN TAKEN HOSTAGE! THE PEASANTS MOCK US! DON'T YOU EVEN CARE?!
YOU CALL YOURSELVES SAMURAI?! THE DEFENDERS OF ODAWARA?! IF THIS HAD BEEN A BATTLE, WHERE WOULD WE BE?!
PARALYZED BY A NAMELESS, RAGGED RŌNIN?! HE WALKED ALL OVER YOU!
HAH! THE GREAT ODAWARA HANSHI!
KANAE-SAMA. YOU SPEAK RASHLY.
WHAT?!
YOUR FATHER THE GO-JŌDAI-SAMA CHOSE TO GO OF HIS OWN FREE WILL. AS I, TOO, CHOSE TO REMAIN.
ODAWARA'S FUTURE HANGS IN THE BALANCE, TEETERING BETWEEN LIFE AND DEATH. PLEASE...CALM YOURSELF.
S-SILENCE!!
STILL ACTING TOUGH, PEASANT SCUM?! IF IT WEREN'T FOR MY FATHER'S ORDERS, YOUR HEAD WOULD BE FROM YOUR BODY THIS VERY INSTANT!
TAKE HIM AWAY!

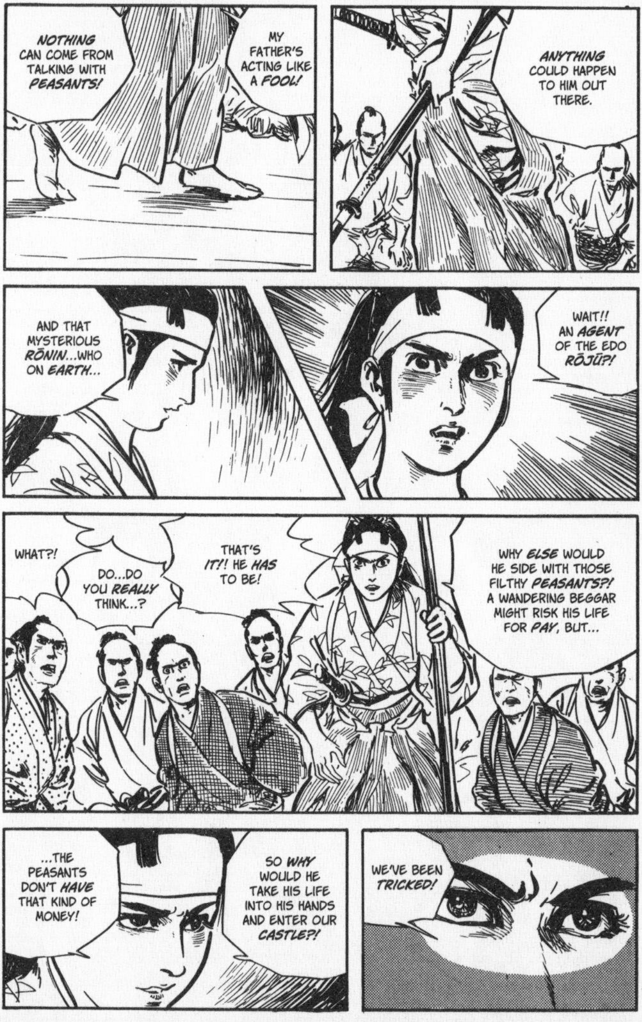
NOTHING CAN COME FROM TALKING WITH PEASANTS!
MY FATHER'S ACTING LIKE A FOOL!
ANYTHING COULD HAPPEN TO HIM OUT THERE.
AND THAT MYSTERIOUS RŌNIN...WHO ON EARTH...
WAIT!! AN AGENT OF THE EDO RŌJŪ?!
WHAT?!
DO...DO YOU REALLY THINK...?
THAT'S IT!! HE HAS TO BE!
WHY ELSE WOULD HE SIDE WITH THOSE FILTHY PEASANTS?! A WANDERING BEGGAR MIGHT RISK HIS LIFE FOR PAY, BUT...
...THE PEASANTS DON'T HAVE THAT KIND OF MONEY!
SO WHY WOULD HE TAKE HIS LIFE INTO HIS HANDS AND ENTER OUR CASTLE?!
WE'VE BEEN TRICKED!

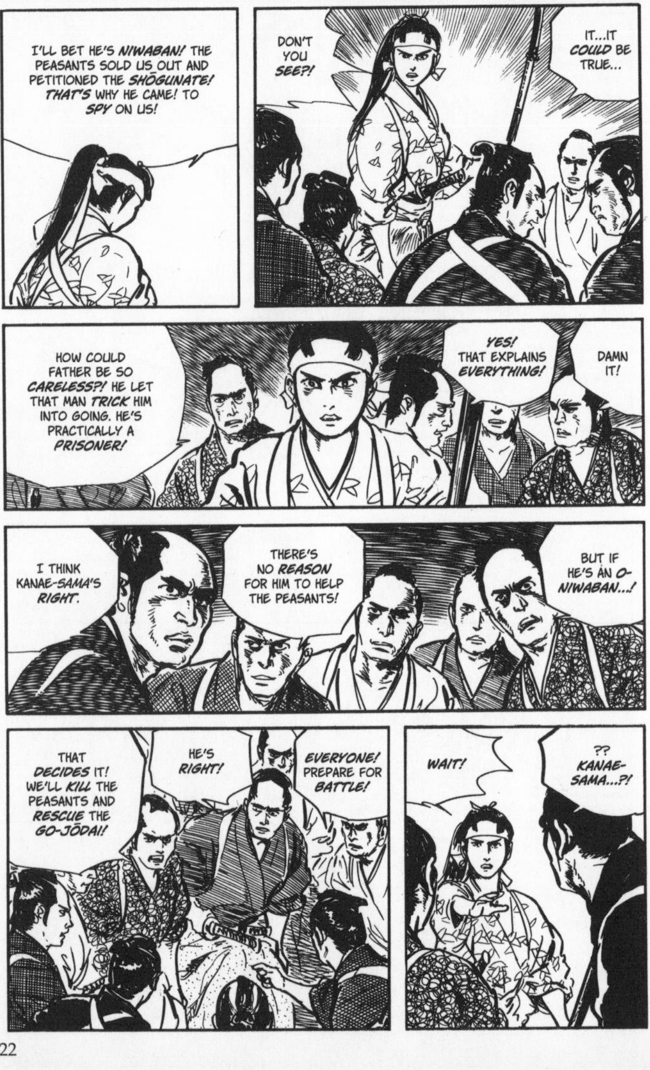
I'LL BET HE'S NIWABAN! THE PEASANTS SOLD US OUT AND PETITIONED THE SHŌGUNATE! THAT'S WHY HE CAME! TO SPY ON US!
DON'T YOU SEE?!
IT...IT COULD BE TRUE...
HOW COULD FATHER BE SO CARELESS?! HE LET THAT MAN TRICK HIM INTO GOING. HE'S PRACTICALLY A PRISONER!
YES! THAT EXPLAINS EVERYTHING!
DAMN IT!
I THINK KANAE-SAMA'S RIGHT.
THERE'S NO REASON FOR HIM TO HELP THE PEASANTS!
BUT IF HE'S AN O-NIWABAN...!
THAT DECIDES IT! WE'LL KILL THE PEASANTS AND RESCUE THE GO-JŌDAI!
HE'S RIGHT!
EVERYONE! PREPARE FOR BATTLE!
WAIT!
?? KANAE-SAMA...?!

HE'S A *MASTER SWORDSMAN!* IF WE'RE NOT CAREFUL, HE'LL KILL FATHER *FIRST.*

BUT IF WE CAN GET RID OF *HIM,* THE REST IS EASY!

THAT'S *IT!* BRING ME MY *KOTO!*

YOUR... *KOTO?* WHAT *FOR?!*

YOU HEARD ME! MY *THIRTEEN-STRING KOTO!*

I HAVE A *PLAN!*

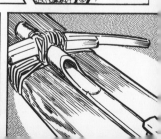

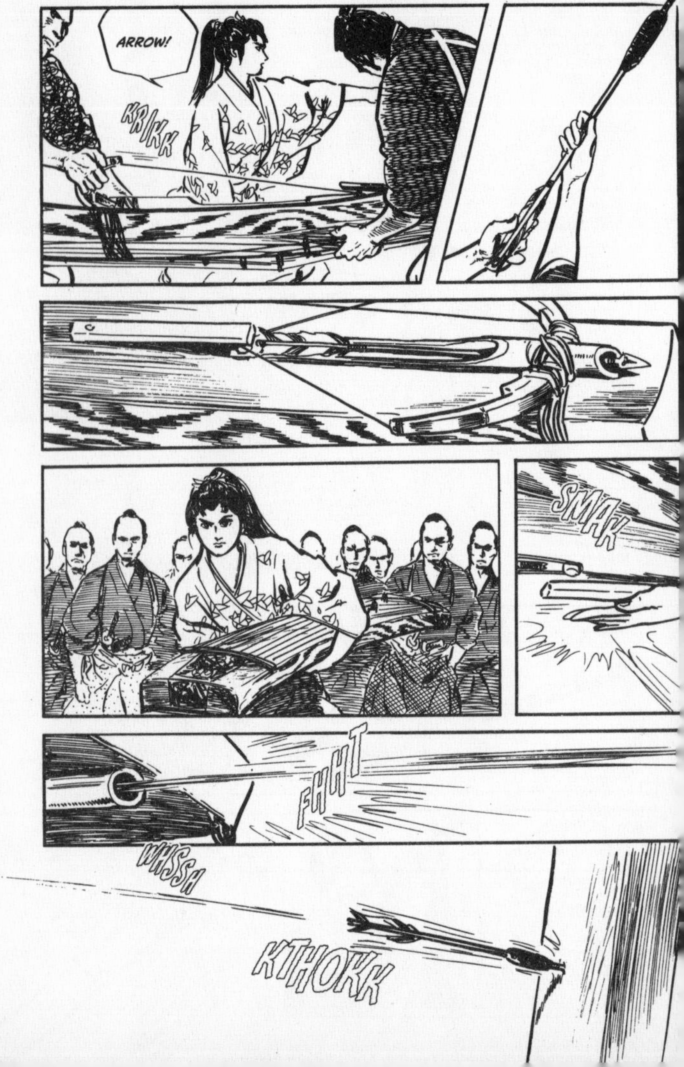
ARROW!
KRIKK
SMAK
FHHT
WHSSH
KTHOKK

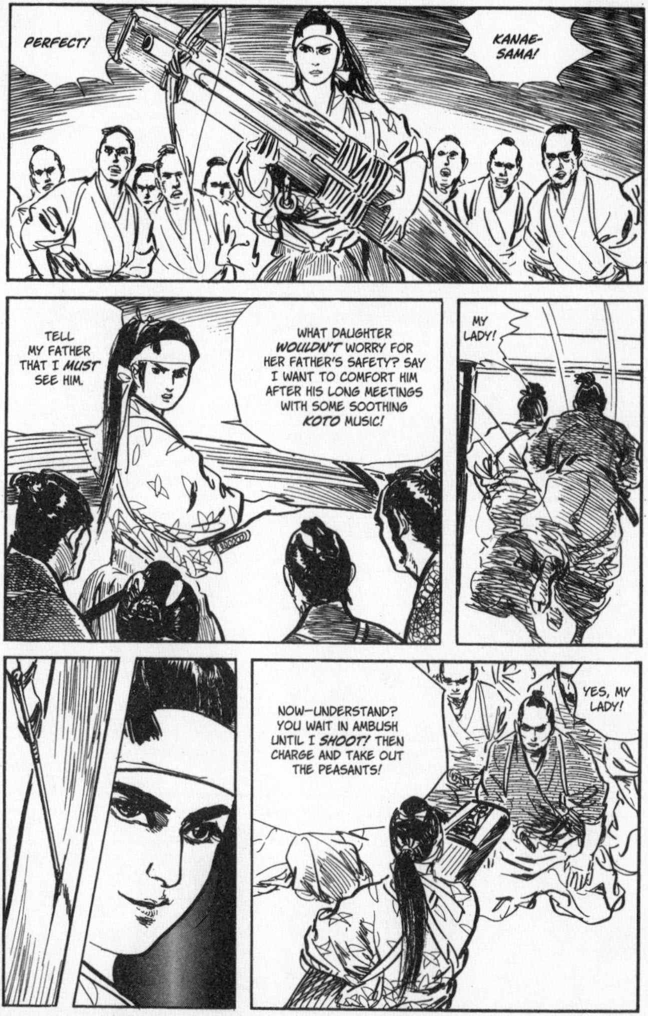
PERFECT!
KANAE-SAMA!
TELL MY FATHER THAT I MUST SEE HIM.
WHAT DAUGHTER WOULDN'T WORRY FOR HER FATHER'S SAFETY? SAY I WANT TO COMFORT HIM AFTER HIS LONG MEETINGS WITH SOME SOOTHING KOTO MUSIC!
MY LADY!
NOW—UNDERSTAND? YOU WAIT IN AMBUSH UNTIL I SHOOT! THEN CHARGE AND TAKE OUT THE PEASANTS!
YES, MY LADY!

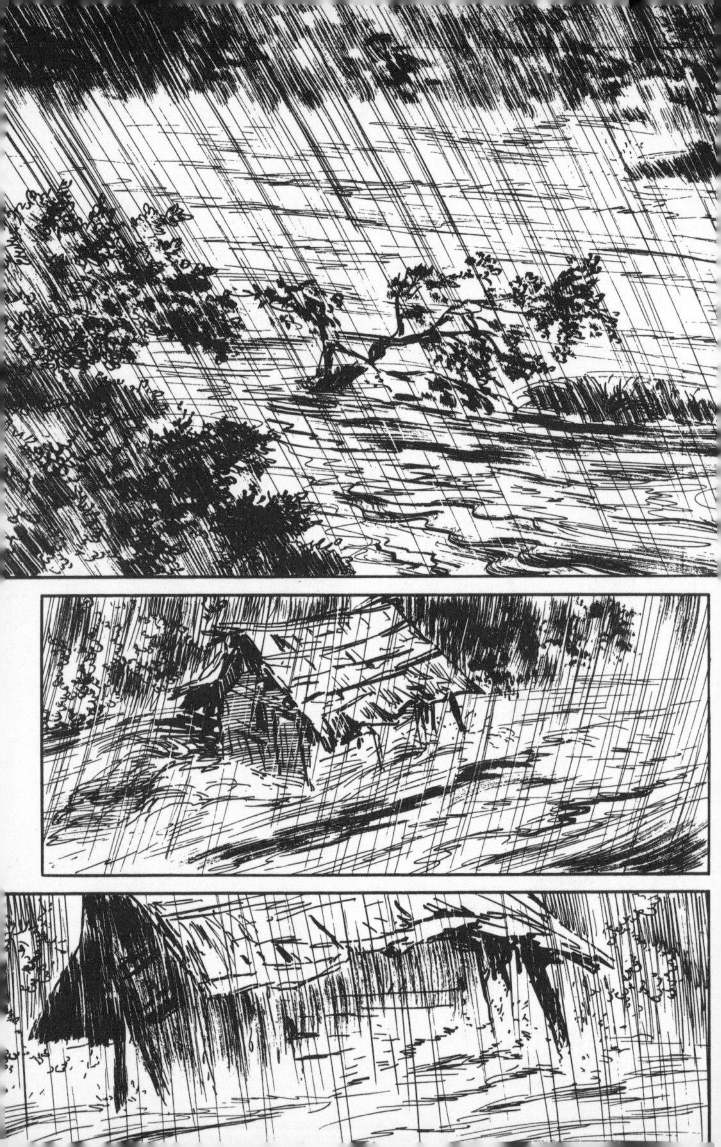

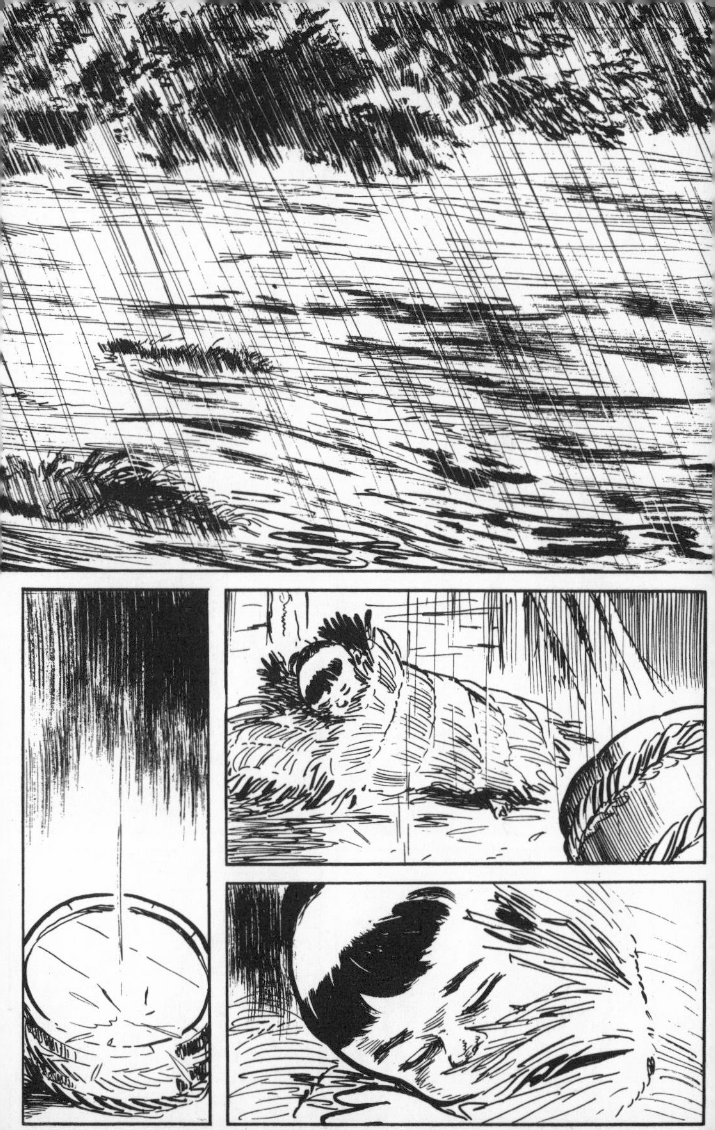

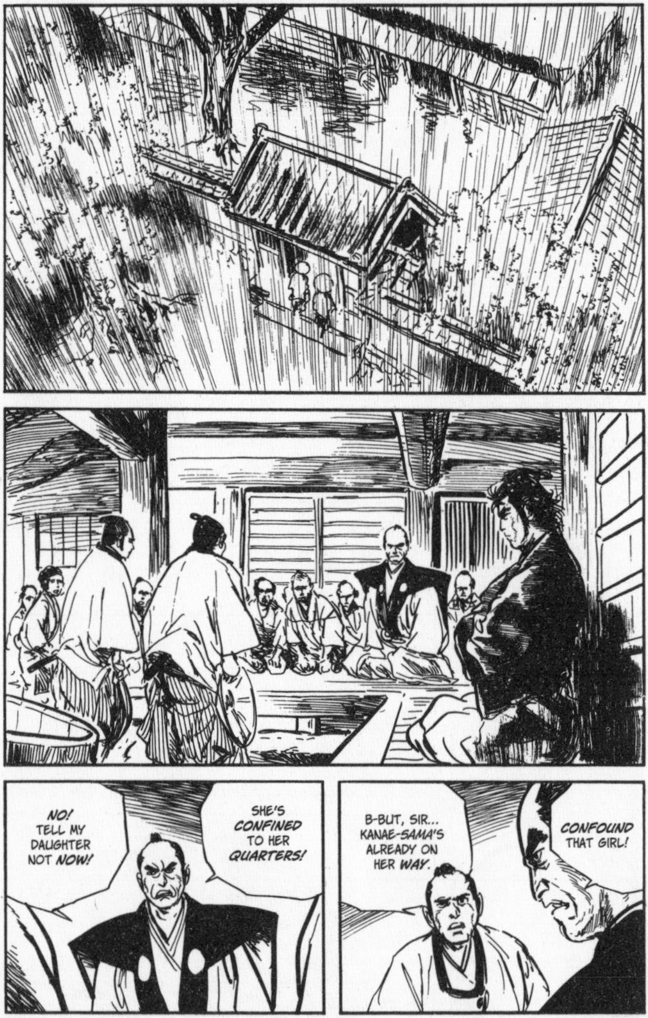
NO! TELL MY DAUGHTER NOT NOW!
SHE'S CONFINED TO HER QUARTERS!
B-BUT, SIR... KANAE-SAMA'S ALREADY ON HER WAY.
CONFOUND THAT GIRL!

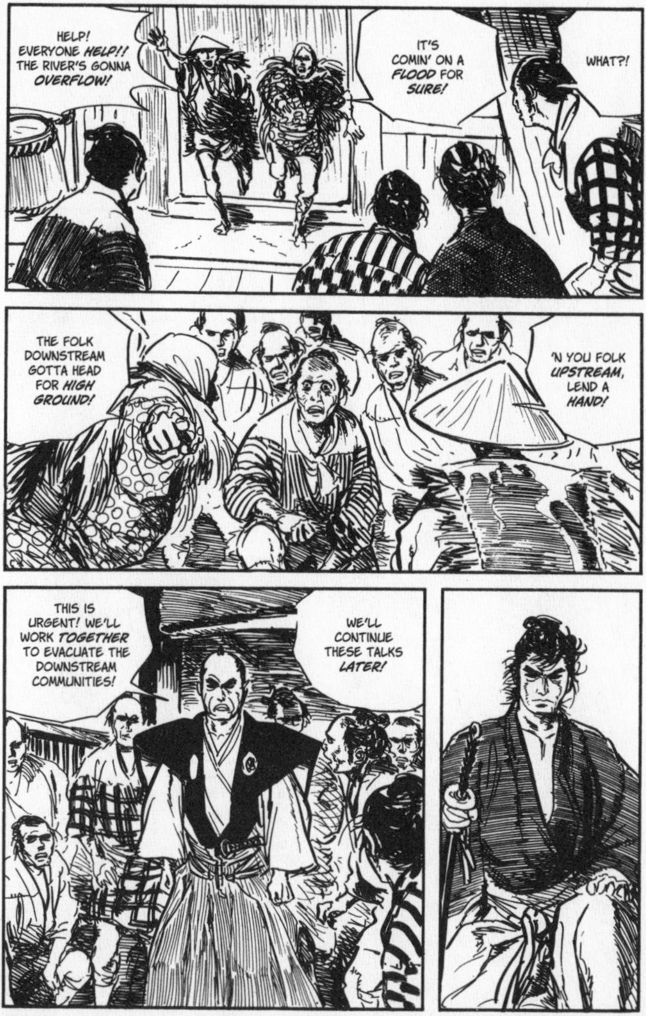
HELP! EVERYONE HELP!! THE RIVER'S GONNA OVERFLOW!
IT'S COMIN' ON A FLOOD FOR SURE!
WHAT?!
THE FOLK DOWNSTREAM GOTTA HEAD FOR HIGH GROUND!
'N YOU FOLK UPSTREAM, LEND A HAND!
THIS IS URGENT! WE'LL WORK TOGETHER TO EVACUATE THE DOWNSTREAM COMMUNITIES!
WE'LL CONTINUE THESE TALKS LATER!

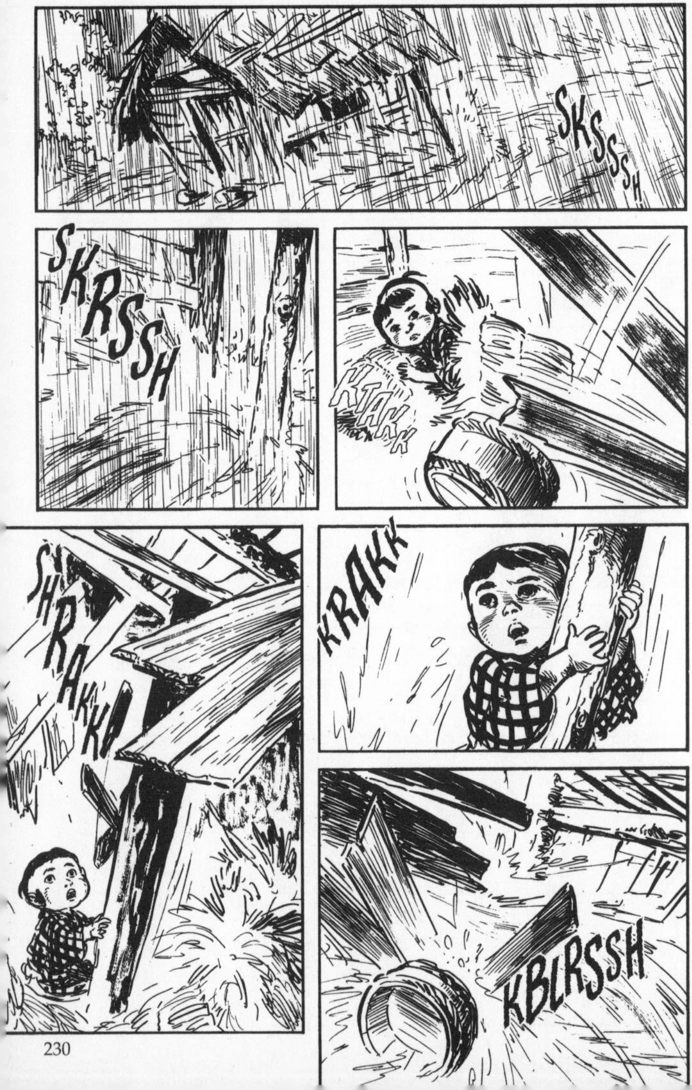
SKSSSSH!
SKRSSSH
KRAKK
SHRAKKK
KRAKK
KBLRSSH

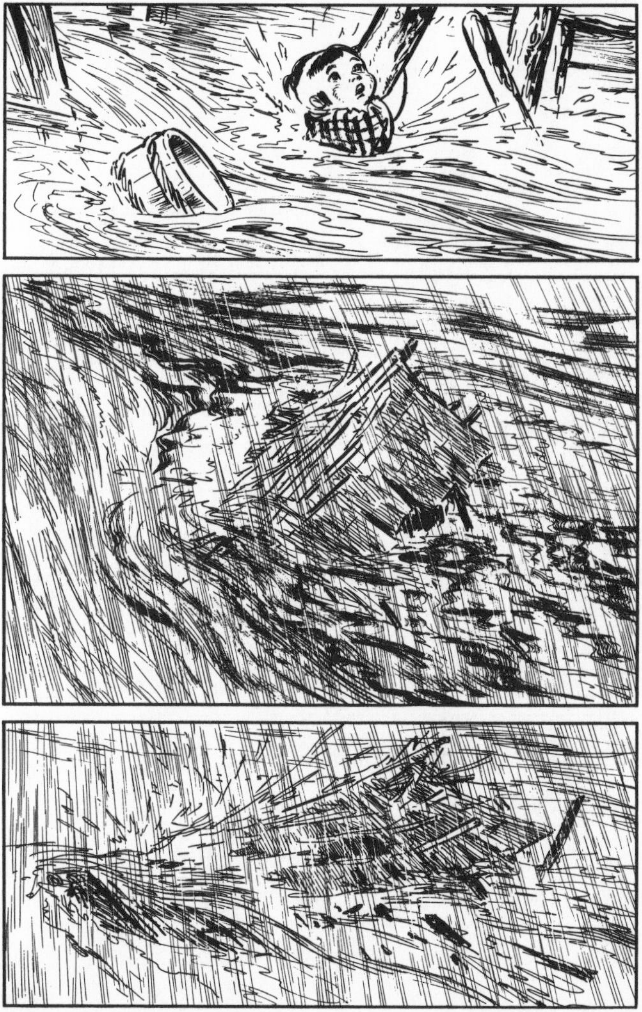

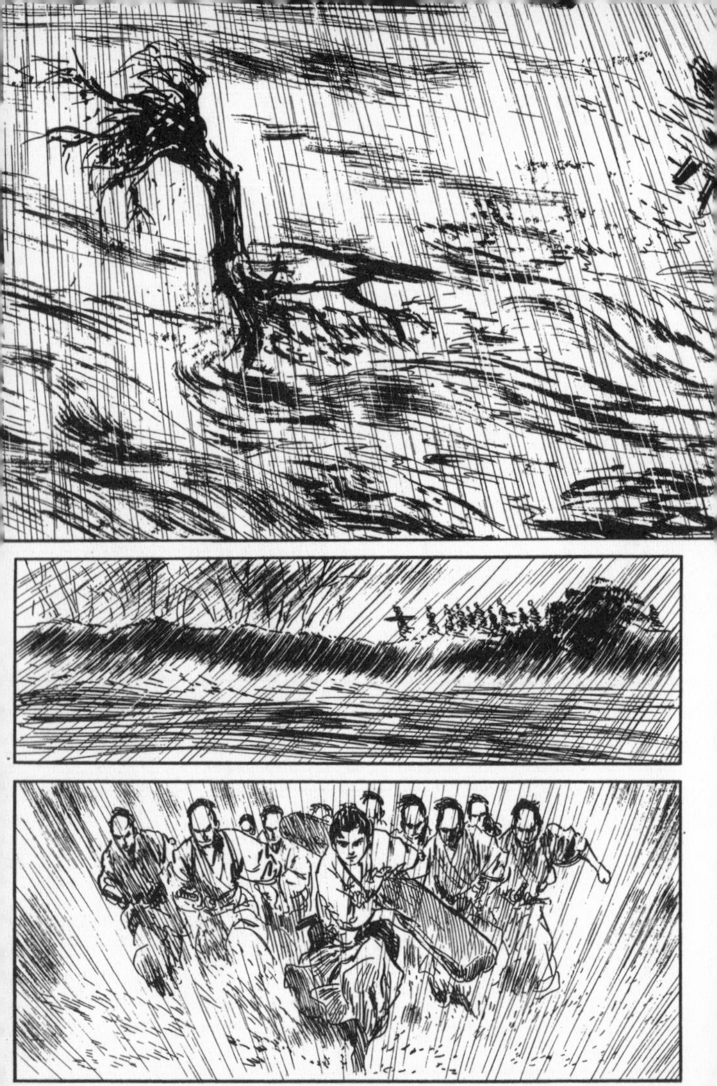

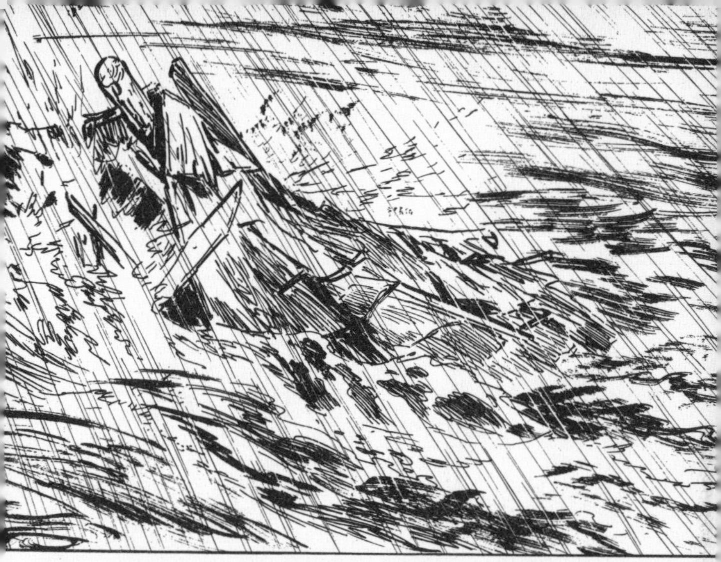
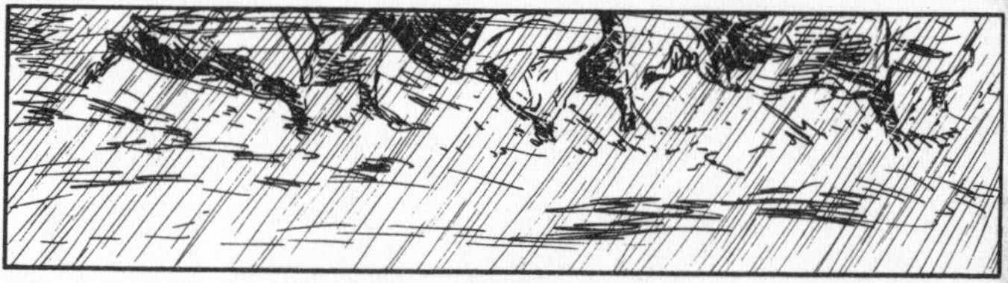
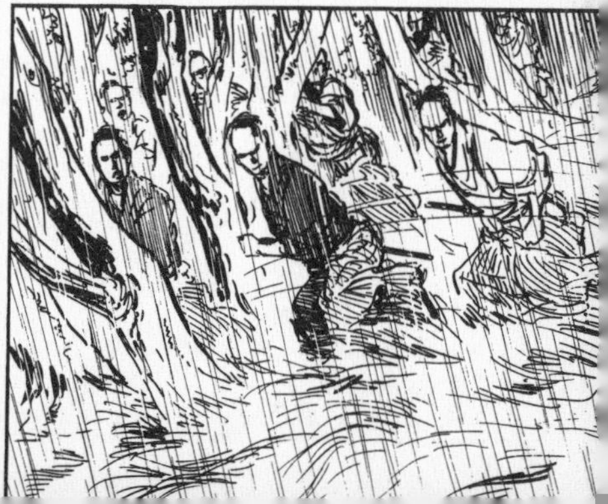
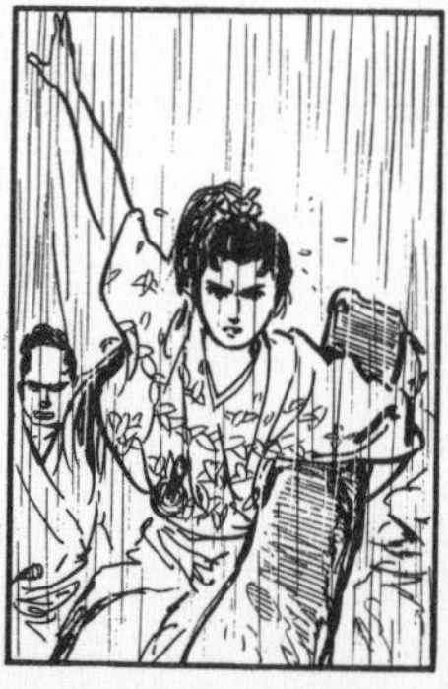

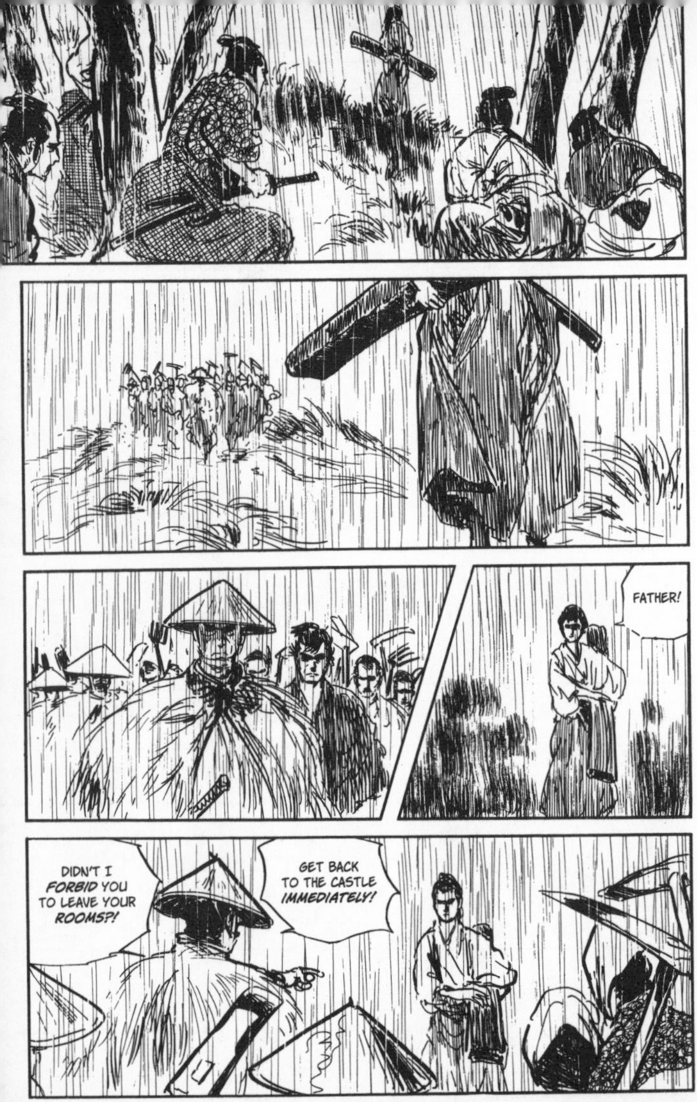
FATHER!
DIDN'T I *FORBID* YOU TO LEAVE YOUR *ROOMS?!*
GET BACK TO THE CASTLE *IMMEDIATELY!*

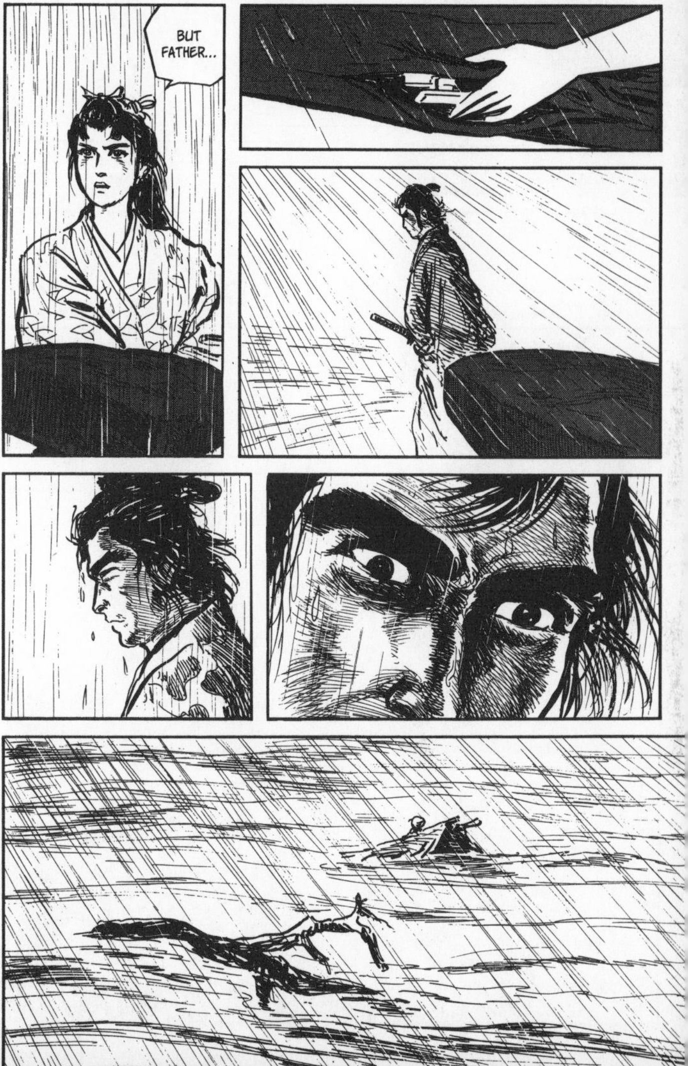
BUT FATHER...

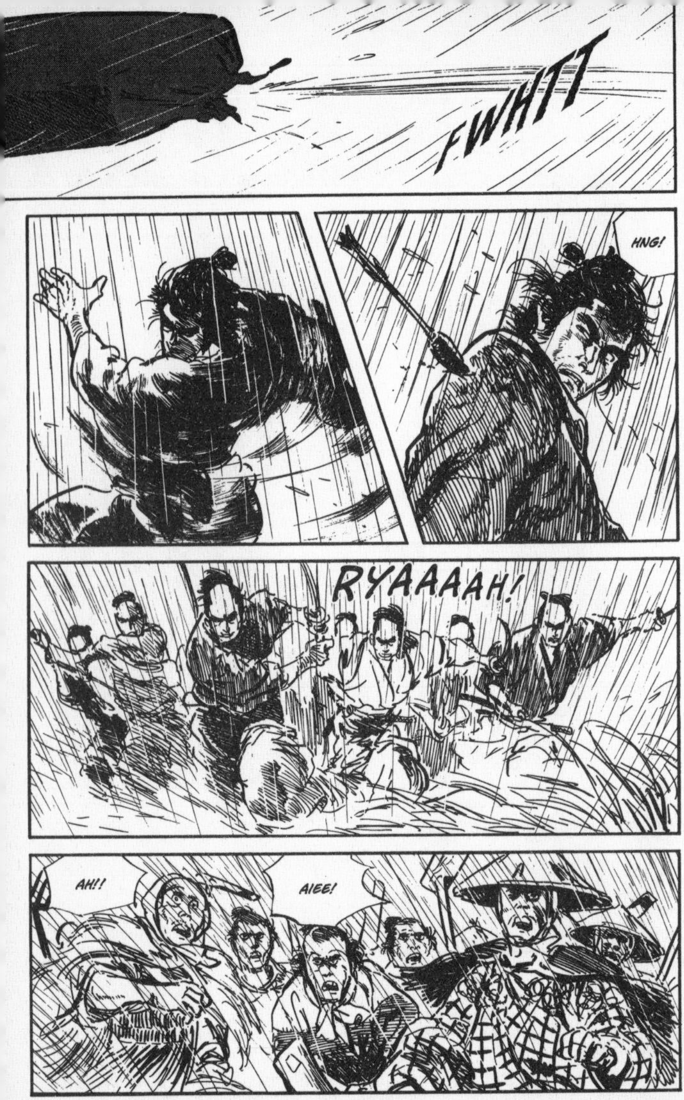
FWHTT
HNG!
RYAAAAH!
AH!!
AIEE!

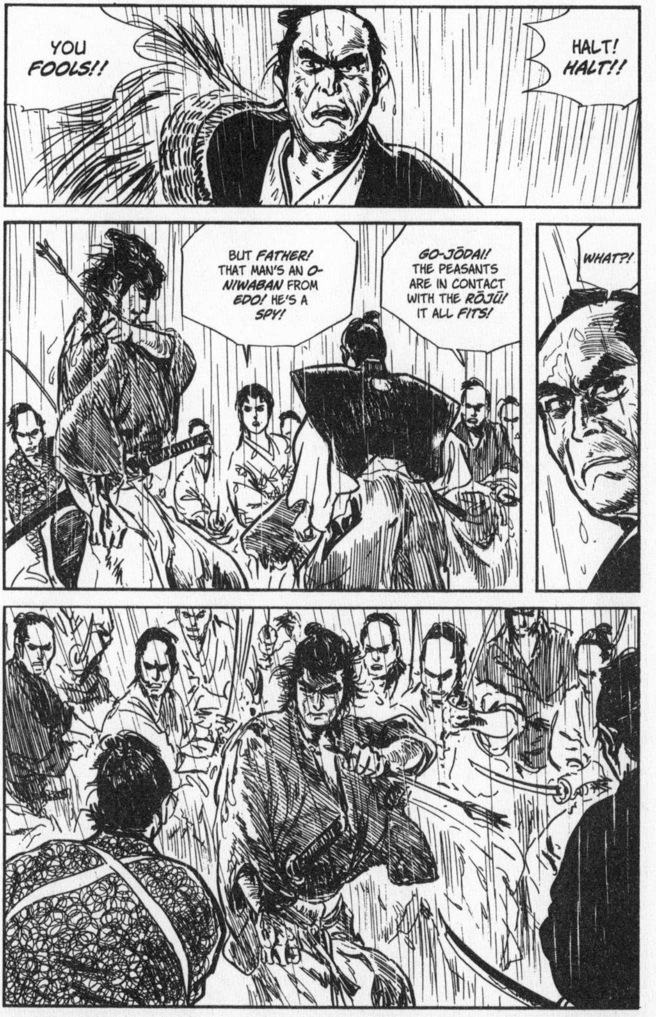
YOU FOOLS!!
HALT! HALT!!
BUT FATHER! THAT MAN'S AN O-NIWABAN FROM EDO! HE'S A SPY!
GO-JŌDAI! THE PEASANTS ARE IN CONTACT WITH THE RŌJŪ! IT ALL FITS!
WHAT?!

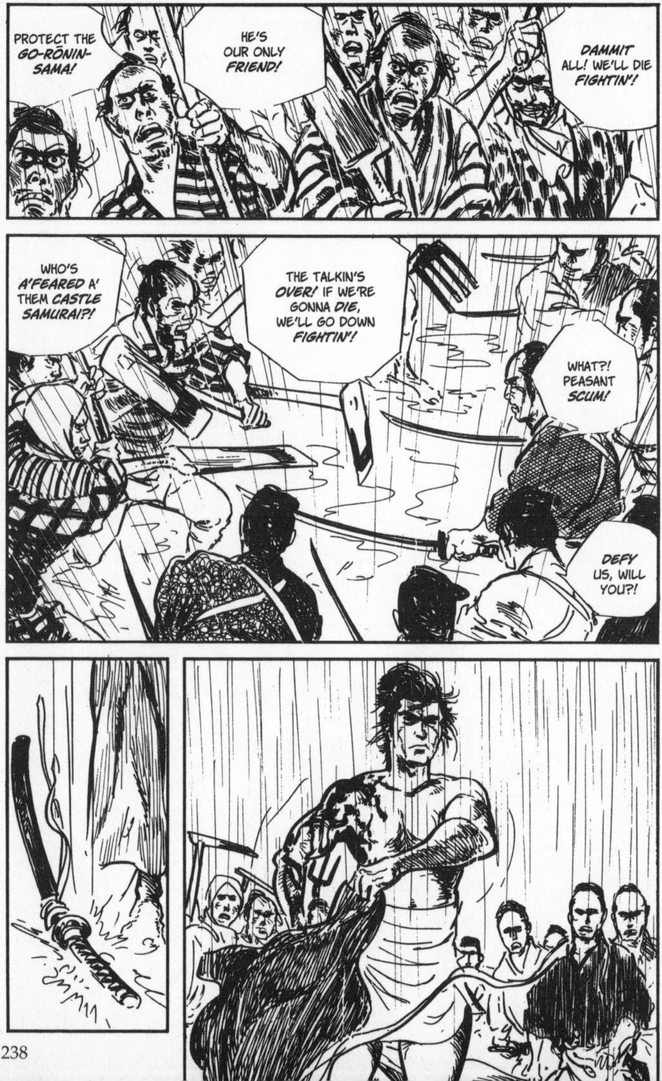
PROTECT THE GO-RŌNIN-SAMA!
HE'S OUR ONLY FRIEND!
DAMMIT ALL! WE'LL DIE FIGHTIN'!
WHO'S A'FEARED A' THEM CASTLE SAMURAI?!
THE TALKIN'S OVER! IF WE'RE GONNA DIE, WE'LL GO DOWN FIGHTIN'!
WHAT?! PEASANT SCUM!
DEFY US, WILL YOU?!

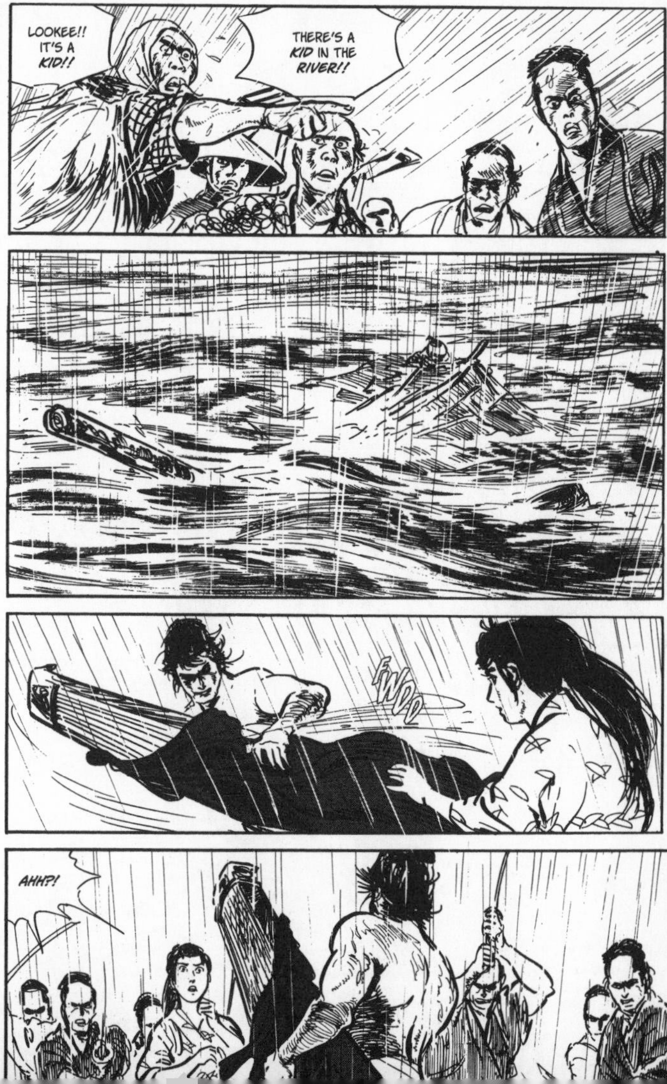
LOOKEE!! IT'S A KID!!
THERE'S A KID IN THE RIVER!!
FWOO
AHH?!

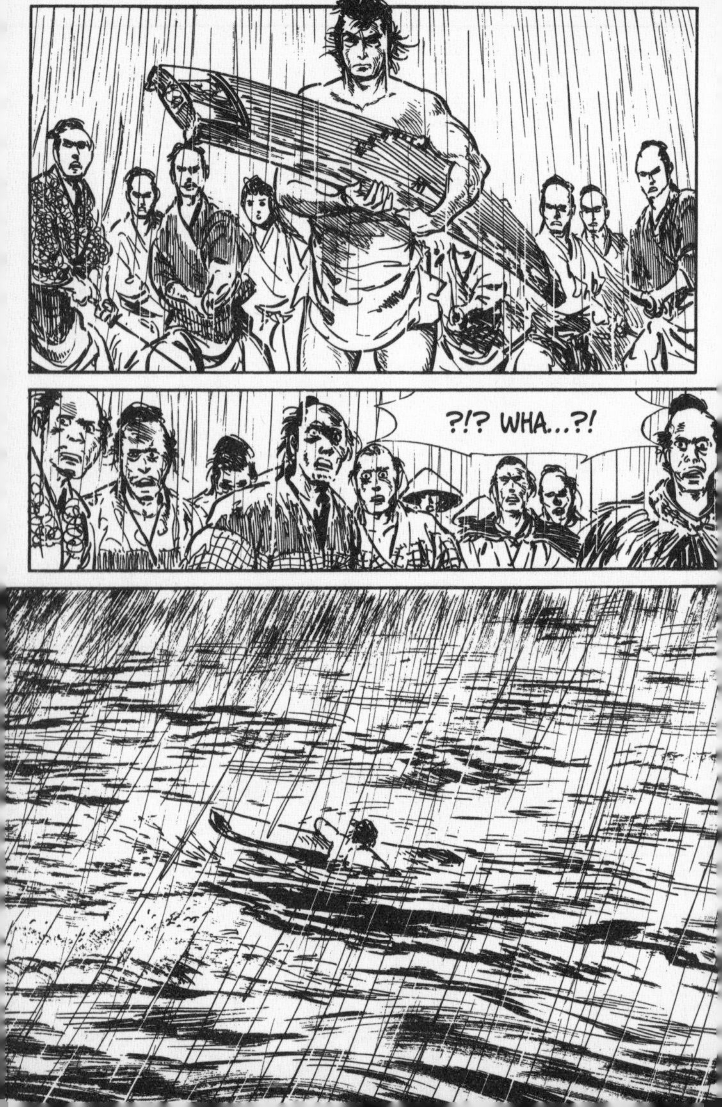
?!? WHA...?!

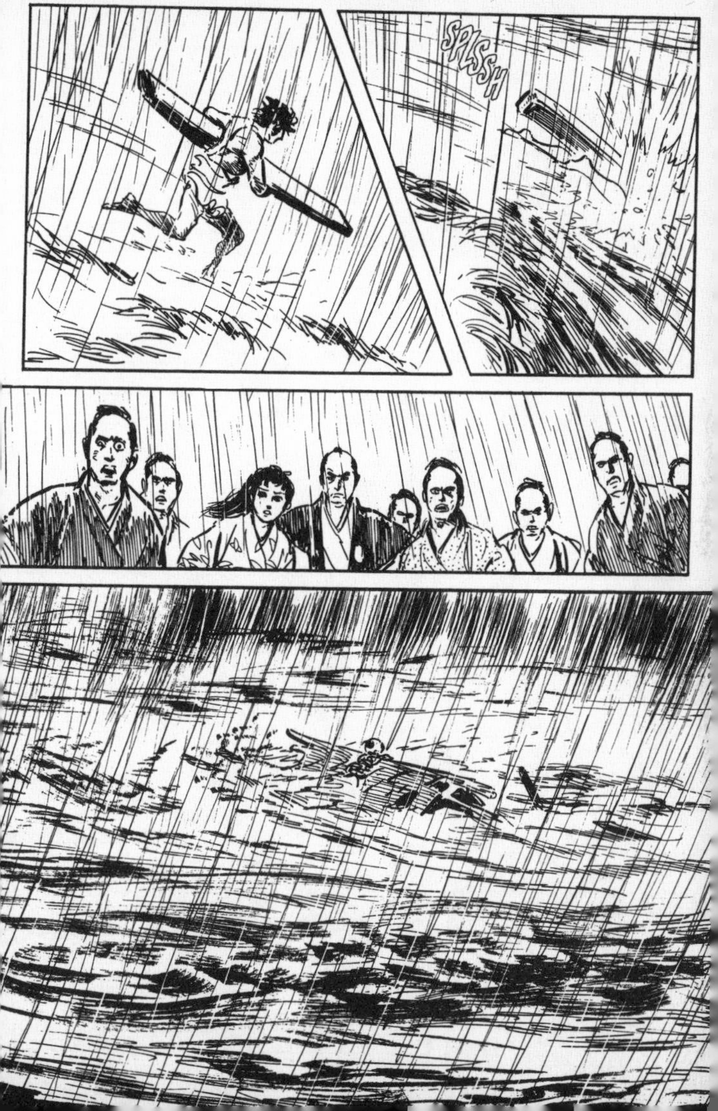
SPLSSH

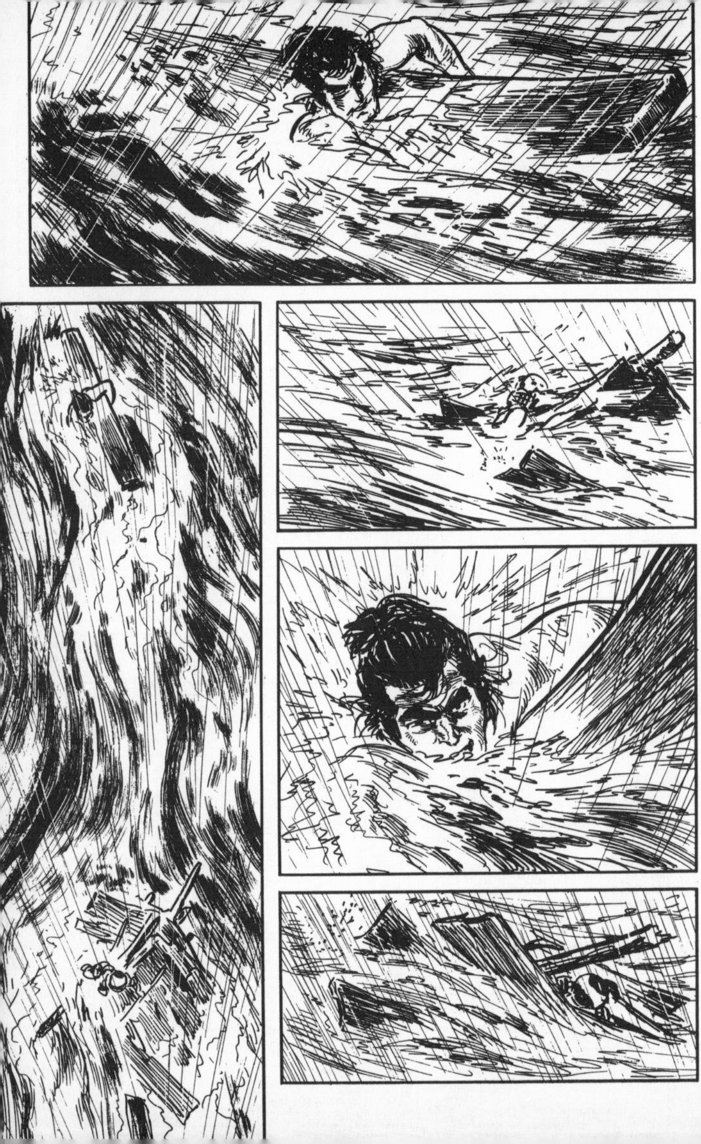

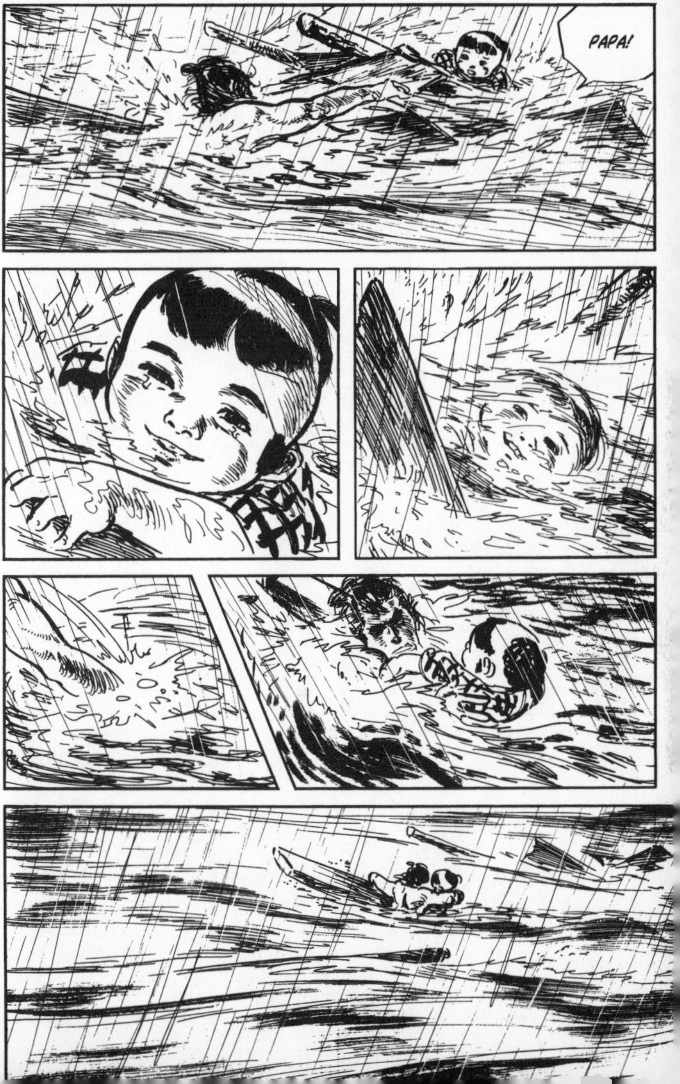
PAPA!

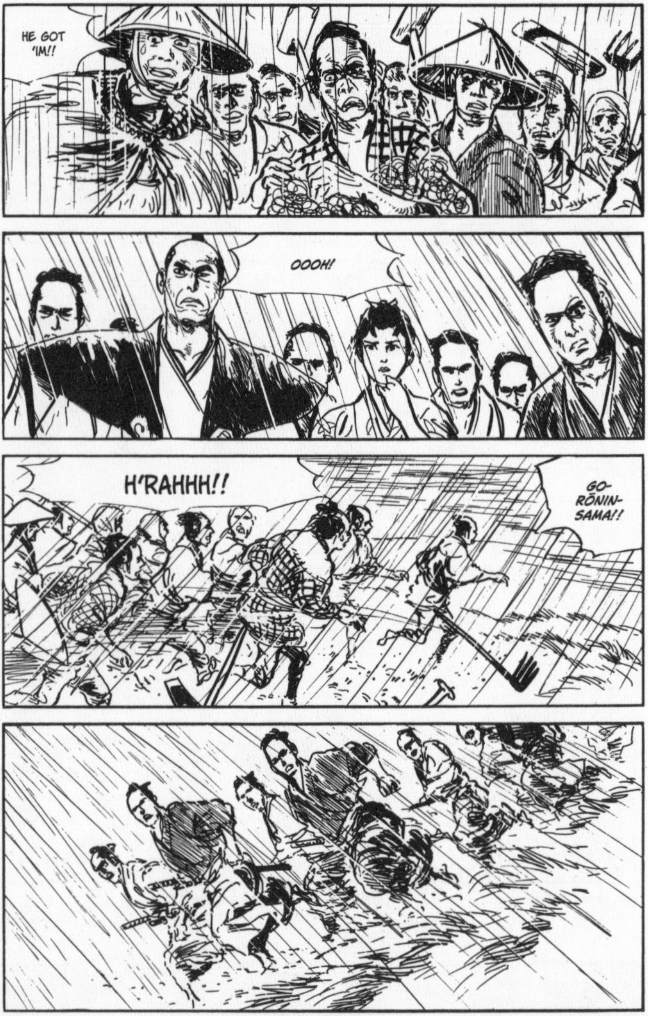
HE GOT 'IM!!
OOOH!
H'RAHHH!!
GO-RŌNIN-SAMA!!

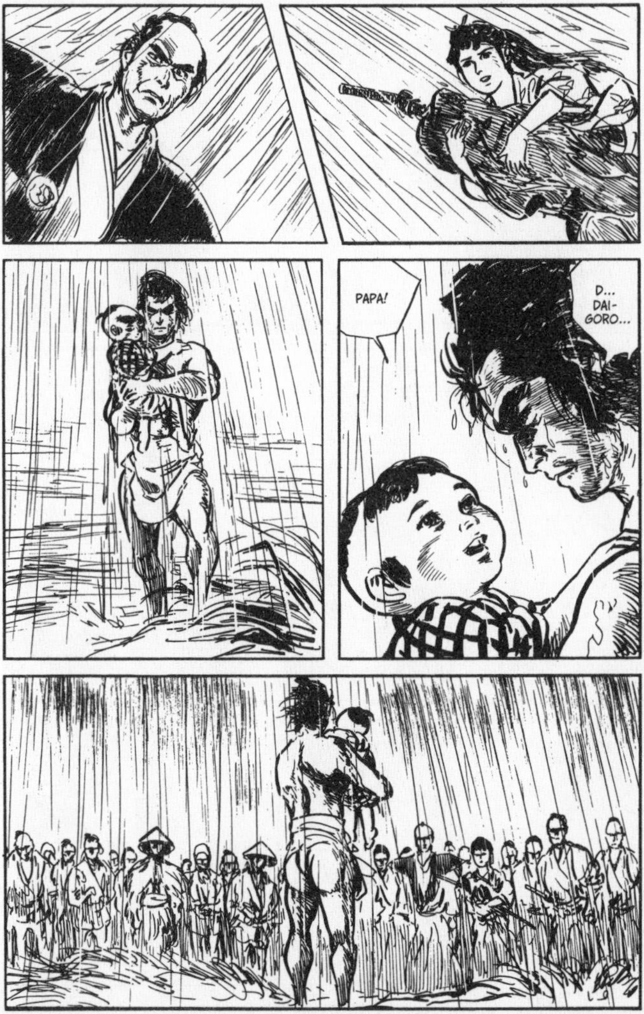
PAPA!
D... DAI-GORO...

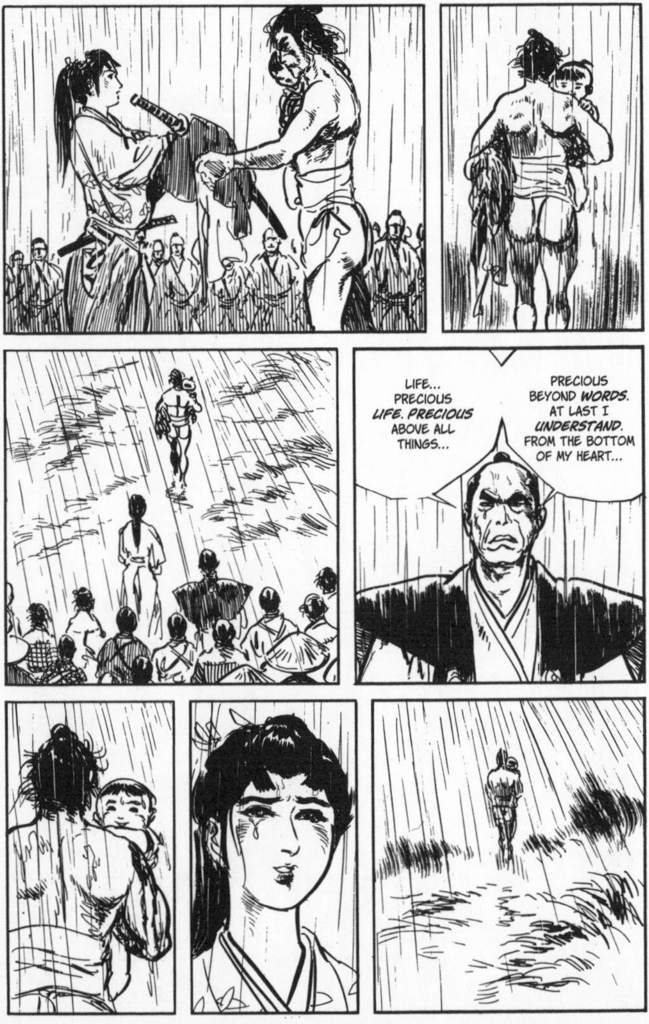
LIFE... PRECIOUS LIFE. PRECIOUS ABOVE ALL THINGS...
PRECIOUS BEYOND WORDS. AT LAST I UNDERSTAND. FROM THE BOTTOM OF MY HEART...

the fifty-eighth

A Poem for the Grave

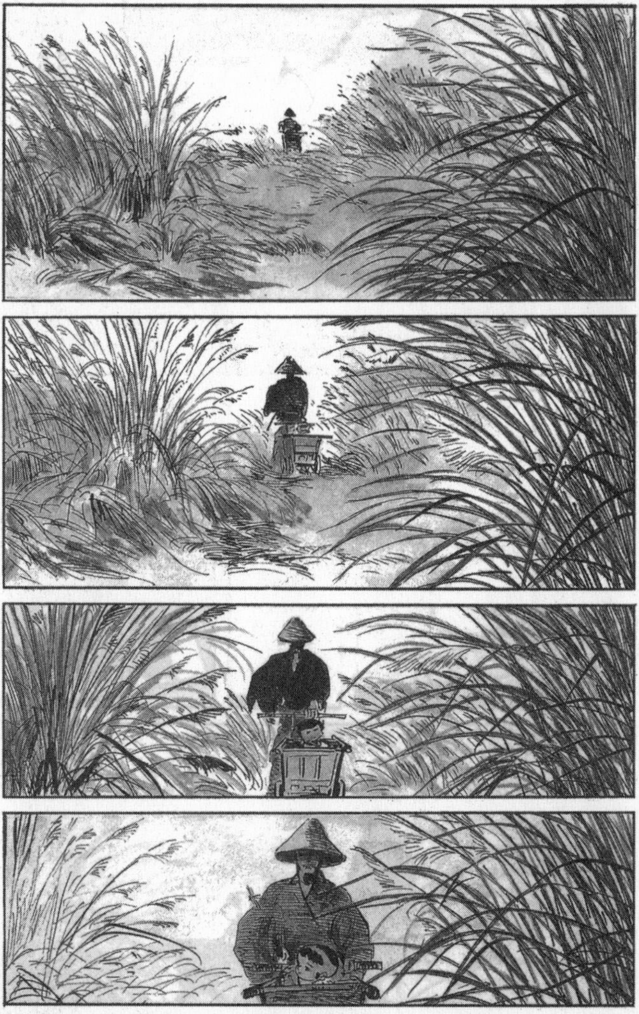

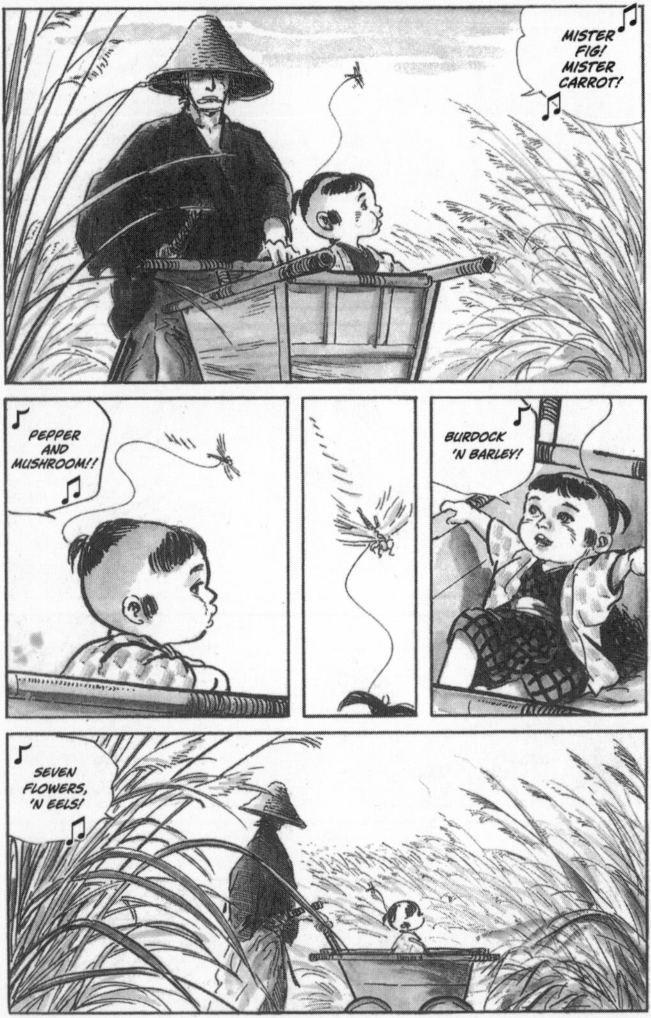
MISTER FIG! MISTER CARROT!
PEPPER AND MUSHROOM!!
BURDOCK 'N BARLEY!
SEVEN FLOWERS, 'N EELS!

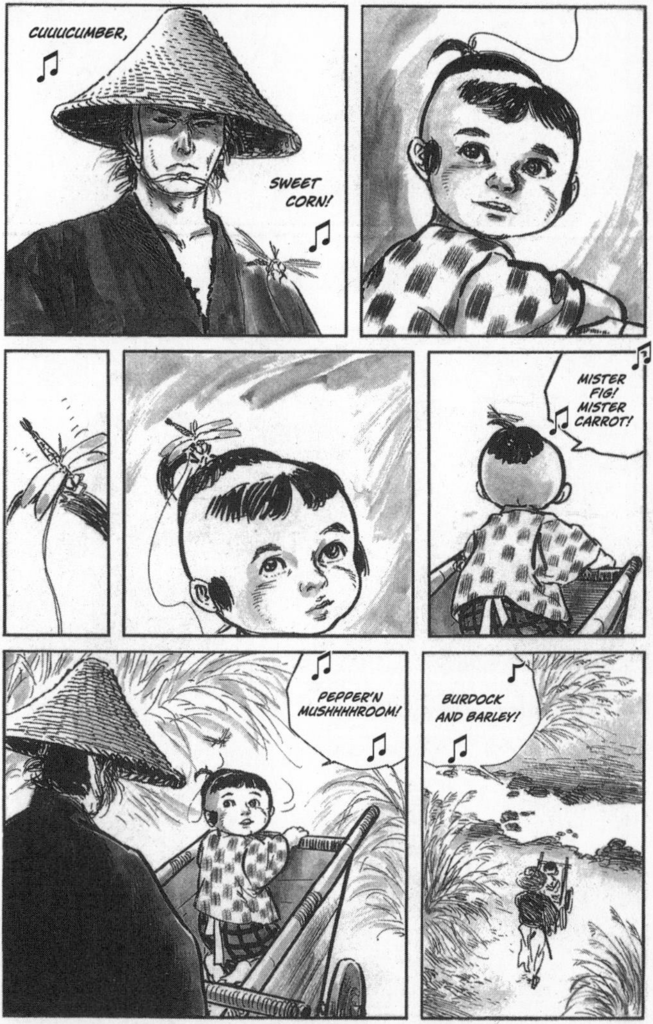
CUUUCUMBER,
SWEET CORN!
MISTER FIG! MISTER CARROT!
PEPPER'N MUSHHHHROOM!
BURDOCK AND BARLEY!

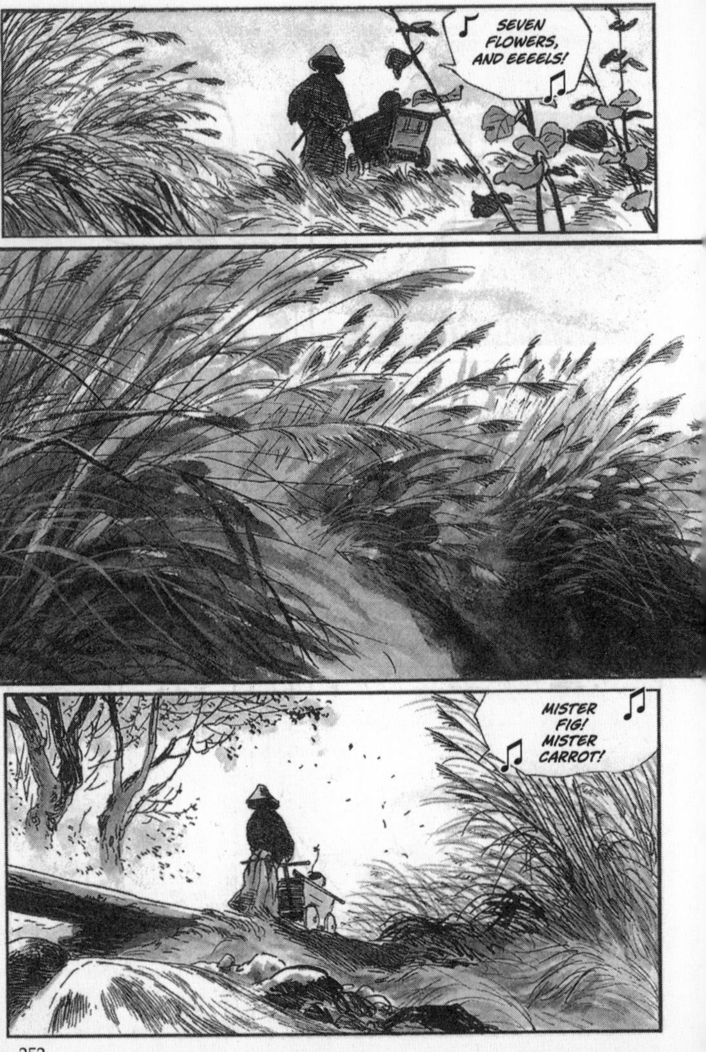
SEVEN FLOWERS, AND EEEELS!
MISTER FIG! MISTER CARROT!

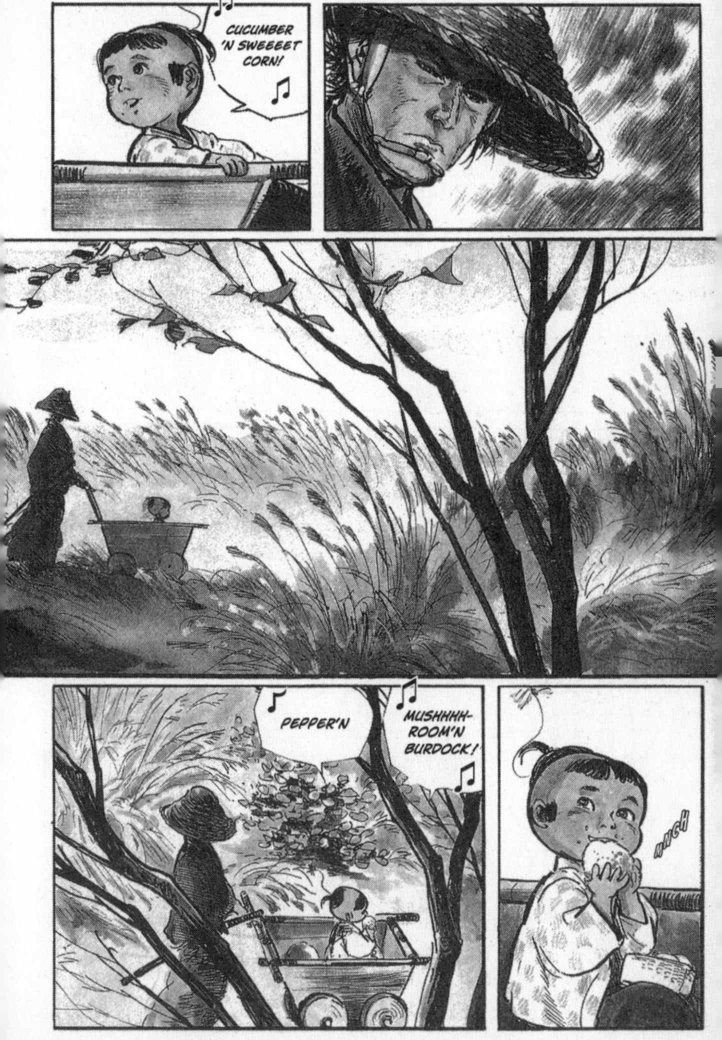
CUCUMBER 'N SWEEEET CORN!
PEPPER'N
MUSHHHH-ROOM'N BURDOCK!
MNCH

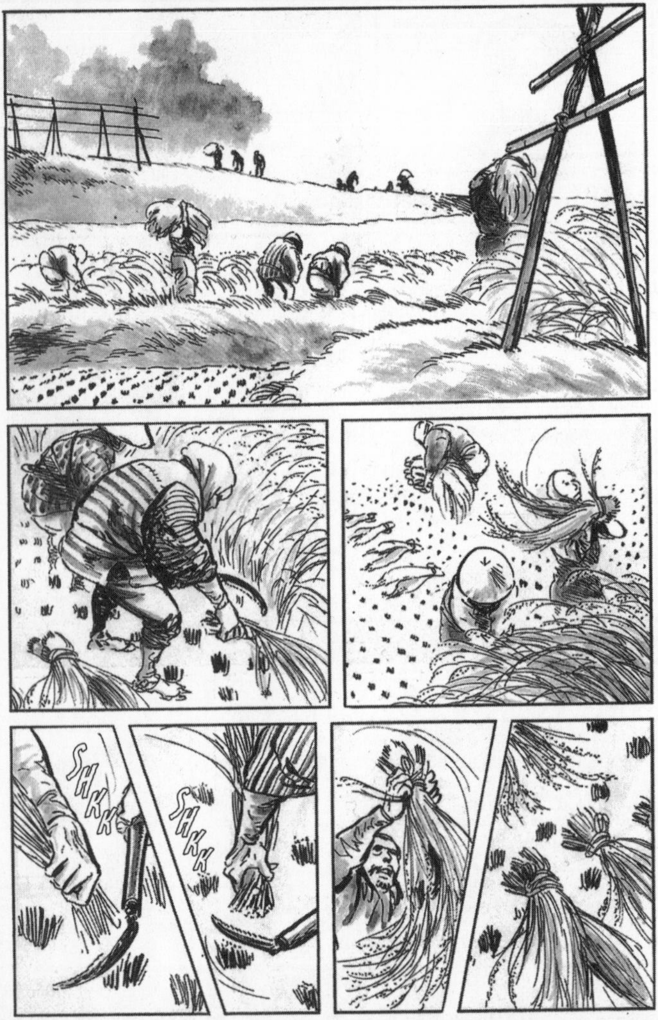
SHKK
SHKK

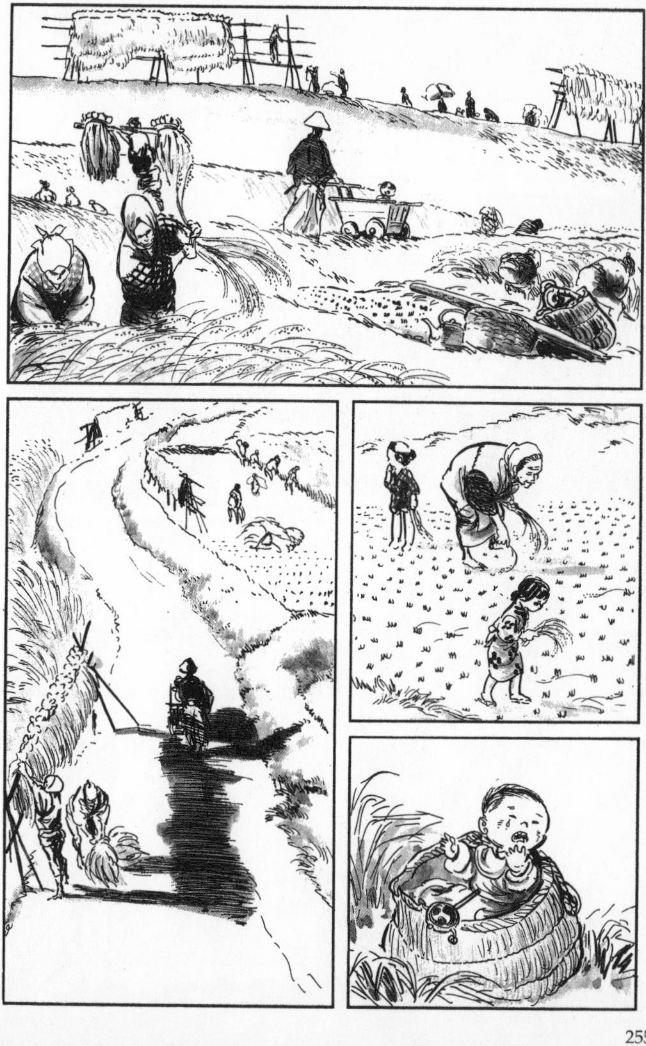

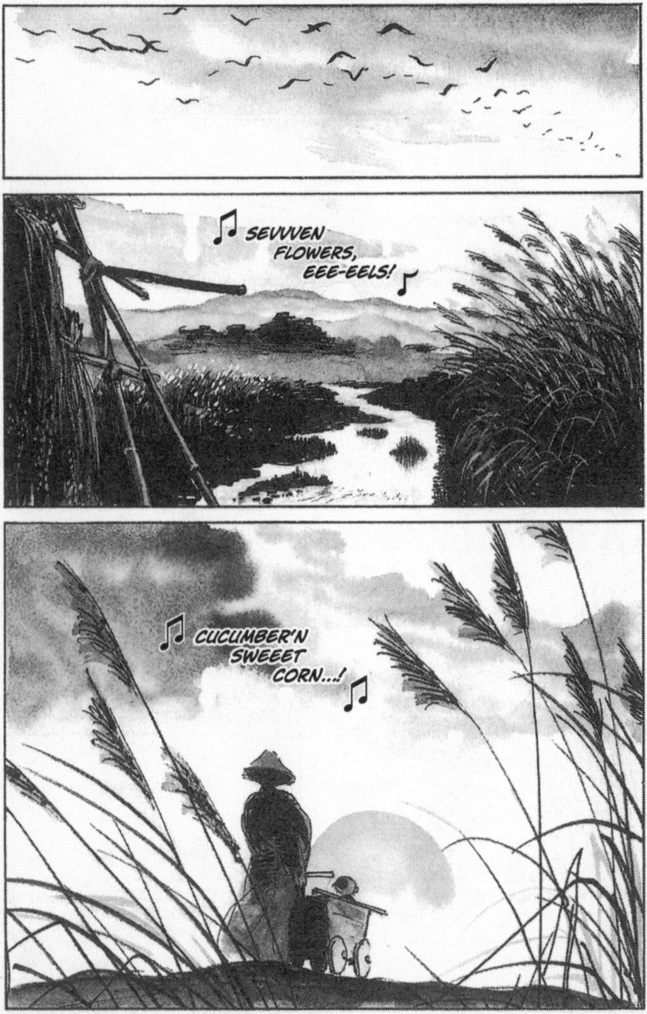
SEVUVEN FLOWERS, EEE-EELS!
CUCUMBER'N SWEEET CORN...!

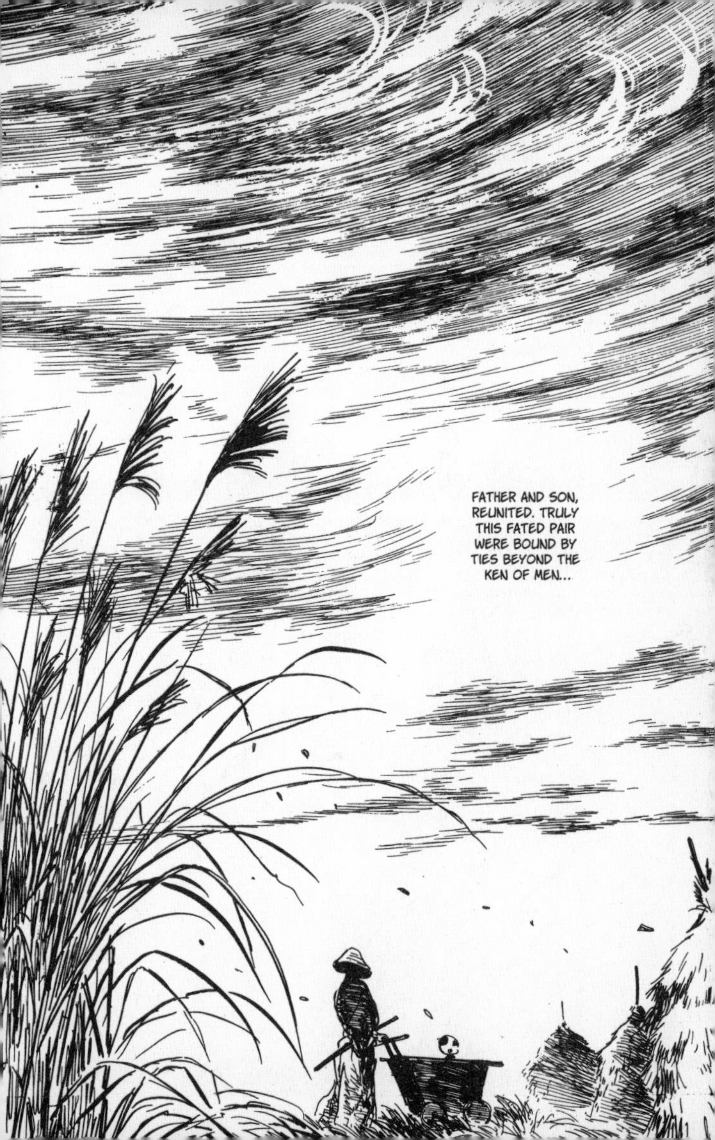
FATHER AND SON, REUNITED. TRULY THIS FATED PAIR WERE BOUND BY TIES BEYOND THE KEN OF MEN...

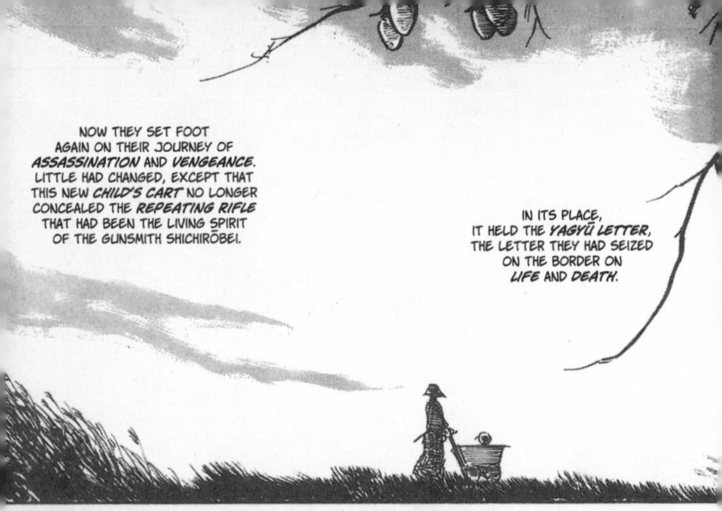
NOW THEY SET FOOT AGAIN ON THEIR JOURNEY OF ASSASSINATION AND VENGEANCE. LITTLE HAD CHANGED, EXCEPT THAT THIS NEW CHILD'S CART NO LONGER CONCEALED THE REPEATING RIFLE THAT HAD BEEN THE LIVING SPIRIT OF THE GUNSMITH SHICHIRŌBEI.
IN ITS PLACE, IT HELD THE YAGYŪ LETTER, THE LETTER THEY HAD SEIZED ON THE BORDER ON LIFE AND DEATH.

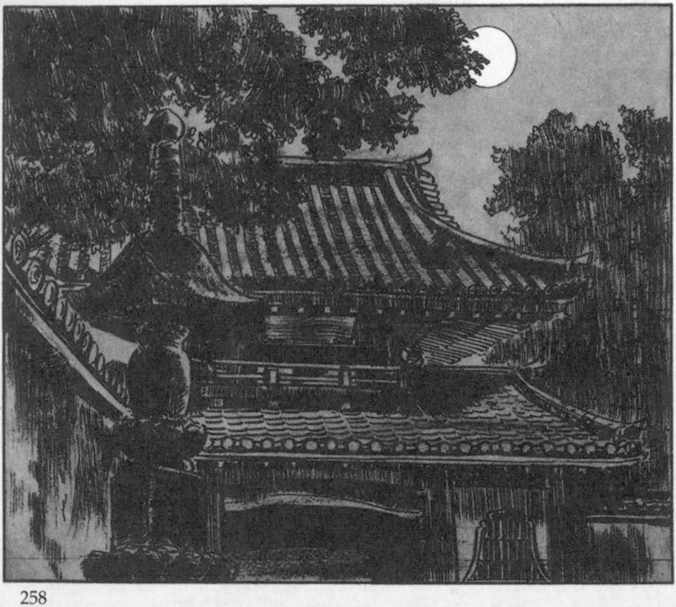

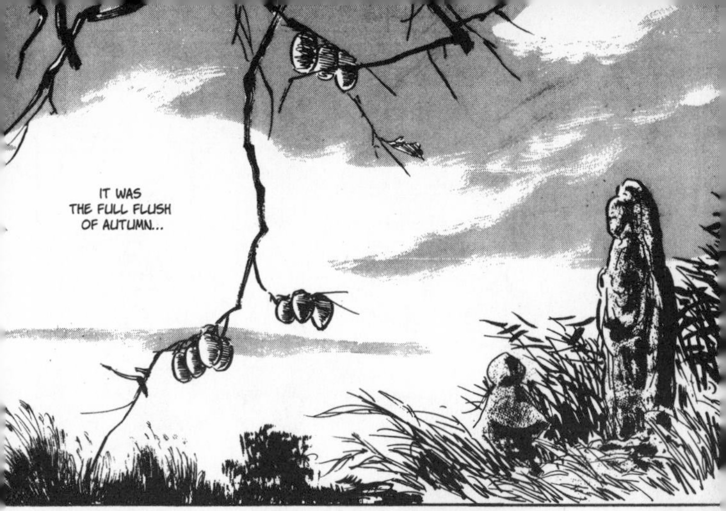
IT WAS THE FULL FLUSH OF AUTUMN...

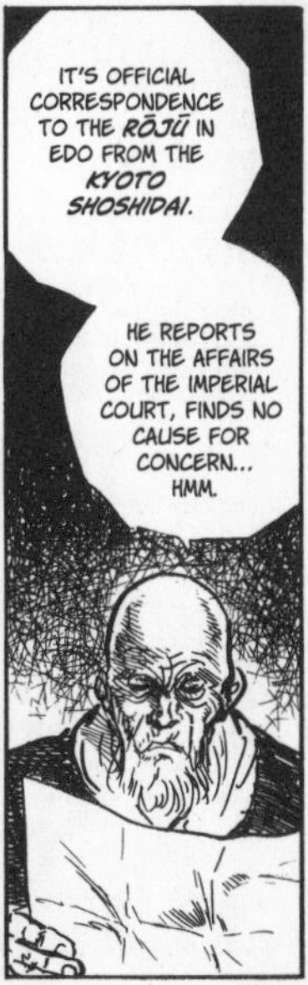
IT'S OFFICIAL CORRESPONDENCE TO THE *RŌJŪ* IN EDO FROM THE *KYOTO SHOSHIDAI.*
HE REPORTS ON THE AFFAIRS OF THE IMPERIAL COURT, FINDS NO CAUSE FOR CONCERN... HMM.

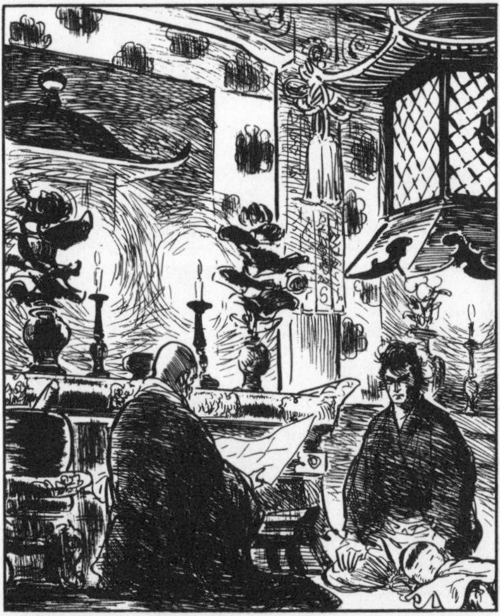

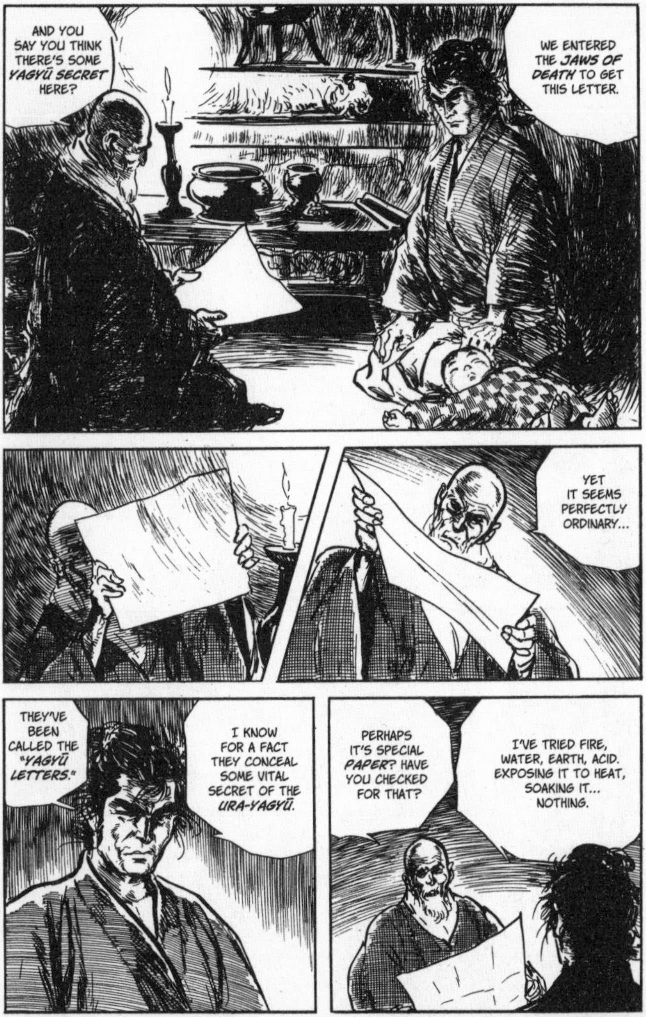
AND YOU SAY YOU THINK THERE'S SOME *YAGYŪ SECRET* HERE?
WE ENTERED THE ***JAWS OF DEATH*** TO GET THIS LETTER.
YET IT SEEMS PERFECTLY ORDINARY...
THEY'VE BEEN CALLED THE "*YAGYŪ LETTERS*."
I KNOW FOR A FACT THEY CONCEAL SOME VITAL SECRET OF THE *URA-YAGYŪ*.
PERHAPS IT'S SPECIAL *PAPER*? HAVE YOU CHECKED FOR THAT?
I'VE TRIED FIRE, WATER, EARTH, ACID. EXPOSING IT TO HEAT, SOAKING IT... NOTHING.

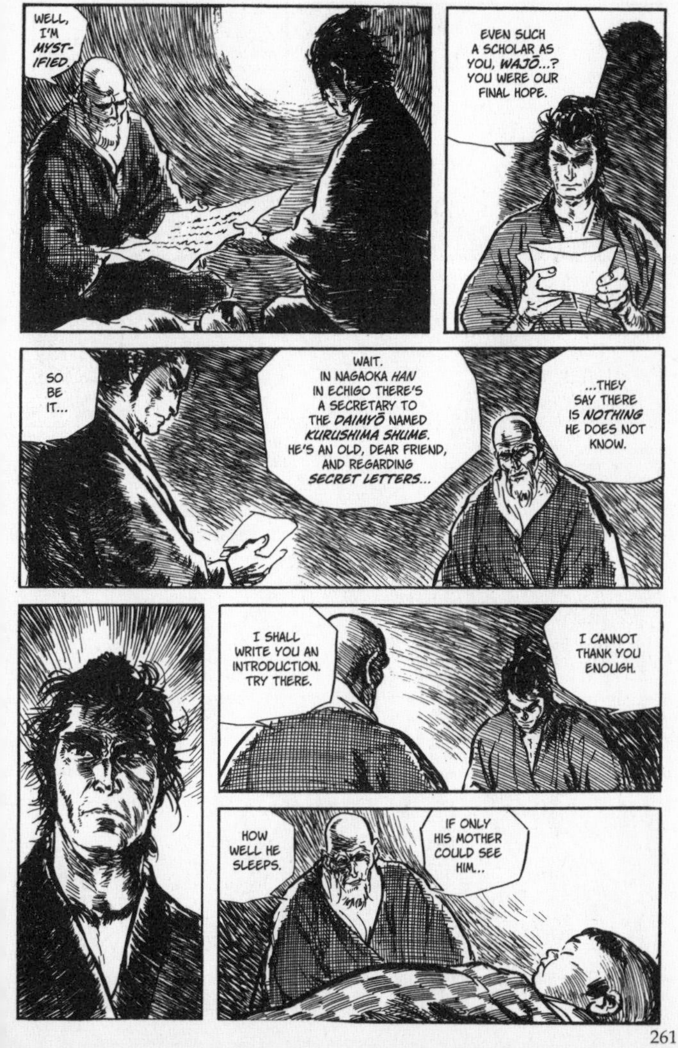
WELL, I'M MYST-IFIED.
EVEN SUCH A SCHOLAR AS YOU, WAJŌ...? YOU WERE OUR FINAL HOPE.
SO BE IT...
WAIT. IN NAGAOKA HAN IN ECHIGO THERE'S A SECRETARY TO THE DAIMYŌ NAMED KURUSHIMA SHUME. HE'S AN OLD, DEAR FRIEND, AND REGARDING SECRET LETTERS...
...THEY SAY THERE IS NOTHING HE DOES NOT KNOW.
I SHALL WRITE YOU AN INTRODUCTION. TRY THERE.
I CANNOT THANK YOU ENOUGH.
HOW WELL HE SLEEPS.
IF ONLY HIS MOTHER COULD SEE HIM..

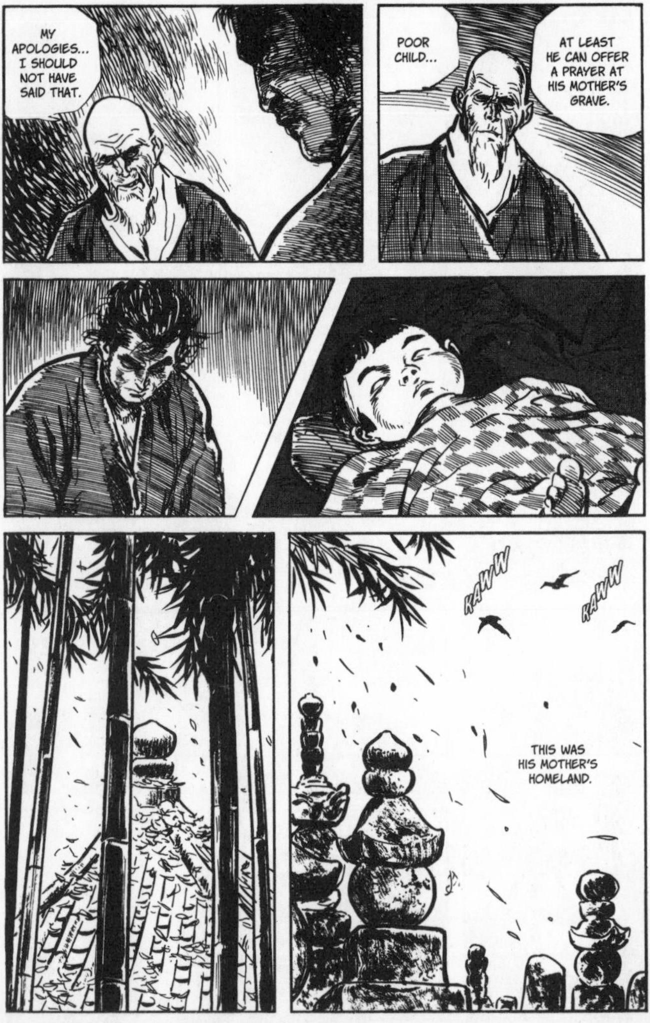
MY APOLOGIES... I SHOULD NOT HAVE SAID THAT.
POOR CHILD...
AT LEAST HE CAN OFFER A PRAYER AT HIS MOTHER'S GRAVE.
KAWW
KAWW
THIS WAS HIS MOTHER'S HOMELAND.

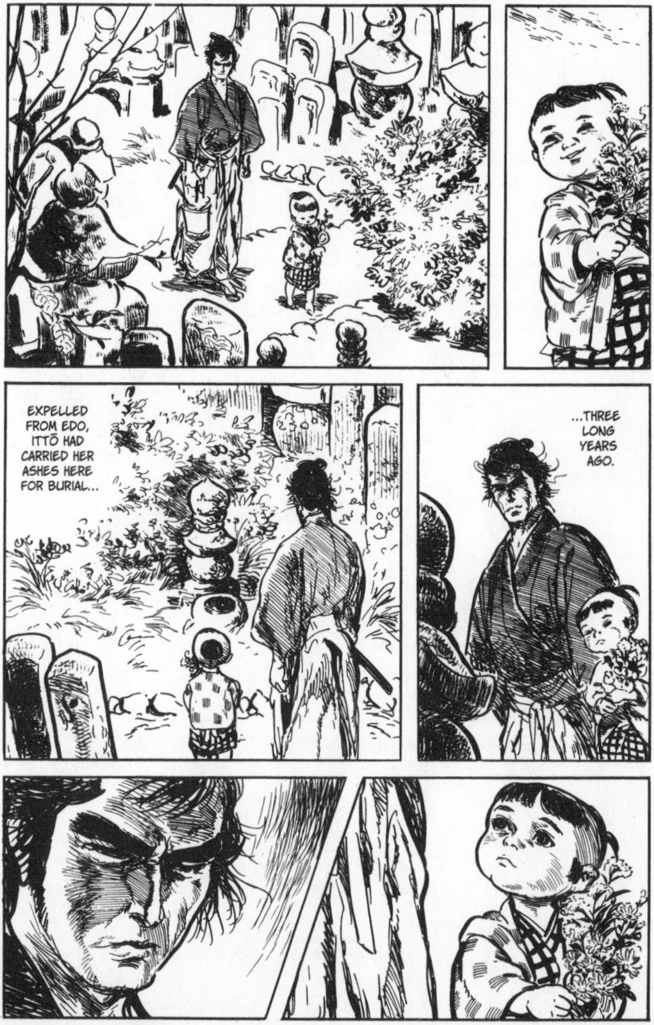

EXPELLED FROM EDO, ITTŌ HAD CARRIED HER ASHES HERE FOR BURIAL...
...THREE LONG YEARS AGO.

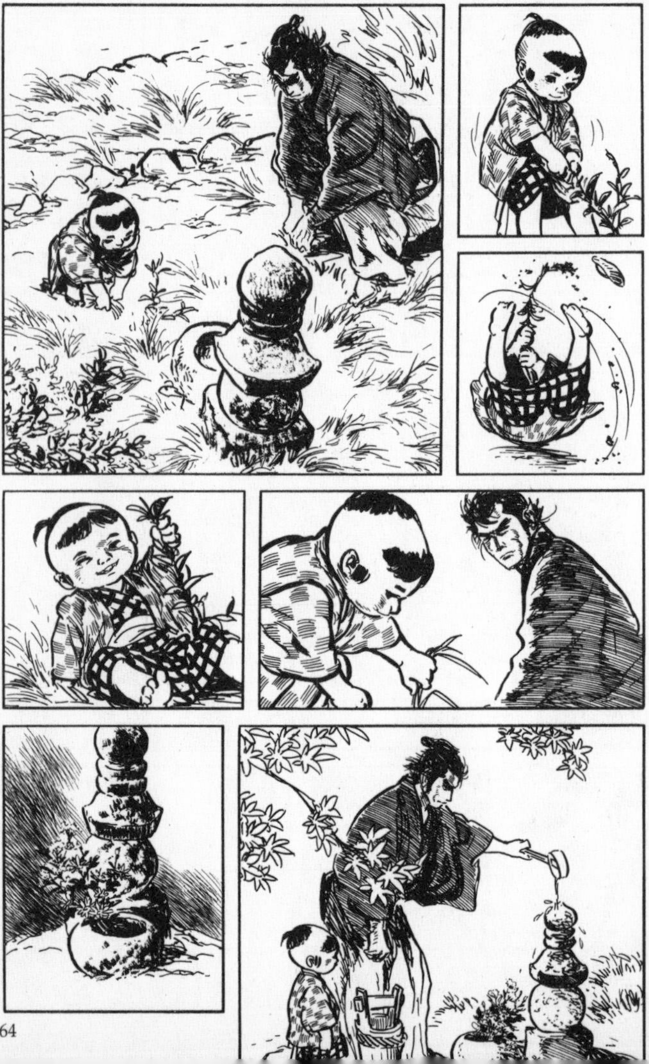

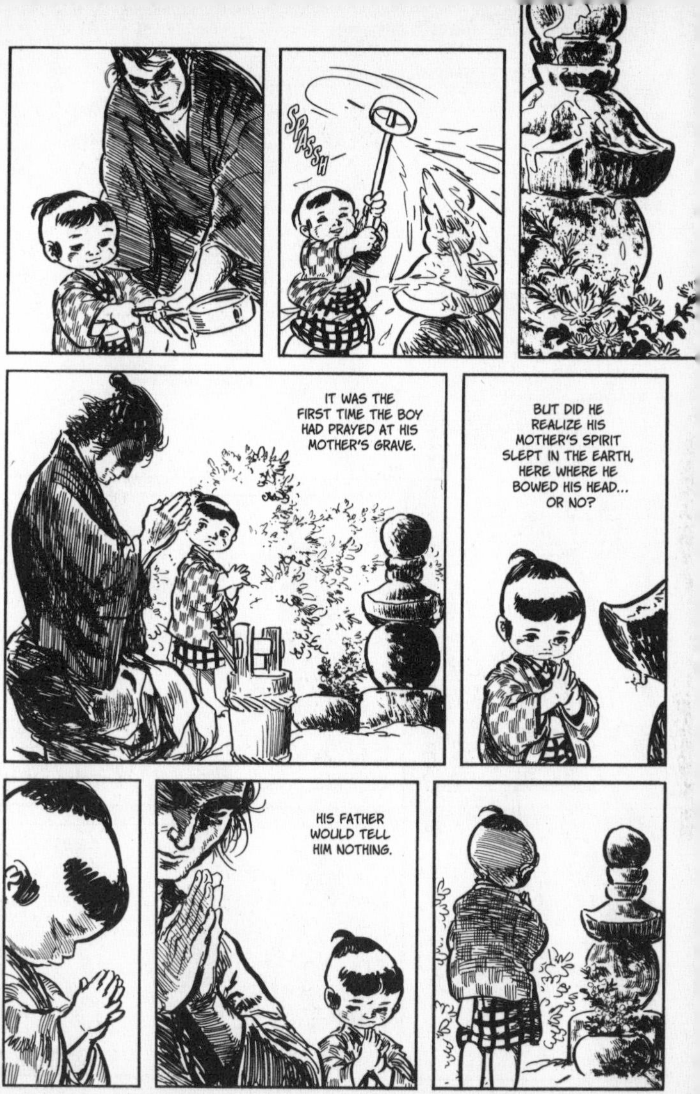
SPASSH
IT WAS THE FIRST TIME THE BOY HAD PRAYED AT HIS MOTHER'S GRAVE.
BUT DID HE REALIZE HIS MOTHER'S SPIRIT SLEPT IN THE EARTH, HERE WHERE HE BOWED HIS HEAD... OR NO?
HIS FATHER WOULD TELL HIM NOTHING.

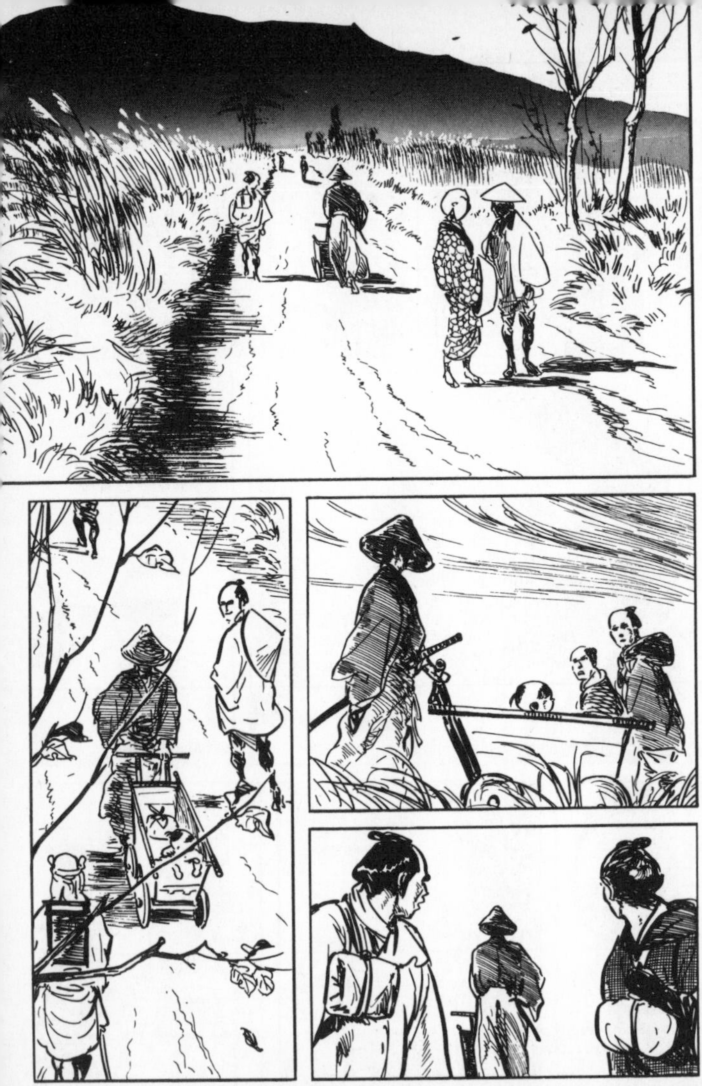

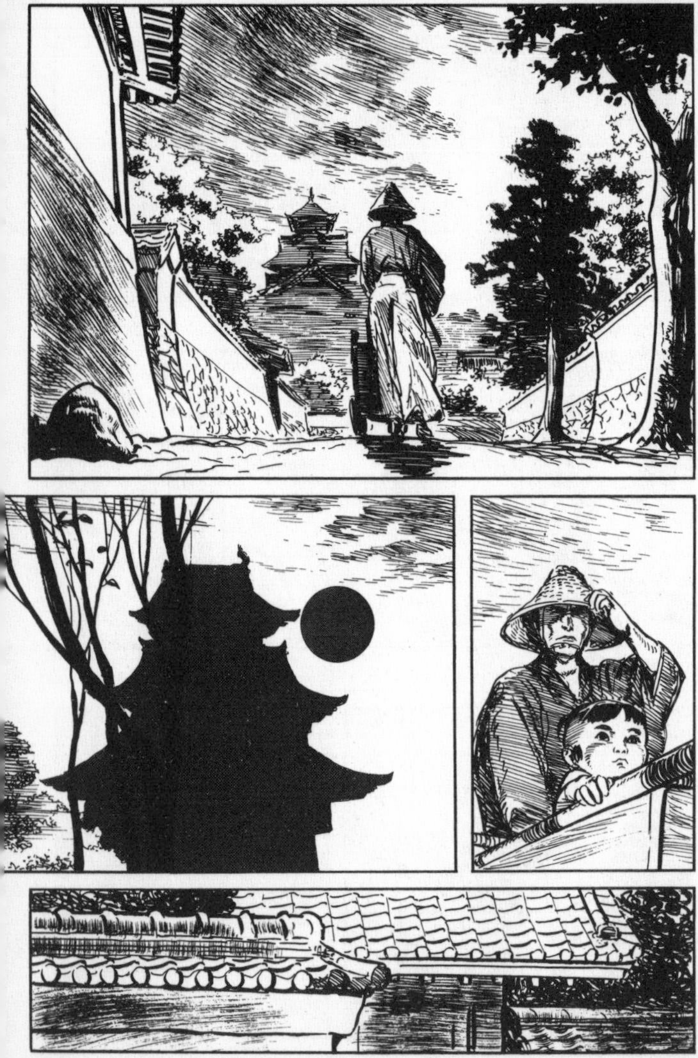

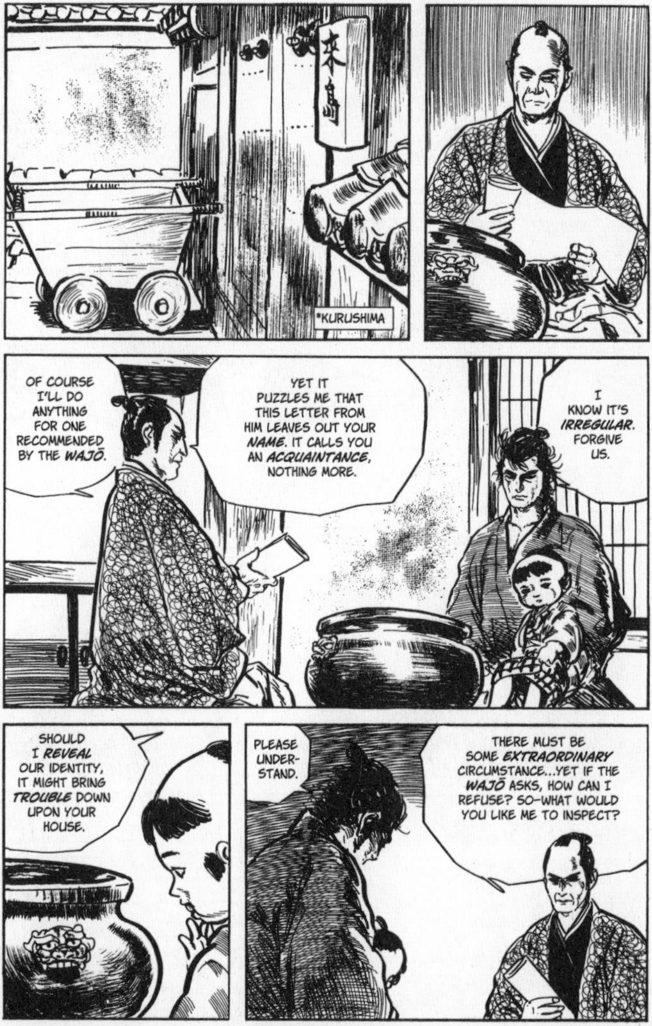

*KURUSHIMA
OF COURSE I'LL DO ANYTHING FOR ONE RECOMMENDED BY THE WAJŌ.
YET IT PUZZLES ME THAT THIS LETTER FROM HIM LEAVES OUT YOUR NAME. IT CALLS YOU AN ACQUAINTANCE, NOTHING MORE.
I KNOW IT'S IRREGULAR. FORGIVE US.
SHOULD I REVEAL OUR IDENTITY, IT MIGHT BRING TROUBLE DOWN UPON YOUR HOUSE.
PLEASE UNDER-STAND.
THERE MUST BE SOME EXTRAORDINARY CIRCUMSTANCE...YET IF THE WAJŌ ASKS, HOW CAN I REFUSE? SO—WHAT WOULD YOU LIKE ME TO INSPECT?

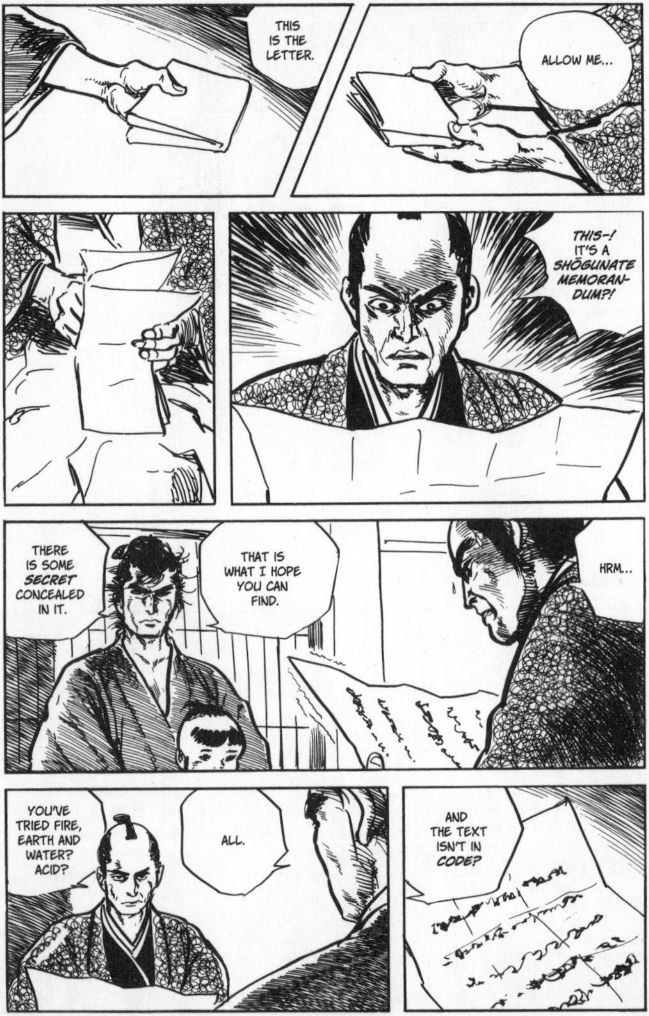
THIS IS THE LETTER.
ALLOW ME...
THIS-! IT'S A SHŌGUNATE MEMORANDUM?!
THERE IS SOME SECRET CONCEALED IN IT.
THAT IS WHAT I HOPE YOU CAN FIND.
HRM...
YOU'VE TRIED FIRE, EARTH AND WATER? ACID?
ALL.
AND THE TEXT ISN'T IN CODE?

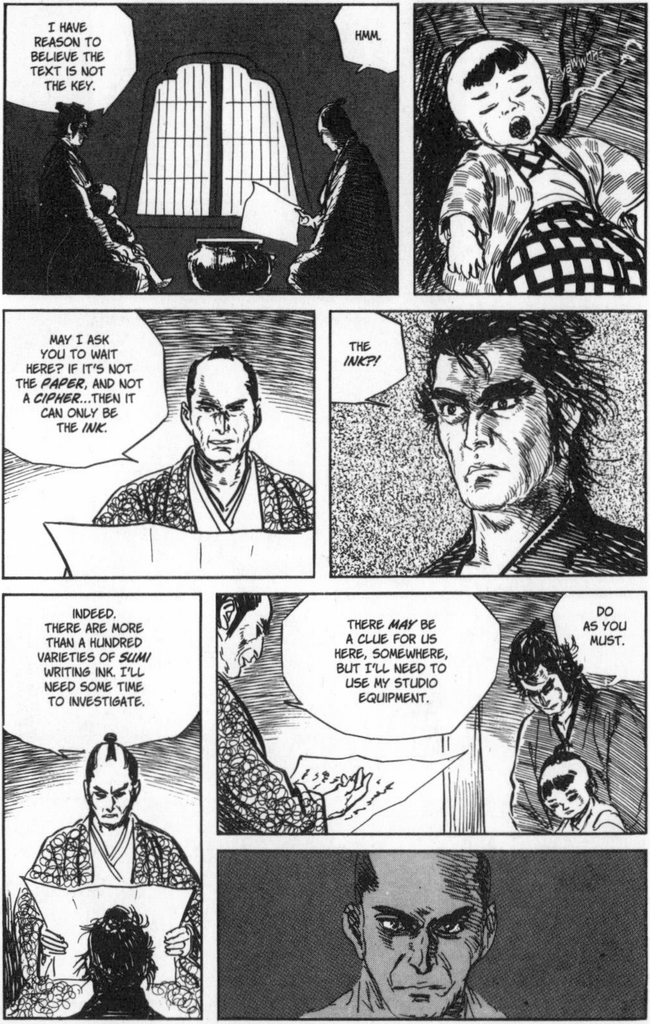
I HAVE REASON TO BELIEVE THE TEXT IS NOT THE KEY.
HMM.
MAY I ASK YOU TO WAIT HERE? IF IT'S NOT THE *PAPER*, AND NOT A *CIPHER*...THEN IT CAN ONLY BE THE *INK*.
THE *INK?!*
INDEED. THERE ARE MORE THAN A HUNDRED VARIETIES OF *SUMI* WRITING INK. I'LL NEED SOME TIME TO INVESTIGATE.
THERE *MAY* BE A CLUE FOR US HERE, SOMEWHERE, BUT I'LL NEED TO USE MY STUDIO EQUIPMENT.
DO AS YOU MUST.

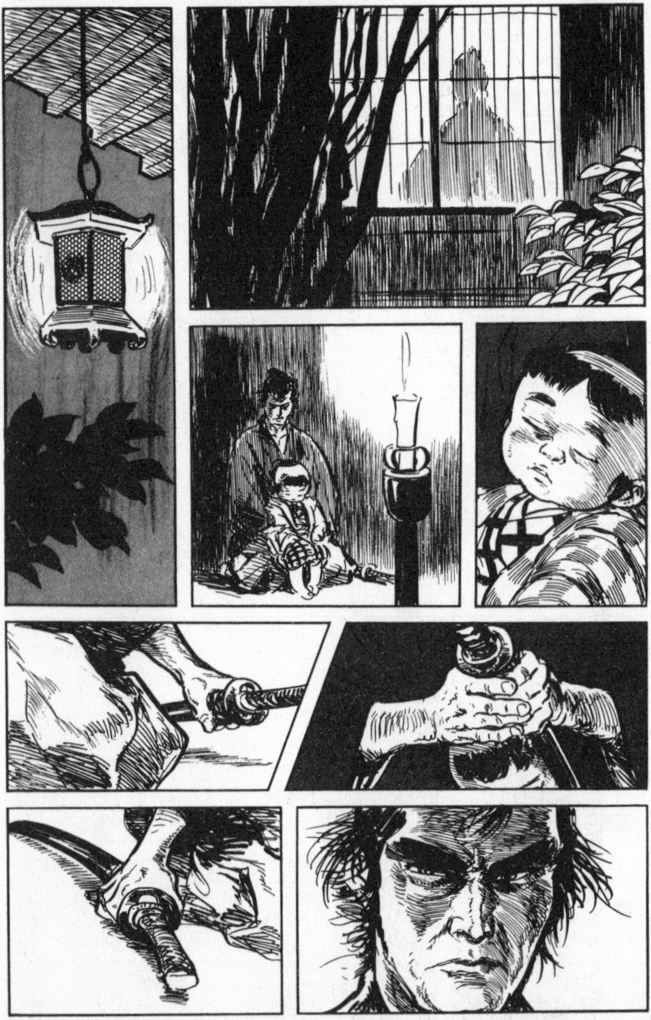

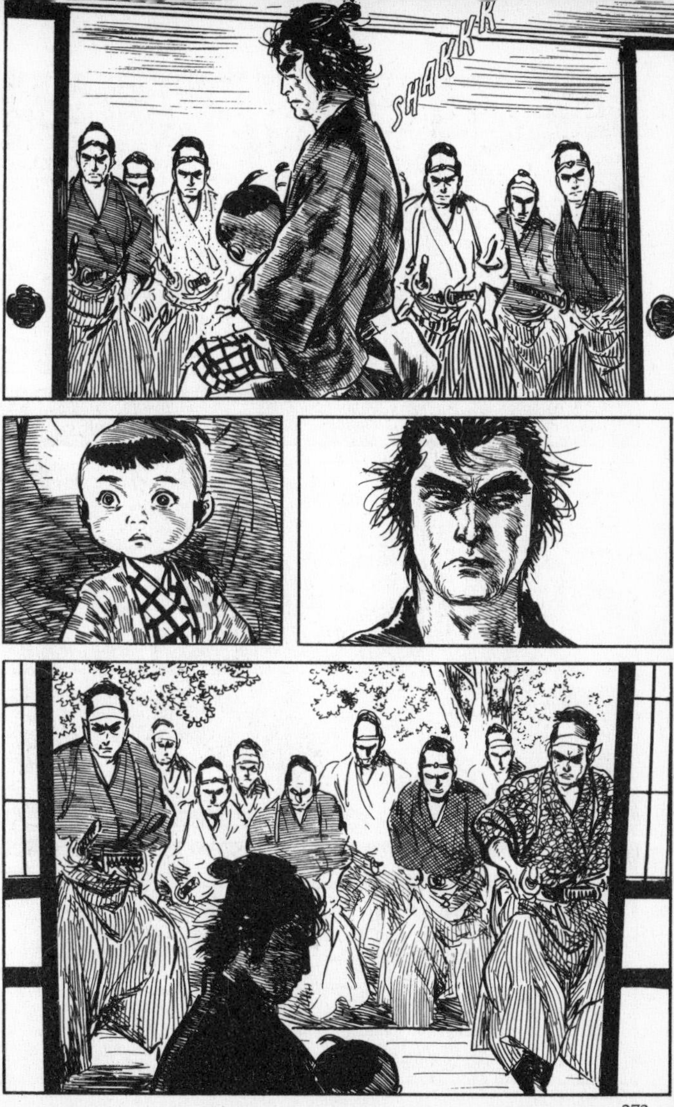
SHAKKK

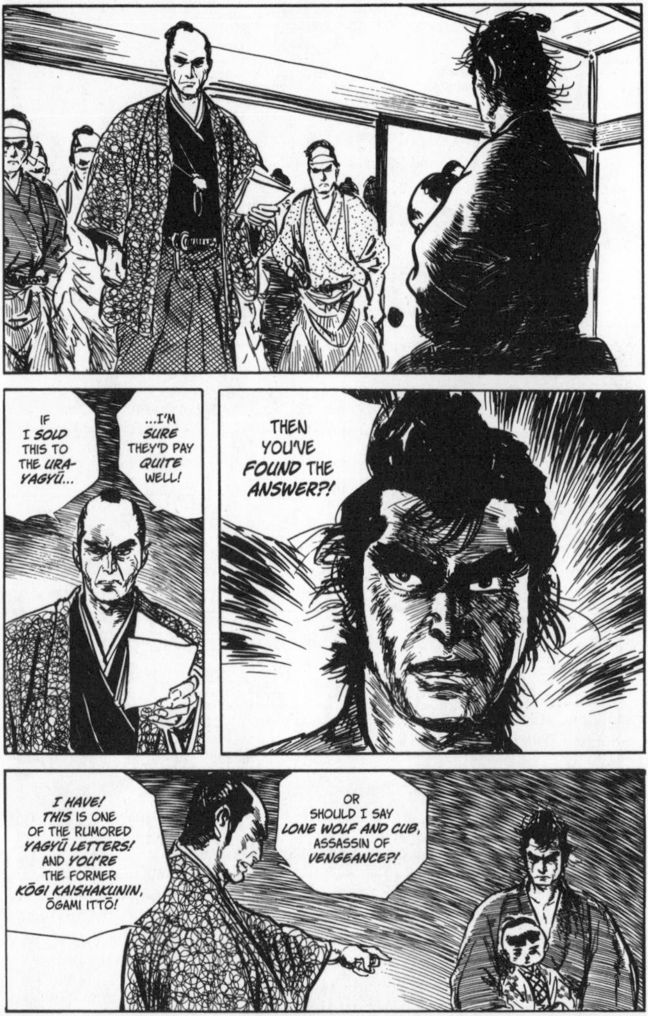
IF I SOLD THIS TO THE URA-YAGYŪ...
...I'M SURE THEY'D PAY QUITE WELL!
THEN YOU'VE FOUND THE ANSWER?!
I HAVE! THIS IS ONE OF THE RUMORED YAGYŪ LETTERS! AND YOU'RE THE FORMER KŌGI KAISHAKUNIN, ŌGAMI ITTŌ!
OR SHOULD I SAY LONE WOLF AND CUB, ASSASSIN OF VENGEANCE?!

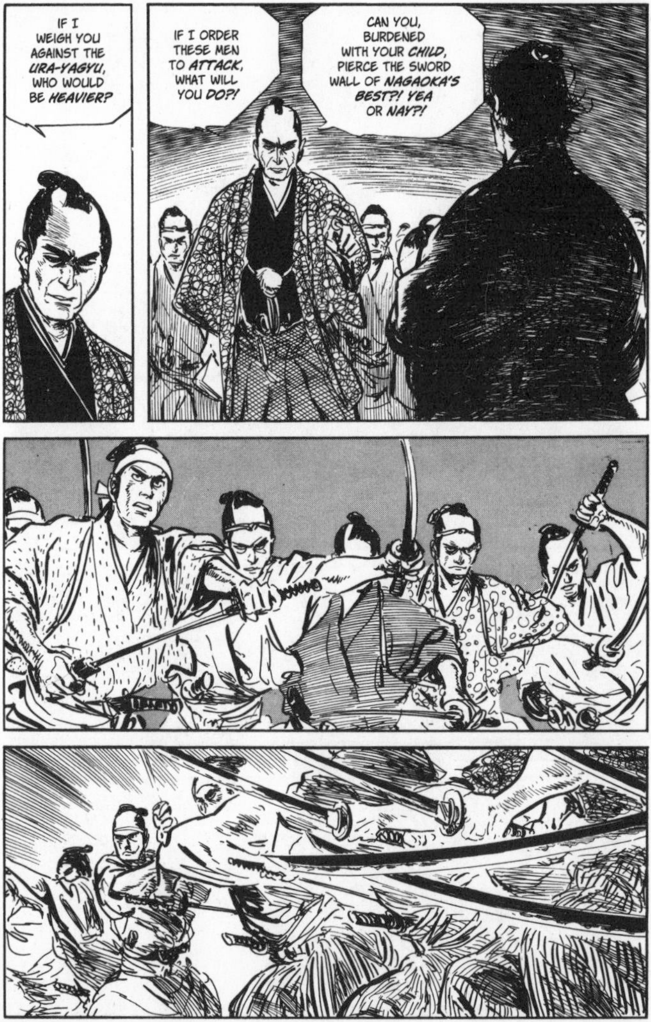
IF I WEIGH YOU AGAINST THE URA-YAGYU, WHO WOULD BE HEAVIER?
IF I ORDER THESE MEN TO ATTACK, WHAT WILL YOU DO?!
CAN YOU, BURDENED WITH YOUR CHILD, PIERCE THE SWORD WALL OF NAGAOKA'S BEST?! YEA OR NAY?!

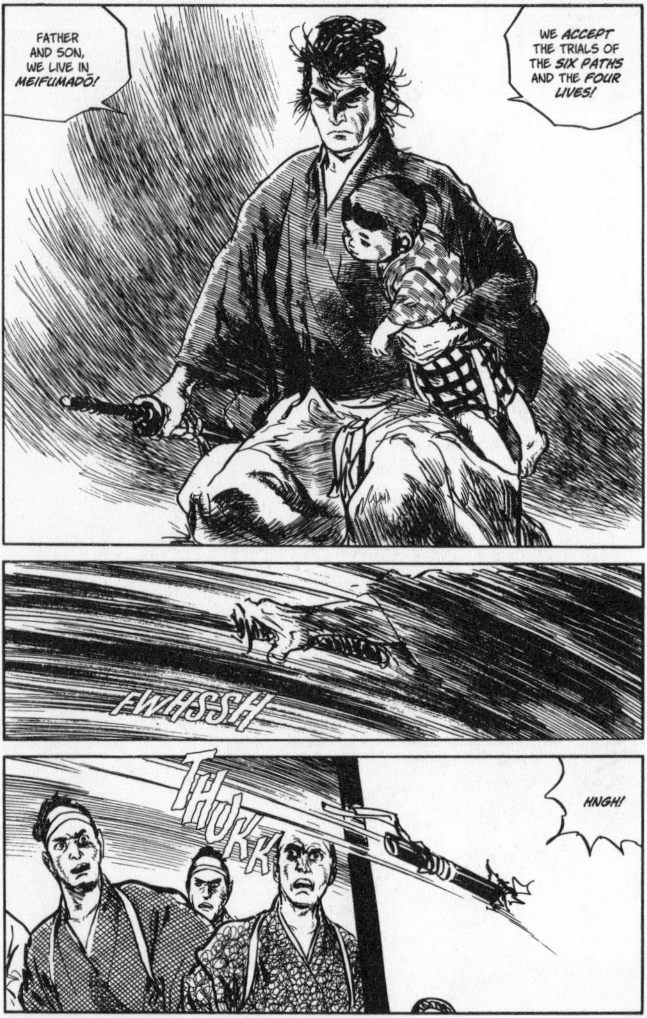
FATHER AND SON, WE LIVE IN *MEIFUMADŌ!*
WE *ACCEPT* THE TRIALS OF THE *SIX PATHS* AND THE *FOUR LIVES!*
FWHSSH
THUKK
HNGH!

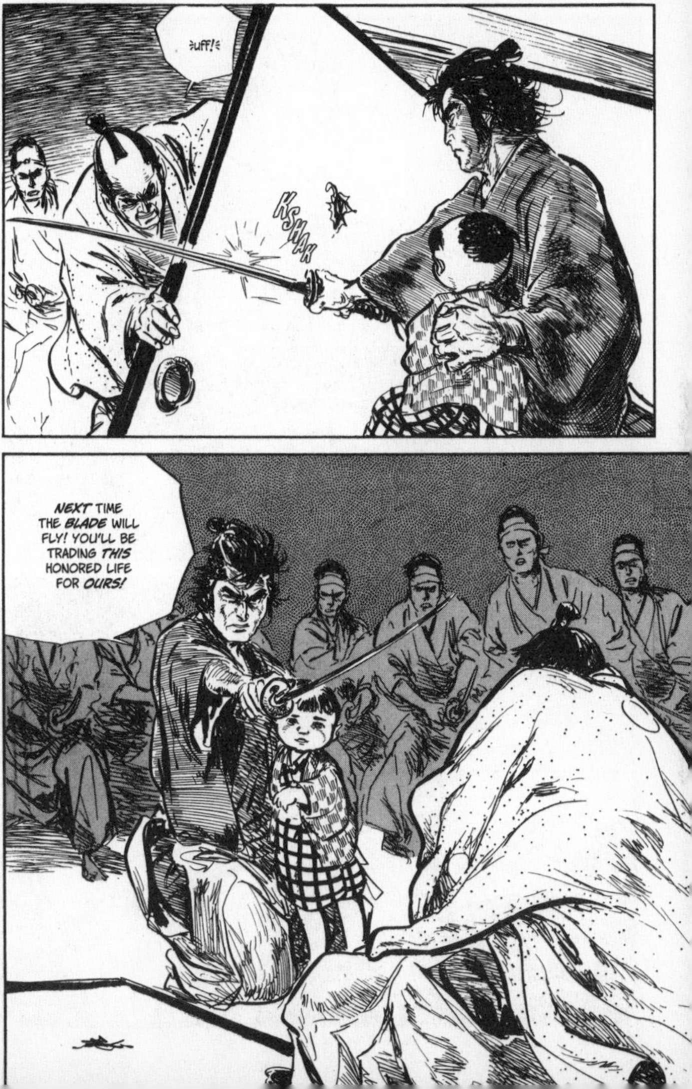

≥UFF!≤
KSHAK
NEXT TIME THE BLADE WILL FLY! YOU'LL BE TRADING THIS HONORED LIFE FOR OURS!

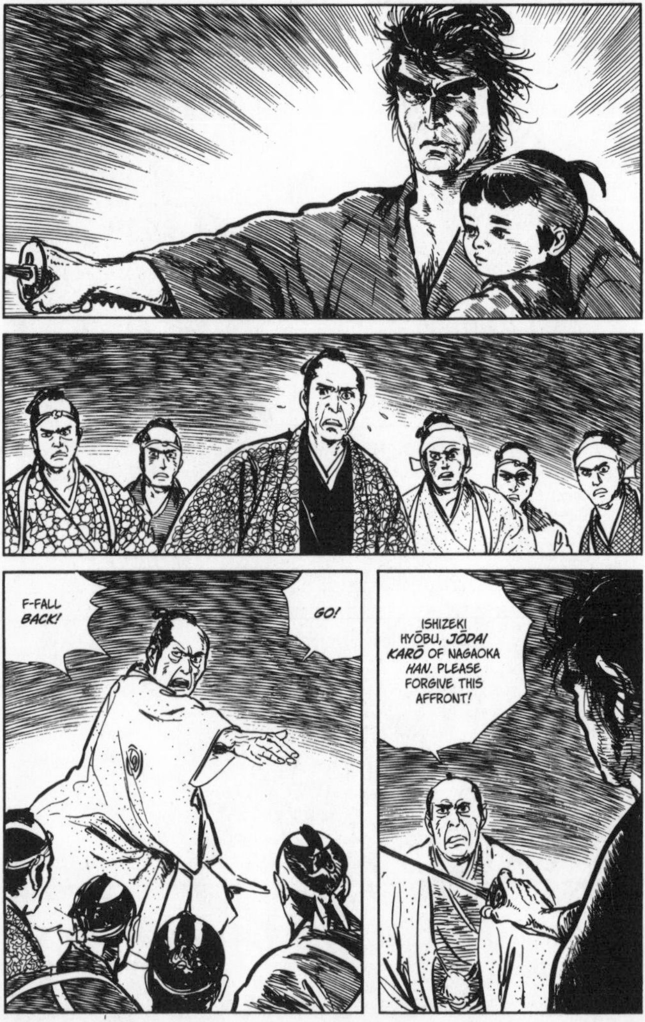
F-FALL *BACK!*
GO!
ISHIZEKI HYŌBU, ***JŌDAI KARŌ*** OF NAGAOKA *HAN*. PLEASE FORGIVE THIS AFFRONT!

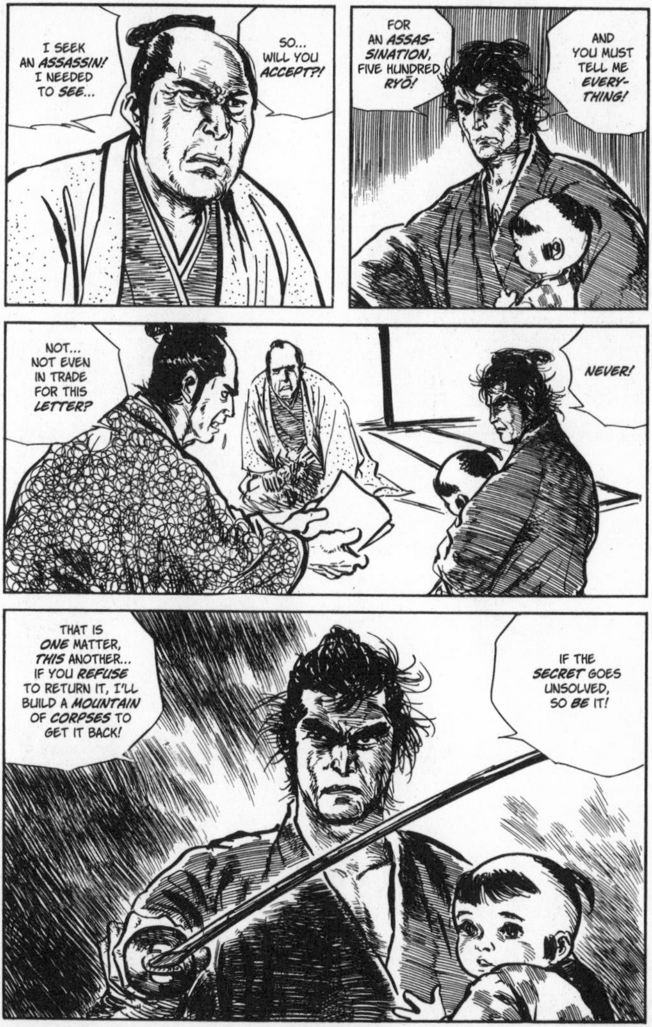
I SEEK AN ASSASSIN! I NEEDED TO SEE...
SO... WILL YOU ACCEPT?!
FOR AN ASSASSINATION, FIVE HUNDRED RYŌ!
AND YOU MUST TELL ME EVERYTHING!
NOT... NOT EVEN IN TRADE FOR THIS LETTER?
NEVER!
THAT IS ONE MATTER, THIS ANOTHER... IF YOU REFUSE TO RETURN IT, I'LL BUILD A MOUNTAIN OF CORPSES TO GET IT BACK!
IF THE SECRET GOES UNSOLVED, SO BE IT!

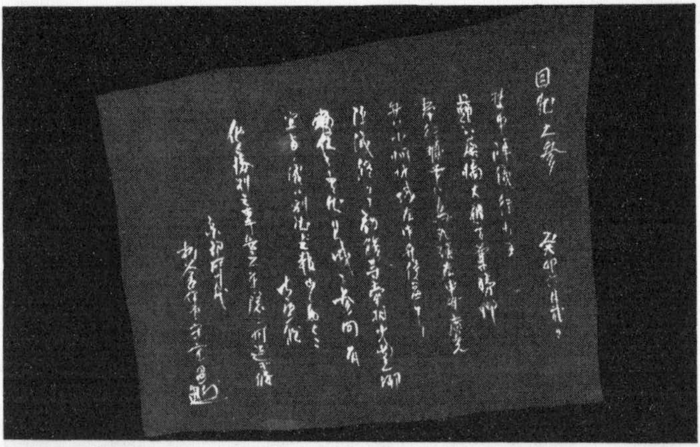
回状之参

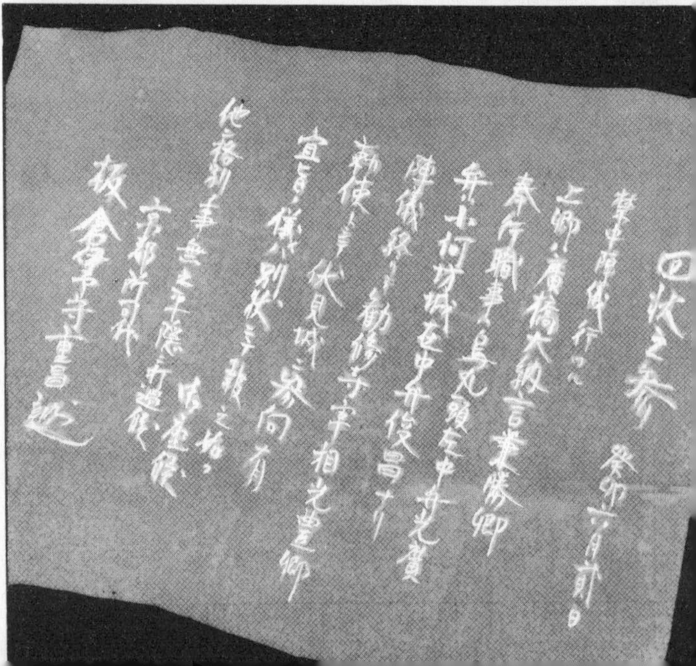
回状之参

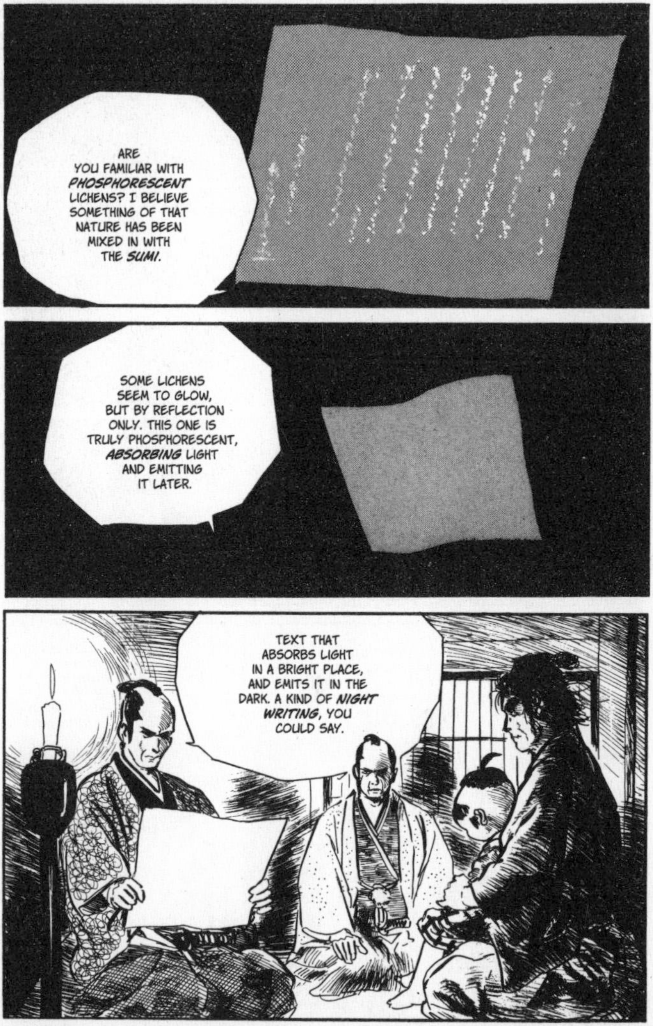
ARE YOU FAMILIAR WITH *PHOSPHORESCENT* LICHENS? I BELIEVE SOMETHING OF THAT NATURE HAS BEEN MIXED IN WITH THE *SUMI*.
SOME LICHENS SEEM TO GLOW, BUT BY REFLECTION ONLY. THIS ONE IS TRULY PHOSPHORESCENT, *ABSORBING* LIGHT AND EMITTING IT LATER.
TEXT THAT ABSORBS LIGHT IN A BRIGHT PLACE, AND EMITS IT IN THE DARK. A KIND OF *NIGHT WRITING*, YOU COULD SAY.

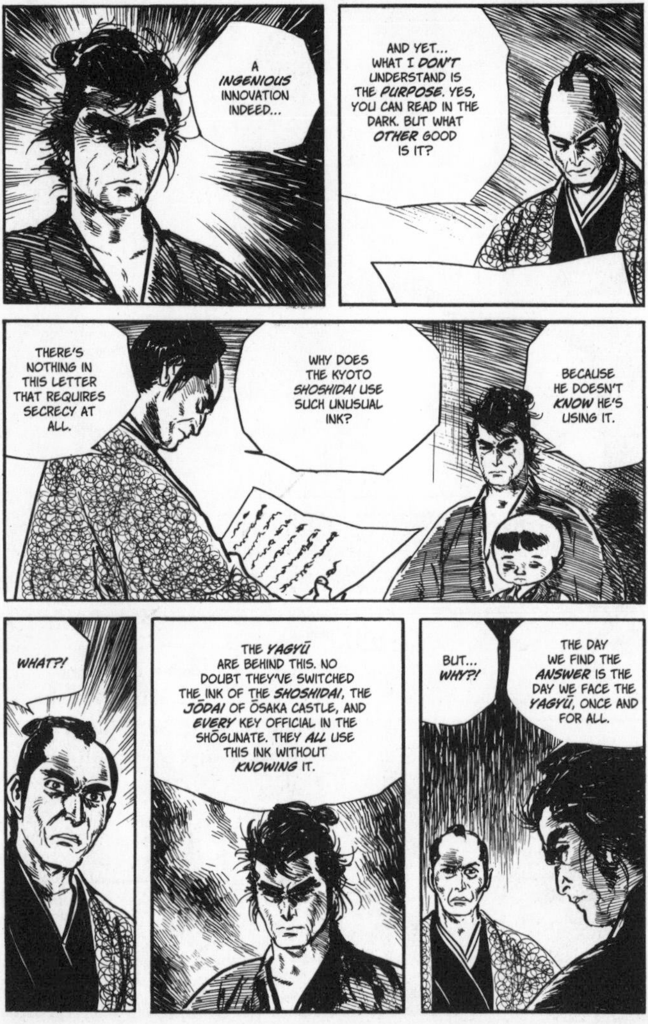

A *INGENIOUS* INNOVATION INDEED...
AND YET... WHAT I *DON'T* UNDERSTAND IS THE *PURPOSE*. YES, YOU CAN READ IN THE DARK. BUT WHAT *OTHER* GOOD IS IT?
THERE'S NOTHING IN THIS LETTER THAT REQUIRES SECRECY AT ALL.
WHY DOES THE KYOTO *SHOSHIDAI* USE SUCH UNUSUAL INK?
BECAUSE HE DOESN'T *KNOW* HE'S USING IT.
WHAT?!
THE *YAGYŪ* ARE BEHIND THIS. NO DOUBT THEY'VE SWITCHED THE INK OF THE *SHOSHIDAI*, THE *JŌDAI* OF ŌSAKA CASTLE, AND *EVERY* KEY OFFICIAL IN THE SHŌGUNATE. THEY *ALL* USE THIS INK WITHOUT *KNOWING* IT.
BUT... *WHY?!*
THE DAY WE FIND THE *ANSWER* IS THE DAY WE FACE THE *YAGYŪ*, ONCE AND FOR ALL.

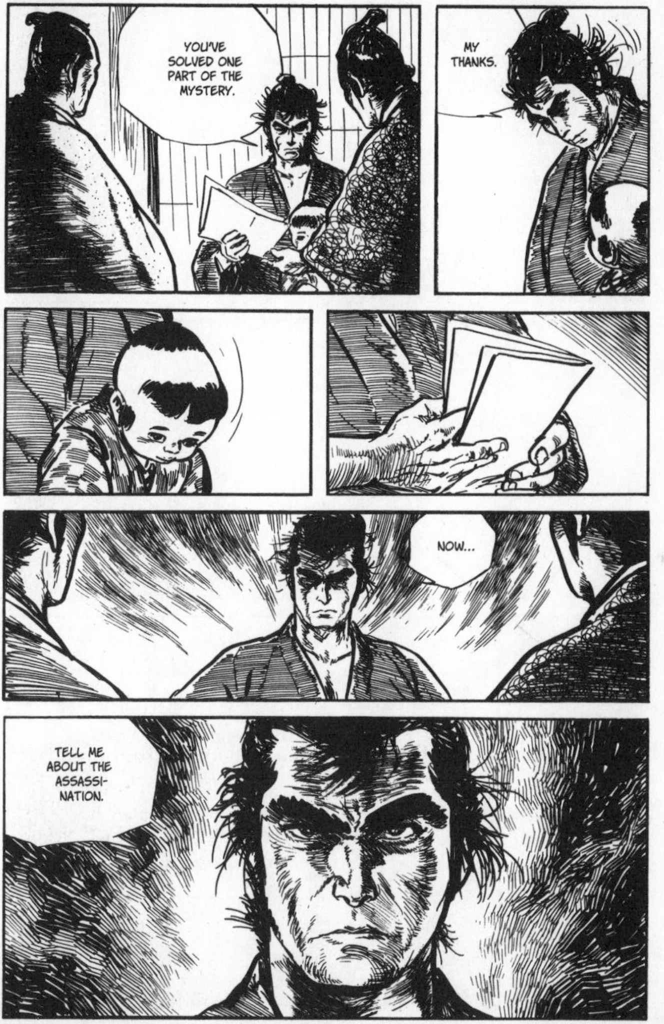
YOU'VE SOLVED ONE PART OF THE MYSTERY.
MY THANKS.
NOW...
TELL ME ABOUT THE ASSASSI- NATION.

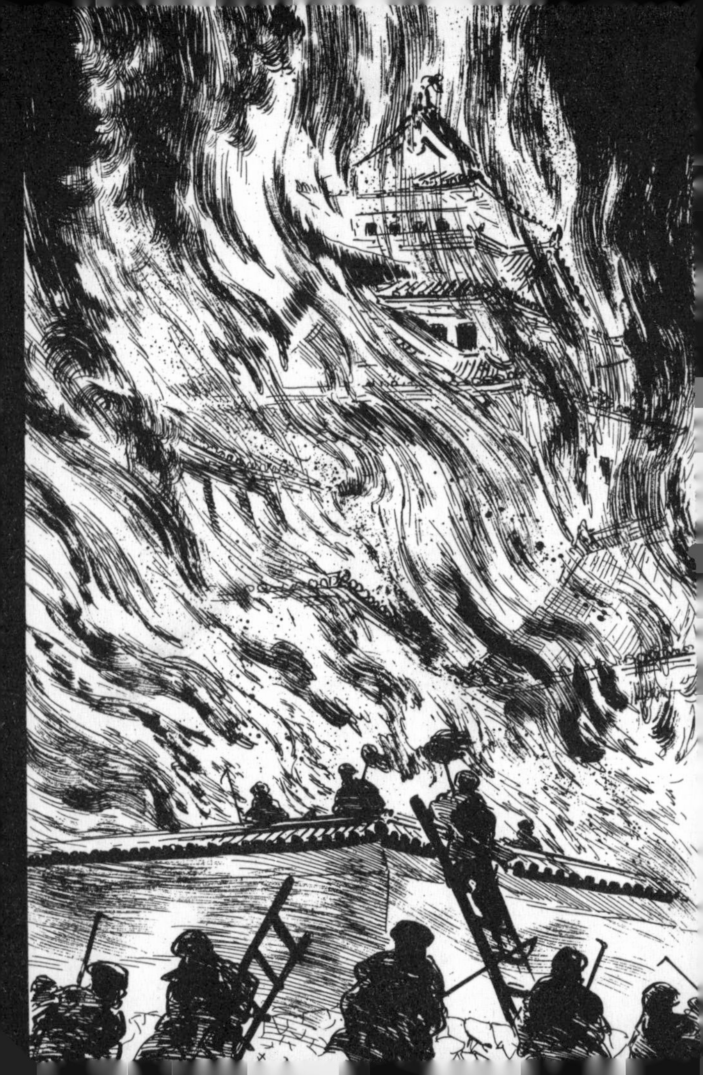

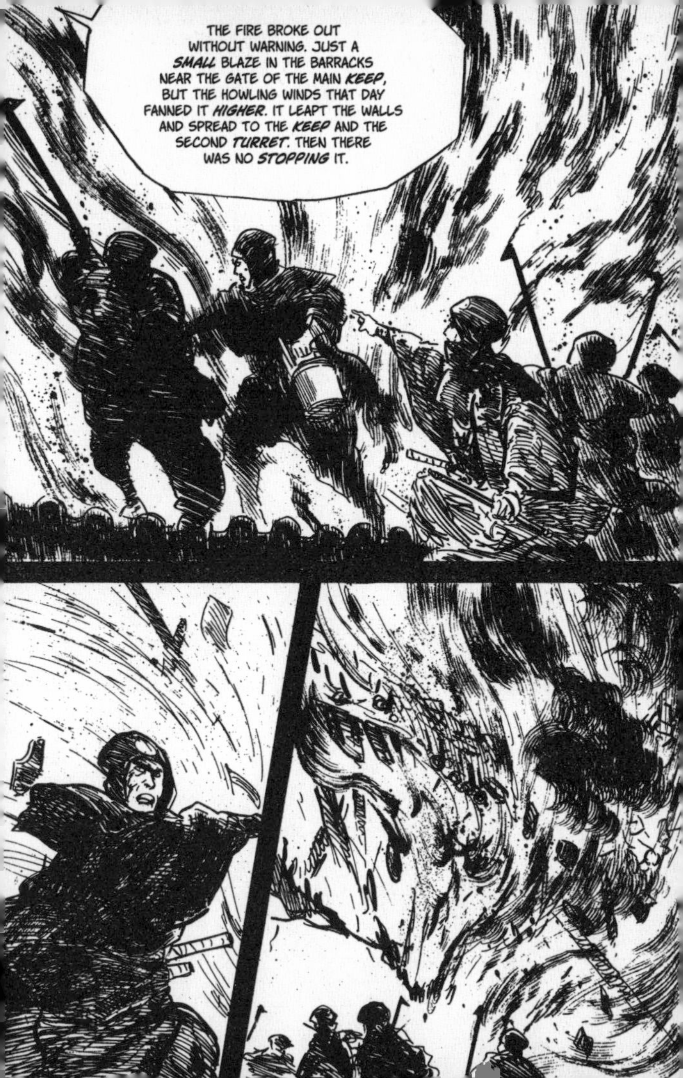
THE FIRE BROKE OUT WITHOUT WARNING. JUST A SMALL BLAZE IN THE BARRACKS NEAR THE GATE OF THE MAIN KEEP, BUT THE HOWLING WINDS THAT DAY FANNED IT HIGHER. IT LEAPT THE WALLS AND SPREAD TO THE KEEP AND THE SECOND TURRET. THEN THERE WAS NO STOPPING IT.

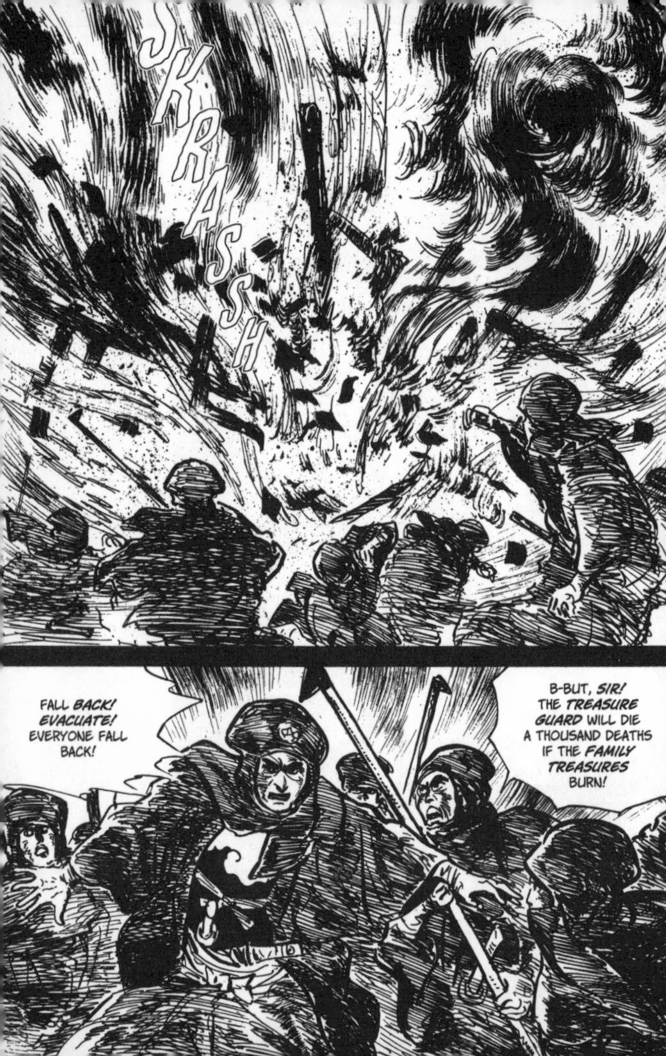
SKRASSH
FALL BACK! EVACUATE! EVERYONE FALL BACK!
B-BUT, SIR! THE TREASURE GUARD WILL DIE A THOUSAND DEATHS IF THE FAMILY TREASURES BURN!

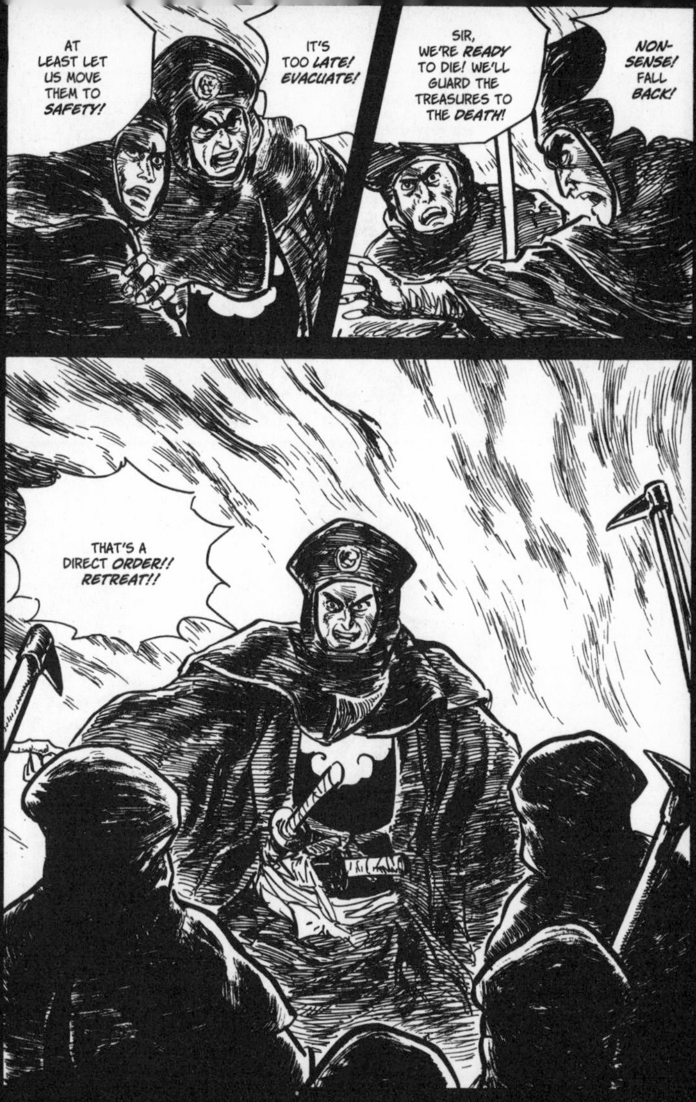
AT LEAST LET US MOVE THEM TO *SAFETY!*
IT'S TOO *LATE! EVACUATE!*
SIR, WE'RE *READY* TO DIE! WE'LL GUARD THE TREASURES TO THE *DEATH!*
NON-SENSE! FALL *BACK!*
THAT'S A DIRECT *ORDER!! RETREAT!!*

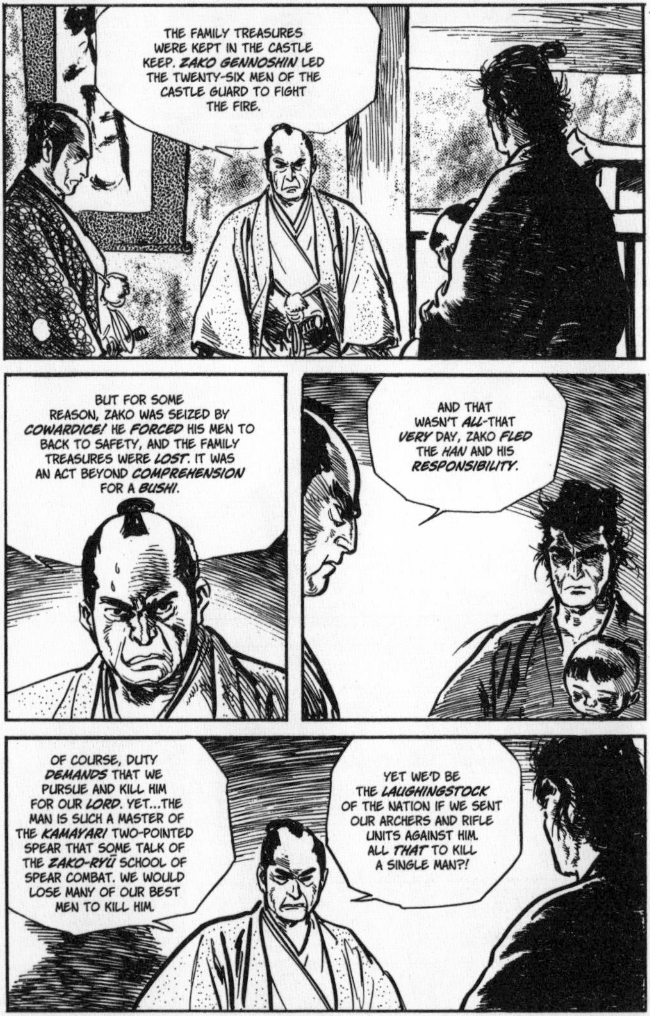
THE FAMILY TREASURES WERE KEPT IN THE CASTLE KEEP. ZAKO GENNOSHIN LED THE TWENTY-SIX MEN OF THE CASTLE GUARD TO FIGHT THE FIRE.
BUT FOR SOME REASON, ZAKO WAS SEIZED BY COWARDICE! HE FORCED HIS MEN TO BACK TO SAFETY, AND THE FAMILY TREASURES WERE LOST. IT WAS AN ACT BEYOND COMPREHENSION FOR A BUSHI.
AND THAT WASN'T ALL-THAT VERY DAY, ZAKO FLED THE HAN AND HIS RESPONSIBILITY.
OF COURSE, DUTY DEMANDS THAT WE PURSUE AND KILL HIM FOR OUR LORD. YET...THE MAN IS SUCH A MASTER OF THE KAMAYARI TWO-POINTED SPEAR THAT SOME TALK OF THE ZAKO-RYŪ SCHOOL OF SPEAR COMBAT. WE WOULD LOSE MANY OF OUR BEST MEN TO KILL HIM.
YET WE'D BE THE LAUGHINGSTOCK OF THE NATION IF WE SENT OUR ARCHERS AND RIFLE UNITS AGAINST HIM. ALL THAT TO KILL A SINGLE MAN?!

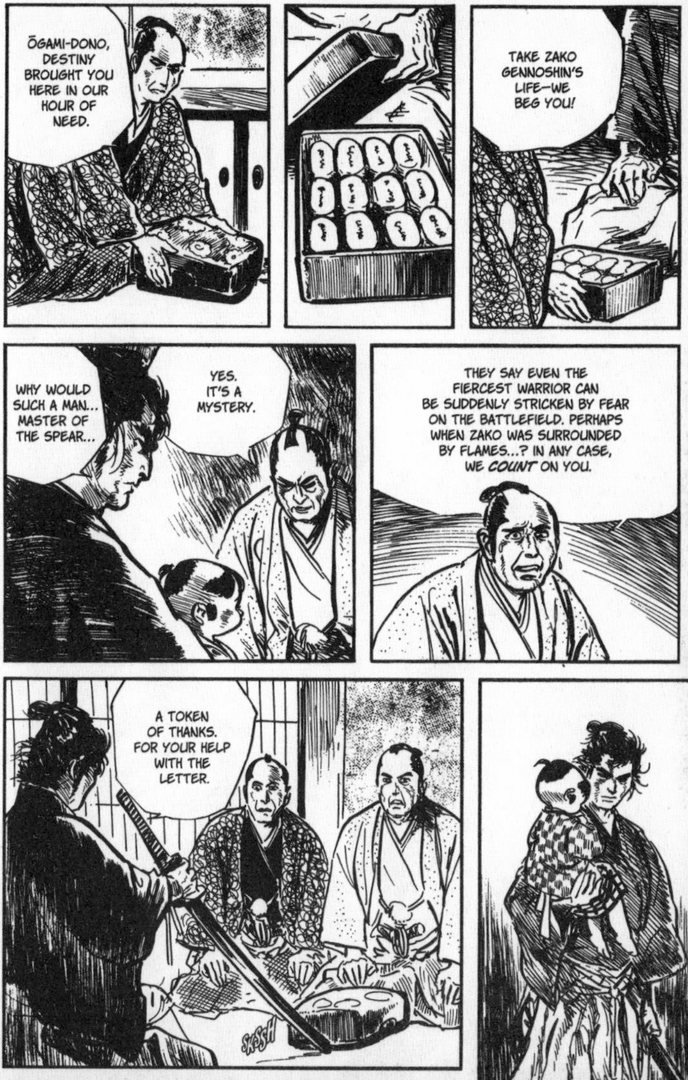
ŌGAMI-DONO, DESTINY BROUGHT YOU HERE IN OUR HOUR OF NEED.
TAKE ZAKO GENNOSHIN'S LIFE—WE BEG YOU!
WHY WOULD SUCH A MAN... MASTER OF THE SPEAR...
YES. IT'S A MYSTERY.
THEY SAY EVEN THE FIERCEST WARRIOR CAN BE SUDDENLY STRICKEN BY FEAR ON THE BATTLEFIELD. PERHAPS WHEN ZAKO WAS SURROUNDED BY FLAMES...? IN ANY CASE, WE *COUNT* ON YOU.
A TOKEN OF THANKS. FOR YOUR HELP WITH THE LETTER.
SKSSH

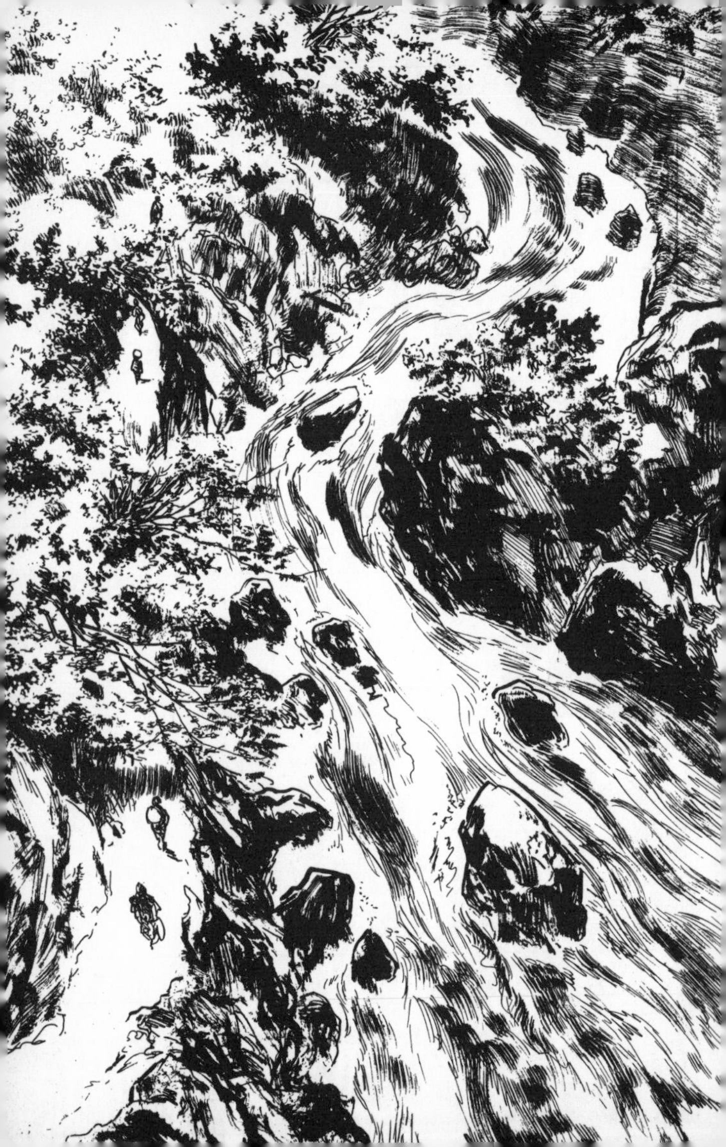

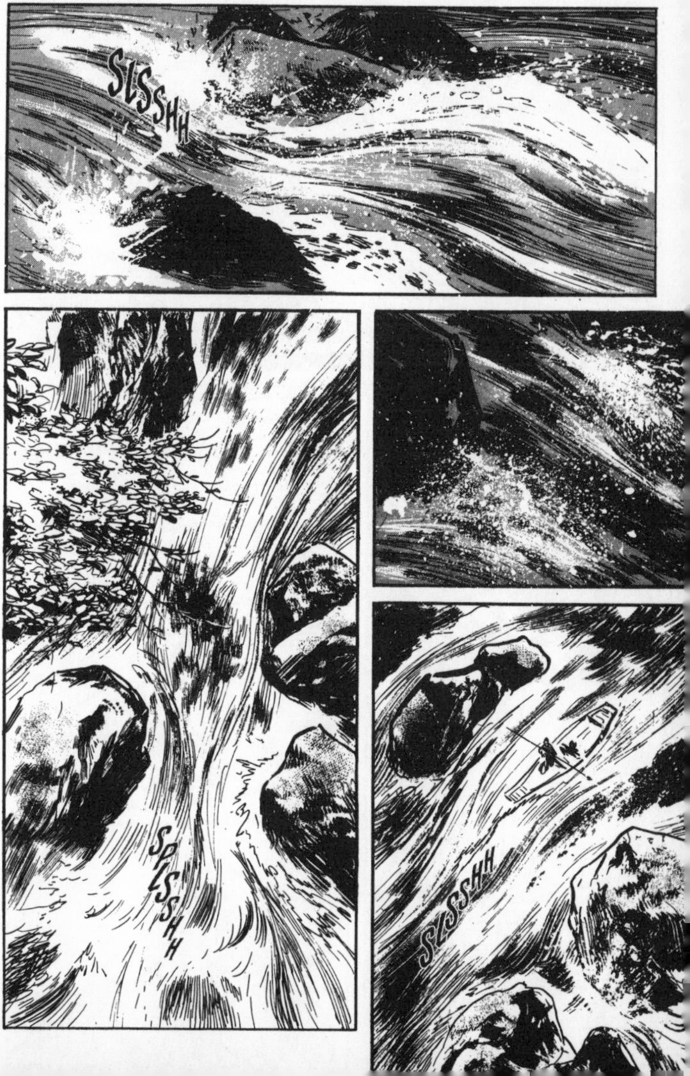
SLSSHH
SPLSSHH
SLSSHH

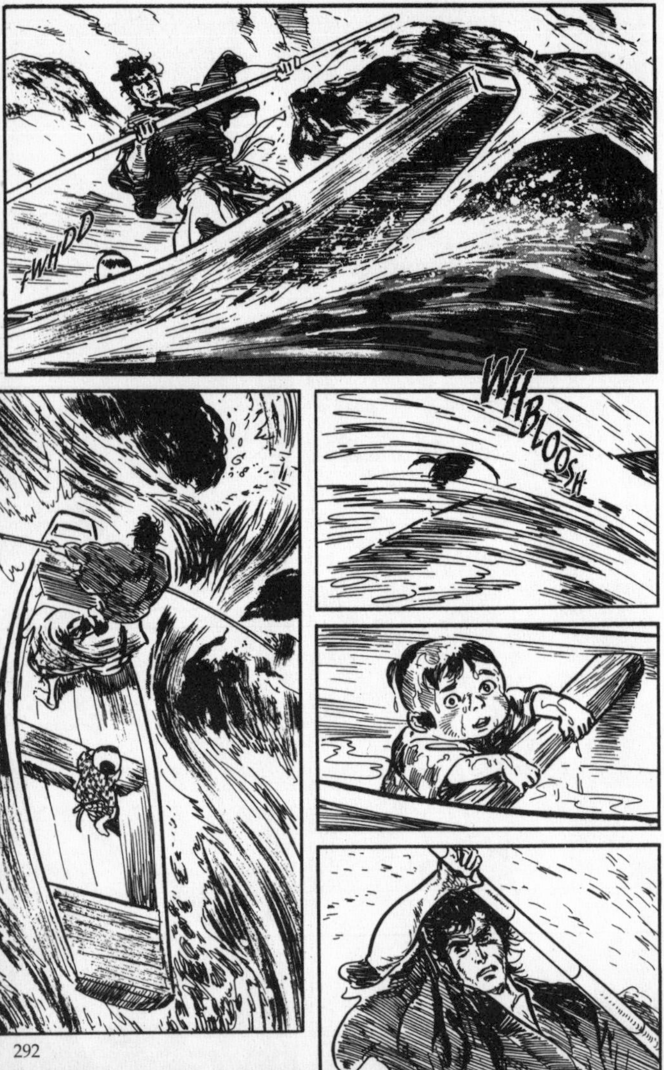
FWHDD
WHBLOOSH

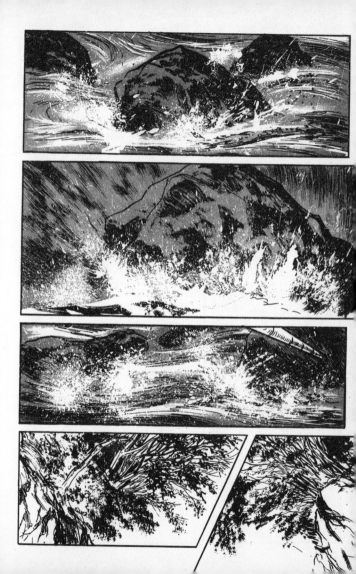

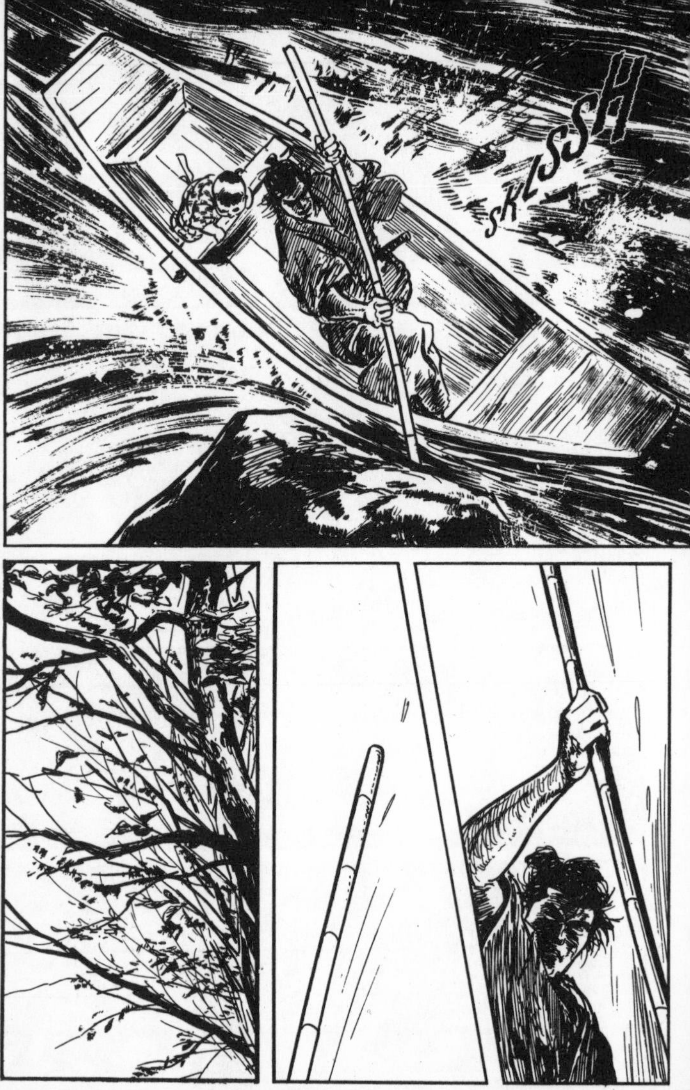
SKLSSSH

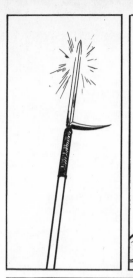

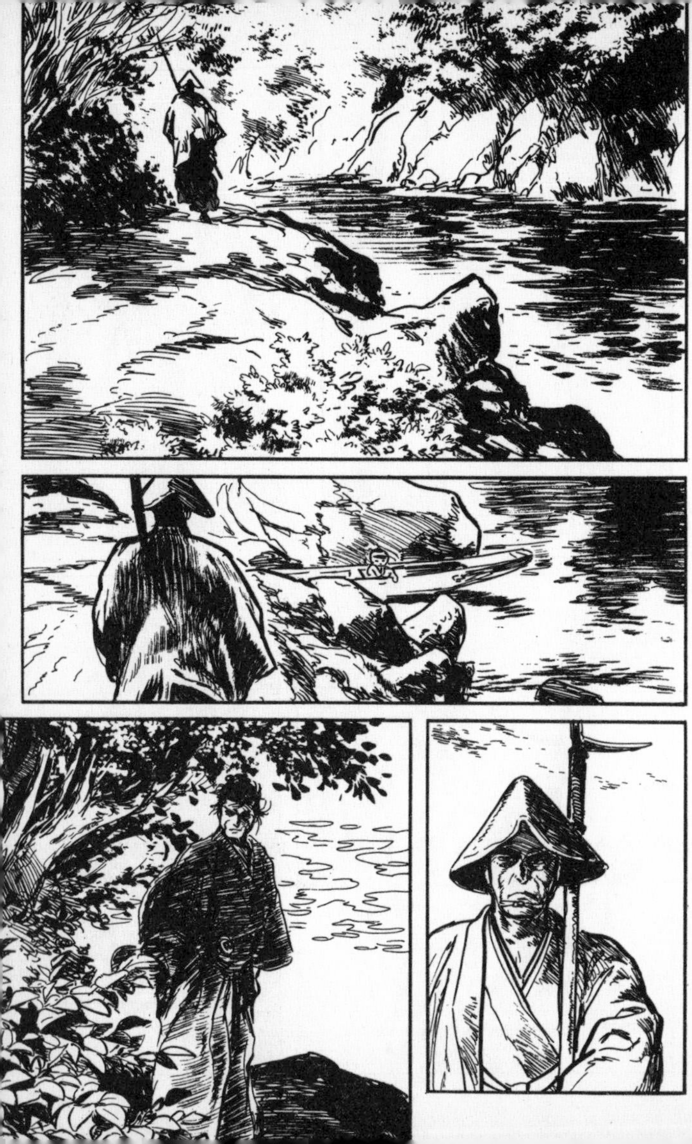

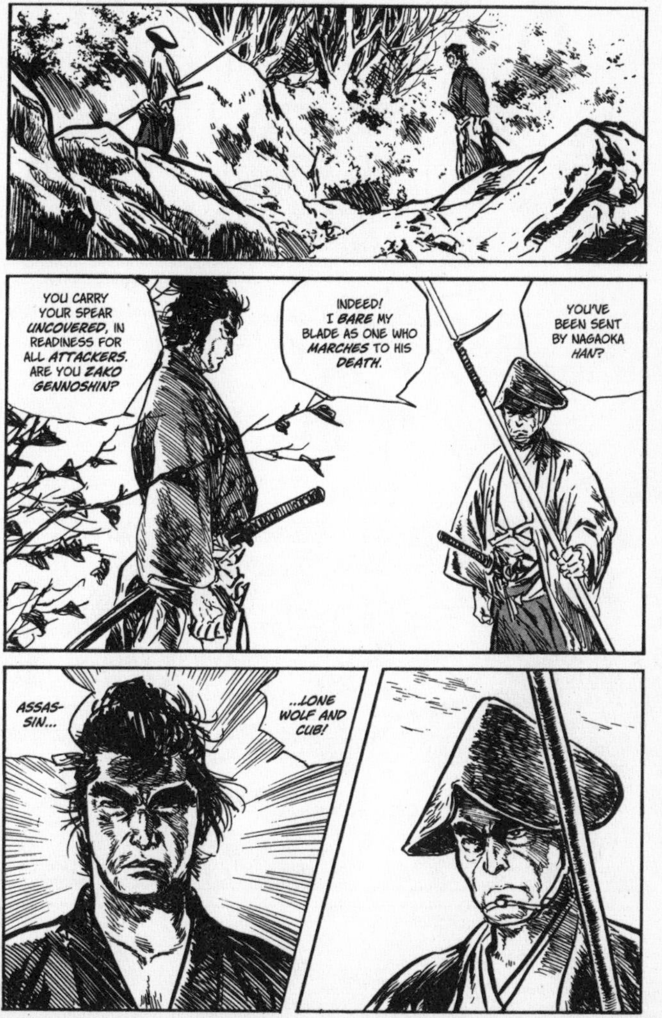
YOU CARRY YOUR SPEAR UNCOVERED, IN READINESS FOR ALL ATTACKERS. ARE YOU ZAKO GENNOSHIN?
INDEED! I BARE MY BLADE AS ONE WHO MARCHES TO HIS DEATH.
YOU'VE BEEN SENT BY NAGAOKA HAN?
ASSAS-SIN...
...LONE WOLF AND CUB!

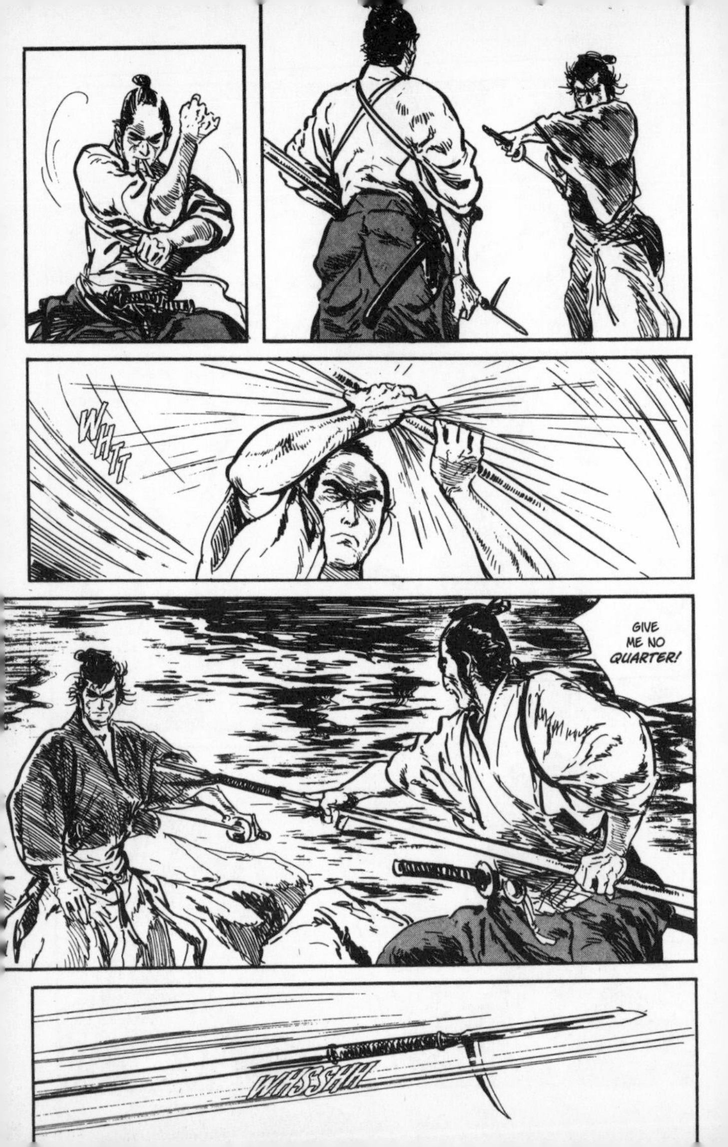
WHITT
GIVE ME NO QUARTER!
WHSSHH

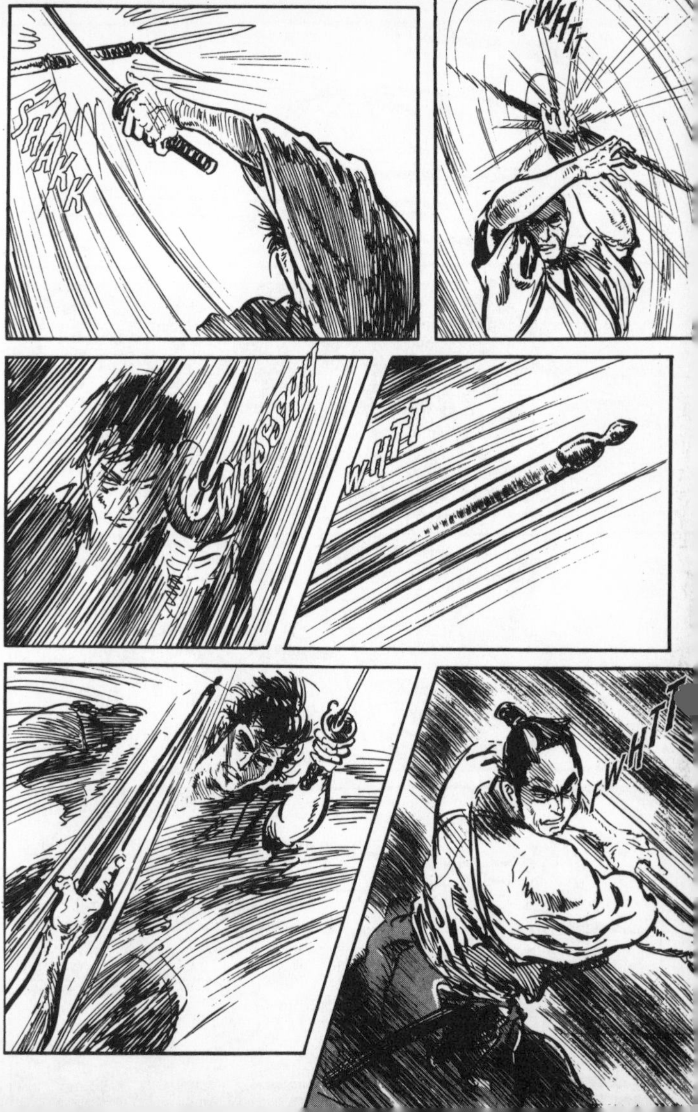
SHAKK
VWHTT
WHSSSHH
WHTT
WHTT

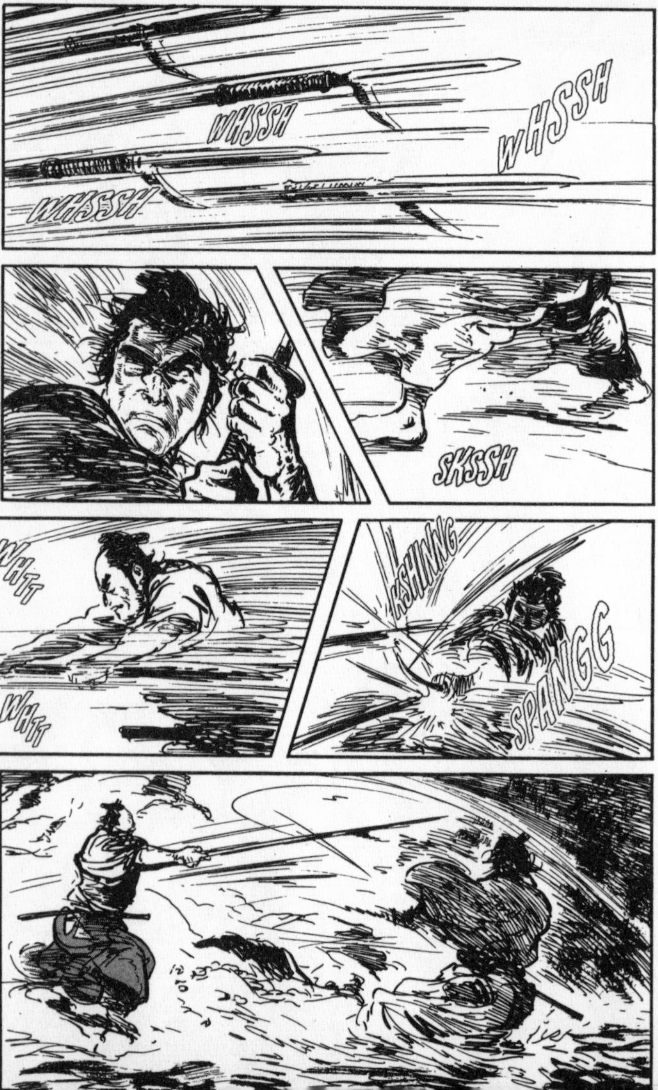
WHSSH
WHSSH
WHSSSH
SKSSH
WHTT
WHTT
KSHINNG
SPANGG

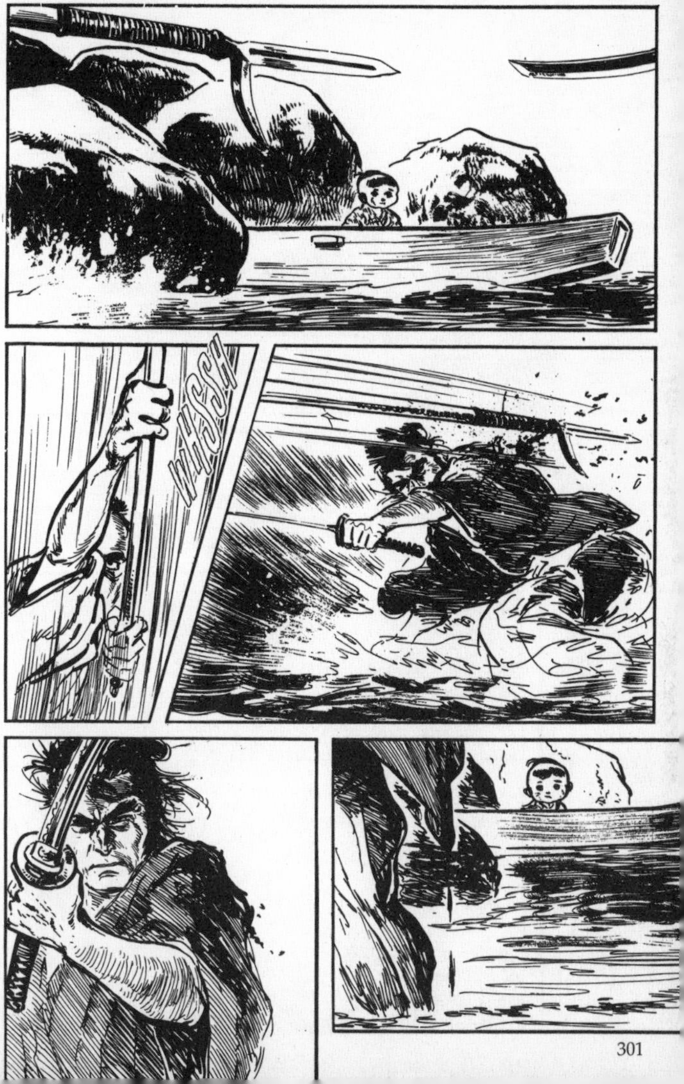
WHSSH

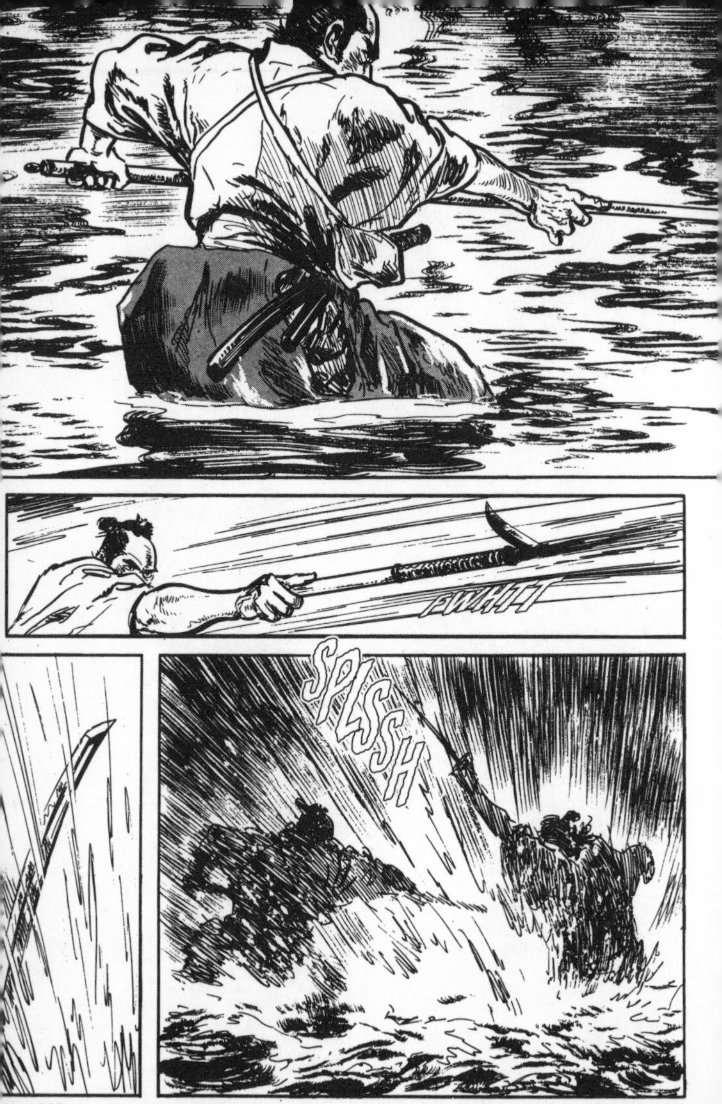
FWHTT
SPLSSH

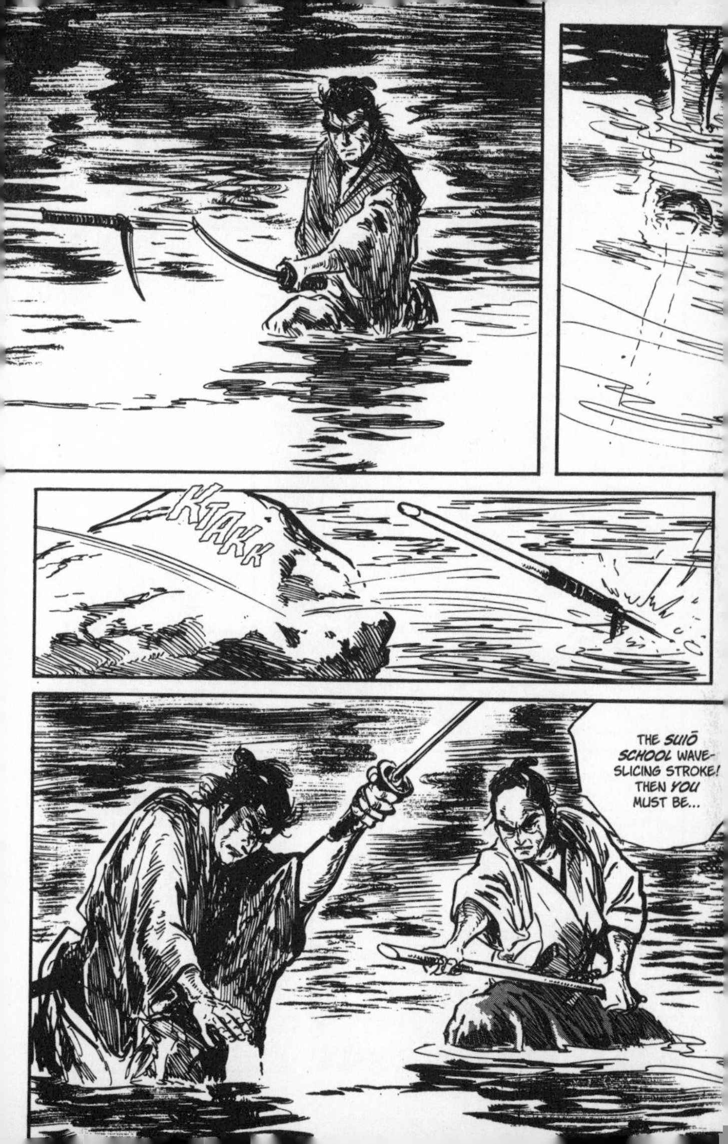
KTAKK
THE SUIŌ SCHOOL WAVE-SLICING STROKE! THEN YOU MUST BE...

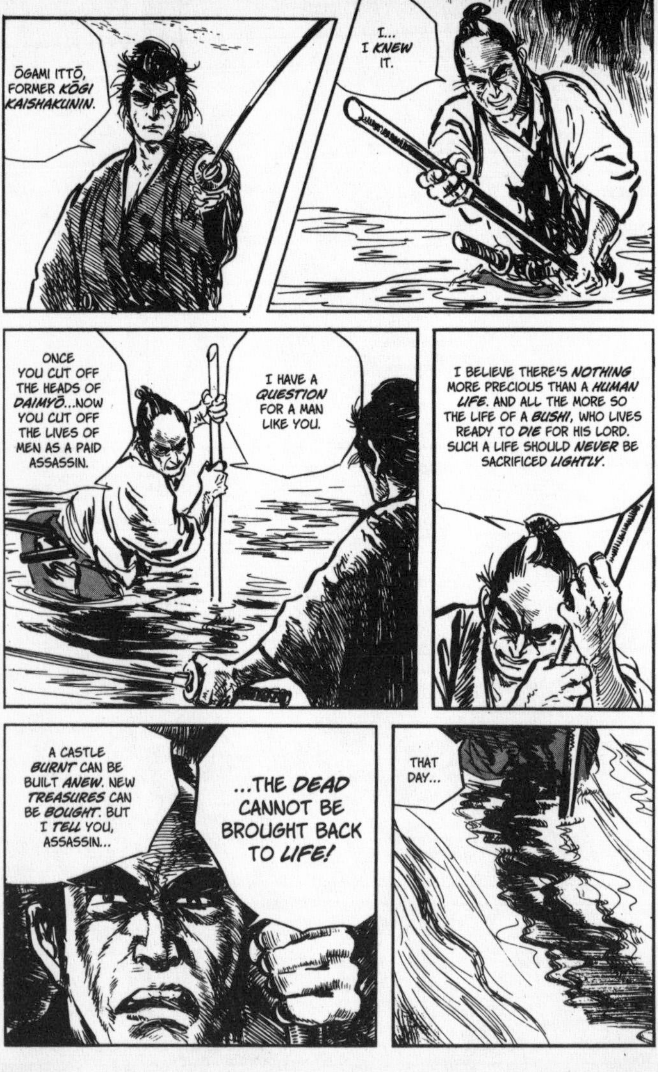
ŌGAMI ITTŌ, FORMER KŌGI KAISHAKUNIN.
I... I KNEW IT.
ONCE YOU CUT OFF THE HEADS OF DAIMYŌ...NOW YOU CUT OFF THE LIVES OF MEN AS A PAID ASSASSIN.
I HAVE A QUESTION FOR A MAN LIKE YOU.
I BELIEVE THERE'S NOTHING MORE PRECIOUS THAN A HUMAN LIFE. AND ALL THE MORE SO THE LIFE OF A BUSHI, WHO LIVES READY TO DIE FOR HIS LORD. SUCH A LIFE SHOULD NEVER BE SACRIFICED LIGHTLY.
A CASTLE BURNT CAN BE BUILT ANEW. NEW TREASURES CAN BE BOUGHT. BUT I TELL YOU, ASSASSIN...
...THE DEAD CANNOT BE BROUGHT BACK TO LIFE!
THAT DAY...

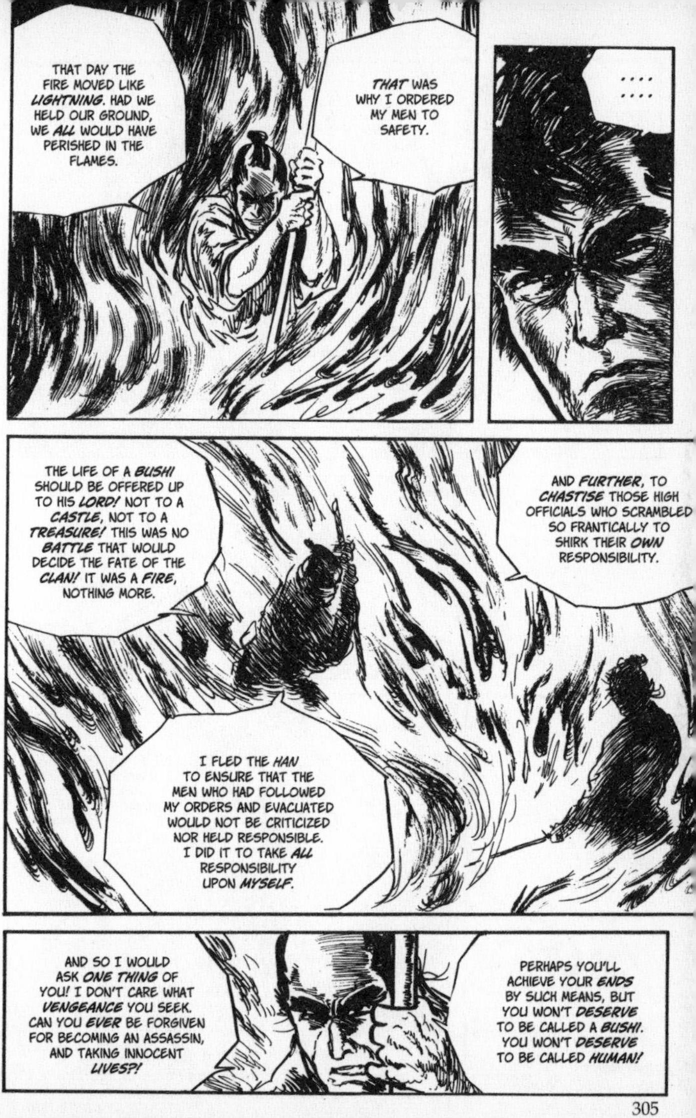
THAT DAY THE FIRE MOVED LIKE LIGHTNING. HAD WE HELD OUR GROUND, WE ALL WOULD HAVE PERISHED IN THE FLAMES.
THAT WAS WHY I ORDERED MY MEN TO SAFETY.
....
....
THE LIFE OF A BUSHI SHOULD BE OFFERED UP TO HIS LORD! NOT TO A CASTLE, NOT TO A TREASURE! THIS WAS NO BATTLE THAT WOULD DECIDE THE FATE OF THE CLAN! IT WAS A FIRE, NOTHING MORE.
AND FURTHER, TO CHASTISE THOSE HIGH OFFICIALS WHO SCRAMBLED SO FRANTICALLY TO SHIRK THEIR OWN RESPONSIBILITY.
I FLED THE HAN TO ENSURE THAT THE MEN WHO HAD FOLLOWED MY ORDERS AND EVACUATED WOULD NOT BE CRITICIZED NOR HELD RESPONSIBLE. I DID IT TO TAKE ALL RESPONSIBILITY UPON MYSELF.
AND SO I WOULD ASK ONE THING OF YOU! I DON'T CARE WHAT VENGEANCE YOU SEEK. CAN YOU EVER BE FORGIVEN FOR BECOMING AN ASSASSIN, AND TAKING INNOCENT LIVES?!
PERHAPS YOU'LL ACHIEVE YOUR ENDS BY SUCH MEANS, BUT YOU WON'T DESERVE TO BE CALLED A BUSHI. YOU WON'T DESERVE TO BE CALLED HUMAN!

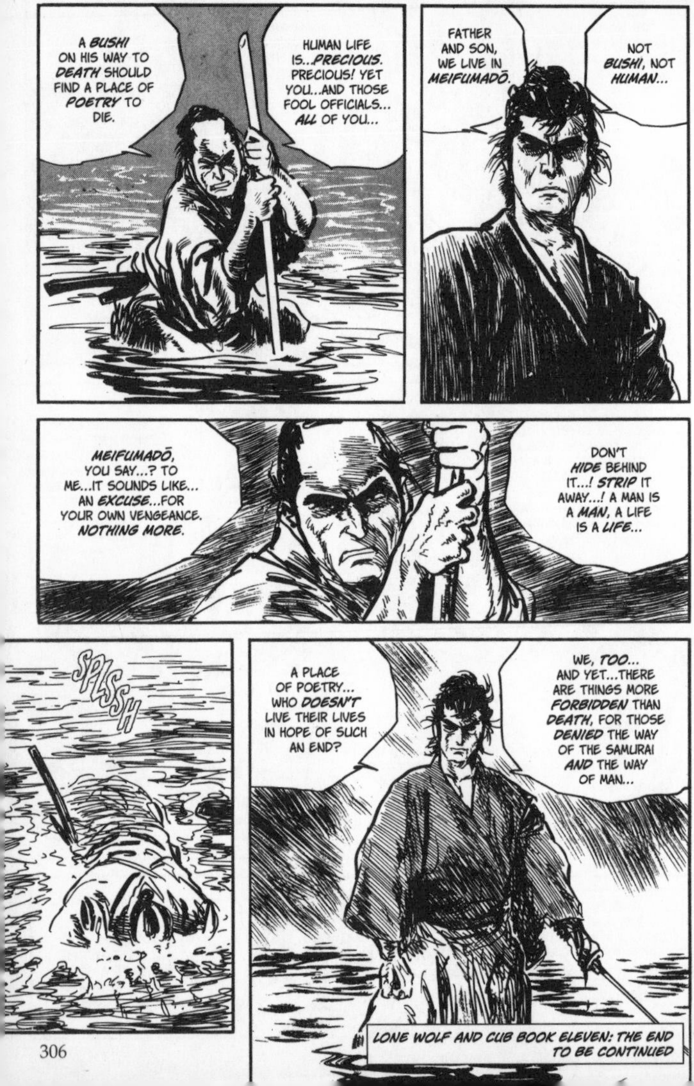
A BUSHI ON HIS WAY TO DEATH SHOULD FIND A PLACE OF POETRY TO DIE.
HUMAN LIFE IS...PRECIOUS. PRECIOUS! YET YOU...AND THOSE FOOL OFFICIALS... ALL OF YOU...
FATHER AND SON, WE LIVE IN MEIFUMADŌ.
NOT BUSHI, NOT HUMAN...
MEIFUMADŌ, YOU SAY...? TO ME...IT SOUNDS LIKE... AN EXCUSE...FOR YOUR OWN VENGEANCE. NOTHING MORE.
DON'T HIDE BEHIND IT...! STRIP IT AWAY...! A MAN IS A MAN, A LIFE IS A LIFE...
SPLSSH
A PLACE OF POETRY... WHO DOESN'T LIVE THEIR LIVES IN HOPE OF SUCH AN END?
WE, TOO... AND YET...THERE ARE THINGS MORE FORBIDDEN THAN DEATH, FOR THOSE DENIED THE WAY OF THE SAMURAI AND THE WAY OF MAN...
LONE WOLF AND CUB BOOK ELEVEN: THE END
TO BE CONTINUED

GLOSSARY

bushi
A samurai. A member of the warrior class.

bushidō
The way of the warrior.

chūsei
The old educational system's equivalent to high-school students.

daimyō
A feudal lord.

daisei
The old educational system's equivalent to college students.

dōtanuki
A battle sword. Literally, "sword that cuts through torsos."

Edo
The capital of medieval Japan and the seat of the shōgunate. The site of modern-day Tokyo.

han
A feudal domain.

hanshi
Samurai in the service of a *han*.

hatamoto
Daimyō considered utterly loyal to the Tokugawa clan, with the right to meet the shōgun face to face. Their title, "standard bearers," came from history, when the warriors who would be promoted in peacetime to *hatamoto* had been the most trusted allies of Tokugawa Ieyasu, the first of the Tokugawa shōguns.

honorifics
Japan is a class and status society, and proper forms of address are critical. Common markers of respect are the prefixes *o* and *go*, and a wide range of suffixes. Some of the suffixes you will encounter in *Lone Wolf and Cub*:
dono – archaic; used for higher-ranked or highly respected figures
sama – used for superiors

jōdai
Castle warden. The ranking *han* official in charge of a *daimyō's* castle and *han* when the *daimyō* was in residence in Edo.

kago-sho
A peasant petition to the shōgunate, indicting a *han's* leadership for abuses. Those delivering such a petition did so knowing that they would be executed for insolence, whether the *han* was found guilty or not.

karō
Elders, usually the senior advisor to a *daimyō*. Since the daimyō was required to alternate each year between life in his castle in the han and his residence in Edo, there was usually an *Edo-karo* (Edō elder) and a *kuni-karō* (*han* elder), who would administer affairs when their lord was away.

katsu
The shout of a Zen priest, meant to jolt a student into self-awareness.

kōgi kaishakunin
The shōgun's own second, who performed executions ordered by the shōgun.

koto
A traditional Japanese zither. The thirteen silk strings are tuned by moving individual ivory bridges.

Kyoto shoshidai
The shōgun's emissary to the Imperial Court in Kyoto. Although real power lay with the shōgun in Edo, the shōgunate maintained the fiction that the emperor was the ultimate authority in Japan. The *shoshidai* maintained contact with the imperial household and the aristocracy, and oversaw tax collection and other shōgunate business in the old capital.

meifumadō
The Buddhist Hell. The way of demons and damnation.

Meirin-kan
Each *han* had its own school for the children of *hanshi* retainers. The school in Hagi was called the Meirin-kan.

o-niwaban
A ninja. Literally, "one in the garden." Ninja had their heyday in the time of warring states before the rise of the Tokugawa clan. Originally mercenaries serving different warlords, by the Edo period they were in the service of the central government. The most famous were the ninja of Iga and Kaga, north of Kyoto. The Kurokuwa that appear in *Lone Wolf and Cub* were officially the laborers and manual workers in Edo Castle. Whether they truly served as a secret spy corps is lost in history.

Ōsaka Castle
The largest castle outside of Edo, originally built by Hideyoshi Toyotomi, the first unifier of Japan. After the Tokugawa clan took the castle by siege, it became their stronghold in western Japan, from which they monitored the activities of the unruly western *han*.

rōjū
Senior councilors. The inner circle of councilors directly advising the shōgun. The *rōjū* were the ultimate advisory body to the Tokugawa shogunate's national government.

rōnin
A masterless samurai. Literally, "one adrift on the waves."

ryō
A gold piece, worth 60 *monme* or 4 *kan*.

ryū
Often translated as "school." The many variations of swordsmanship and other martial arts were passed down from generation to generation to the offspring of the originator of the technique or set of techniques, and to any *deishi* students that sought to learn from the master.

Shōheikō
The shōgunate's institute of higher learning, founded in Edo in 1691. It was named after the birthplace of Confucius.

shosei
The old educational system's equivalent to middle-school students.

sōmeishu
A master village chieftain. In Edo Japan, a select handful of *meishu* (village chieftains) were assigned official duties by the *machi-bugyō* (Edo city commissioner) and local *daikan* (magistrate). Peasants were forbidden to bear arms and had no family names, but these select few were given special dispensation to wear a sword and pass down their family name. A *sōmeishu* spoke for all the *meishu* of the *han*.

sumi
Japanese ink, used for calligraphy and *sumi-e* (ink paintings). It comes in a solid block and is wetted with water in a tray.

urameshiya
"Vengeance." The traditional wail of Japanese ghosts. A threat of this sort was considered very real and frightening.

Wajō
A term of respect for a high priest or the head of a temple.

KAZUO KOIKE

Though widely respected as a powerful writer of graphic fiction, Kazuo Koike has spent a lifetime reaching beyond the bounds of the comics medium. Aside from co-creating and writing the successful *Lone Wolf and Cub* and *Crying Freeman* manga, Koike has hosted television programs; founded a golf magazine; produced movies; written popular fiction, poetry, and screenplays; and mentored some of Japan's best manga talent.

Lone Wolf and Cub was first serialized in Japan in 1970 (under the title *Kozure Okami*) in *Manga Action* magazine and continued its hugely popular run for many years, being collected as the stories were published, and reprinted worldwide. Koike collected numerous awards for his work on the series throughout the next decade. Starting in 1972, Koike adapted the popular manga into a series of six films, the *Baby Cart Assassin* saga, garnering widespread commercial success and critical acclaim for his screenwriting.

This wasn't Koike's only foray into film and video. In 1996, *Crying Freeman*, the manga Koike created with artist Ryoichi Ikegami, was produced in Hollywood and released to commercial success in Europe and is currently awaiting release in America.

And to give something back to the medium that gave him so much, Koike started the *Gekiga Sonjuku*, a college course aimed at helping talented writers and artists — such as *Ranma 1/2* creator Rumiko Takahashi — break into the comics field.

The driving focus of Koike's narrative is character development, and his commitment to character is clear: "Comics are carried by characters. If a character is well created, the comic becomes a hit." Kazuo Koike's continued success in comics and literature has proven this philosophy true.

GOSEKI KOJIMA

Goseki Kojima was born on November 3, 1928, the very same day as the godfather of Japanese comics, Osamu Tezuka. While just out of junior high school, the self-taught Kojima began painting advertising posters for movie theaters to pay his bills.

In 1950, Kojima moved to Tokyo, where the postwar devastation had given rise to special manga forms for audiences too poor to buy the new manga magazines. Kojima created art for *kami-shibai*, or "paper-play" narrators, who would use manga story sheets to present narrated street plays. Kojima moved on to creating works for the *kashi-bon* market, bookstores that rented out books, magazines, and manga to mostly low-income readers. He soon became highly popular among *kashi-bon* readers.

In 1967, Kojima broke into the magazine market with his series *Dojinki*. As the manga magazine market grew and diversified, he turned out a steady stream of popular series.

In 1970, in collaboration with Kazuo Koike, Kojima began the work that would seal his reputation, *Kozure Okami* (*Lone Wolf and Cub*). Before long the story had become a gigantic hit, eventually spinning off a television series, six motion pictures, and even theme-song records. Koike and Kojima were soon dubbed the "golden duo" and produced success after success on their way to the pinnacle of the manga world.

When *Manga Japan* magazine was launched in 1994, Kojima was asked to serve as consultant, and he helped train the next generation of manga artists.

In his final years, Kojima turned to creating original graphic novels based on the movies of his favorite director, Akira Kurosawa. Kojima passed away on January 5, 2000 at the age of 71.

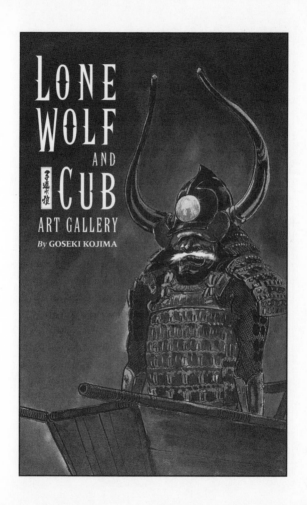

LONE WOLF AND CUB

ART GALLERY

By **GOSEKI KOJIMA**

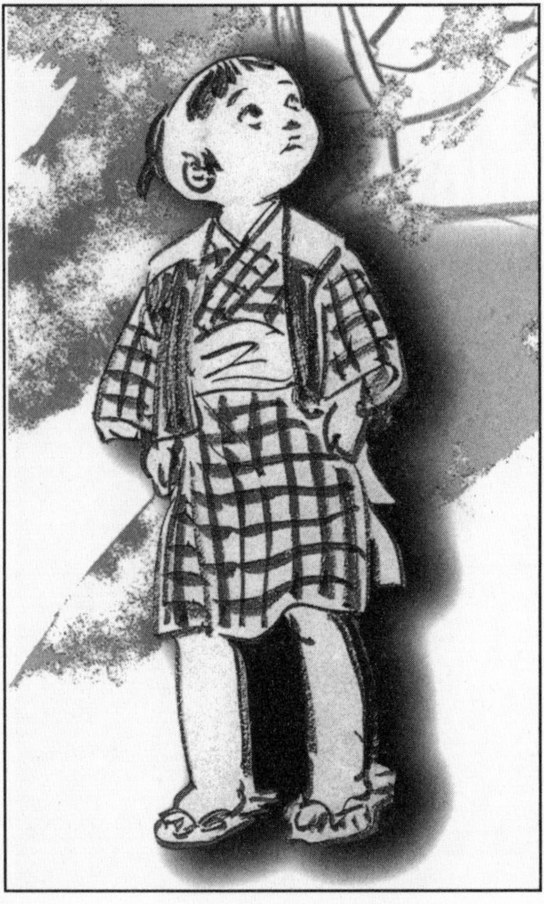

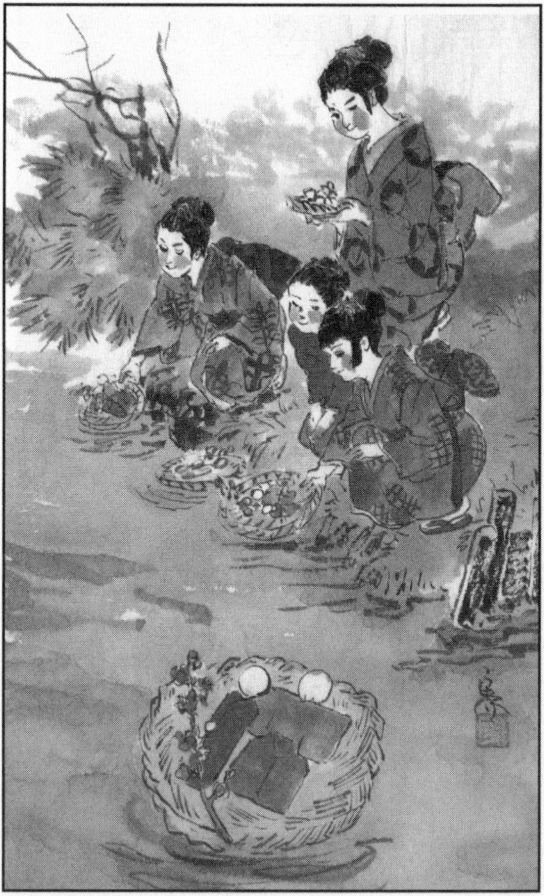

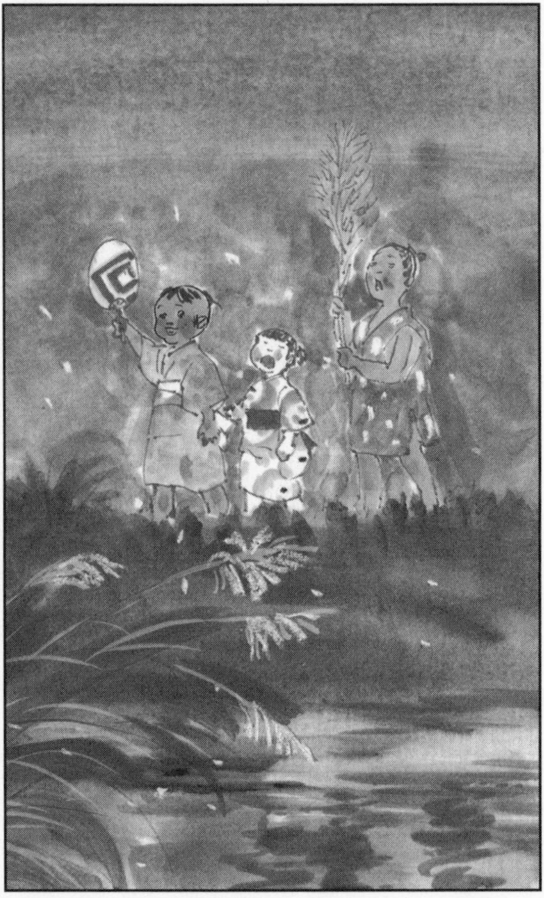

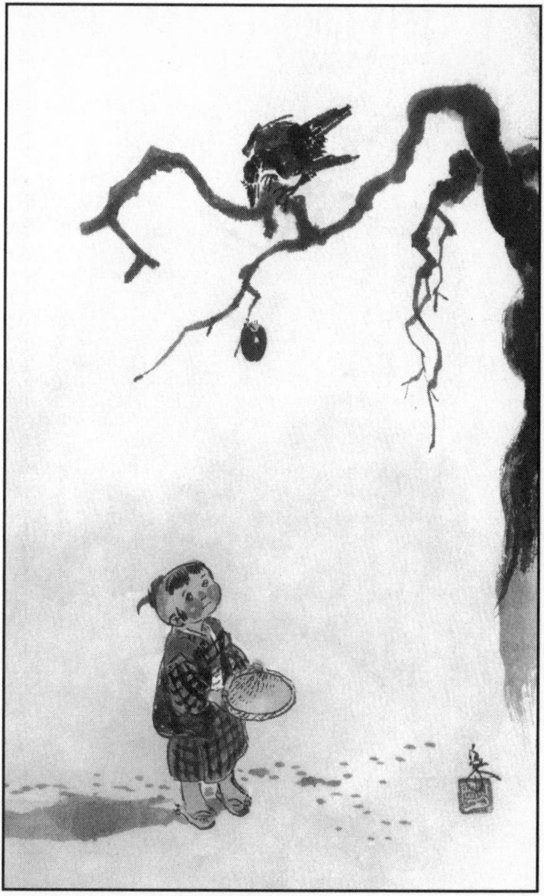

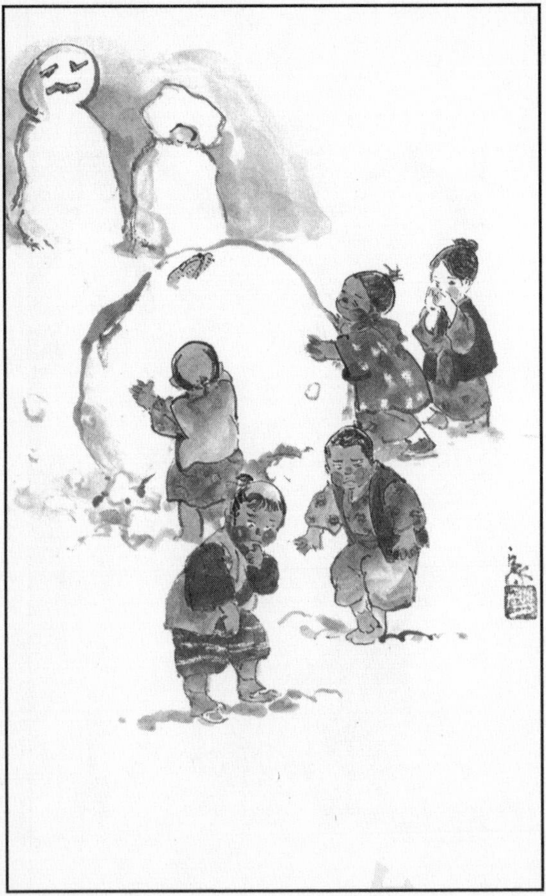

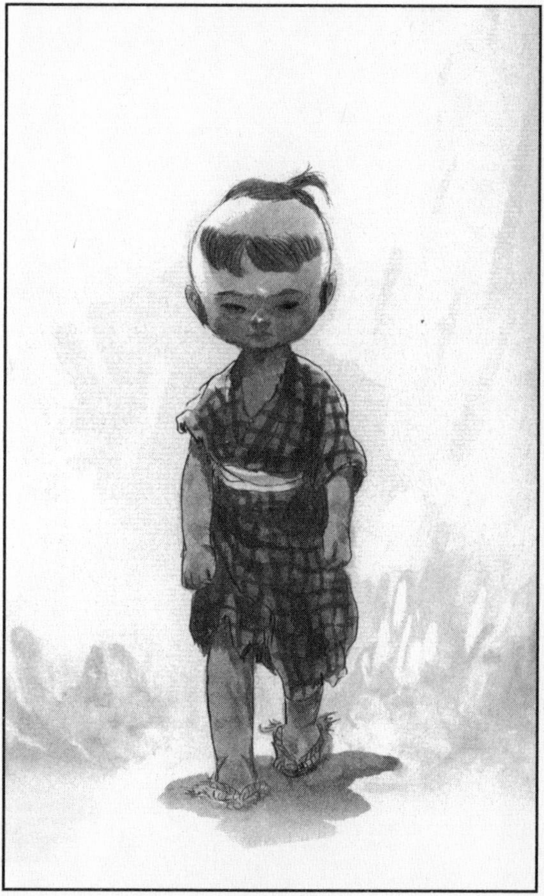

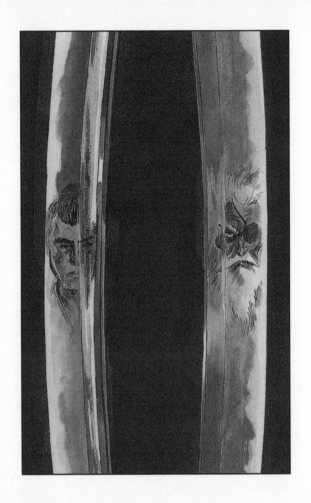

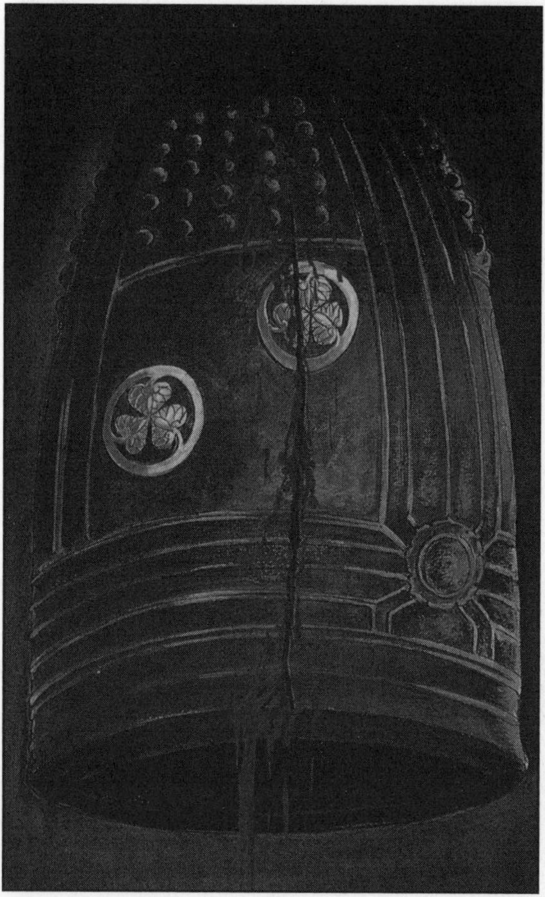

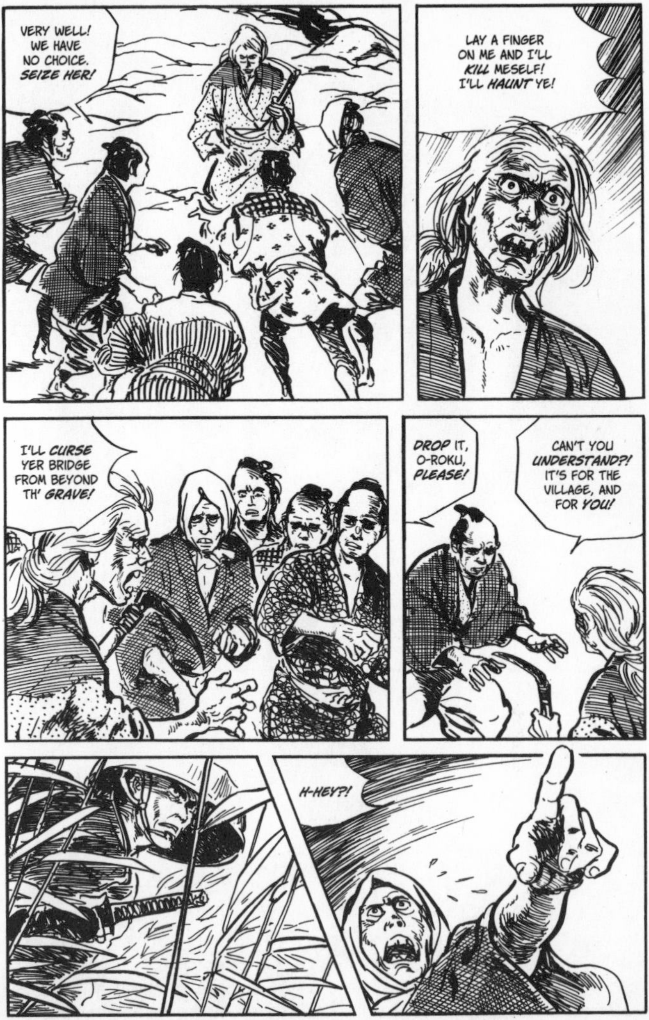
VERY WELL! WE HAVE NO CHOICE. SEIZE HER!
LAY A FINGER ON ME AND I'LL KILL MESELF! I'LL HAUNT YE!
I'LL CURSE YER BRIDGE FROM BEYOND TH' GRAVE!
DROP IT, O-ROKU, PLEASE!
CAN'T YOU UNDERSTAND?! IT'S FOR THE VILLAGE, AND FOR YOU!
H-HEY?!

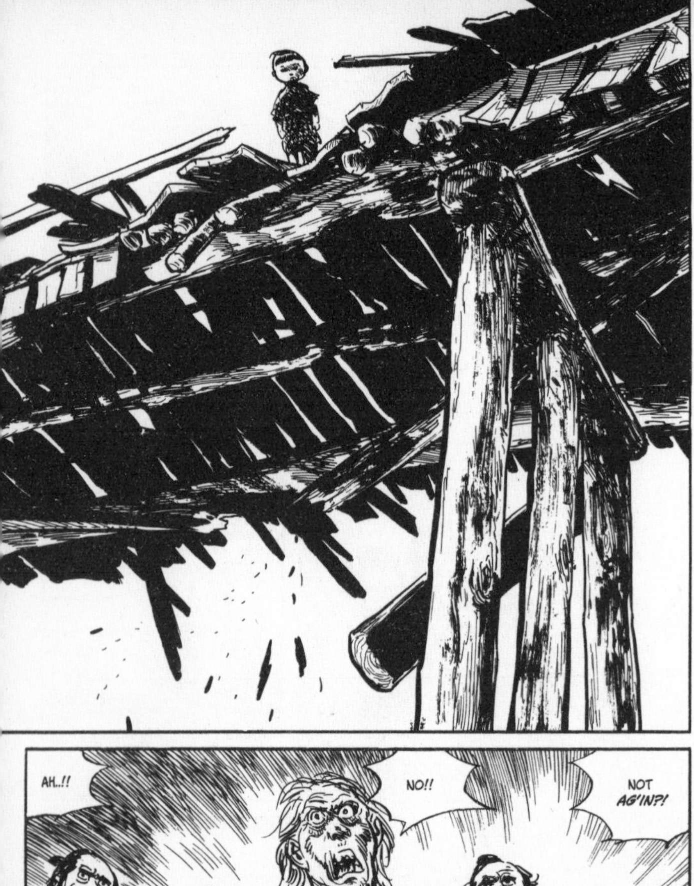

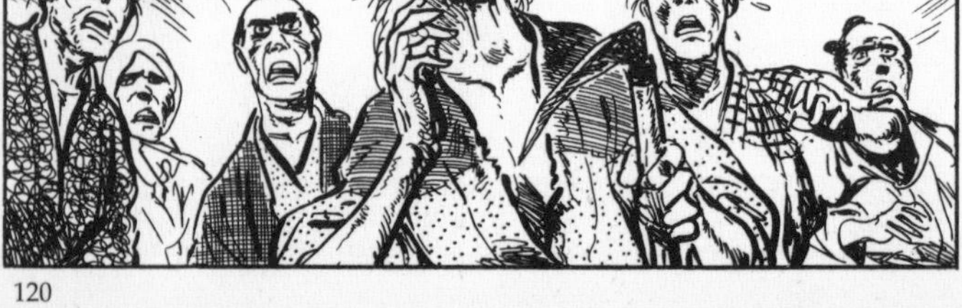
AH..!!
NO!!
NOT AG'IN?!

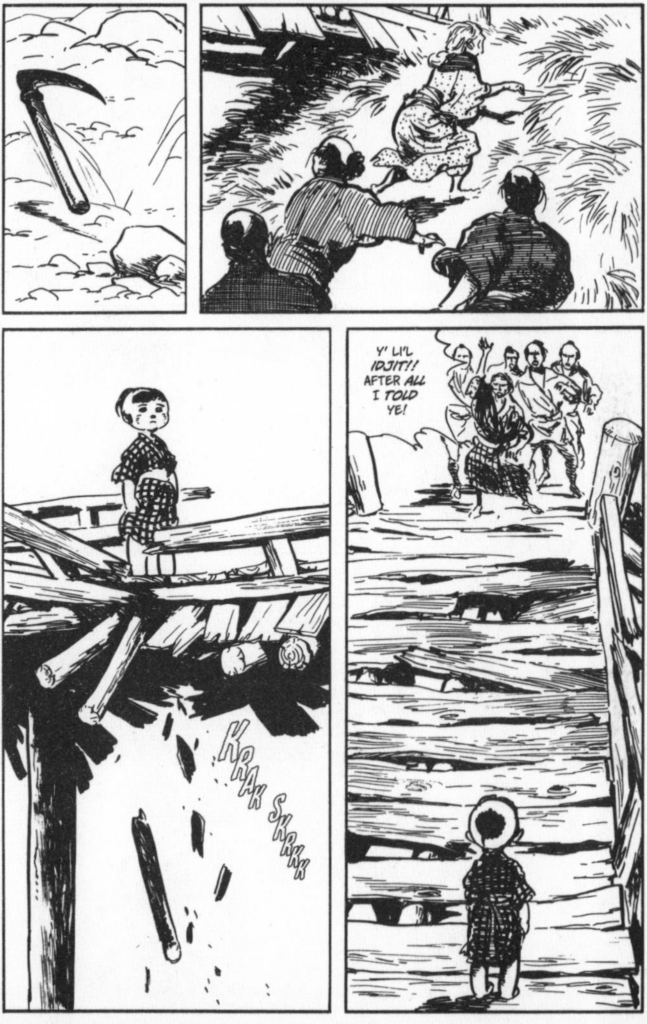

Y' LI'L IDJIT!! AFTER ALL I TOLD YE!
KRAK SKRKK

C-COME 'ERE! RIGHT NOW!

SLOW... SLOW...JES' EDGE ON OVER...

aah! D-DON'T TELL ME...?!

IS...IS THET IT, SWEETIE...?

Y' THOUGHT IF Y' WENT ON THE BRIDGE, THEM MEDDLERS'D... IS THET IT...?

FER... FER ME? Y' WENT OUT THERE FER ME?

122

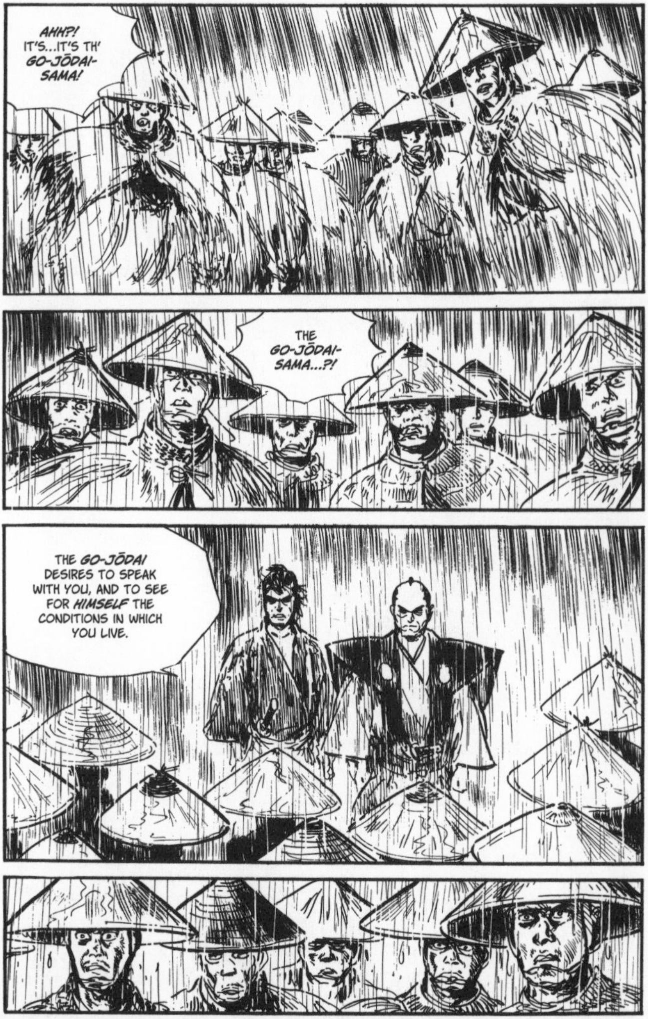
AHH?! IT'S...IT'S TH' GO-JŌDAI-SAMA!
THE GO-JŌDAI-SAMA...?!
THE GO-JŌDAI DESIRES TO SPEAK WITH YOU, AND TO SEE FOR HIMSELF THE CONDITIONS IN WHICH YOU LIVE.

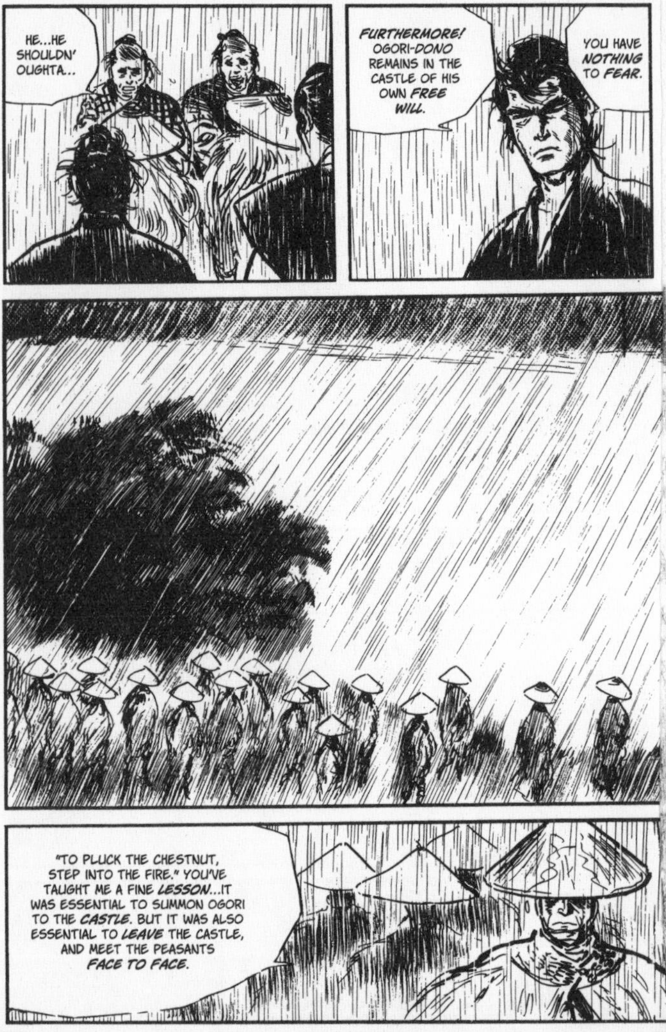
HE...HE SHOULDN' OUGHTA...
FURTHERMORE! OGORI-DONO REMAINS IN THE CASTLE OF HIS OWN FREE WILL.
YOU HAVE NOTHING TO FEAR.
"TO PLUCK THE CHESTNUT, STEP INTO THE FIRE." YOU'VE TAUGHT ME A FINE LESSON...IT WAS ESSENTIAL TO SUMMON OGORI TO THE CASTLE. BUT IT WAS ALSO ESSENTIAL TO LEAVE THE CASTLE, AND MEET THE PEASANTS FACE TO FACE.

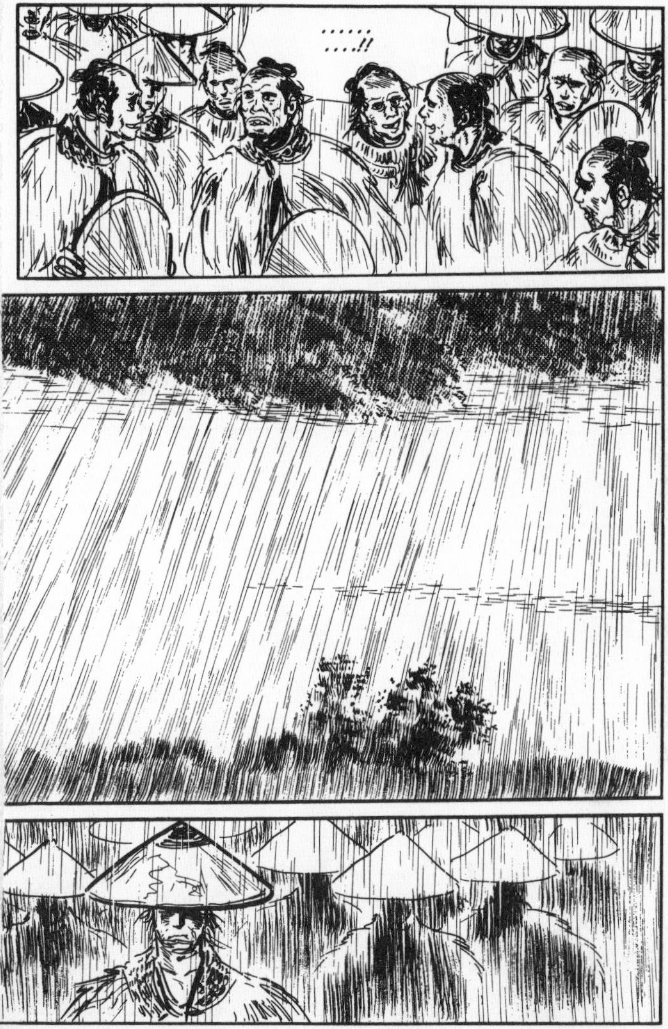
......
....!!

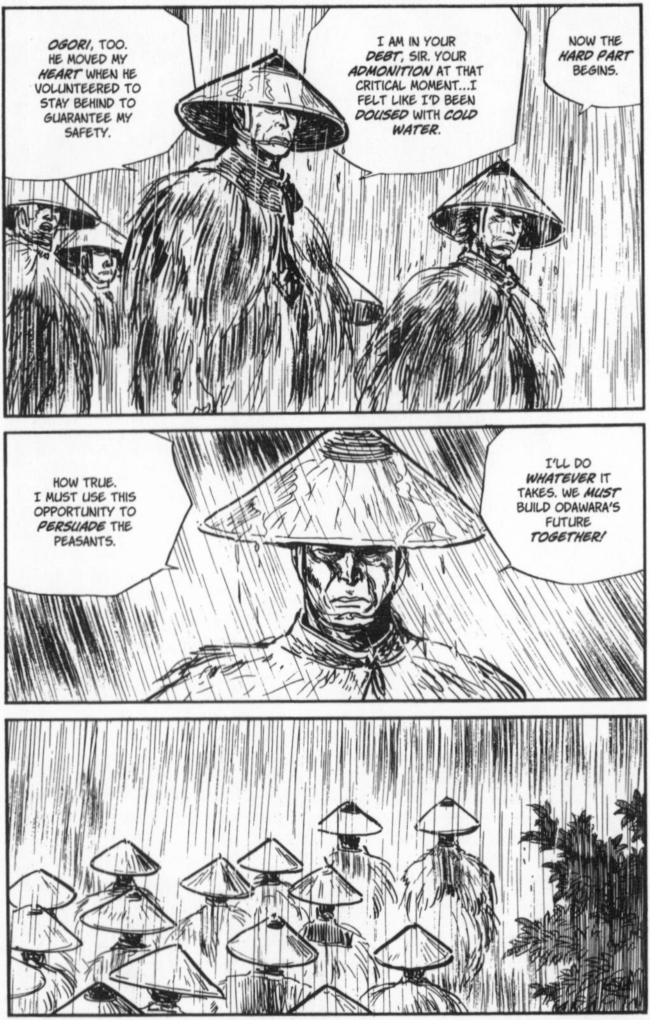
OGORI, TOO. HE MOVED MY HEART WHEN HE VOLUNTEERED TO STAY BEHIND TO GUARANTEE MY SAFETY.
I AM IN YOUR DEBT, SIR. YOUR ADMONITION AT THAT CRITICAL MOMENT...I FELT LIKE I'D BEEN DOUSED WITH COLD WATER.
NOW THE HARD PART BEGINS.
HOW TRUE. I MUST USE THIS OPPORTUNITY TO PERSUADE THE PEASANTS.
I'LL DO WHATEVER IT TAKES. WE MUST BUILD ODAWARA'S FUTURE TOGETHER!

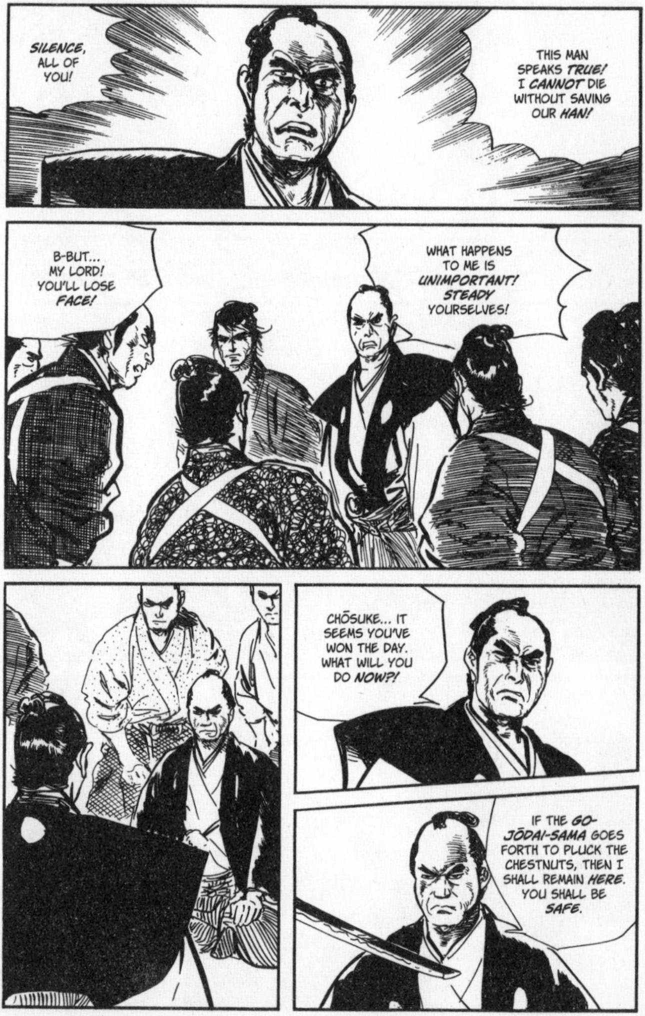
SILENCE, ALL OF YOU!
THIS MAN SPEAKS TRUE! I CANNOT DIE WITHOUT SAVING OUR HAN!
B-BUT... MY LORD! YOU'LL LOSE FACE!
WHAT HAPPENS TO ME IS UNIMPORTANT! STEADY YOURSELVES!
CHŌSUKE... IT SEEMS YOU'VE WON THE DAY. WHAT WILL YOU DO NOW?!
IF THE GO-JŌDAI-SAMA GOES FORTH TO PLUCK THE CHESTNUTS, THEN I SHALL REMAIN HERE. YOU SHALL BE SAFE.

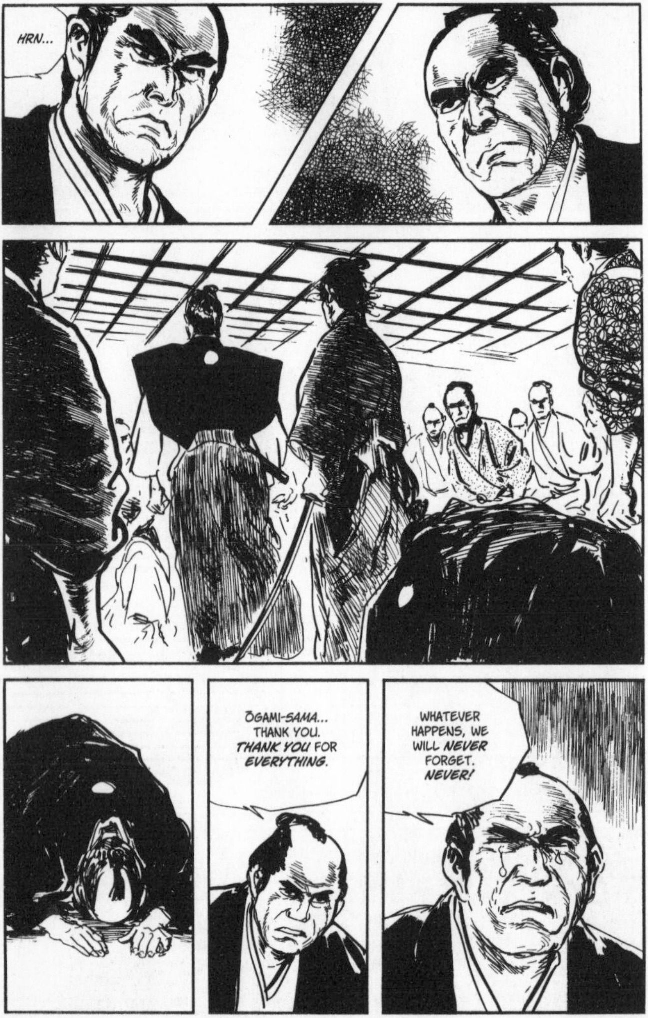
HRN...
ŌGAMI-SAMA... THANK YOU. THANK YOU FOR EVERYTHING.
WHATEVER HAPPENS, WE WILL NEVER FORGET. NEVER!

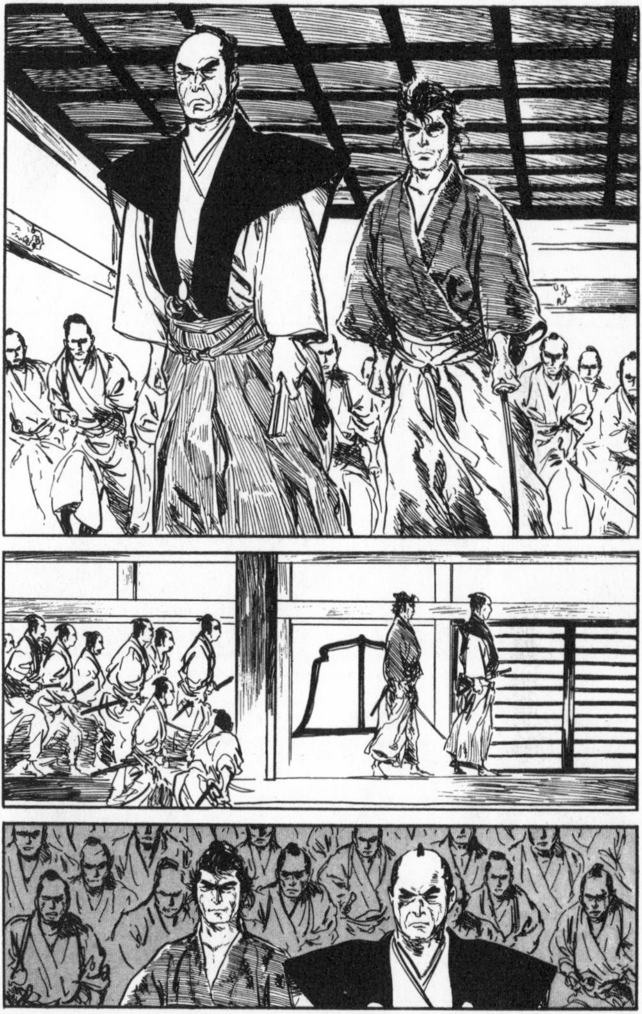

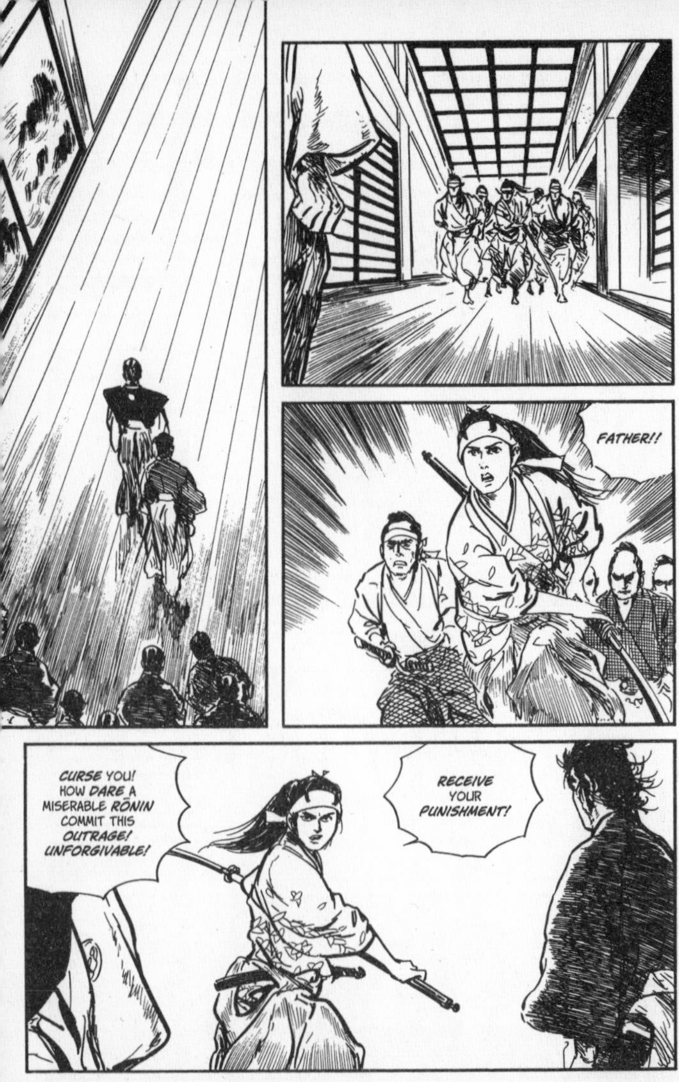
FATHER!!
CURSE YOU! HOW DARE A MISERABLE RŌNIN COMMIT THIS OUTRAGE! UNFORGIVABLE!
RECEIVE YOUR PUNISHMENT!